SHERLOCK HOLMES
BY GAS-LAMP

SHERLOCK HOLMES BY GAS-LAMP

Highlights from the
First Four Decades of

Edited by
PHILIP A. SHREFFLER

Fordham University Press
New York

TO
THE MOST WINNING WOMAN
I EVER KNEW

CONTENTS

A NOTE ON THE TEXT

At the conclusion of each offering in this volume is a date that represents the month and year in which the foregoing piece appeared in THE BAKER STREET JOURNAL. As shall be quite apparent, however, in some cases the date of composition much preceded the date of publication in the JOURNAL.

INTRODUCTION

In 1944, one of the first major anthologies of essays and other pieces about Sherlock Holmes to treat the Master Detective as a historical figure was published by Simon and Schuster. The book was *Profile by Gaslight*, edited by Edgar W. Smith who, two years later, would found THE BAKER STREET JOURNAL. And at the beginning of *Profile by Gaslight* Smith slyly modified that standard legal disclaimer common to works of fiction:

> The characters in this book are real persons. Any resemblance to fictitious characters, living or dead, is purely accidental.

No more succinct statement was ever made summarizing the nature of the intellectual divertissement undertaken by the Baker Street Irregulars and the now-many thousands of other Sherlockians around the world. When formally established by author and *Saturday Review of Literature* editor Christopher Morley as a society of Holmes devotees in 1934, the Baker Street Irregulars published their *Constitution and Buy-Laws* (sic), a document that made clear at the outset the Irregulars' mission of "study[ing] the Sacred Writings"—a mission further delineated by the certificate of membership in the organization as "keeping green the Master's memory." Above all, what studying the Sacred Writings and keeping green Sherlock Holmes's memory meant to the Irregulars was *writing* about Holmes and his adventures as historical reality, historical fact.

And why not? Has the site of 221B Baker Street not been identified (and with it the site of Camden House, the empty edifice across the road from which the craggy and degraded Colonel Sebastian Moran sought to dispatch Sherlock Holmes)? As the reader of this book will discover, they have. Do we not know much of the Baker Street *dramatis personae* (the Master, Dr. John H. Watson, Mrs. Hudson, Inspector Lestrade, Professor Moriarty, Irene Adler, and the rest) that is only hinted at or inferred by the published stories about them? We do.

And all of this is the felicitous result of the Sherlockian brains and pens that have been turned toward the explication of those fundamental truths inherent in the magical Holmesian cosmos—that world where "it is always 1895." The flinty-eyed "realist," the dour professor, the critical mythmonger of the late twentieth century—none of these shall ever convince the comfortably-settled Sherlockian that the assertion of Holmes's being fictional is anything but the rankest absurdity. Indeed, numerous critics who ought to have known better have been stung by the Sherlockians' blithe spirit of certitude in this regard. Among the most recent of these is Professor Pasquale Accardo who is responsible for these astonishing words:

> The pseudoscholarship prevalent in the literature of Sherlock Holmes testifies indirectly and obscurely to the existential vitality of the characters and events narrated in the original stories. In the annals of popular literature, the "writings upon the writings" reflect a phenomenon perversely unique for two reasons; first, they contribute little or nothing to explain the immense popularity of the characters whether in the original Doyle stories or in their countless plagiarisms, pastiches, parodies, and other incarnations. Second, they accept their basic principles of critical analysis from the original tales themselves and apply Holmes's rules for detection to unsolved and artifactual pseudoproblems inherent in the narrative. . . . The irony of extant Sherlockian scholarship is that it has focused on the [non-Iconic] level of meaning, especially informants (boring minutiae Victorianae), the least revealing component of the narrative structure. Further, while these informants have been tortured to surrender conclusions both inconsequential and questionable, their relevance to the structure of discourse has been almost totally ignored. Needless to say, such detailed textual analyses yield results that quite simply violate the canons of elementary psychology and outrage common sense.[1]

Forgive us, Professor, for we have sinned.

And we began our sinning early. Even before the formation of the Baker Street Irregulars, there were Sherlockians sounding deeply into the Holmes Canon, discovering therein innumerable inconsistencies seemingly emanating from Dr. Watson's poor memory, faulty perception, or deliberate discretionary obfuscation of the facts in Holmes's cases. These crying out for clarification, Sherlockian scholarship was born. Had Watson two wives or three? A wound in the shoulder or the leg? A flourishing practice or a failing career? Was Holmes's university Oxford or Cambridge? His parents British or American? His use of cocaine pathological or benign? His feelings toward Irene Adler love or respect?

In 1934, a small group of American Sherlockians, the Baker Street Irregulars, gathered for the first time in New York, put drinks in their hands and such problems on the table. They were writers and editors, professors and physicians—and they did what they did without any thought to the subsequent humorless rancor that their activities might arouse among a small gaggle of annoyed academic idiopaths. They just did it.

By 1944, Edgar W. Smith, a vice president of the General Motors Corporation and an especially literate and articulate early Irregular, concluded that the time had come to commit some of the Irregulars' Canonical investigations to paper: thus *Profile by Gaslight*. In the months that followed *Profile's* publication, Smith's thoughts turned to the possibility of a Sherlockian journal representing the Baker Street Irregulars. And in January of 1946, with Smith as Editor and New York bookseller (and later fellow BSI) Ben Abramson as Publisher, the first issue of the quarterly BAKER STREET JOURNAL appeared.

It was an attractive artifact, that first JOURNAL: yellow-backed, its wrappers printed in Victorian typography, its signatures stitched, and featuring 108 pages of analytical essays, verse, musings, illustrations, and news about the Holmesian *mise en scène*. Owing to Smith's enthusiasm and Abramson's grandiose plans for its future, the JOURNAL was printed in a press run of several thousand—some going to subscribers, some sold through Abramson's Argus Book Shop on West 47th Street, many being remaindered by Abramson personally to the book department of Macy's. The masthead listed Smith as Editor; the impressive roster of Associate Editors included Christopher Morley, Ellery Queen, Lee Wright (mystery editor at Simon and Schuster), publishers' representative W. S. Hall, and Charles Honce, head of the New York office of the Associated Press. The Honorary Associates were H. W. Bell, the Sherlockian chronologist, and Vincent Starrett, bookman and *Chicago Tribune* columnist.

In this lavish format, however, the JOURNAL survived only thirteen issues; perhaps its novelty and esoteric nature, for all its sophistication, were against it—and certainly the expense of producing it was. Subscription receipts and sporadic over-the-counter sales could not sustain it. And when this Original Series of THE BAKER STREET JOURNAL folded with the January 1949 issue, it may well have appeared as if the Irregulars' pursuit of Sherlock Holmes on the printed page would be stymied by the arbitrary barrier of 1950.

But the devotion of Edgar Smith to this well-beloved offspring was greater than that. And in 1951, funded now by Smith himself, the JOURNAL reappeared with Volume 1, Number 1 of the New Series. Physically, this new JOURNAL was a radical departure from what its early readers had become accustomed to: it comprised forty pages of reduced typescript printing, the signatures punched and held together with three large brads, its light-green cover bearing the original JOURNAL logo, plus a silhouette of Sherlock Holmes. And, as if apologizing for the JOURNAL's now-less-than-resplendent clothing, Smith wrote: "In this modified and modest format, THE BAKER STREET JOURNAL continues publication."

Of course, Smith had no reason to apologize. The Irregulars' readership welcomed that single sentence and the JOURNAL's recrudescence similarly to the way in which Holmes himself was welcomed back to the world of the living in *The Adventure of the Empty House*. Here again was THE BAKER STREET JOURNAL—even if only in a press run of about 150—with all its familiar departments: Smith's "Editor's Gas-Lamp" editorial, Morley's column "Clinical Notes by a Residential Patient," "The Scion Societies" that reported the doings of the Sherlockian clubs that had begun to spring up throughout the United States, and "From the Editor's Commonplace Book," which summarized or reprinted Holmesian gleanings from the popular press. And the featured articles demonstrated clearly that the JOURNAL's new, "modest" apparel would have no negative effect on the by-now-expected articulate and witty quality of their contents. In short, it was—happily—the same old JOURNAL.

The next year, 1952, saw the JOURNAL return to its original yellow wrappers, and it was now staple-bound. With the very able and considerable assistance of his secretary at General Motors, Ruth L. Freiberg (who was listed as Associate Editor), Smith continued to see the JOURNAL into print four times a year

4

throughout the 1950s, an avocational editorship, in sum, rather remarkable.

The JOURNAL's next major crisis occurred in 1960 with Edgar Smith's premature and unexpected death. Smith had edited, since 1946, fifty-three issues plus five "Christmas Annuals"— extra issues in Decembers of the late 1950s—, and now was a moment at which THE BAKER STREET JOURNAL itself might have passed into that "swift oblivion" from which Smith sought to preserve Sherlockian writing by founding the publication. But, once again, faithful service to the cause beyond the call of duty turned what might have been a disaster into an opportunity.

Julian Wolff, a New York physician, stepped handily into the breach. Dr. Wolff was no stranger either to the Irregulars or to the JOURNAL. He received his Investiture in the BSI in 1944, the year that *Profile by Gaslight* was published, and he was listed as an Associate Editor of the JOURNAL in the late Original Series issues. Wolff's accession to the editorship was characterized by a reassuring stance. Paraphrasing Winston Churchill in the "Editor's Gas-Lamp" department, Wolff wrote: "I did not come here to preside over the dissolution of THE BAKER STREET JOURNAL." Nor did he. For between 1961 and 1977, Wolff edited a total of sixty-six issues.

If Smith's editorship of the New Series seemed a one-man operation, Wolff's was in fact just that. Those who were privy to the editorial process during those sixteen years report how the dining room table of Wolff's Riverside Drive apartment was commonly heaped with JOURNAL-related papers and manuscripts, how Wolff quarterly pulled order out of chaos, pecked on his old manual typewriters, dummied the issues where (and often when) dinner was to be served, carried copy himself to the printer, retrieved the bound JOURNALS the same way, and then hauled them to the post office for mailing to subscribers (of whom there were by then about 600). It was all a Herculean effort, made not easier but more difficult by the fact that the Sherlockian world was growing in popularity, and now contributions came in by the hundreds instead of by scores. But the good doctor, Sherlock Holmes's most valuable medical amanuensis since Watson, was equal to it.

Beginning with the March 1975 issue, the JOURNAL changed its physical appearance substantially for the first time since

5

1952; it was now being typeset again, as it had been through all of the Original Series issues. Owing to the good offices of George Fletcher, Julian Wolff's close friend, fellow Irregular, and Director of Fordham University Press, the university undertook the JOURNAL's publication, with Wolff still at the helm as Editor. In a matter of a little less than thirty years' time, the JOURNAL had come rather full circle—again a very attractive artifact, again piloted by a thoroughly-devoted Editor. When Dr. Wolff stepped down as Editor in 1977 in favor of a younger man, he was able to look back over a tenure that included the virtually knightly rescue of the JOURNAL and the publication of more issues even than under Edgar Smith's editorship.

Following Wolff's retirement came a succession of able Irregular Editors. John M. Linsenmeyer, Peter E. Blau, and George Fletcher (the pseudonymous Fred Porlock, aided and abetted by certain BSI cronies) carried the JOURNAL through 1984, at the end of which the editorship devolved upon the author of these words.

And certain it must be that those of us who have followed in the train of both Smith and Wolff, we who have labored in the subtle glow of The Editor's Gas-Lamp, have also felt the call to preserve THE BAKER STREET JOURNAL from that "swift oblivion" about which Smith wrote in his first editorial. Indeed, it is pleasant to be able to report that the JOURNAL currently has a greater number of subscribers than it ever has—numbering not in the hundreds but over two thousand—and an international readership, from Sweden, Denmark, and Great Britain to Japan and Australia. The Baker Street Irregulars and their JOURNAL have made a home for Sherlock Holmes in this century so alien to him.

Still, though, there are those today—all ignorant of the love, even of the occasional passion with which Sherlockians regard the Holmes Canon and with which they invest their writings upon the Writings—who consider puerile or even (as we have seen) shocking the pursuit of the variety of scholarship represented by THE BAKER STREET JOURNAL. To the Sherlockian, of course, this is perfectly delightful—not only because Sherlockians can be as disputatious as Sherlock himself (and as dry and scathing in the doing) but because it is so diverting to see these antagonists confused.

Perhaps the Irregulars and the JOURNAL and the Sherlockian movement as a whole have done too good a job of keeping green Holmes's memory. That they choose to do so in scholarly form and that so many have taken up the exercise seems to have perplexed a good many people. And Sherlockian scholarship's having been indulged in by such a diversity of individuals, including the likes of Ellery Queen, Basil Rathbone, Isaac Asimov, and Franklin Roosevelt—Irregulars all—is probably more perplexing still.

Of course, it is certainly not the true Sherlockian's intention to bewilder; quite to the contrary, his is to enlighten about the rarest and finest of worlds surrounding Baker Street and beyond. And as did one British Holmesian when asked the question "Sherlock Holmes, fact or fiction?," the best devotees will answer straight from the shoulder: "Yes." No hesitation. No equivocation.

That affirmation is what THE BAKER STREET JOURNAL has been about since its inception in 1946, and it is what this book is about. Selecting the present volume's contents from among the many thousands of JOURNAL pages has been a more-than-daunting procedure, and one hesitates single-handedly to essay any such anthology. But whether or not one agrees that these contents comprise the best of the JOURNAL, what is important is that they capture its spirit—what Edgar Smith called "the spirit of adventurous emprise."

And plainly, adventuring through the byways of London and across the rural moors in the company of Sherlock Holmes and the wise Dr. Watson is the only enterprise that the JOURNAL ever sought to foster. There are some paths in life that we may follow only with our intellects; some that we may follow only with our hearts. But only occasionally do we find paths like these that we may follow with both.

—PHILIP A. SHREFFLER

NOTE

1. Pasquale Accardo, *Diagnosis and Detection: The Medical Iconography of Sherlock Holmes* (Rutherford, Madison, and Teaneck, N.J.: Fairleigh Dickenson University Press, 1987), pp. 14–15.

7

ACKNOWLEDGMENTS

I wish to express my grateful appreciation to the following members of The Baker Street Irregulars whose valuable advice and assistance contributed positively and substantially to this project: Peter E. Blau, Benjamin S. Clark, Saul Cohen, George Fletcher, Robert G. Harris, William D. Jenkins, Michael Kean, Christopher Redmond, Donald A. Redmond, Thomas L. Stix, Jr., and Robert E. Thomalen.

WHAT IS IT THAT WE LOVE IN SHERLOCK HOLMES?

THE GAME IS AFOOT!

by EDGAR W. SMITH

IT IS ALTOGETHER FITTING that Sherlock Holmes should be honored by the publication of a journal devoted to a critical analysis of his life and times. No other man has ever been so honored before him—but then no other life has ever lent itself so completely to affectionate dissection; no other times have offered quite so full a flavor of the stuff of which our dreams are made.

While yet the memory of Sherlock Holmes is green—and that will be as long as the spirit of adventurous emprise is still astir in human hearts—there will be those who will be moved to write in loving tribute to the master and his works. They will address themselves, in their devotion, to the man himself and to the things he thought and said and did: and they will take within their scope as well the London street in which he lived, and the room in which he sat, and the brave, devoted friend who stood and fought beside him when he sallied forth upon the chase.

It is well that this is so. The urge is in us all to give expression to the things we think and feel, and Holmes himself, it will be recalled, endorsed this literary bent in no uncertain terms. Speaking to Victor Hatherley, when that epollicate engineer had poured his story forth (and how we might wish he had been speaking to John H. Watson instead!) he made his dictum plain: "You have only to put it into words," he said, "to gain the reputation of being excellent company for the remainder of your existence."

And since Holmes was never one to give voice to apothegms in a vacuum, he practiced what he preached. He "put into words," over the years, his observations and conclusions on an amazing variety of subjects, from tobacco ashes and tattoo marks to the tracing of footsteps and the art of malingering. He

11

Edgar W. Smith, editor of the JOURNAL, receives the first copy of Volume I Number 1 from Ben Abramson, publisher, at the B.S.I. meeting at the Murray Hill Hotel on January 11th. Fletcher Pratt is seen entering his subscription.

produced, among his other masterpieces, two profound philological treatises, a definitive work on the polyphonic motets of Lassus, a highly specialized anatomical exegesis, and—for measure not so good—two pot-boiling detective stories. Yet all of these fruits of Holmes's genius are lost to us today with the exception of his relatively feeble contributions to the field of fiction, and, through the single precious copy which has survived, his *Practical Handbook of Bee Culture, With Some Observations Upon the Segregation of the Queen.*

The disappearance of this great body of Holmesian literature, to mankind's irreparable loss, can be ascribed only to the fact that the master had no regular, ready, and sympathetic repository for the products of his pen. Too often his "small brochures" and "trifling monographs" were entrusted to the hands of the private printer or given to one of those obscure magazines which catered so exclusively to the undiscerning that they can now themselves no longer be discerned. His "Book of Life,"

Christopher Morley, B.S.I. Gasogene-cum-Tantalus, who presided at the meeting, also puts himself down as a charter subscriber.

it is true, found its way into a publication presumably of some pretensions (was it the *Cornhill Magazine?*) despite Watson's offhand appraisal of the piece as "ineffable twaddle." The essay on the conformation of the human ear appeared—in two instalments, circa 1884—in the *Anthropological Journal,* which cannot now, for some unfortunate reason, be located in the libraries of the world. And there is, of course—but this probably merely in fulfillment of a long-established Watsonian tradition—the selection of *The Strand Magazine* in November and December, 1926, for the not-brief-enough excursion into the field of fiction. Otherwise, Holmes's choice of media for the recording and transmission of his genius was, as the result has proved, incredibly bad.

To those who follow in his footsteps, there is no longer any danger that a similar descent into limbo will be the inevitable fate of their outgivings. We have already had, as warranty of this, our *Baker Street Studies,* our *221B,* our *Profile by Gaslight,* and our *Baker Street Four-Wheeler,* with the promise that other volumes of collectanea will make their appearance in the years to come. And now, as a current and continuing medium for preserving to posterity the writings in the Holmesian lore, we have this BAKER STREET JOURNAL.

The JOURNAL is dedicated to the proposition that there is still infinitely much to be said about the scene in Baker Street, and that it is of the first importance to safeguard the meritorious offerings laid upon our common shrine from that swift oblivion to which, by a heedless and unheeding world, they might otherwise be condemned. In that purpose and intent, which honors by its very terms the name and fame of Sherlock Holmes, the JOURNAL's course of destiny will run.

—January 1946

THE IMPLICIT HOLMES

by EDGAR W. SMITH

WHAT IS IT that we love in Sherlock Holmes?

We love the times in which he lived, of course: the half-remembered, half-forgotten times of snug Victorian illusion, of gaslit comfort and contentment, of perfect dignity and grace. The world was poised precariously in balance, and rude disturbances were coming with the years; but those who moved upon the scene were very sure that all was well: that nothing ever would be any worse nor ever could be any better. There was no threat to righteousness and justice and the cause of peace on earth except from such as Moriarty and the lesser villains in his train. The cycle of events had come full turn, and the times were ripe for living—and for being lost. It is because their loss was suffered before they had been fully lived that they are times to which our hearts and longings cling.

And we love the place in which the master moved and had his being: the England of those times, fat with the fruits of her achievements, but strong and daring still with the spirit of imperial adventure. The seas were pounding, then as now, upon her coasts; the winds swept in across the moors, and fog came down on London. It was a stout and pleasant land, full of the flavor of the age; and it is small wonder that we who claim it in our thoughts should look to Baker Street as its epitome. For there the cabs rolled up before a certain door, and hurried steps were heard upon the stair, and England and her times had rendezvous within a hallowed room, at once familiar and mysterious. . . .

But there is more than time and space and the yearning for things gone by to account for what we feel toward Sherlock Holmes. Not only there and then, but here and now, he stands before us as a symbol—a symbol, if you please, of all that we are

15

not, but ever would be. His figure is sufficiently remote to make our secret aspirations for transference seem unshameful, yet close enough to give them plausibility. We see him as the fine expression of our urge to trample evil and to set aright the wrongs with which the world is plagued. He is Galahad and Socrates, bringing high adventure to our dull existences and calm, judicial logic to our biased minds. He is the success of all our failures; the bold escape from our imprisonment.

Or, if this be too complex a psychological basis to account for our devotion, let it be said, more simply, that he is the personification of something in us that we have lost, or never had. For it is not Sherlock Holmes who sits in Baker Street, comfortable, competent and self-assured; it is we ourselves who are there, full of a tremendous capacity for wisdom, complacent in the presence of our humble Watson, conscious of a warm well-being and a timeless, imperishable content. The easy chair in the room is drawn up to the hearthstone of our very hearts—it is *our* tobacco in the Persian slipper, and *our* violin lying so carelessly across the knee—it is *we* who hear the pounding on the stairs and the knock upon the door. The swirling fog without and the acrid smoke within bite deep indeed, for we taste them even now. And the time and place and all the great events are near and dear to us not because our memories call them forth in pure nostalgia, but because they are a part of us today.

That is the Sherlock Holmes we love—the Holmes implicit and eternal in ourselves.

—April 1946

16

Each of us has first encountered Holmes in his or her
own special way, Ellery Queen's included; yet there is a
commonality in all our experiences. . . .

My First Meeting with Sherlock Holmes

by Ellery Queen

I WANT TO TELL YOU the unforgettable circumstances that led to
my first meeting with Sherlock Holmes.

When I was a small child my family lived in a small town in
western New York. I didn't realize it then, but I was given a colossal gift early in life—a Huckleberry Finn–Tom Sawyer boyhood spent, by a strange coincidence, in the very town in which
Mark Twain lived shortly before I was born.

Does any man with a spark of boyhood still in his heart ever
forget his home town? No—it's an unconquerable memory.
Most of us never return, but none of us forgets.

I remember we had a river at our back door—the gentle
Chemung. I remember how, in the cycle of years, the spring
torrents came down from the hills; how they overflowed our
peaceful valley—yes, over the massive concrete dikes that towered with grim Egyptian austerity above the shallow bed of the
Chemung. I remember how old man river burst through our
back door, flooding our kitchen and parlor, driving us—temporary refugees—to our top floor. Happy days for a wide-eyed
boy, proud in his hip-boots and man's sou'wester, with a prospect of daily trips by rowboat—voyages of high adventure—to
the nearest grocer!

I remember the unpaved streets—the heavily rutted road that
slept in the sun before our house. I have a queer memory about
those ruts. Every 4th of July we boys would plant our fire-
crackers deep in the soft earth of those ruts. Then we'd touch
our smoking punks to the row of seedling fuses, run for cover,
and watch the "thunderbolts" (that's what they were called in
those days) explode with a muffled roar and send heavenward—
at least three feet!—a shower of dirt and stones. It wasn't so
long after the Spanish–American War that we couldn't pretend

17

we were blowing up the *Maine*—in some strangely perverted terrestrial fashion only small boys can invent.

I remember the long walks to and from public school—three miles each way, in summer mud and winter drifts; the cherry trees and apple trees and chicken coops and dogs—the long succession of dogs ending with that fine hunter that was killed by a queer-looking machine called an "automobile." I remember the all-day trips to the brown October hills, gathering nuts; the wood fires and the popping corn; the swimming hole that no one knew about but ourselves; the boyhood secret society and its meeting place in the shed behind my best friend's house. We called it "The League of the Clutching Hand"—can you guess why?

But I started to tell you how I first met Sherlock Holmes. Somehow I cannot think of Holmes without succumbing to a wave of sentimental nostalgia. I find myself fading back—far, far back in the remembrance of things past.

As a boy my reading habits were pure and innocent. I confess now that I never read a Nick Carter until I was past thirty. My literary childhood consisted of Horatio Alger and Tom Swift and the Viking legends and the multi-colored Lang fairy books and—yes, the Oz stories. I can reread the Oz stories even today—and I do. Somehow crime and detection failed to cross my path in all those happy days, except in the movies—"The Clutching Hand," remember? The closest I might have come to blood and thunder would have been TOM SAWYER, DECTEC-TIVE—I say "might have come," because oddly enough I have no recollection of TOM SAWYER, DETECTIVE as part of my early reading.

When I was twelve years old, my family moved to New York City. For a time we lived with my grandfather in Brooklyn. It was in my grandfather's house, only a few weeks after my arrival in fabulous New York, that I met Sherlock Holmes. Oh, unforgettable day!

I was ill in bed. In those days I was afflicted periodically with an abscess of the left ear. It came year after year, with almost astronomical regularity—and always, I remember, during the week of school exams. My grandfather had an old turnip of a watch that he used to place flat against my left ear, and it always astounded him that, even after the ordeal of having had my ear lanced, I still couldn't hear his Big Ben tick.

I was lying in bed, a miserable youngster, on just such a day as Dr. Watson has so often described—a "bleak and windy" day with the fingers of winter scratching at the window pane. One of my aunts walked in and handed me a book she had borrowed at the near-by public library.

It was the ADVENTURES OF SHERLOCK HOLMES.

I opened the book with no realization that I stood—rather, I sat—on the brink of my fate. I had no inkling, no premonition, that in another minute my life's work, such as it is, would be born. My first glance was disheartening. I saw the frontispiece of the Harper edition—a picture of a rather innocuous man in dress coat and striped trousers holding the arm of a young woman in bridal gown. *A love story,* I said to myself—for surely this unattractive couple were in a church about to be married. The quotation under the illustration—"The gentleman in the pew handed it up to her"—was not encouraging. In fact, there was nothing in that ill-chosen frontispiece by Sidney Paget to make a twelve-year-old boy sit up and take notice—especially with his left ear in agony.

Only an unknown and unknowable sixth sense prompted me to turn to the table of contents—and then the world brightened. The first story—*A Scandal in Bohemia*—seemed to hold little red-blooded promise, but the next story was, and always will be, a milestone.

A strange rushing thrill challenged the pain in my ear. *The Red-Headed League!* What a combination of simple words to skewer themselves into the brain of a hungry boy! I glanced down quickly—*The Man with the Twisted Lip*—*The Adventure of the Speckled Band*—and I was lost! Ecstatically, everlastingly lost!

I started on the first page of *A Scandal in Bohemia* and truly, the game was afoot. The unbearable pain in my ear—vanished! The abyss of melancholy into which only a twelve-year-old boy can sink—forgotten!

I finished the ADVENTURES that night. I wasn't sad—I was glad. It wasn't the end—it was the beginning. I had knocked fearlessly on the door of a new world and I had been admitted. There was a long road ahead—even longer than I dreamed.

That night, as I closed the book, I knew that I had read one of the greatest books ever written. And today I realize with amazement how true and tempered was my twelve-year-old critical sense. For in the mature smugness of my present literary judgment, I still feel—unalterably—that the ADVENTURES is one of the world's masterworks.

I could not have slept much that night. If I did, I merely passed from one dreamworld to another—with the waking dream infinitely more wondrous. I remember when morning came—how symbolically the sun shone past my window. I leaped from bed, dressed, and with that great wad of yellow-stained cotton still in my ear, stole out of the house. As if by instinct I knew where the public library was. Of course it wasn't open, but I sat on the steps and waited. And though I waited hours, it seemed only minutes until a prim old lady came and unlocked the front door.

But, alas—I had no card. Yes, I might fill out this form, and take it home, and have my parents sign it, and then after three days—three days? three eternities!—I could call and pick up my card.

I begged, I pleaded, I implored—and there must have been something irresistible in my voice and in my eyes. Thank you now, Miss Librarian-of-Those-Days! Those thanks are long overdue. For that gentle-hearted old lady broke all the rules of librarydom and gave me a card—and told me with a twinkle in her eyes where I could find books by a man named Doyle.

I rushed to the stacks. My first reaction was one of horrible and devastating disappointment. Yes, there were books by Doyle on the shelves—but so few of them! I had expected a whole libraryful—rows and rows of Sherlock, all waiting patiently for my "coming of age."

I found three precious volumes. I bundled them under my arm, had them stamped, and fled home. Back in bed I started to read—A STUDY IN SCARLET, the MEMOIRS (with a frontispiece that almost frightened me to death), THE HOUND OF THE BASKERVILLES. They were food and drink and medicine—and all of the Queen's horses and all the Queen's men couldn't put Ellery together again.

But my doom had been signed, sealed, and delivered in the ADVENTURES. The books which followed merely broadened the picture, filled in the indelible details. That tall, excessively lean man. His thin razor-like face and hawk's-bill of a nose. The curved pipe, the dressing gown. The way he paced up and down the room, quickly, eagerly, his head sunk upon his chest. The way he examined the scene of a crime, on all fours, his nose to the ground. The gaunt dynamic figure and his incisive speech. The gasogene, the Persian slipper, and the coal scuttle for the cigars. The bullet-pocks on the wall, the scraping violin. The hypodermic syringe—what a shock to my fledgling sensibilities! The ghostly hansom cab—with a twelve-year-old boy clinging by some miracle of literary gymnastics to its back as it rattled off through the mist and fog. . . .

Reader, I had met Sherlock Holmes.[1]

—April 1946

NOTE

1. Adapted from the introduction to *The Misadventures of Sherlock Holmes* (Boston: Little, Brown, 1944).

CALIX MEUS INEBRIANS
QUAMPRAECLARUS EST

by VINCENT STARRETT

AS MAN TO MAN, now, what sort of murder do you particularly adore? I mean, of course, in a book. What is your secret passion in the way of fictive corpses? A nameless body with a jeweled dagger still quivering in the warm flesh? A bullet-slain card expert, clutching the jack of hearts in his lifeless fingers? A hideous gargoyle swaying beneath a blackened rafter? Or do you fancy a still, cold form about whose pale lips the transcendent fathomer detects the familiar odor of bitter almonds?

And, in the matter of fathomers, what will you have? A hulking bully from Headquarters, with a gob of tobacco in his cheek? A lean scientist with high-domed brow, speaking a jargon of the higher mathematics? A dull inspector from the Yard, pursuing his investigations in the stodgy precincts of an English village? A cheeky amateur of unbelievable intuition, with a passion for tea and sausages? Or an amiable dilettante with mismated eyes? Or a blind polyglot, retired? Or a grave professor from the universities? Or Father Brown?

Thank you! I will myself take Mr. Sherlock Holmes of Baker Street. I will take him, if need be—in two handsome omnibus volumes—to a desert island, and do without the Bible, the *Iliad,* and Shakespeare.

Darkness is setting in, a storm is rising, and there is potential danger in every creak and whisper of the locked-up house. But it is only a short stroll to the bookcase—a short *dash.* One passes the windows going and returning. So! I am back in the big chair now, and all is well; all save that queer bulge in the curtains, and that recurrent sound in the stair. . . .

Sherlock Holmes and Dr. Watson! I first met them on a doorstep in Toronto. The story was *The Speckled Band,* which I was reading out of turn in a book discovered in the family bookcase. My age, I think, was not yet ten. The attractive title of the volume had taken my eye; I was reading at random. A little later, with pounding pulse, I hurried to the beginning, to read what had gone before. That afternoon life really began for me, a lifetime of almost single-minded devotion.

Did he really live? I wondered. I know now that he did and does; and the old house still stands in Baker Street to prove it. The address as reported by Watson was obviously selected to mislead autograph seekers; but I could find it tomorrow morning. Not even the Hunnish bombs were able to destroy it. It will continue to stand, as Mr. Irving Dilliard has said, as long as the cold London fog rolls in with the winter and mischief is planned and thwarted and books are written and read.

"You are a benefactor of the race," said Watson to Sherlock Holmes, in *The Red-Headed League.*

I am content that the last word shall be Watson's.

—January 1946

"Yes, Virginia, There Is a Sherlock Holmes"

by Julian Wolff, m.d.

In the *Manchester Guardian Weekly* of 20 April 1961 Michael Frayn wrote: "Not enough credit, I sometimes feel, is given to the energy and imagination of those devoted souls who contribute to our newspapers not for sordid gain but for pure love. I mean the people who write letters to the editors."

Well, we have singled out for credit and special attention this most interesting communication from one of our readers and the editor's reply to it.

> Dear Mister Editor:
>
> I am a young blonde girl (38–22–36) and all my friends in our chorus line laugh at me because I believe in Sherlock Holmes. They say that there is no such person and that he was invented just to fool people.
>
> I asked my sugar daddy and he said to write to The Baker Street Journal, because if you see it in the Journal, it's so. Please tell me, is there a Sherlock Holmes?
>
> Virginia B. G. West

Dear Virginia, your daddy is correct. If you see it in The Baker Street Journal, it is so—and so it is. Your friends are all wrong, and you are right. There has to be a Sherlock Holmes. How can we dismiss the existence of such a great man whose adventures have given so much pleasure to so many people? Just because he has become a legend one does not have to stop believing in him. Many other great men have become legends, and everybody believes in them. None of your friends ever saw Abraham Lincoln or George Washington (or maybe even Babe Ruth and Diamond Jim Brady—two really fabulous characters) but they believe in them all. They are certainly legendary figures. King Arthur and Robin Hood are too, and many, many others, too numerous to list here. No one doubts their reality, even though we must depend on stories printed in books for what we know about them.

And what stories, and what books we have about Sherlock Holmes! How can anyone read Vincent Starrett's *Private Life of Sherlock Holmes* and then say that he does not exist? Who can read Dr. Watson's reminiscences without *knowing* that there *must* be a Sherlock Holmes? How can a person visit those famous places connected with him, Baker Street, the Criterion Bar, the Reichenbach, all marked with plaques, and then be so silly as to believe that there never was such a man? What is more, Sherlock Holmes enjoys one great advantage over all those other legendary people: he is immortal, and we shall always have him with us.

No Sherlock Holmes, indeed! The next thing your misguided friends will say is that there is no Santa Claus—and in this month of the year, too. Or, to be completely ridiculous, somebody may insist that there is no Dr. Watson, who gave us all those wonderful stories.

The world is in a bad enough state as it is. Let us not make it worse by removing one of the fixed points in a changing age, one of the few influences for good among so many that tend to move in the opposite direction.

Yes, Virginia, there is a Sherlock Holmes, and I am glad that you wrote to me because I enjoyed this opportunity to say what I thought about that great and good man who has gladdened my heart and the hearts of so many others all over the world.

And in closing, even though it is a little early, I shall quote from *The Blue Carbuncle* and wish you and all my readers "the compliments of the season."

—December 1961

THE EXTRAORDINARY CASE OF THE SIX UNKNOWN STORIES

by DUNCAN MACDOUGALD, JR.

"SIX NEW SHERLOCK HOLMES STORIES DISCOVERED," shriek the *Second Coming* headlines, as hagiologists of the Canon all over the planet collapse in a beatific swoon, too blissful to even grasp for their gasogenes. "Material Said to Contain," the sub-caption ecstatically proclaims, "Some of Author's Greatest Writing!"

It may be unequivocally stated that such an announcement would unleash more primordial bliss to devotees of Sherlock Holmes than any other piece of intelligence the human mind could possibly ever contemplate. However, and horrendously enough, it seems highly improbable that such a miraculous discovery will ever be made.

Yet on the other hand, there is at least one perfervid reader of the Sacred Writings who has that ineffable prospect, namely, the reading for the first time of six of the stories before him. And with outrageous gloating and shameless smirks of smugness I am enchanted to announce that I am that fortunate mortal!

It happened like this. I first came across the *Corpus scriptorum sanctissimorum* when I was twelve or thirteen years old. At that time the sterling doings of Tom Swift totally swamped my attention. To be sure, the Sherlock Holmes stories were fairly interesting; but it was the indomitable Tom's adventures that really roused a seething interest in me.

About five years later, I returned to Sherlock Holmes; this time the impression was much more acute and I experienced a strange new feeling of satisfaction while following the Master as he nimbly but inexorably ferreted out the enemies of society and brought them to bay.

Some four years later, possessed of a brand-new degree from

26

Princeton, and having read a passel of the World's Greatest Authors in six or seven languages, I returned to the Canon. Then and there, at some twenty-one years of age, I discovered once and for all, like Keats peeking into Chapman's Homer, the greatness—nay, the Absolute Uniqueness—of the author's art.

Now, although I had rummaged through such standard classics as Homer and Sophocles in Greek, Horace and Lucretius in Latin, Dante and Leopardi in Italian, Cervantes and Espronceda in Spanish, Molière and Balzac in French, Goethe and Heine in German, Shakespeare and Shelley in English, to say nothing of platoons of others, I had never come across anything like or anything that even remotely approached Sherlock Holmes!

A ghastly, shriveling thought seized me: how many stories were there in the entire extant corpus? And how many had I read? After frenetically thumbing through the *Editio Princeps,* I ascertained that of the total 60 stories I had already read no fewer than the horrifying total of 52! I was panic-stricken! *Corpo di Baccho!* What should I do?

The whole idea was so hideous that I sat down and started figuring. Although I had read a warehouse full of Greek, Latin, Italian, Spanish, French, German, and English literature, there were still hundreds of great works which I had never touched. But of Sherlock Holmes—The Great, The Miraculous, The Mirific, The Absolutely Incomparable—there remained—beastially enough—only eight stories that I did not know!

Obviously I could do only one thing: namely, keep on reading and re-reading the stories I had read, and save for the last—for some dire misfortune, for some catastrophe unspeakable—the eight unknown adventures in all their pristine glory.

This I have done to this day, with the exception of two stories I read after two calamities in the annals of the race—the Fall of lovely Paris in June, 1940, and December the Seventh, 1941. Of the 60 stories, I have now read 54 of them from fifteen to fifty times each. But six of these priceless tales I have never even begun! And so there awaits me the indescribable joy of reading for the first time—if some unutterable misfortune should befall me—one of the six virginal adventures of the Master.

Nor is this all. Obviously I have tracked, with spine a-tingle, *The Hound of the Baskervilles.* Indeed I have read it at least thirty times. *But,* I have only read some 95% of it, as I have never yet dared to force myself to finish it! And I rejoice in being one of the few idolators of the Canon on the globe—perhaps the only one—who still can speculate about the solution to this intriguing mystery.

Furthermore, despite the fact that broadcasts of the Sherlock Holmes stories have been going on for a number of years, I have shunned them with singular assiduity. For that would be, according to the way I feel, sheer heresy. Or more accurately, sheer apostasy.

Nor have I ever seen a film dealing with—or rather purporting to deal with—Sherlock Holmes—oh, no—perish that vilest of thoughts! For I recoil in mortal horror at viewing any cinematic debacle which Hollywood would make of this transcendent character.

In addition, I have still another unusual reaction to the Canon. Although I, as a philologist, have groaned through the intense exegesis of vast piles of "sacred writings," in which emphasis has been laid—in the fashion of the ancient hagiologists—upon the smallest detail in the text, I must confess that I have only a relatively superficial knowledge of all aspects of the stories. This is because I have on purpose read them abstractly—almost vaguely, so to speak—without trying to learn and memorize all the marvelous and exciting details. For example, I don't remember, and I am delighted that I don't, the name of the doctor whose practice Watson acquired; or which one of Sherlock's ancestors came from France and when, etc., etc., etc.

Finally there still remains the extensive body of exegetical studies by many and great students of the Canon. Although I have occasionally peeked surreptitiously at them, I shall never study them seriously. That pleasure is for others—but not for me, for I, for my part, prefer to do my hagiography on far less important questions—say the origin of the human race, or the development of writing. I might add here that I have pursued Sherlock not only in English, but in translation in four or five other languages. This in itself is a great pleasure because the stories appear in a somewhat different light. Although the characters and the plot remain, of course, the same, the fact that they are clothed in a foreign tongue gives them a different, altogether intriguing flavor and atmosphere.

So, as far as Sherlock Holmes is concerned, I only want—for once—to chase every one of my scantilly-clad Circassian dancing girls out of the apartment, and settle 'way back in an easy chair on a drizzling night with a copy of the *Gesamtausgabe*, perhaps some Camembert, *Knåckebrød,* and several bottles of Pilsener.

Let others hold their learned disquisitions about the Master! All I want to do is relax and forget myself in the utterly wondrous and unique world that Sherlock Holmes—and only he—in the entire recorded history of the world's literature has been able to conjure up.

—October 1951

221B

by VINCENT STARRETT

Here dwell together still two men of note
Who never lived and so can never die:
How very near they seem, yet how remote
That age before the world went all awry.
But still the game's afoot for those with ears
Attuned to catch the distant view-halloo:
England is England yet, for all our fears—
Only those things the heart believes are true.

A yellow fog swirls past the window-pane
As night descends upon this fabled street:
A lonely hansom splashes through the rain,
The ghostly gas lamps fail at twenty feet.
Here, though the world explode, these two survive,
And it is always eighteen ninety-five.

THE WRITINGS UPON
THE WRITINGS

Shall the rich vein of Sherlockian topics that may be subjected to our scrutiny ever be exhausted? As Mr. Smith points out, Hamlet would sooner so expire. . . .

THE WRITINGS ABOUT THE WRITINGS

by EDGAR W. SMITH

WHEN THE POSSIBILITY of publishing a journal of Sherlockiana was first discussed, back in 1945, there was much argument as to how often, and with what number of pages, such a periodical might be made to appear. Quite a few desirable items had been crowded out of *Profile by Gaslight,* when it came forth in 1944, and these, it was felt, could form a nucleus around which an Irregular annual, or even a semi-annual, could safely be built, with each issue containing, perhaps, some fifty or sixty pages. There was great skepticism that anything more ambitious than this should be attempted—but the bolder spirits among the organizers prevailed, fortunately, and we know now, in retrospect, how right their counsels were.

The old BAKER STREET JOURNAL was launched as a quarterly in January, 1946, and thirteen issues in all were published, containing an aggregate of 1700-odd closely-printed pages, devoted exclusively to the life and times of Sherlock Holmes. In January, 1951, the new JOURNAL began to issue, and to this date another 280 pages have been added to the saga of the Saga— and the end is, happily, nowhere in sight. "Never," as Christopher Morley put it when he saw the material that was rolling in and weighed it against the JOURNAL's subscription list, "has so much been written by so many for so few." Here, in the writings about the Writings, has been found, by those who feel the kindred urge, a bottomless well of wisdom and delight.

What is it that makes this subject inexhaustible? Why do those who read the magic tales, for all the utter satisfaction their reading gives them, insist on adding something to the lore themselves? Whence comes the irresistible impulse to dig deeper into the meaning of things Sherlockian, and to seek a closer identification or interpretation of the truth?

There is nothing like it, to one's knowledge, in all the field of literature. Not Robinson Crusoe, nor Mr. Pickwick, nor yet great Hamlet has been so honored by the imp of the inquisitive. Do Alice and Don Quixote inspire long hours of research to determine the whys and wherefores of some foible they displayed, or do Pitti-Sing and Madame Buttlerfly compel erudite analyses of the crowded box-rooms of their minds? Ivanhoe and Hiawatha, Dr. Jekyll and David Copperfield, Hercules and George Babbitt—who cares if they were married once or twice, or how profound their knowledge of the Solar System may have been? We know just where Achilles had his wound, and we let it go at that; and we know, too, what college Tom Brown attended and what kind of snake it was that Cleopatra took into her bosom. We know so very much of all the figures that move upon the literary scene, and, knowing, cease to care or question.

But Sherlock Holmes is different. Of him we know, of course, as much as any other—and yet he still remains the great enigma; the one of all the lot we fain would know as we would know ourselves. There is some kind of empathy, perhaps, that moves us to the endless search; that makes us never satisfied with what has been revealed. Or what we do in probing out the inner things is done, it may well be, in emulation of his own approach to life, and as a tribute to his master mind.

Whatever it may be, we know it will go on: we know that men will write of Sherlock Holmes, and what he thought and did and was, for many years to come. The surface, up to now, has not been scratched.

—April 1952

THREE POEMS

by CHRISTOPHER MORLEY

What opiate can best abate
    Anxiety and toil?
Not aspirins, nor treble gins,
    Nor love, nor mineral oil—
My only drug is a good long slug
    Of Tincture of Conan Doyle.

      *   *   *   *

God rest us merry, gentlemen,
    Let nothing us disturb;
So be it we may hear again
    The wheels grind at the kerb,
    Regard, with mien acerb,
    The boots with muddy spots on,
    The tardy German verb. . . .
    You know my methods, Watson!

[This unfinished ballade was composed by Mr. Morley in a hot tub, and was recited by him at the dinner of The Baker Street Irregulars, 5 January 1945. The remaining lines were promised for the 1946 dinner, but they were never delivered.]

      *   *   *   *

If Baker Street required a mate
    Or Reason crowned a queen,
The only one to segregate
    Would be, of course, IRENE.

—September 1961

*A devout Sherlockian warns us not to twist fact to suit
theories in what we accept as true of the Holmes
Canon. . . .*

A Plea for Respect for the Canon
With Some Observations on *The Three Gables*

by Walter Pond

ALL SHERLOCKIAN SCHOLARSHIP must be based on the thesis
that, with four exceptions, the stories which the Canon com-
prises are reports of the great detective's cases written by Dr.
Watson, and that Sir Arthur Conan Doyle was Dr. Watson's literary agent. Once this thesis is abandoned, the foundation of
Canonical research is undermined and Sherlockians will find
themselves adrift on uncharted seas.

For this reason, it is deeply disturbing that some commentators have arrogated to themselves the right to determine, on
the basis of their own predilections, which of the stories are
genuine and which are not, and to declare some of the stories to
be spurious and fictional rather than reports of Holmes's actual
cases. There are two obvious objections to such a position: First,
it is not explained why Dr. Watson should have permitted, without protest, the use of his name in the publication of spurious
reports, and second, the conclusion would be inevitable that Sir
Arthur, as literary agent, participated in a fraud when he placed
the stories for publication. This, of course, is unthinkable.

Moreover, when we examine the reasons given for the rejection of specific stories, we find them without merit. A glaring
example of this is found in the attacks on *The Adventure of the
Three Gables*. An examination of this story may be particularly
appropriate because of an Editorial Note on page 147 of the
September 1977 issue of the JOURNAL, which calls attention to
the fact that some respectable modern scholars view *The Three
Gables* as obviously apocryphal, citing Dakin's *Sherlock Holmes
Commentary*. While Mr. Dakin undoubtedly is a respectable modern scholar, it is clear, upon analysis, that his conclusions have
no validity.

The main reason given by Dakin for his conclusion that the story is spurious relates to the "cheap gibes at the Negro Steve Dixie." According to Dakin, "No admirer of Holmes can read these scenes without a blush. For Holmes was a gentleman; and one thing no gentleman does is to taunt another man for his racial characteristics."[1]

A recent refutation of Dakin's position is found in an article by William P. Collins, entitled "Norbury and Steve Dixie: Holmes and Victorian Racial Attitudes."[2] Mr. Collins shows that there was prejudice against non-white peoples in Victorian England and that it was not considered reprehensible to express it.

Mr. Collins' view is confirmed by G. K. Chesterton's Father Brown. Nobody will accuse Father Brown of being what today is referred to as a racist. But in "The God of the Gongs"[3] the villain is a Negro prize-fighter, like Steve Dixie, who is called "Nigger Ned." Also, like Steve Dixie, he is flashily dressed: "He was buttoned and buckled up to his bursting eyeballs in the most brilliant fashion. A tall black hat was tilted on his broad black head. . . . It is needless to say that he wore white spats and a white slip inside his waistcoat." His teeth are described as "apish." Looking after him, Flambeau says: "Sometimes I am not surprised that they lynch them." And Father Brown states: "That negro who has just swaggered out is one of the most dangerous men on earth, for he has the brains of a European, with the instincts of a cannibal."

This makes Holmes's "cheap gibes" look pretty mild. The fact is that our grandfathers were not as sensitive to racial equality as we are today. Consequently, it is sheer folly to reject a story as spurious because Holmes's attitude does not conform to what we deem desirable today. In this post-Watergate era, are we to declare *Charles Augustus Milverton* a forgery because Holmes commits a burglary and a gentleman like Holmes would not violate poor Milverton's constitutional rights? It seems clear that the only proper attitude is to take Holmes as we find him and not to attempt to determine the authenticity of the stories on the basis of our personal notions of ethics, or plausibility. Otherwise, no part of the Canon would be safe.

Moreover, far from being justification for rejection, Holmes's treatment of Steve Dixie is affirmative proof of the authenticity of the story. For it has always been typical of Holmes to adopt an attitude of languid sarcasm when a bully threatened him with physical violence.

This can be seen as early as 1883 in Holmes's treatment of the villainous Dr. Grimesby Roylott in the *Speckled Band*. Here is the dialogue. Dr. Roylott says: "My stepdaughter has been here. I have traced her. What has she been saying to you?"

"It is a little cold for the time of year," said Holmes.

"What has she been saying to you?" screamed the old man furiously.

"But I have heard that the crocuses promise well," continued my companion imperturbably.

After Dr. Roylott called Holmes a meddler, a busybody, and the Scotland Yard Jack-in-office, Holmes chuckled heartily, and said, "Your conversation is most entertaining. When you go out close the door, for there is a decided draught."

Again, in *The Problem of Thor Bridge*, when Neil Gibson "raised his great knotted fist," Holmes smiled languidly and reached for his pipe, saying: "Don't be noisy, Mr. Gibson. I find that after breakfast even the smallest argument is unsettling."

Thus, when Dr. Watson tells us in *The Three Gables* that after Steve Dixie had burst into the room like "a mad bull" Holmes raised his pipe with a languid smile, this is completely in character. Holmes's attitude in the face of Steve Dixie's threats is exactly what we should expect it to be, and confirms the genuineness of the story.

Mr. Dakin's second reason for rejecting *The Three Gables* as spurious is that no real man would have the name of Langdale Pike. On that basis, we should also eliminate *The Adventure of the Priory School* from the Canon on the ground that no real man would have the name of Thorneycroft Huxtable. This objection is patently frivolous; how frivolous can be seen from an article in the issue of *New York* magazine for 31 October 1977, entitled "Remarkable Names of Real People." Examples of real names given there include "Colonel Clarence Clapsaddle," "Humperdink Fangboner," "Madonna Ghostly," "Positive Wasserman Johnson," and "Toilet Jacobs." This makes "Langdale Pike" look fairly ordinary.

Mr. Dakin states as a third reason for his view that *The Three Gables* was not written by Dr. Watson that "the plot is fantastic and improbable." Of course, this objection has been raised with respect to many of the stories in the Canon. Can there be anything more improbable than the plot of *The Yellow Face*? Mr. Dakin himself has stated that the events described in *The Final Problem* are fantastic and improbable. If that were enough to remove stories from the Canon, very little would be left. We must never forget that Holmes "refused to associate himself with any investigation which did not tend towards the unusual, and even the fantastic."[4]

The only proper attitude for the Sherlockian scholar is to have confidence in the integrity of Dr. Watson and his literary agent and to accord proper respect to all the stories, whether or not they conform to our own notions of ethics or plausibility.

—March 1978

NOTES

1. D. Martin Dakin, *A Sherlock Holmes Commentary* (New York: Drake, 1972), p. 252.

2. BSJ (ns) 27 (1977), 149.

3. *The Father Brown Omnibus* (New York: Dodd, Mead, 1951), p. 368.

4. *The Speckled Band.*

Two Acrostic Sonnets

Cum Laude: The Baker Street Journal
by Belden Wigglesworth

S irs, here we have the medium that we
H ave long desired, through which we can express,
E ach one of us, with fervent eagerness . . .
R eluctantly . . . or otherwise with free
L ogicians' minds, the truth of truths we see
O nce overlooked in Baker Street. Ah yes,
C onfession's good, and here we'll all confess
K ing, prince, and commoner, religiously.

H ere we will give our Watson his full due;
O r, seeking other avenues, explain
L ess happily for Scotland Yard the crimes
M ishandled by Lestrade and Gregson: clue
E ngenders clue to end in Sherlock's gain,
S ince he remains the master of our times.

Cum Laude: Sherlock Holmes
by Bliss Austin

S irs, you're welcome to Dupin and Poe;
H ave also Queen, and if you like say prayers
E ach night to Peter Wimsey and Miss Sayers.
R ex Stout is yours, and corpulent Nero;
L ikewise Lecoq and E. Gaboriau,
O r yet Van Dine and Vance. For aught one cares
C hoose Chesterton and Father Brown's affairs,
K nox, or Mrs. Christie and Poirot.

H ave all of these, I say; but as for me,
O nce I have been in Baker Street by night
L ooking upon his profile by gaslight,
M y sight's too strained such lesser lights to see.
E xcuse me, Sirs! To me no substitute
S erves half so well as: "Come, the game's afoot!"

—January 1946

Everyone knows how Sherlock Holmes has been depicted physically in the popular media; but getting to know the character behind the caricature reveals a level of profundity. . . .

SHERLOCK HOLMES—THE INNER MAN

by GEORGE SIMMONS

IT IS THE MIND, the character, and the philosophy of Sherlock Holmes that have made him one of the landmarks in English literature, and in his own day made him a world figure.

Perhaps the strongest feature of the Holmes legend is one which Watson passed on to us through his own somewhat foggy perception, for it is quite erroneous. Not entirely without reason, casual readers have come to think of Holmes as a thinking machine, a mind without a soul behind it. Watson once remarked, in connection with the almost impenetrable wall of reserve which the detective built around himself:

> During my long and intimate acquaintance with Mr. Sherlock Holmes I had never heard him refer to his relations, and hardly ever to his own early life. This reticence upon his part had increased the somewhat inhuman effect which he produced upon me, until I sometimes found myself regarding him as an isolated phenomenon, a brain without a heart, as deficient in human sympathy as he was preeminent in intelligence. His aversion to women and his disinclination to form new friendships were both typical of his unemotional character, but not more so than his complete suppression of every reference to his own people.

This was, of course, nearly a half-dozen years after the fateful meeting of the two friends, and since Holmes had still failed to mention the fact that he had an elder brother living in London, Watson's conclusions were perhaps justified to a certain extent. In one of his rare gregarious moods, however, Holmes finally did get around to a few words about his early life, in his recital of the goings-on in the case of *The "Gloria Scott."* The circumstances of this, Holmes's first recorded case, began with a vacation invitation from one Victor Trevor, the only friend he made in his two years at college. Holmes himself comments:

42

> I was never a very sociable fellow, Watson, always rather fond of mop-
> ing in my rooms and working out my own little methods of thought, so
> that I never mixed much with the men of my year. Bar fencing and box-
> ing I had few athletic tastes, and then my line of study was quite distinct
> from that of the other fellows, so that we had no points of contact at all.

"I was never a very sociable fellow," he says. What a classic understatement! What a bohemian soul he must have had, to
make but one friend in college, where most men make so many!
R. K. Leavitt, in his little study *"Nummi in Arca*; or, the Fiscal
Holmes,"[1] observed that many youths, who are of introspective
disposition, and who have a taste for solitude, develop astonishing powers. So it was with Holmes. Watson, at this stage of their
friendship, still had not begun to plumb the depths of Holmes's
extraordinary character.

T. S. Blakeney has made a very apt comparison between
Holmes and the Iron Duke of Wellington. He says:

> In both, despite an outwardly cold aspect, we are vouchsafed glimpses
> of an emotional (not sentimental) nature kept in strong control, re-
> pressed, perhaps, from a sense that any display was a sign of weakness.
> Both were keen musicians, and music is the most emotional of all the
> arts; both could be delightful with children, who instinctively know real
> from feigned affability. The Iron Duke broke down seldom, but those
> breaks were very complete; the other side of Holmes's nature peeps
> through even less thoroughly, but not less certainly.

Recall the experiment with *radix pedis diaboli*, in *The Devil's Foot*;
recall the occasion when Watson was shot while apprehending
Killer Evans, in *The Three Garridebs*. Watson, in the second instance, said:

> It was worth a wound—it was worth many wounds—to know the
> depths of loyalty and love which lay behind that cold mask. The clear,
> hard eyes were dimmed for a moment, and the firm lips were shaking.
> For the one and only time I caught a glimpse of a great heart as well as a
> great brain. All my years of humble but single-minded service culmi-
> nated in that moment of revelation.

Deficient in human sympathy, indeed! It seems that Watson was
as poor a student of human nature as he was a logician. But
"one and only" is again wide of the mark. There is another passage of this kind in *The Six Napoleons*. Holmes has just built a
situation to a high pitch of dramatic excitement in one of those

masterful denouements of his, and he brings it off with a true artist's touch:

> Lestrade and I sat silent for a moment, [said Watson,] and then, with a spontaneous impulse, we both broke out clapping, as at the well-wrought crisis of a play. A flush of color sprang to Holmes's pale cheeks, and he bowed to us like the master dramatist who receives the homage of his audience. It was at such moments that for an instant he ceased to be a reasoning machine, and betrayed his human love for admiration and applause. The same singularly proud and reserved nature which turned with disdain from popular notoriety was capable of being moved to its depths by spontaneous wonder and praise from a friend.

Watson says it admirably. Holmes, rather than being a mere machine, and something scarcely human, was a man even as you and I—but he had himself well in hand. He knew himself, and, like the old Greek, had attained the mastery of self and serenity of spirit which are the results of self-knowledge.

As a philosopher he was neither profound nor original, but he was a close observer of life; he drew conclusions, and he thought about them. His was neither optimism nor pessimism, cynicism nor fatalism, but a subtle blend of many traits, which varied with his mood. He was, however, notably free from external influences which so roughly use our own whims and caprices. His ability to concentrate was very great, and it took only an effort of will for his mind to be freed for a time of mundane matters.

His religious views, if any, are the most obscure parts of his makeup. On only one occasion did he speak definitely of religion, and that was a rather strange and incongruous one. In the midst of his cross-questionings in *The Naval Treaty*, he suddenly commented: "What a lovely thing a rose is!" Then he walked across the room, and held up a drooping moss-rose, saying,

> There is nothing in which deduction is so necessary as in religion. It can be built up as an exact science by the reasoner. Our highest assurance of the goodness of Providence seems to me to rest in the flowers. All other things, our powers, our desires, our food, are all really necessary for our existence in the first instance. But this rose is an extra. Its smell and colour are an embellishment of life, not a condition of it. It is only goodness which gives extras, and so I say again that we have much to hope from the flowers.

His listeners received this statement with astonishment, and Watson most of all. He well knew how small a part the appreciation of nature and its beauties played in his friend's mental processes. It is interesting to note that after almost a score of years of close association, Watson was still as much in the dark as ever as to what went on in that strange mind. Holmes seemed at one time to have a hope for another life; witness his comment to the Veiled Lodger: "The ways of fate are indeed hard to understand. If there is not some compensation hereafter, then the world is a cruel jest."

He inclined in his later years to the opinion that that very hope, which sustains so many in their constant strivings to ward off life's manifold sorrows and satisfy its endless needs, is but a hope and a dream, and contains no part of reality. In *The Retired Colourman,* Holmes put forth the dreary question: "But is not all life pathetic and futile? Is not his story a microcosm of the whole? We reach. We grasp. What is left in our hands in the end? A shadow. Or worse than a shadow—misery."

He maintained a partly humorous, partly cynical attitude through most of his life. His sense of humor was acid and dry, but strong. A vein of fatalism threaded persistently through the whole.

However active he might be in the heat of the chase, part of him was always the onlooker, reluctant to lapse out of a spectator's interest in what was going on. This, perhaps, is part of the secret of the inhuman composure with which he met every situation, and which he preserved without a marring wrinkle through the most trying circumstances.

He found great interest in the vagaries and paradoxes of human existence, and derived from it the slightly sardonic attitude which is so often that of those who are well aware of what "fools these mortals be." "My dear fellow," he once said to Watson, across their fireplace,

"life is infinitely stranger than anything which the mind of man could invent. We would not dare to conceive the things which are really mere commonplaces of existence. If we could fly out of that window, hand in hand, hover over this great city, gently remove the roofs, and peep in at the queer things which are going on, the strange coincidences, the plannings, the cross-purposes, the wonderful chains of events, working through generations, and leading to the most *outré* results, it would make all fiction with its conventionalities and foreseen conclusions most stale and unprofitable."

When Holmes was at college he undoubtedly read very widely. Many of his pet methods of thought were picked up from the more brilliant among his proxy tutors, and the lessons stuck, which is really extraordinary among undergraduates, when you come to think about it. He made many remarks on the folly of prejudice. One—"I make a point of never having any prejudices and of following docilely wherever fact may lead me."—has an interesting phraseology. Compare it with that of Thomas Henry Huxley: "Sit down before fact as a little child, be prepared to give up every preconceived notion, follow humbly and to whatever abysses nature leads, or you shall learn nothing."

Holmes keenly appreciated the great value of an open mind, and it seems that he was acquainted with Huxley's ideas on the subject. Again, he laid great stress on the importance of detail: "It has long been a maxim of mine that the little things are infinitely the most important." "It is of course a trifle, but there is nothing so important as trifles."

This phrase goes back even farther. It was the opinion of Michelangelo that "Trifles make perfection, but perfection is no trifle." Perhaps Holmes acquired some of that dilettante's knowledge of art, about which Watson ragged him, from reading of the great Italian master.

The credulous people of the world are sometimes deceived, but often they gain far more than they lose. This is a good attitude to take when reading the chronicles of the good Watson. Give yourself up to the magic of his pen, and you will be gently wafted into a different world, and a fascinating one. If you are the blunt realist who says "Holmes never lived, so why the fuss?" you are beyond hope; for he *did* live. His was and is a far more permanent reality than that of legions who have passed across the sands of life and have been forced to make their imprints with the transient flesh. His was the realm of subjective fancy, and many kings and warriors and statesmen may well envy him his immortality, he who shall never die. There is no reality too strong to blot out the vision of that pale, gaunt figure, curled in the chair by the fireplace, with his pipe sending forth its tenuous whorls.

Should the kind gods ever grant me a visit into some page of the past, there can be no doubt as to which I should choose. Some might prefer to sit by the side of Socrates in the market place of Athens, and discourse with him and with his small following. Others might like to visit the dinner table at Ferney, and listen to the blithe Voltaire, most intrepid and persistent of all the generals in the great perennial war upon intolerance and injustice. A large group would doubtless wend their way to the tavern in which Marlowe, Jonson, and Shakespeare used to spend jolly evenings. You and I, fellow believer, would of a certainty choose to be in Baker Street some gloomy night, with the yellow London fog blotting out the houses across the way. We would sit in the light of the flickering fire, and gaze into it to the accompaniment of Holmes's violin, as it brings to him the peace for which he yearns; or as it lifts his great mind to new heights of power and clarity. Let us have the commissionaire bring in a note, one of those which have presaged so many a long chase. We shall then attain a clear glimpse of that iridescent bubble Adventure—beautiful, rich with tints of romance, and tinged with hints of happiness, finely shaded with heroism.

—April 1947

NOTE

1. In *221B: Studies in Sherlock Holmes.*

*Lurking behind the Master Detective's devotion to
justice may—just may—have been a higher
calling. . . .*

THE RELIGIOUS SHERLOCK HOLMES

by EDGAR S. ROSENBERGER

WAS SHERLOCK HOLMES religious? Offhand, no. He smoked,[1] drank,[2] swore,[3] gambled,[4] took dope,[5] and pursued women of dubious virtue[6]—the last not, as every reader knows, on the common earthly plane, but in the intellectual stratosphere in which he lived. He once took part in a barroom brawl,[7] once threw a man over a cliff,[8] once threatened to horsewhip a man,[9] gave another a black eye,[10] five times burgled a house,[11] and once, with the aid of Watson, shot a man dead in cold blood.[12] There is no evidence that he danced, played cards, or told off-color stories, but he lied,[13] cheated,[14] and blackmailed.[15]

Yet to call Sherlock Holmes an unrighteous man because of all this would be to convict him on technicalities alone. "My business is that of every good citizen—to uphold the law," he coolly told the blustering Sir Robert Norberton.[16] And in that grave hour when he faced the heroic end of his brilliant career he remarked to Watson, "In over a thousand cases I am not aware that I have ever used my powers on the wrong side."[17] In Watson's own words, he was the foremost champion of the law of his generation.[18] He was "the best and the wisest man" whom Watson ever knew.[19] Need more be said?

"All things, as the poet says, 'Beauty take from those who loved them in other days,' and Baker Street has been less uninteresting since Sherlock Holmes, with his pipe and dressing-gown, took up his abode in it, and listened sympathetically to the stories of a succession of pale young ladies dressed in black." So wrote J. C. Squire in *A London Reverie*.[20] Mr. Squire is evidently an impressionist, and while his version of the Baker Street scene is factually reprehensible, in a symbolic sense it is acceptable. Sherlock Holmes was indeed a kind man, a fact that Watson corroborates with his assertion that "Holmes was acces-

48

sible upon the side of flattery, and also, to do him justice, upon the side of kindliness."[21] He had, Watson further informs us, a remarkable gentleness and courtesy in his dealings with women, and one sees the trembling Helen Stoner, the fatuous Mary Sutherland, and the persistent Mrs. Warren—total strangers all—treated by Sherlock Holmes as deferentially as if they had been his daughters.

His icy coldness and his deadpan emotional objectivity were obviously a defense mechanism. It would never do for Brooks, or Woodhouse, or any of the fifty men who had good reason for taking his life—to say nothing of the stalwart men of Scotland Yard—to think of him as a gentle, good-hearted old goat. Henry Staunton, whom he helped to hang, surely had no such illusions. It remained for Watson, to the undoubted annoyance of his friend, to reveal the finer nature of Sherlock Holmes. "We have had the good fortune to bring peace to many troubled souls," Holmes told the distraught Grant Munro.[22] And in that contemptible little scamp, James Ryder, he saw a soul to be saved, in that frosty Christmas season long ago.[23] "Besides," said Holmes, "it is the season of forgiveness." While all emotions were abhorrent to his cold, precise but admirably balanced mind, and he never spoke of the softer passions save with a gibe or a sneer, he was nevertheless shaken to the very depths of his being when the life of his only true friend in the world was endangered by Killer Evans, alias John Garrideb. "It was worth a wound," wrote Watson, "it was worth many wounds to know the depth of loyalty and love which lay behind that cold mask. The clear, hard eyes were dimmed for a moment, and the firm lips were shaking. For the one and only time I caught a glimpse of a great heart as well as of a great brain."[24] This, coming from Watson, is ample proof that Sherlock Holmes was more than a mere thinking machine. Verily, he had a soul.

But even as Sherlock Holmes could soothe the troubled and the bewildered, so he could flay mercilessly the rich and the mighty who had transgressed the moral law. The Duke of Holdernesse, one of the most revered names in all England, stood speechless as Holmes berated him within his own ducal hall.[25] That personification of rugged individualism, Neil Gibson, the American Gold King, who was accustomed to getting what he wanted and laying down the law to others, had the law laid down to him by Mr. Sherlock Holmes. "Some of you rich men," lectured Holmes, himself a rich man, "have to be taught that all the world cannot be bribed into condoning your offences."[26] In a lighter moment he advised the wheezy, profane Susan Stockdale, "It's a wicked thing to tell fibs."[27] He accused his friend of the same vice, saying, "Your morals don't improve, Watson. You have added fibbing to your other vices."[28] Watson's fib was his assertion that his medical practice was not too demanding, when it was obvious to the trained eye of Sherlock Holmes that he was a busy man.

It is clear, from a careful study of the Canon, that Sherlock Holmes had a religious early upbringing. His pious parents— would that we knew more of them!—saw to it that he was properly versed in the Scriptures, though it is as regrettable as it is obvious that in his adult years his passion for criminology crowded out his biblical erudition. "My biblical knowledge is a trifle rusty, I fear," he said, referring to the affair of Uriah and Bathsheba, "but you will find the story in the first or second of Samuel."[29] And fretting and fuming over the state of affairs at the Copper Beeches he cried, "I can't make bricks without clay."[30] If his metaphor referred, as it undoubtedly did, to the travail of the children of Israel in the land of Egypt, he meant bricks without straw. In that delightful little game of deduction in which Holmes and Watson sought to discover the key to the cryptic message from Fred Porlock that marked the beginning of the long trail to the Valley of Fear, Watson, knowing his friend well, triumphantly exclaimed, "The Bible!"[31] There is no reason to doubt that Holmes owned a Bible, for he replies, with a touch of subtle humor, "Even if I accepted the compliment for myself, I could hardly name any volume which would be less likely to lie at the elbow of one of Moriarty's associates."

The religious element interested Holmes even in the field of drama and music. His brilliant conversation, during the little repast with Watson and Athelney Jones that preceded that wild and never-to-be-forgotten chase down the Thames in pursuit of the great Agra treasure, included the subject of miracle plays.[32]

And during the whole of that memorable day when the fate of England hung in the balance because of the theft of the Bruce-Partington plans, he refreshed his great mind with his

50

celebrated monograph upon the polyphonic motets of Lassus.[33] On another occasion it was probably one of these motets, weirdly chanted by the supposedly delirious Holmes, that sent cold chills down Watson's spine as he descended the stairs to set forth upon his quest for the rascally Culverton Smith.[34]

Humility is one of the true signs of a religious as well as a great personality. Sherlock Holmes was humble. Though having no misgivings about his extraordinary talents, he nevertheless regarded them as a gift from a higher power. Shaken to his soul by the tragic death of John Openshaw, he said, "If God sends me health, I shall set my hand upon this gang."[35] Hitting suddenly upon the solution of the disappearance of Lady Frances Carfax, he exclaimed, "What has become of any brains that God has given me?"[36] Recognizing his limitations, he remarked half-humorously to Dr. James Mortimer, "In a modest way I have combatted evil, but to take on the Father of Evil himself would, perhaps, be too ambitious a task."[37]

Further unmistakable evidence of Sherlock Holmes's early religious conditioning is to be found in his extraordinary respect for the clergy. One fancies that he readily dropped all but the most urgent cases to oblige a member of the ecclesiastical hierarchy. In the year '95 he carried out his famous investigation of the sudden death of Cardinal Tosca—an inquiry which was carried out by him at the express desire of His Holiness the Pope.[38] The public owes a debt of gratitude to Dr. James Mortimer, M.R.C.S., for his persistence in bringing the affair of the Hound of the Baskervilles to the attention of Sherlock Holmes. "I had observed some newspaper comment at the time," said Holmes, "but I was exceedingly preoccupied by that little affair of the Vatican cameos, and in my anxiety to oblige the Pope I lost touch with several interesting English cases." Again, he regarded the affair of the two Coptic Patriarchs as of more importance than the strange disappearance, at Lewisham, of Mrs. Josiah Amberley and Dr. Ray Ernest.[39] Once, strangely enough, he played a trick on a clergyman, but it backfired on poor Watson. The vicar of Little Purlington, whom Holmes used to decoy his friend and Josiah Amberley while he burgled the latter's house, proved to be not the kindly, white-haired old gentleman whom Holmes had probably assumed him to be, but an explosive choleric individual who quickly showed his callers the door.[40] Holmes also had a weakness for disguising himself as a clergyman, which is understandable in view of his high regard for members of the cloth. It was as a simple-minded Nonconformist clergyman that he played upon the sympathies of the kind-hearted if worldly Irene Adler in order to gain admittance to her residence.[41] As a venerable Italian priest he deceived not only Professor Moriarty, who was in hot pursuit, but even the good Watson, who sat opposite him in a railway carriage.[42]

But it is in the field of homiletics that we perceive the truly religious nature of Sherlock Holmes. Again and again throughout the tales we see Holmes the philosopher, Holmes the theologian, Holmes the humble minister of the gospel. Even as the prophets of old, he pondered the infinite mysteries of life, and sought an answer. "God help us!" he fervently exclaimed, as the aged, pathetic John Turner tottered out of the room.[43] "Why does fate play such tricks with poor, helpless worms? I never hear of such a case as this that I do not think of Baxter's words, and say, 'There, but for the grace of God, goes Sherlock Holmes.'" But he not only bemoaned the cruel fate of this world; he believed in the stern fact of moral law in the universe. "You are yourself aware," he told the same John Turner, "that you will soon have to answer for your deed at a higher court than the Assizes." Of the misguided Mary Holder he said, "Whatever her sins are, they will soon receive a more than sufficient punishment."[44] To the unfortunate Henry Wood, who had been wronged by Colonel James Barclay, he said, "You have at least the satisfaction of knowing that for thirty years of his life his conscience bitterly reproached him for his wicked deed."[45] Sherlock Holmes, who knew the criminal underworld of London as few men knew it, saw how terrible a toll justice exacts from those who follow the paths of evil. "The wages of sin, Watson—the wages of sin!" he exclaimed, as he listened, pale and shaken, to Watson's account of the ghastly climax of the career of the suave and murderous Baron Adelbert Gruner.[46] "Sooner or later it will always come. God knows, there was sin enough." Again Sherlock Holmes echoed the precepts of truth that he had learned in his early home.

Sherlock Holmes believed, as all believers must, that mankind has a destiny, that there is purpose and direction in this often disordered cosmos. Yet like all good souls, seeing the misery of the world, he sometimes had to pause and ask, Why, Why? "What is the meaning of it, Watson?" he solemnly asked, after reading Jim Browner's confession of the murder of Mary Cushing and her lover.[47] "What object is served by this circle of misery and violence and fear? It must tend to some end, or else our universe is ruled by chance, which is unthinkable. But what end? There is the great standing perennial problem to which human reason is as far from an answer as ever." Holmes was right; man has sought an answer to that question since the early dawn of history, and hasn't found it yet. But perhaps Holmes answered the question himself, not only for his own satisfaction, but for that of all mankind, when he said, "Mr. Neil Gibson has learned something in that schoolroom of sorrow where our earthly lessons are taught."[48]

"Consider the lilies of the field, how they grow; they toil not, neither do they spin: And yet I say unto you, That even Solomon in all his glory was not arrayed like one of these."[49] These words were uttered by a greater man than Sherlock Holmes, yet how like them is the only passage in the long saga in which Holmes speaks forthrightly of religion. Stumped for the time being by the baffling disappearance of the Naval Treaty, he became lost in a dream reverie in that world of changeless beauty that is mankind's spiritual heritage. "What a lovely thing a rose is!" he exclaimed, to the consternation of Percy Phelps and his fiancée. "There is nothing in which deduction is so necessary as in religion. It can be built up as an exact science by the reasoner. Our highest assurance of the goodness of Providence seems to me to rest in the flowers. All other things, our powers, our desires, our food, are all really necessary for our existence in the first instance. But this rose is an extra. Its smell and its colour are an embellishment of life, not a condition of it. It is only goodness which gives extras, and so I say again that we have much to hope from the flowers."

Surely this passage should dispel any doubts we might have concerning Sherlock Holmes's higher nature. Here we see not the master detective running down the fugitive from justice, but the kindly clergyman, bringing hope and comfort to a distressed parishioner. To many a troubled soul Holmes might say, "You see, but you do not observe." Even as his amazing intellect tracked down the doer of an evil deed, so it saw the eternal verities shining through where others saw only darkness.

It is in the worst of the tales that Sherlock Holmes rises to his greatest spiritual heights.[50] It was not a detective, but a counselor whom Eugenia Ronder sought. "Poor girl, poor girl," he said, patting her hand with a show of sympathy such as Watson had seldom known him to exhibit. "The ways of fate are indeed hard to understand. If there is not some compensation hereafter, then the world is a cruel jest." One deduces that Holmes himself believed in the immortality of the soul. As he had sent more than one wicked man to the gallows, so now he intervened to save a worthy life. "Your life is not your own," he told the unhappy woman who felt she had nothing more to live for. "Keep your hands off it." "What use is it to anyone?" she protested. "How can you tell?" he replied. "The example of patient suffering is in itself the most precious of all lessons to an impatient world." Here we see Sherlock Holmes far afield from the science of crime detection, teaching that the victory of the spirit over life's cruelties and injustices is the greatest of all conquests. His brief sermon paid off well, for he shortly received a bottle of prussic acid, with the message, "I send you my temptation. I will follow your advice."

Like all mortals, Sherlock Holmes had his times of doubt and misgiving. "Is not all life pathetic and futile?" he complained to Watson, speaking of the wretched Josiah Amberley.[51] "Is not his story a microcosm of the whole? We reach. We grasp. And what is left in our hands at the end? A shadow. Or worse than a shadow—misery." But again he sought man's higher nature even when the outward signs of it were lacking. "Dirty-looking rascals," he said, as home-going workmen swarmed under the gaslight out of Jacobson's Yard, on the Surrey side of the Thames.[52] "But I suppose every one has some little immortal spark concealed about him. You would not think it, to look at them. There is no *a priori* probability about it. A strange enigma is man!" Yet again he reaffirmed his belief in the spiritual when he said, speaking of the effects of H. Lowenstein's monkey serum on Professor Presbury,[53] "There is danger there—a very real danger to humanity. Consider, Watson, that the material, the sensual, the worldly would all prolong their worthless lives.

The spiritual would not avoid the call to something higher." Holmes would not have mentioned that "something higher" had he not experienced it in his own life.

The Mystery of the Early Retirement has not yet been solved. Why did Sherlock Holmes retire from active practice when, according to the consensus of experts, he was not yet fifty years of age? Perhaps some day one of the more brilliant minds among the learned scions of Baker Street will come forward with a theory that will rock the Holmesian world to its very foundations, but in the meantime the question remains a moot one. True, as early as 1891 Holmes was on Easy Street for life—thanks largely to the crowned heads of Europe, who dipped freely into their ample exchequers in grateful recognition of his assistance in helping them out of embarrassing predicaments. Yet Sherlock Holmes was a man of action whose mind rebelled at stagnation, and one cannot imagine that loafing had any attraction for him. Well, the fact of the matter is that he hated his profession, even as the captain hates the sea. His real desire was to be a minister of the gospel. His penchant for sermonizing, his fawning servility toward the clergy, his irrepressible urge to masquerade as one of them, point to no other conclusion.

As a young man he was frustrated in that direction, and his energies were of necessity diverted into the channels of crime detection. Perhaps he fell flat as a public speaker, or lacked other necessary qualities for the ministry. Brilliance in one field of endeavor is sometimes a form of compensation for frustration in another—a sort of neurosis—and so it may well have been with Holmes. In spite of his sensational achievements as a detective he still suffered from a sense of inadequacy because of failure to enter his chosen field, and would lie around for days on end in a mood of blackest depression. So, having made his pile, he retired to the Sussex Downs and gave himself up to the study of philosophy—including theology—and to the dream he had dreamed so long of moving the multitudes with his eloquence—from the pulpit of St. Paul's, or St. Martin's-in-the-Fields, or the City Temple.

—April 1948

55

1. Tales too numerous to mention.
2. Ibid.
3. *A Study in Scarlet, The Final Problem.*
4. *Silver Blaze.*
5. *The Sign of the Four,* et al.
6. *A Scandal in Bohemia, The Three Gables.*
7. *The Solitary Cyclist.*
8. *The Empty House.*
9. *A Case of Identity.*
10. *The Naval Treaty.*
11. *Charles Augustus Milverton, The Valley of Fear, The Illustrious Client, The Bruce-Partington Plans, The Retired Colourman.*
12. *The Sign of the Four.*
13. *The Missing Three-Quarter.*
14. *The Cardboard Box.*
15. *The Three Gables.*
16. *Shoscombe Old Place.*
17. *The Final Problem.*
18. Ibid.
19. Ibid.
20. New York: Macmillan, 1937.
21. *The Red Circle.*
22. *The Yellow Face.*
23. *The Blue Carbuncle.*
24. *The Three Garridebs.*
25. *The Priory School.*
26. *Thor Bridge.*
27. *The Three Gables.*
28. *The Mazarin Stone.*
29. *The Crooked Man.*
30. *The Copper Beeches.*
31. *The Valley of Fear.*
32. *The Sign of the Four.*
33. *The Bruce-Partington Plans.*
34. *The Dying Detective.*
35. *The Five Orange Pips.*
36. *Lady Frances Carfax.*

37. *The Hound of the Baskervilles.*
38. *Black Peter.*
39. *The Retired Colourman.*
40. Ibid.
41. *A Scandal in Bohemia.*
42. *The Final Problem.*
43. *Boscombe Valley.*
44. *The Beryl Coronet.*
45. *The Crooked Man.*
46. *The Illustrious Client.*
47. *The Cardboard Box.*
48. *Thor Bridge.*
49. Matthew 6:28, 29
50. *The Veiled Lodger.*
51. *The Retired Colourman.*
52. *The Sign of the Four.*
53. *The Creeping Man.*

One can sooner picture Captain Ahab sans harpoon
than Sherlock Holmes without his pipe. Herewith, an
examination of the Master and his famous habit. . . .

No Fire Without Some Smoke

by John L. Hicks

"Genius," says William James, Sherlock Holmes's great contemporary, "in truth, means little more than the faculty of perceiving in an unhabitual way."[1] The Great Detective of course had that faculty in a higher degree than any other man of his time. Another philosopher, Thomas Carlyle, who was also living during the period of Holmes's early cases, speaks of genius as the "transcendent capacity for taking trouble first of all,"[2] and Holmes again undoubtedly qualified. In *A Study in Scarlet* he remarks, "To a great mind, nothing is little."

But where and how, one may ask, did he acquire the "faculty" of observation and the "capacity" for taking pains? His musical talent, his aptitude for scholarship, his scientific ability— these were doubtless all inherited from ancestors that produced the French artist Vernet and the American scholar and scientist Oliver Wendell Holmes. The Master himself says, in *The Adventure of the Empty House*: "I have a theory that the individual represents in his development the whole procession of his ancestors. . . ." He would not have evolved such a theory if his own qualities had not offered evidence supporting it. "To some extent," also, as he declares in *The Greek Interpreter,* "systematic training" increased his facility. His power of observation and his faculty of patiently attending to details, however, cannot be wholly explained in this manner. Moreover, his ability to use the data he gathered by observing carefully and not neglecting details—his great power of deduction—could not have been due entirely to heredity and training. It is true that in *The Greek Interpreter* he attributes his artistry in reasoning partly to his artistic ancestors and offers as proof the superior abilities of Mycroft, but this is only a partial explanation.

A close study of the Sacred Writings reveals that Sherlock

58

Holmes's powers as a logician were due largely to his pipe—and primarily to his briar pipe. Mycroft, of the keen mind and capacious memory, was exceedingly lazy; indeed, he could be greatly moved only when, as in *The Bruce-Partington Plans,* the welfare of his country was threatened. He received inspiration from tobacco, but the tobacco was in the form of snuff. Sherlock was not only a thinker but also a man of action, and he, significantly, smoked a pipe. The difference in the forms in which the two brothers used tobacco explains their dissimilarity in temperament.

No one can seriously question that the Master preferred a pipe to cigars and cigarettes. He smokes a pipe in thirty-five of the sixty cases in the Canon, probably does in three others, and in still another talks about his pipe without, as far as the reader knows, actually lighting it.[3] He smokes nothing but a pipe in twenty-nine or, if one includes the doubtful instances, thirty-two. He indulges in cigars definitely in eight tales and probably in one other, and in cigarettes definitely in nine and probably in one other. In only ten cases does he smoke cigars and/or cigarettes but not a pipe. In eleven tales there is no mention of smoking by Holmes, but there is no reason to believe that the great man stopped the habit at any time, especially since these cases are scattered throughout his career. Holmes very likely smoked a pipe during the adventures recorded in the eleven tales in which there is no reference to smoking, as well as during those of the ten in which Watson names only cigars and cigarettes.

The great man's liking for a pipe began early in life and lasted long; in fact, one cannot doubt that he still smokes one as he contemplates the industrious bee. The earliest mention of Holmes's lighting a pipe is in *A Study in Scarlet,* which records an adventure of 1882.[4] The pipe that he enjoys in *The "Gloria Scott"* is, of course, on "one winter's night" when he tells Watson of his first case. The last reference to a pipe is in *The Creeping Man,* whose date of occurrence is 1903, the year of his retirement.

Most admirers of Sherlock Holmes have believed that his favorite pipe was made of clay. "Let us consider our data." In six tales Watson specifically mentions a clay pipe,[5] and since in three of these accounts it is a "black clay pipe," perhaps the "old black pipe" of *The Creeping Man* is also clay. Watson tells us in *A*

59

Case of Identity that the "old and oily clay pipe" was to Holmes "as a counsellor" and in *The Copper Beeches* that a cherry-wood pipe "was wont to replace his clay when he was in a disputatious rather than a meditative mood." The latter statement might at first seem to indicate that the clay was the favorite among Holmes's pipes, and it is undeniable that the Master was fond of his clay. But since *The Copper Beeches* is concerned with a case of the year 1890 and was published only two years later, the pronouncement can apply only to the first fifteen years of Holmes's professional career and may apply only to the time of the *Adventures*.

Concerning the "old black pipe" of *The Creeping Man,* Watson says, "As an institution I was like the violin, the shag tobacco, the old black pipe, the index books, and others perhaps less excusable." This remark occurs in an adventure of 1903, and the pipe referred to would seem to have been an "institution" during nearly all of Holmes's professional career. *The Creeping Man,* however, was not published until 1923, and it is hardly necessary to add that the doctor's memory was not always reliable, even for periods of much less than twenty years. As Mr. Anthony Boucher has pointed out,[6] another "institution" in this list, the violin, was not, according to the available evidence, played by Holmes after 1891. It may be that the "old black pipe" is not a particular pipe, but all the pipes that Holmes smoked, confused and blended in the mind of the somewhat elderly Watson. Finally, the Master did not treat his clay pipe as a devoted pipe smoker would treat a favorite: in *Charles Augustus Milverton* he even "lit it at a lamp."

Now let us consider the briar. In only two of the adventures—*The Sign of the Four* and *The Man with the Twisted Lip*—does Dr. Watson say that Sherlock Holmes smoked a briar pipe. In the former tale it is an "old brier-root pipe" and in the latter and "old briar pipe." The adjective *old* is significant. When these two cases occurred, Holmes was probably thirty-four and thirty-five years old. Since a devotee of pipes does not call a pipe old unless it has been in use for at least nine or ten years, and since Watson as well as Holmes was a veteran pipe smoker, the latter very likely had cherished this pipe from the time of early manhood. His clay pipe, it is true, is once called old; but for Holmes, who was careless in his habits, a destructible clay pipe would have been old if he had kept it six months. In addition to the two above-mentioned adventures there are others in which, although the word *briar* is not used, the pipe is almost certainly a briar.

One can hardly doubt that when, in *Shoscombe Old Place*, Holmes lit "the oldest and foulest of his pipes," he was lighting the "old briar pipe" of *The Man with the Twisted Lip*—a pipe mellowed by eight more years of devoted attention. In *The Priory School*, the events which occurred twelve years after those of *The Man with the Twisted Lip*, Watson speaks of the "reeking amber" of Holmes's pipe. A briar pipe might have an amber stem, but not a clay pipe. The old briar pipe of *The Man with the Twisted Lip* Holmes smoked at The Cedars, the home of Neville St. Clair, and it was presumably the same pipe that he smoked on the journey to The Cedars. A man who planned his course of action as carefully as did Holmes would carry a durable briar rather than a breakable clay when he went abroad. For that reason the pipe he smoked on the doorstep of Pondicherry Lodge, in *The Sign of the Four*, was likely a briar, as was the pipe he had with him at Poldhu Cottage, in *The Devil's Foot*. In *Charles Augustus Milverton*, disguised as a "rakish young workman," he did descend to the street with a clay pipe in his mouth, but that pipe was part of his disguise. In *The Yellow Face*, speaking of the pipe that Mr. Grant Munro left behind in the sitting room at 221B, Holmes affectionately calls it a "nice old briar," and points out that it has been given careless treatment, for it is charred down one side as a result of being lighted at lamps and gas-jets.

In twenty-two tales Holmes smokes a pipe of which the material is neither identified nor implied. Who can deny that in each instance the pipe is every bit as likely to be a briar as it is to be a clay? The evidence supports the theory that Holmes liked a briar pipe better than any other kind, and that he lit his "old briar pipe" oftener than he did any other.

One might infer from many of the tales that Holmes had only one pipe at some periods; for example, in *The Illustrious Client* he says to Watson, "Put my pipe on the table." If there are several pipes from which to choose, how does Watson know which one to put on the table? Holmes had in mind, of course, his favorite—his well-loved briar. Briar, clay, and cherrywood pipes are, by the way, the only ones mentioned in the Sacred Writings. Neither Holmes nor Watson ever mentions a curved stem; it is possible, however, that the Master followed the fashion of his time and did have one or more pipes with curved stems.

Watson divers times speaks of the help that Holmes received from his pipe. He calls it "the companion of his deepest meditation"[7] and his "meditative pipe."[8] When the Master attacked the mystery of the death of Sir Charles Baskerville, he prepared to spend several hours of "intense mental concentration" by asking Watson to leave and to have the tobacconist send up a pound of the strongest shag.[9] When he was working on the problem of the disappearance of Neville St. Clair, he sat up all night with a briar pipe and an ounce of shag—and of course he solved the mystery.[10] He smoked a pipe when he tackled the problem of the abduction of the only son of the Duke of Holdernesse,[11] when he pondered the mystery of the disappearing bridegroom of Miss Mary Sutherland,[12] and when he became "lost in the deepest thought" concerning the problem brought to him by Lord Bellinger and the Right Honourable Trelawney Hope.[13] Frequently, when he had a particularly difficult matter to consider, he smoked two or more pipefuls in succession: for example, in *The Hound of the Baskervilles* and *The Man with the Twisted Lip* (these incidents are referred to above); in *The Red-Headed League,* which was a "three-pipe problem"; in *Thor Bridge,* in which he smoked two pipefuls in a row; in *The Crooked Man,* in which, having gathered some facts, he "smoked several pipes over them, trying to separate those which were crucial from others which were merely incidental"; and in *Silver Blaze,* in which he devoted a whole day to rambling "about the room with his chin upon his chest and his brows knitted, charging and recharging his pipe with the strongest black tobacco." The evidence is so great that one might easily conclude that Holmes did not solve a single difficult case without the help of his pipe. It is true that in *The Norwood Builder* the Master spent a sleepless night smoking innumerable cigarettes; but it is also true that on the following morning he was nervous and pessimistic about the prospects of his client.

Colonel R. D. Sherbrook-Walker, in a recent article, states that Holmes was not a discriminating user of tobacco, but was merely a slave of habit.[14] He cites the great man's choice of shag;

his custom of smoking a before breakfast pipe "composed of all the plugs and dottles left from his smokes of the day before, all carefully dried and collected on the corner of the mantelpiece";[15] his puffing too rapidly (he allotted fifty minutes to three pipefuls[16]); his practice of keeping his tobacco in the toe of a Persian slipper, where it would dry out and become covered with dust. No real lover of pipes and good tobacco can help deploring the lack of refinement of the Master's palate[17] and the carelessness of his habits. But it is unjust for one who likes the more subtle and expensive blends of tobacco to assert that a smoker who prefers a strong, coarse variety of the leaf does not enjoy his pipe. Sherlock Holmes was faithful to shag because he liked it. His uneducated palate and eccentric habits, moreover, did not detract from the aid and sustenance he received from his pipe and his shag.

It is reported that on one occasion when William Makepeace Thackeray visited his friend Alfred Tennyson, they smoked shag tobacco while praising Miss Barrett's poetry.[18] Great Victorians, both early and late, had a preference for shag as an aid to ratiocination.

—January 1955

NOTES

1. *Psychology,* ch. xx.

2. *Frederick the Great,* bk. IV, ch. 3.

3. I am indebted to the references in the concordance by Jay Finley Christ (*An Irregular Guide to Sherlock Holmes*), but I have made the following emendations. Dr. Christ includes *The Mazarin Stone* among the tales in which Holmes smokes a pipe, but one cannot be sure he lights it. Holmes smokes a pipe in *Shoscombe Old Place,* which Dr. Christ does not list. And Dr. Christ includes *The "Gloria Scott"* among the tales in which Holmes smokes a cigar, but his instance seems to me to be doubtful.

4. I am using the chronology suggested by Edgar W. Smith in "Dr. Watson and the Great Censorship," BSJ (NS) 2 (1952), 138.

5. *The Blue Carbuncle, Charles Augustus Milverton, The Copper Beeches, The Hound of the Baskervilles, A Case of Identity, The Red-Headed League.*

6. "Was the Later Holmes an Impostor?" in *Profile by Gaslight.*

7. *The Valley of Fear.*

8. *The Solitary Cyclist.*

9. *The Hound of the Baskervilles.*

10. *The Man with the Twisted Lip.*

11. *The Priory School.*

12. *A Case of Identity.*

13. *The Second Stain.*

14. "Holmes, Watson, and Tobacco," *The Sherlock Holmes Journal,* 1 No. 2 (September 1952), 7–12.

15. *The Engineer's Thumb.*

16. *The Red-Headed League.*

17. Lack of refinement in regard to tobacco, but not to food. See Fletcher Pratt, "The Gastronomic Holmes," BSJ (NS) 2 (1952), 94–99. [Reprinted in the present volume.]

18. Lionel Stevenson, *The Showman of Vanity Fair* (London, 1947), p. 105.

On the Ashes of the Various Tobaccos

(A Dim View, by a Non-Smoker)

by Florence H. Clum

Whenas our Sherlock hied himself about,
  Resolving London's more abstruse arcana,
His daily round was marked by a devout
  Attachment to the herb Nicotiana.
And when betimes he sat him down at home
  To do an evening's stint of pure deducing,
The Weed's mephitic vapor straight did gloam
  All Baker Street, a deeper murk unloosing
    Than e'er before had poisoned London's air.
    (High Holborn felt it, too, and Portman Square.)

Whatever may be said of his excess,
  Whatever heights his budget may have hiked to,
'Twas not induced by propaganda's stress—
  He smoked the wretched stuff because he *liked* to!
He lived before the battle controversial
  'Twixt brands of rival guild and corporation.
Not his to curse the radio commercial,
  Nor auctioneer's impassioned ululation.
    And (though he scorned them oft) convention's trammels
    Spared him the sight of ladies smoking Camels.

He liked whate'er he puffed on, and his puffs
  Went everywhere. His cigarettes were legion.
Cigars he loved, but drew the line at snuffs
  (We hope). Tobacconists about the region
Of Oxford Street wist well his Jovian ire,
  Should negligence of theirs deny his lips

The polished cherry-wood or fragrant brier;
And so the homely shag, the reeking "ship's"
Came in from Bradley's by the bale and caseful,
Till even Watson called the smudge disgraceful.

And yet this human chimney-pot, whose pall
  Of fumes beclouded home, street, park, and pleasance,
Had the consummate hardihood to call
  The air of London sweeter for his presence!

—July 1948

Sherlock Holmes has often been accused of cocaine addiction—but anyone who knows him well is aware that his taste was more refined than that. . . .

UP FROM THE NEEDLE

by EDGAR W. SMITH

THE REPUTATION attributed to Sherlock Holmes for addiction to cocaine and morphine has served, unfortunately, to obscure the name he more justly deserves for a sound and civilized attitude toward the narcotics in their more venial form. In the early days of his career, when cases were few and far between, it is beyond denying that he turned to the crystalline alkaloids for solace:[1] he tells us in his own words[2] that he found their influence so transcendentally stimulating and clarifying to the mind as to make him careless of the ravages inevitable upon his body and soul. Yet we know that he was never a slave to the vice, in the clinical sense of the term, for despite indulgence at one period in his life in doses of a seven-per-cent cocaine solution "three times a day for many months,"[3] he was always able to cast off the spell, and to find inspiration instead in the exhilaration of the chase.

The fact that Holmes's resort to the lethal drugs was sporadic and voluntary is proof in itself that his reputation for addiction is undeserved. We have further evidence, however,[4] that Watson's doggedly virtuous urgings, abetted progressively by the greater frequency and increasing importance of Holmes's professional preoccupations, were to result at last in his abandoning the practice entirely. How long the reformation took we do not know, but we can feel quite certain that by the time the zenith of his powers had been attained, and queen and potentate and pontiff were inclining themselves before him in suppliance for his aid, the master had learned without remorse and without regret to reach for the gasogene instead of the needle.[5]

This noble implement of aqueous dilution, gone in a modern age with the oil-lamp and the four-wheeler, stands symbolic of a simpler and more wholesome field of indulgence in which

Sherlock Holmes acquitted himself intelligently and well. His tastes were catholic and comprehensive: he loved the grape as well as the barley, and he loved both of them in their naturally fermented states as well as in their more potent distillate forms. In their use as gastronomic adjuncts, he was logical and precise—he had the great good sense to wash down a plate of cold roast beef with a draught of foaming plebeian beer,[6] but when it came to the consumption of oysters and a brace of grouse we are gratified to know that he insisted upon something a little choice in the way of white wine.[7] That he did not ignore the concentrated and more fiery spirit, for the convivial as distinct from the gustatory effect, we are given abundant evidence: early in his career we find him offering Athelney Jones a whisky and soda,[8] and we know that the tantalus sat handy in the corner, side by side with the gasogene itself.[9]

Other references to Holmes's interest in the traditional drink of his countrymen appear recurrently.[10] No deliberate restraint seems to have been put upon access to the store of spirit maintained in the room, but always the indulgence is occasional and gracious, and never is there evidence of excessive or habitual use. In other days,[11] a subtle change steals unaccountedly upon the Baker Street scene—perhaps with the advent of greater affluence—and it is brandy, rather than the dew of Scotland, which finds the greater favor. It is interesting, for example, that it was this costlier imported spirit that Watson himself had handy, impecunious medico though we have thought him to be, when Holmes found opportunity to rescue him from his first and only fainting spell.[12]

But it is Holmes's taste in wines, after all, that excites our greatest interest and commands our greatest respect. Whisky is whisky, and beer is beer, and even the most ignorant may stumble upon the choicest and best and consume it appropriately in time and place. In the realm of the natural grape, however, a sense of discrimination is essential to even a modest reputation for *savoir boire*, and this quality the Master possessed to a unique degree.

At base, his preference was francophile. There is, of course, the reference to a glass of port imbibed in his younger days,[13] and to the Imperial Tokay (from Franz Josef's special cellar in the Schoenbrunn) provided reluctantly by the villain Von

Bork;[14] but it was definitely to the Bordeaux and the Burgundies that Holmes's natural tastes were inclined. Surprisingly, for an Englishman of his generation, he seems to have shunned the hocks completely. Nowhere are the vintages of the Moselle and the Rhineland given mention in the tales, and we are led to wonder if, foreseeing the part he was to play in the Great War, he did not take it upon himself to set up a sort of individual boycott before the fact.

We can be sure, in any event, that the group of ancient and cobwebby bottles sent in by the confectioners to help regale Mr. and Mrs. Francis Hay Moulton[15] had seen their origin in some first-rate château in the Gironde, and that Holmes searched the labels beneath the accumulated dust to verify the fact of their local *mise en bouteille*. So, too, with the Beaune which helped to incline Watson sentimentally toward Mary Morstan: we can assume—if Holmes shared the doctor's repast, as he presumably did—that he made sure of his hospice and his bottling before he partook.[16]

A happy commentary on Holmes's wisdom in the art of drinking is to be found in an obscure passage in the tale of Eugenia Ronder's tragic experience.[17] There, before setting out for South Brixton where the horribly mutilated beauty pondered self-destruction, he discourses sagely to his companion on the futility of speculation when facts are lacking; then abruptly he changes the subject. "There is a cold partridge on the side board, Watson," he says, "and a bottle of Montrachet. Let us renew our energies before we make a fresh call upon them."

Montrachet! It is a compliment to a noble vintage that Sherlock Holmes should have chosen it for restoration when his mind was troubled and distraught; that he would have come, even so late in life, to prefer it to hypodermic and gas-ogene alike. But it is a finer tribute still to the man himself, and to his taste and discernment, that he should have fixed upon what Courtépée has called, with delightful understatement, "*le plus excellent vin blanc d'Europe.*" The presence of Montrachet on the Baker Street sideboard was, we must assume, a matter of studied and deliberate choice, and it stamps Sherlock Holmes, in the matter of his ultimate preference in the narcotics, with the hall-mark of *savant* and *connoisseur*.

—January 1947

1. Dr. Charles S. Goodman believes that Holmes first took to cocaine not from boredom but from toothache: he was, as Dr. Goodman has convincingly established, a chronic sufferer from pyorrhea. Cf. "The Dental Holmes," in *Profile by Gaslight.*

2. *The Sign of the Four.*

3. Ibid.

4. *The Missing Three-Quarter.*

5 T. S. Blakeney believes that the practice had not begun at the time of Holmes's meeting with Watson, but that it had become strongly pronounced by 1888, and that it lasted only intermittently until perhaps 1897. Cf. *Sherlock Holmes: Fact or Fiction?*

6. *A Scandal in Bohemia.*

7. *The Sign of the Four.*

8. Ibid.

9. *A Scandal in Bohemia.*

10. *The Red-Headed League, The Noble Bachelor,* etc.

11. *The Engineer's Thumb, Wisteria Lodge,* etc.

12. *The Empty House.*

13. *The "Gloria Scott."*

14. *His Last Bow.*

15. *The Noble Bachelor.*

16. *The Sign of the Four.*

17. *The Veiled Lodger.*

For those of us who would emulate Holmes's prandial epicureanism, Mr. Pratt offers some suggestions. . . .

THE GASTRONOMIC HOLMES

by FLETCHER PRATT

IT IS MOST UNEXPECTED to discover a new talent in the extraordinary man in whose honor we meet. But the available evidence—and what evidence is available except the Sacred Writings?—allows one to believe, nay, convinces one entirely, that Holmes was one of the true epicures of history, one of the great names in that long line which is supposed to begin with Lucullus and Petronius Arbiter and which extends in unbroken sequence to Lucius Beebe and Rex Stout. I say "supposed to begin" because I doubt whether any modern gourmet could contemplate with pleasure or even satisfaction such a dish as the pheasants sculptured entirely from roast pork with which the so-called epicures of Rome decorated their tables. Also, they watered their wine. It is a horrible fact but a proved one.

There is no doubt about the palates of Mr. Beebe and Mr. Stout. But they live in an age and a place where high honor is paid to distinguished cookery. The point I wish to emphasize is that Holmes did not have their advantages. It was all pure talent on his part. During his active period he was living in London, the capital of the world's worst cookery, unless that title can be claimed by Chicago, and the active period runs through the late Victorian years in which cookery was probably at the lowest level it had attained in centuries. His whole background and training must have been such as would prepare him to accept, if not to enjoy, that worst of all meals—the average English dinner, with the over-done joint of beef or mutton, the brussels sprouts, and the slightly gelid boiled potato swimming in its little lake of grease.

Yet what do we find on examining the record? A genuine gourmet, in both food and wine; a man who will not allow his delicate palate to be insulted, who will eat a basic food such

71

as bread rather than put up with the merely mediocre. One must always recognize the limits imposed upon Holmes by place and time, by the fact that really good food was rarely available, and when it was available, there was seldom anyone who knew how to cook it properly. One must also recognize the fact that Watson had practically no palate at all—a man who takes brandy and soda with his lunch obviously could not—and therefore Watson omitted recounting to us the more vivid of the repasts that must have been consumed at 221b.

But there remain enough details to permit certain deductions. I quote from *The Sign of the Four,* the point at the end of Chapter Nine, when in the midst of an intricate case, Holmes insists upon Athelney Jones's remaining to dine: "I have oysters and a brace of grouse, with something a little choice in white wines—Watson, you have never yet recognized my merits as a housekeeper." I submit that we have here the outline of a repast that would have received the approval of Mr. Beebe or the far more censorious Mr. Stout. The English oysters, with their strong flavor of copper, are not the best preparation for a meal, but they were the best the market afforded and an excellent prelude to grouse. As for the grouse themselves, there is clearly no question as to how they were served. One brace of grouse would be insufficient for three men, of whom one was Watson, who did nothing to preserve his figure. Therefore there must have been three brace, one to each of the eaters; and if that is the case, they could only have been served in the classic manner prescribed by both Brillat-Savarin and Escoffier—roasted with the breasts only served, accompanied by a bread sauce, potato chips, and a gravy made from the unused portions of the birds. All these materials were easily available. As to the identity of the white wine, I make no pronouncement; I would suspect a Montrachet in a domaine bottling, but I am unfamiliar with the vintages of the period and will leave to some more learned Irregular the determination of the precise year. I am also inclined to the opinion that Mrs. Hudson could not possibly have cooked the meal. It must have come from a good caterer and have been prepared under Holmes's personal supervision. There is no mention of a salad, and probably none was served. There was probably no dessert either, unless the walnuts and cheese which would have gone effectively with the port that Holmes very properly poured when the meal was complete. Parenthetically, it is to be noted that Holmes poured it himself; another sign of the true gourmet, who would rather let a gorilla handle his sister than a waiter touch his port.

But the really important point, which establishes Holmes's reputation as a gourmet beyond cavil, is what happened after this little dinner. The great detective became very gay and talkative, discussed medieval pottery, miracle plays, Stradivarius violins, and warships of the future, and ended by pouring two more rounds of port—quite enough in view of the serious work ahead, but very indicative all the same. For it is only the non-gourmet, the melancholy fellow, who becomes solemn after dinner and sits grumping over the scotch and soda which furnishes the offices of digestion the cook should have accomplished. A truly great eater is exhilarated by an exhibition of the art of cooking as a truly great critic is exhilarated by a masterpiece from the hand of Rembrandt.

It is unfortunate that we have been left the description of only one other meal, and even that in a semi-complete state, to illustrate Holmes's taste in food. This was the cold supper laid out for Lord St. Simon in *The Noble Bachelor* and Mr. and Mrs. Francis Hay Moulton. It consisted of a brace of cold woodcock, a pheasant, a paté de foi gras pie, and a number of ancient and cobwebby bottles. There are several very interesting deductions to be drawn from this meal. In the first place there is food enough for four but not for five, although five places were laid. One woodcock or half a pheasant is exactly a portion, and since the paté pie would be required as garnish, it was evidently not intended to serve the fifth eater. That is, Holmes must have deduced that Lord St. Simon would not remain to share the repast; a point which Watson completely missed.

In the second place, the means of preparing woodcock and pheasant, when they are to be served cold, approach each other very closely, and the difference is only perceptible to a delicate palate. Holmes was subtly flattering his guests by assuming that although they were Americans, they would know enough about the *haute cuisine* to be able to express an intelligent choice between the cold woodcock and the cold pheasant; that they would savor the fine distinction between the two, and perhaps take a slice of each.

I think that there can be little doubt about how the woodcock and pheasant were served. At least one of them must have been *à la buloz* and the other chaud-froid. There are only two other possible recipes, the Bohemian, in which the bird appears in aspic in the center of a block of ice—which was impossible because the supper had to wait from 5 until after 9—and the recipe *à la croix de berny,* which involves paté, and would have been in conflict with the paté already on the table in the pie. Therefore, the pheasant almost undoubtedly appeared in aspic, sliced and decorated with truffles coated with a sauce and served on a low bed of semolina. The woodcock would be gently poached, their skins removed, and the birds themselves served coated with chaud-froid sauce and aspic, surrounded by cockscombs and mushrooms.

I must admit that the ancient and cobwebby bottles have given me a good deal of trouble. Surely, with his fine taste in wines, Holmes would never have served reds beside pheasant and woodcock; and I am not now aware of a white that could stand enough age to become cobwebby without also becoming vinegar. I can only suggest that he was once more exercising his delicate taste and immense knowledge by providing a Portuguese rosé, which as a wired wine can stand much longer storage and, indeed, improves by it. The fact that there was not one, but a number of the ancient and cobwebby bottles, is very significant; quite clearly and very properly, Holmes expected to continue whatever drinking was done after the meal from the contents of these bottles. A Portuguese rosé would serve this purpose admirably.

The occasions mentioned are the only two in which the menu is given. In *The Cardboard Box,* Holmes sits for half an hour over a bottle of claret after a lunch, which again is perfectly correct; except that we do not know what was eaten for lunch. As far as Watson was concerned, it might as well have been horsemeat. Once more, in *The Naval Treaty,* there is at least the adumbration of a meal; a breakfast this time. The great detective offers Phelps a choice of curried chicken or ham and eggs. It is noteworthy that Watson takes the ham and eggs and also that the epicurean Holmes remarks that Mrs. Hudson's cuisine is a little limited, another proof that she could not possibly have prepared the grouse dinner.

There remain the cases when Holmes ate out. In *The Hound of the Baskervilles* he and Watson had time to stop in at Marcini's for a little dinner before going to hear the De Reszkes. In *The Bruce-Partington Plans* he meets Watson at Goldini's. In *The Dying Detective* there is something nutritious at Simpson's, and he was once attacked by Moriarty's thugs outside the Café Royale, though this does not positively tell us whether he had been eating within.

This makes a total of four cases of restaurant eating, of which two of the restaurants were Italian, with the third one doubtful. Of Simpson's I confess I know nothing and submit it for future research. The Italian restaurants of London in this period are, however, easier to identify in a culinary sense, and they do Holmes almost as much credit as the two recorded meals in Baker Street. One must not consider them as the common Italian restaurant of New York or even of America, which is run by Sicilians, who have no culinary ideals but that of bloating their customers with large amounts of spaghetti and getting them out into the street. The Italian restaurant of London at the time was entitled to respect, and it still is. In the kitchen there is usually a good cook from the Romagna or Piedmont who will provide you with a decent soup, an honest roast of veal, and an equally good roast of poultry, followed by a salad and a zabaglione. As far as my researches extend there were few good French restaurants in London at the time, and there had as yet been no Swedish or German invasion.

There remain two cases in which Holmes is seen eating informally. In *The Five Orange Pips,* having had nothing to eat all day, he devours large pieces of a loaf of bread and washes them down with water. In the Baskerville case, while he is camping out in the hut on the moor, Cartwright brings him bread, as requested, but also a can of tongue and a can of peaches. Holmes eats the bread and leaves the tongue and peaches. I cannot find it in my heart to blame him for what Watson considers his eccentricities in these two cases. "You are hungry," says the Doctor on the first occasion. Indeed Holmes was, and I have no doubt that the sight of the repulsive left-overs Watson would have around the place drove him to bread and water. As for the case on the moor, consider what the flavor of the British tinned tongue and peaches of 1889 must have been like. It honors the memory of Holmes that he refused to eat them and preferred plain bread.

—April 1952

(This paper by Mr. Pratt was read at the Annual Dinner of The Baker Street Irregulars on 11 January 1952.)

OBSERVATIONS ON SHERLOCK HOLMES
AS AN ATHLETE AND SPORTSMAN

by H. T. WEBSTER

NO READER of the Sacred Writings can fail to note, as did Dr. Watson, that Sherlock Holmes possessed a considerable degree of natural athleticism, and that he was an adept at several athletic skills. Very early in the Canon, Watson puts on record his illustrious friend's ability as a singlestick player, a boxer, and swordsman.[1] Only the last of these accomplishments suggests a purely recreational motive on Holmes's part, and since there is no later reference to his swordsmanship, we may conclude that he gave it up to fill in his early ignorance of belles-lettres. Holmes's generally utilitarian attitude toward sports is clearly indicated by the fact that he chose to sacrifice the delicate and exacting art of fencing to the comparatively crude singlestick and boxing glove. There is no reason to believe that Holmes ever touched a foil or épée after his early acquaintance with Watson.

Though his singlestick work gave him an invaluable background for the wielding of a hunting crop, which Watson declares was his favorite weapon,[2] it is Holmes's skill as a boxer which Watson emphasizes most appreciatively. This may owe partly to a British and American predilection for boxing among the more combative sports. But there can be no doubt that Holmes was an accomplished performer in the ring.

Presumably, in the early days of their friendship, Watson had watched Holmes work out in the rooms of Professor Ned Donnelly, or in some other well-known academy of self-defense on or near the Strand, for there is no mention of boxing equipment at Baker Street. Perhaps Watson himself, as his health improved, was rash enough to put on the gloves with Holmes occasionally, but a more frequent gentleman sparring partner was

77

doubtless Watson's literary agent, a man named Conan Doyle, who was known to be handy with the muffles or mawleys, and was himself the author of some stories of the prize ring.[3] Another possible sparring partner for Holmes was Bernard Shaw, a well-known figure in the academies of self-defence of the period, who recorded his impressions of them in *Cashel Byron's Profession*.

Holmes was most fortunate in his physical endowment as a boxer. The long-limbed rangy sort of individual has always done well in the ring, for reach is a great advantage when it is joined with speed and strength. We know that Holmes was unusually fast and active on his feet. This is perhaps most authoritatively demonstrated in *The Hound of the Baskervilles*, where Watson, reckoned fleet of foot himself, declares: "Never have I seen a man run as Holmes ran that night." He also had exceptional strength; indeed, he was able to straighten a poker bent by such a giant as Dr. Grimesby Roylott of Stoke Moran, and straightening it seems a more difficult feat than bending it.

Holmes evidently learned something of boxing during his university days.[4] Mr. E. B. Mitchell, *The Badminton Library*'s authority on boxing and sparring (1889), concedes that there was an excellent school of boxing at the elder university, though he is generally contemptuous of provincial boxers. However, once Holmes came to London, the boxing capital of the empire, he rapidly polished his style, until by 1884 he was good enough in his bout with McMurdo in Allison's rooms to merit the latter's unreserved compliments four years later.[5] Now, accolades of this sort are rare. In some branches of athletics, swimming for example, the amateur is able to compete on more or less equal terms with the professional, but in boxing there have been very few amateurs who could even give a workout to a high-grade professional like McMurdo. The complete disparity in such competition can best be realized if one imagines the box-office reaction to a match between Joe Louis and any holder of an amateur heavyweight championship. Holmes had, however, brought his boxing by this time to a level where Watson declares: "He was undoubtedly one of the finest boxers of his weight I have ever seen. . . ."[6] It will be noted that Watson does not limit his comparison to the amateur ranks alone, and it is probable that Holmes did most of his later sparring with professionals.

What was Holmes's weight? Presumably about the same as McMurdo's; and McMurdo, described as short and deep-chested, sounds like a typical middleweight. Holmes was six feet tall, according to his own word,[7] and probably weighed about 11 stone, which would make him resemble the celebrated Bob Fitzsimmons in build. This impression is confirmed by the authentic portraits from the hands of Sidney Paget and Frederick Dorr Steele, though some of the apocryphal ones would make him appear a little heavier. But a man of eleven stone can pack plenty of wallop. Neither Fitzsimmons nor Carpentier weighed much more than that, though they were sometimes credited with extra poundage for publicity purposes.

McMurdo was particularly impressed with Holmes's "cross punch under the jaw." The right cross is indeed the characteristic Sunday punch of the tall rangy type of boxer, as the left hook is the main reliance of the short and stocky one. This punch, to the head or body, is delivered straight from the shoulder but with a slight pivoting motion of the body which gives it something of the character of a hook. It is called a cross, because it must cross either over or under the opponent's left arm to land. It is the natural counter to a left jab, and unskilled boxers commonly leave themselves open to it when they begin to carry their lefts too far forward to serve as an effective guard. The fact that McMurdo says nothing about Holmes's left does not indicate that it was not a good one, but simply that in three rounds it had not yet given him much trouble. Very few left jabs in the history of the ring have been powerful enough to conquer rugged and skilled opposition in a few rounds. On the other hand, Holmes's left proved sufficiently formidable when applied to the features of a mere slogging ruffian like Roaring Jack Woodley, who, it will be remembered, had to be carried home in a cart.[8]

In general, then, we can reconstruct Holmes's boxing style as somewhat like that of Jem Mace, Jim Corbett, and Mike Gibbons. (There are so few master boxers today that one is at a loss for a ready contemporary parallel.) He stood up straight in the classic style, used his extraordinary speed of foot to avoid the infighting which is likely to be troublesome to a man with a lightly armored body, staggered his opponent with a straight left which was punishing but not lethal, and finished him with that powerful right cross.

Holmes's skill at boxing was more than once of practical value to him. It enabled him to subdue Mr. Joseph Harrison in *The Naval Treaty,* and Roaring Jack Woodley in *The Solitary Cyclist,* and to defend himself against the anonymous rough with the bludgeon in *The Final Problem.* But before 1892, Holmes had clearly perceived that boxing alone was not a sufficient means of self-defense against villains like Professor Moriarty and Colonel Sebastian Moran, both of whom had to be subdued by wrestling; and he had no doubt supplemented it with the less sportsmanlike, but more practical baritsu—which one takes to be something like modern judo. This was of course entirely necessary as a means of defense against villains who have an instinctive disregard for either Queensberry or London Prize Ring Rules. Such depths of uninhibited and almost un-British behavior were revealed to Holmes at latest in 1887 by the atrocious behavior of the two Cunninghams.[9]

In his early days, Holmes knew so little about wrestling[10] that he was unaware that wrestlers as well as boxers have cauliflower ears, but once the need for a skill in it became obvious he proved his ready adaptability, and learned the baritsu well enough to employ it in most later hand-to-hand encounters with really dangerous opponents. It was evidently by means of some baritsu hold that he quickly overpowered the young and vigorous Von Bork in his last recorded case.

Neither boxing nor wrestling was more useful to Holmes than his skill with the singlestick, which served as a means of defense in a number of tight spots. It is doubtful if Holmes engaged in any singlestick competition after his early days in London, but his youthful practice with it made the cane or hunting crop an unusually formidable weapon in his hands. Watson declared that the latter was Holmes's favorite weapon, and this is understandable, for when available, it spared him the bruised knuckles that frequently resulted when he had his fists alone to rely on,[11] and exhausting hand-to-hand struggles like those in *A Study in Scarlet* and *The Reigate Squires.* Moreover, a loaded cane or hunting crop could be used against a variety of fauna like the swamp adder in *The Speckled Band,* where the bare hands would hardly suffice, and as a defense against ruffians themselves armed with bludgeons.[12] Holmes therefore kept his hunting crop handy in his rooms.[13] On one occasion, at least,[14] he found it effective protection even against a man armed with a pistol.

For situations of the greatest peril, Holmes had to rely upon firearms, however. Neither boxing, nor baritsu, nor for that matter a loaded hunting crop would be adequate defense against an Andaman Islander's blow gun, or a gigantic and possibly spectral hound. Major Robert Keith Leavitt's brilliant and erudite study of Holmes's markmanship[15] leaves little additional to be said about the subject, but in fairness to Holmes that little must be said.

Major Leavitt proves beyond reasonable doubt that Holmes was originally a rifleman, and that as such he had a considerable distrust of the handgun. However, we may assume that in his early London days Holmes found his rifle rather inconvenient to carry, thought it was not necessarily conspicuous, since he could always conceal an arm like the popular Winchester .44-40 carbine under a long coat. This was, however, necessarily at some sacrifice to his own agility. It was probably after he had been incommoded to the point of irritation by his rifle a few times that he impatiently went to the opposite extreme of getting the stubby little Webley Metropolitan Police revolver, with which Major Leavitt arms him, and which proved to be so unsatisfactory in his hands. Now, riflemen are generally contemptuous of the short ranges and relatively large targets at which handgunners shoot, and, probably enough, until Watson came along with his long-barrelled Adams, and demonstrated what a competent pistol shot could really do, it never entered Holmes's head that the pistol shot could supply effective protection at more than point-blank range. Yet with his usual respect for facts, when presented with the evidence that he was a comparatively poor pistol shot with the Webley, he set out to make himself an efficient marksman. No doubt he confided his troubles to François le Villard, who secured for him a long-barrelled Continental hair-trigger pistol, as a good transition piece to convert the skill of an expert rifleman to the less familiar handgun. Holmes's triumphant display with this arm[16] was another of his well-known indulgences in the dramatic. It evidently made Watson feel nettled and envious, for the results were spectacular in all senses of the word, though they were achieved under circumstances that would not have been allowed in competitive pistol shooting. The hair trigger on Holmes's weapon was barred, his sitting posture was characteristic of a rifleman, and it seems probable enough that he had a carbine stock attached to his long-barrelled pistol to further approximate the conditions of rifle shooting.

Nevertheless, it is inconceivable that Holmes allowed himself to be beaten by the tricky handgun. Major Leavitt assumes that the weapon which he refers to as "my old favorite" in *The Three Garridebs*, and which he brings down on Killer Evans' head, is still the impractical little Webley of his early days. Such a weapon would make a very inefficient bludgeon. What, then, is more probable than that Sir Henry Baskerville or some other grateful transatlantic client had presented Holmes with a Colt Frontier Model .45, or some other well-designed American arm which would have been a practicable substitute for either a rifle or a loaded hunting crop? Holmes was not the man to allow himself to be frustrated, and we may be sure that he eventually found means to master the handgun.

In all the saga of Holmesian adventures one finds only one reference to sport practised over a long period of time strictly for its own sake, unless Mr. C. R. Andrew is right in his contention that by 1883 Holmes had become interested in horse racing.[17] But even Mr. Andrew does not suggest that Holmes was himself a rider. Nor is there reason to suppose that he had more than a moderate enthusiasm for fishing, though to be sure he does not disdain to catch a few trout when there is nothing better to do.[18]

But Holmes tells us in *The Lion's Mane* that he enjoys swimming. He probably had at best limited opportunity for this in London, though he could get in a few strokes in the pools which are frequently attached to Turkish baths like the one he and Watson frequented on Northumberland Avenue. The swimming, then, must belong to his youth in Yorkshire, and to his retirement in Sussex. It seems very fitting that the sport in which he had passed early days of leisure, before he became conscious of the world and his mission, should beguile his later days of well-earned and philosophic repose. Bernard Shaw,

Holmes's approximate contemporary, also found a valetudinarian tranquillity in the water, and as the summer seasons roll around, now that the hunting days of these hardy oldsters for villains and hypocrites are past, we can wish them both good swimming.

—January 1948

NOTES

1. *A Study in Scarlet.*
2. *The Six Napoleons.*
3. The relationship of Dr. Doyle to Holmes and Watson needs more thorough investigation. Doyle later became one of Holmes's detractors. In the Foreword to *The Case Book of Sherlock Holmes,* he blusteringly declares: "I had determined to bring the career of Sherlock Holmes to an end," a remark that may have had a sinister *arrière pensée.* It is well known that at least one of Watson's manuscripts is at present suppressed by the Doyle family, for reasons one can only surmise. Rumor has occasionally identified Doyle with Porlock.
4. *The "Gloria Scott."*
5. *The Sign of the Four.*
6. *The Yellow Face.*
7. *The Three Students.*
8. *The Solitary Cyclist.*
9. *The Reigate Squires.*
10. *The "Gloria Scott."*
11. *The Naval Treaty, The Final Problem.*
12. *The Illustrious Client.*
13. *A Case of Identity.*
14. *The Red-Headed League.*
15. "Annie Oakley in Baker Street," in *Profile by Gaslight* (New York: Simon & Schuster, 1944).
16. *The Musgrave Ritual.*
17. "Sherlock Holmes on the Turf," in *A Baker Street Four-Wheeler* (Maplewood: The Pamphlet House, 1944).
18. *Shoscombe Old Place.*

In sorting out the mysteries with which he was
confronted, Holmes is frequently seen to engage in a bit
of breaking-and-entering. Criminal behavior, to be
sure. Or can we agree with Judge Bigelow that

SHERLOCK HOLMES WAS NO BURGLAR

by S. TUPPER BIGELOW

IT HAS BEEN taken for granted for a long time that Sherlock
Holmes did a number of things that scholars have called "burglary." Some may be readily forgiven, because the Master himself seemed to be under the impression on more than one occasion that he was guilty of that offence. Others, however, who
have analyzed the stories from a legal or quasi-legal aspect, cannot so readily be forgiven for their indefensible slur, if not actual libel, on the Master, even though they could plead in miti-
gation of damages that Holmes himself had described himself
as a burglar or had admitted a course of conduct that implicitly
had some criminality about it which the layman would un-
hesitatingly take to be burglary.

For example, in *The Retired Colourman*, Holmes told Inspector MacKinnon: "There being no fear of interruption, I proceeded to burgle the house." And in *The Bruce-Partington Plans*,
Holmes and Watson, equipped with a jemmy, a dark lantern, a
chisel, and a revolver, broke and entered Oberstein's residence,
and Watson reported: "Mycroft Holmes and Lestrade had come
around by appointment after breakfast next day and Sherlock
Holmes had recounted to them our proceedings of the day
before. The professional shook his head over our confessed
burglary."

Homes fancied himself as a burglar, too, had he chosen to
adopt a criminal career. In *Charles Augustus Milverton,* a major
crime-wave in itself, Holmes told Watson: "You know, Watson, I
don't mind confessing to you that I have always had an idea that
I would have made a highly efficient criminal."

Earlier in the story, Holmes had said: "I mean to burgle
Milverton's house to-night," and as he detailed his plans to
Watson, he produced "a neat little leather case out of a drawer,

and opening it, he exhibited a number of shining instruments. 'This,' he said, 'is a first-class, up-to-date burgling kit, with nickel-plated jemmy, diamond-tipped glass-cutter, adaptable keys, and every modern improvement which the march of civilization demands. Here, too, is my dark lantern. Everything is in order.'"

As it most certainly was. The burglar's kit of 1958 could scarcely be better, although perhaps a stout crowbar and a few assorted saws might have been added, although all would hardly fit into "a neat little leather case," and by now, of course, the further march of civilization would substitute a flashlight for a dark lantern.

In *The Retired Colourman,* Holmes told Inspector MacKinnon: "Burglary has always been an alternative profession had I cared to adopt it, and I have little doubt that I should have come to the front."

Moreover, Holmes was apparently an authority on the *mores* of burglars. In *The Abbey Grange,* Holmes told Watson: "As a matter of fact, burglars who have done a good stroke of business are, as a rule, only too glad to enjoy the proceeds in peace and quiet without embarking on another perilous undertaking. Again, it is unusual for burglars to operate at so early an hour" (shortly after 11:00 P.M.), "it is unusual for burglars to strike a lady to prevent her screaming, since one would imagine that was the sure way to make her scream, it is unusual for them to commit murder when their numbers are sufficient to overpower one man, it is unusual for them to be content with a limited plunder when there was much more within their reach, and finally, I should say, that it was very unusual for such men to leave a bottle half empty."

Many scholars of the Canon have stated categorically that Holmes was a burglar. Anatole Chujoy, in "The Only Second Stain,"[1] complacently accepts that assessment. He says: "Jay Finley Christ, in his *An Irregular Guide to Sherlock Holmes of Baker Street,* lists . . . four cases of burglary." This is not strictly accurate. The Christian listings in the incomparable *Irregular Guide* are:

Burglary by Holmes CHAS 678 SIXN 681 BRUC 1090
Sherlock Holmes, Burglar, acts as CHAS 672 GREE 513 BRUC 1090 RETI 1321.

Note the distinction between burglary and acting as a burglar that Christ makes. Far from being a subtle distinction, it is the theme of this thesis that there is a vast distinction from being a burglar and acting as one. In any event, Christ lists only three cases in which Holmes was a burglar and a total of five in which he was or appeared to be a burglar.

Irving M. Fenton in "An Analysis of the Crimes and Near-Crimes at Appledore Towers in the Light of the English Criminal Law,"[2] in an otherwise masterful dissection of the Milverton case, says: "Holmes removes a circle of glass from the study door and turns the key from the inside. At this point, the 'breaking and entering' is complete. Burglary has, in fact, been committed." And later: "Freudians may make what they will of Holmes's often-expressed desire to become a highly efficient criminal, a burglar by choice (*Charles Augustus Milverton* and *The Retired Colourman*)." And still later: "The casual reader detects a note of yearning, but a closer examination discloses a substantial fulfillment (*Charles Augustus Milverton, The Greek Interpreter, The Bruce-Partington Plans, The Illustrious Client, et al.*)."

Ignoring the "*et al.*" for the moment, we should add *The Illustrious Client* to the list for analysis.

The same erudite scholar, in "Holmes and the Law,"[3] says: "Holmes's major crimes such as burglary (*Charles Augustus Milverton, The Retired Colourman, The Bruce-Partington Plans*)" and "He" (Holmes) "even burglarizes Moriarty's residence (*The Valley of Fear*)." And slightly modifying his earlier assessment of Holmes's substantial fulfillment of a desire to become "a highly efficient criminal, a burglar by choice," he says: "In *The Illustrious Client*, Holmes was, in fact, threatened with prosecution for burglary." A little different thing from clearly implying that burglary was committed.

The Valley of Fear is the only story not mentioned in the writings about the Writings discussed so far, so we should add it to the list.

So now we have seven alleged burglaries or pseudo-burglaries. We add to the list, for investigative purposes only, *The Red Circle, The Speckled Band,* and *A Scandal in Bohemia,* since each records Holmes's ostensibly unlawful entry into private premises. Now we have ten. In *Lady Frances Carfax,* Holmes was called a burglar, so we should likewise investigate this charge against him.

What was burglary in England in Holmes's time? The Larceny Act, 1916, was nothing new in the way of law; it was merely a codification of the common law of larceny as it existed up to that time; we can take it that its statutory force in 1916 had had legal effect from the date of the earliest story in the Canon. Section 25 of the Larceny Act, 1916, reads: "Every person who in the night—(1) breaks and enters the dwelling-house of another, having—(a) entered the said dwelling-house with intent to commit any felony therein; or (b) committed any felony in the said dwelling-house, shall be guilty of felony called burglary. . . ."

Section 46 reads: "The expression 'night' means the interval between nine o'clock in the evening and six o'clock in the morning of the next succeeding day."

Section 27 reads: "Every person who with intent to commit any felony therein"—(1) enters any dwelling-house in the night; or (2) breaks and enters any dwelling-house . . . shall be guilty of felony. . . .

We should look at sec. 51 of The Malicious Damage Act, 1861, which describes malicious damage as a misdemeanour rather than a felony, and we should perhaps consult *Russell on Crime*, an authoritative legal text in England, then and now (5th Edition, 1877; 6th Edition, 1896; 7th Edition, 1909; 8th Edition, 1923; 9th Edition, 1936), who said: "In order to constitute the offence of burglary, there must be a breaking of the dwelling-house. If a man enters a house by a door or a window which he finds open, or through a hole which was made there before, and steals goods; or draws goods out of a house through such a door, window or hole, he is not guilty of burglary.—3 Co. Inst. 64; 1 Hawk. c. 38, s.4; 1 Hale 551—2; 4 Bl. Com. 226." This is ancient British law, to be sure, and just as valid today.

The lay reader might think it somewhat captious or hair-splitting to take the high ground that, according to the letter of the law, burglary can take place only at night, when the layman's conception of burglary is breaking and entering at any time of the day or night. Well, then, let us go along with the layman's opinion. We shall call the offense mentioned in sec. 25 of The

Larceny Act, 1916, "burglary," and the offence described in sec. 27 "unlawful entry" and admit, for the purpose of this thesis, that it is a kind of burglary as well.

Now all we have to do is review the cases.

Charles Augustus Milverton

Holmes and Watson broke and entered Milverton's dwelling-house (Appledore Towers) at night, but with no intention of committing a felony; Holmes's only intention, it appears, was to break open Milverton's safe and destroy his blackmailing assets, which was done. This is merely malicious damage—a misdemeanour, not a felony. True, they saw a felony committed, and were accessories after the fact to murder, but that was pure inadvertence. Neither Holmes nor Watson was guilty of either burglary or unlawful entry.

The Six Napoleons

Burglary was committed here, but not by Holmes.

> (Irrelevant and gratuitous Note: Some scholars have accused Holmes of having been a receiver of stolen goods—the Borgia pearl—and in the criminal law, that would appear to be true. But civilly, Holmes's title to the Borgia pearl is good against Mr. Sandeford of Reading but not against the original owner, the Prince of Colonna.)

The Bruce-Partington Plans

Undoubtedly, Holmes and Watson broke and entered Oberstein's dwelling-place, but with no intention of committing a felony. All Holmes was after were some incriminating documents or the Bruce-Partington plans. Having found the former, he and Watson left, and later they re-entered the house with Lestrade and Mycroft. None had any intention of committing a felony on either occasion, unless it might be argued that, if Holmes had found the plans, he would have appropriated them—but as that was what he had been retained for, it could scarcely have been larceny. On the first occasion of entering the house, Holmes did a little malicious damage but, as in Milverton's case, we don't count that.

> (Irrelevant and gratuitous Note: Seems odd that in this story, Holmes didn't know the names of the principal foreign spies in London and had

to ask Mycroft for them, but he was thoroughly familiar with them in *The Second Stain*, an earlier story. Mislaid his index, perhaps?)

The Greek Interpreter

While this story bristles with crime, Holmes surely came out of it unscathed. The villains here were very sinful characters, indeed, as they appear to have been guilty of murder, attempted murder, attempted extortion, abduction twice if not three times, to say nothing of assorted assaults. Holmes, however, was not guilty of burglary. Watson reported that: "The Inspector . . . noted the clever way in which my friend had forced back the catch." But it will be recalled that Watson had earlier said: "It was more than an hour before we could get Inspector Gregson and comply with the legal formalities which would enable us to enter the house." That clearly means that Gregson was busy getting a search-warrant and the delay was occasioned, no doubt, by his difficulty in finding a magistrate or Justice of the Peace, by either of which a search-warrant must be signed, then and now.

With the search-warrant, the police had every right to enter The Myrtles, by force or otherwise, and Holmes was merely their assistant or agent. By no stretch of the imagination could he be charged with burglary or unlawful entry.

(Irrelevant and gratuitous Note: Seems a pity, though, that these desperate characters were not hunted down and punished, even though Harold Latimer and Wilson Kemp—the latter "a man of the foulest antecedents"—killed each other shortly after at or near Buda-Pesth. They were no doubt buried in Austria-Hungary under the provisions of the [Austria-Hungary] Local Improvements Act.)

The Retired Colourman

It will be recalled that Holmes admitted in this case that he "burgled" The Haven, Josiah Amberley's dwelling-house. But we shall not accept that admission of guilt any more than we would accept it in the Milverton case.

While he entered, Holmes had no intention of committing a felony; his only purpose was to find out how and where Mrs. Amberley and Dr. Ray Ernest were murdered.

We are not told how Holmes entered the house, or whether he had to break to enter, but we are told that he "slipped out through the pantry window." Subsection (2) of sec. 25 of The Larceny Act, 1916, does not reach Holmes on this footing either, since no felony was either contemplated or committed.

(Irrelevant and gratuitous Note: An interesting thing about this story is that there is nothing told about how Holmes, Watson, and Inspector MacKinnon get from 221B to The Haven. The dialogue starts at 221B, and half-way through it, they are all at and remain at The Haven. Watson probably was thinking of his fourth wife?)

The Illustrious Client

When Baron Adelbert Gruner heard a noise in his inner study, he rushed in, closely followed by Watson. As Watson described the scene: "Two steps took me to the open door, and my mind will ever carry a clear picture of the scene within. The window leading to the garden was wide open. Beside it, looking like some terrible ghost, his head girt with bloody bandages, his face drawn and white, stood Sherlock Holmes."

Holmes had stolen the Baron's love diary, or as Holmes chose to call it, the "lust diary." If he had broken to enter the inner study, the time of the break-in must surely have been before 9:00 P.M., as Watson's appointment was for 8:30 and Holmes's arrival on the scene would not be long after. So we must acquit Holmes of burglary.

As for unlawful entry, while Holmes had every intention of committing larceny (there is nothing in The Larceny Act, 1916, that says that one may commit larceny if the purpose is beneficent; maybe something can be done about it at the next session of parliament), there is no evidence of breaking in the Canon. The window was open; it might well have been open before Holmes got there, since it was early September; and in every criminal case, if there is reasonable doubt, we must give the benefit of it to the accused. In England and in most enlightened parts of the civilized world, an accused person was and is presumed innocent until he is proved guilty beyond a reasonable doubt. There is unquestionably reasonable doubt here.

(Irrelevant and gratuitous Note: Here we learn that "Lomax, the sub-librarian of the London Library," was a friend of Watson's. Add him to young Stamford (*A Study in Scarlet*) and Thurston, the billiards-player

(*The Dancing Men*), and discount the fact that Holmes said: "He [Watson] was not a man with intimate friends.")

The Valley of Fear

Speaking of Professor Moriarty to Inspector Alec MacDonald, Holmes said: "I have been three times in his rooms, twice waiting for him under different pretexts and leaving before he came. Once—well, I can hardly tell about the once to an official detective. It was on the last occasion that I took the liberty of running over his papers—with the most unexpected results." (As in the case of the dog in the night-time, the results were, of course, that Holmes found "absolutely nothing.") But there was no evidence that there was any breaking, nor is running over another's papers a felony; it's not even a misdemeanour. A lot of people do it with legal impunity and enjoy it.

However, it might be argued that the "once" Holmes referred to was a criminal action of some kind and known to Holmes to be such, and was, in all probability, burglary, since on only two occasions did Holmes wait for Moriarty in his rooms. This argument would appear to be fortified by Holmes's reluctance to tell the Inspector about the third occasion.

Such an argument, it is submitted, is invalid on two footings: first, it was probably another example of Holmes's pawkish sense of humour, often in evidence in the Canon when he was baiting the police; and secondly, there are not enough data. As the master said, "Data, data, data! I can't make bricks without clay" (*The Copper Beeches*), and "The temptation to form premature theories upon insufficient data is the bane of our profession" (*The Valley of Fear*).

Whatever Holmes did, if he did it, there is not a jot or tittle of evidence in the Canon that it was either burglary or unlawful entry. Case dismissed.

The Red Circle

All Holmes did here, in the way of burglary, was to enter a vacant apartment through an open door with the cooperation of the police with no criminal intent whatever. Not that the cooperation or consent of the police can legalize burglary or unlawful entry: the police are merely minions of the law; not the law.

The Speckled Band

Holmes entered an open window in a dwelling-house at night with no consent of the owner, Dr. Grimesby Roylott, but with the tacit consent of one of the house's occupants—indeed, on Miss Stoner's tacit invitation by placing a lamp in the window. But there was no intent to commit a felony, but rather an intent to prevent one being committed and to ascertain how an earlier one had been committed. Not guilty.

A Scandal in Bohemia

Holmes, Watson, and the King of Bohemia entered Irene Adler's vacated premises with intent to commit felony therein, to wit, to steal the compromising photograph. But the door of Briony Lodge was open, so there was no breaking. As for unlawful entry, Mrs. Norton's servant permitted, or at all events made no effort to prevent, the entry, and in any case (see sec. 27, Larceny Act, 1916), the entering was not at night; it was shortly after breakfast-time.

The Disappearance of Lady Frances Carfax

Having traced Holy Peters to a house in Poultney Square, Holmes got his foot in the door and was invited into the house, although somewhat reluctantly. He told Peters he was going to search the house for Lady Carfax.

> "Where is your warrant?" asked Peters.
> Holmes half drew a revolver from his pocket. "This will have to serve till a better one comes."
> "Why, you are a common burglar."
> "So you might describe me," said Holmes cheerfully.

The word "burglar," as used by Holy Peters, was obviously a figure of speech, employed much as a layman uses the word as a generic word for thieves and larcenous characters of all kinds.

CONCLUSION

It must now be apparent to all aficionados of the Master that he has been reviled and traduced over many decades, and it is devoutly hoped that this defense of his allegedly burglarious activities has not come too late to give him solace and comfort on the occasion of his 105th birthday next month in his happy retirement upon the Sussex Downs. May it cheer him, in fact, to the extent that he will live forever, as he undoubtedly will, in any case.

IRRELEVANT AND GRATUITOUS FOOTNOTE

It seems somewhat significant that Holmes's confessed "burglaries" took place after The Great Hiatus. We are bound to respect Watson's assessment in *A Study in Scarlet*: Holmes "has a good practical knowledge of British law," notwithstanding occasional criminal offences committed by Holmes and Watson, consistently with the best intentions.

Scholars have attacked this assessment of Watson's on many grounds, mainly that Holmes wittingly or unwittingly committed a variety of criminal offences; but this criticism seems to be answered by the fact that Holmes committed no criminal offence unless he thought it was for the public good. Other scholars, notably Irving Fenton (in his second article, *op. cit.*) and S. T. L. Harbottle (in "Sherlock Holmes and the Law," *The Sherlock Holmes Journal* 1, No. 3), have endeavoured to prove that Watson's assessment was invalid on the tenuous ground that Holmes was apparently quite ignorant of the law of Wills (*The Norwood Builder*), and so, assuredly, he was. But this captious criticism would seem to be answered by the fact that Holmes had little need to know any civil law; only a knowledge of criminal law was essential to him in his profession. And in any event, *The Norwood Builder* was likewise a case that was undertaken after the Return.

But what of Holmes's colossal ignorance of the law of burglary and unlawful entry after the Return? Even the lowliest recruit in the Police College is well aware of what burglary and unlawful entry are.

It would appear, in fact, that this article provides powerful ammunition for those who espouse the theory of the deutero-Holmes. There is no instance in the Canon before the Return, for example, in which Holmes revealed his contempt for what he believed to be the law so far as burglary was concerned. Nor is there a case in which he thought he had committed burglary or even unlawful entry, before the Return. On the contrary, compare Holmes's respect for a search-warrant in *The Greek Interpreter* with his utter disdain for such a scrap of paper in *Lady Frances Carfax*.

Furthermore, it must be pointed out, Holmes's sublimated yearnings for a criminal career are made evident in the Canon only after the Return. *Vide supra.*

But all that, I dare say, is another story.

—Christmas Annual 1958

NOTES

1. BSJ (NS) 4 (1954), 165.
2. BSJ (NS) 6 (1956), 69.
3. BSJ (NS) 7 (1957), 79.

After one hundred years, the "infallible" test for
hemoglobin developed by Sherlock Holmes is proved to
be no fable. . . .

THE SHERLOCK HOLMES BLOOD TEST:
The Solution to a Century-old Mystery

by CHRISTINE L. HUBER [1]

"I'VE FOUND IT! I've found it," he shouted to my companion, running towards us with a test-tube in his hand. "I have found a re-agent which is precipitated by haemoglobin, and by nothing else. . . . No doubt you see the significance of this discovery of mine?" "It is interesting, chemically, no doubt," I answered, "but practically—" "Why, man, it is the most practical medico-legal discovery for years. Don't you see that it gives us an infallible test for blood stains?"

" . . . Let us have some fresh blood," he said, digging a long bodkin into his finger, and drawing off the resulting drop of blood in a chemical pipette. "Now I add this small quantity of blood to a litre of water. You perceive that the resulting mixture has the appearance of pure water. The proportion of blood cannot be more than one in a million. I have no doubt, however, that we shall be able to obtain the characteristic reaction." As he spoke, he threw into the vessel a few white crystals, and then added some drops of a transparent fluid. In an instant the contents assumed a dull mahogany colour, and a brownish dust was precipitated to the bottom of the glass jar.

"Ha! ha!" he cried, clapping his hands, and looking as delighted as a child with a new toy. "What do you think of that?" "It seems to be a very delicate test," I remarked. "Beautiful! beautiful! The old guaiacum test was very clumsy and uncertain. So is the microscopic examination for blood corpuscles. The latter is valueless if the stains are a few hours old. Now, this appears to act as well whether the blood is old or new. Had this test been invented, there are hundreds of men now walking the earth who would long ago have paid the penalty of their crimes."

"Indeed!" I murmured.

"Criminal cases are continually hinging upon that one point. A man is suspected of a crime months perhaps after it has been committed. His linen or clothes are examined and brownish stains discovered upon them. Are they blood stains, or mud stains, or rust stains, or fruit stains, or what are they? That is a question which has puzzled many an expert, and why? Because there was no reliable test. Now we have the Sherlock Holmes test, and there will no longer be any difficulty."

—*A Study in Scarlet*

A Study in Scarlet, which appeared in *Beeton's Christmas Annual* in 1887, was the first published story to introduce Sherlock Holmes to the world. At the time of its publication and probably for many years to follow, the Sherlock Holmes Test for hemoglobin was regarded as fictional. As Sherlockiana developed, more and more people began approaching the Holmes Test from the standpoint of the chemical tests for blood that were known in Holmes's day. But the true nature of the Holmes Test has withstood Sherlockians' best efforts to plumb its mysteries. Until now.

ERRONEOUS IDENTIFICATIONS

Human blood contains many components, some of which are red blood cells, white blood cells, and many proteins. Hemoglobin is the principal component in red blood cells. The function of hemoglobin is the transportation of oxygen and the exchange of carbon dioxide between tissues.

Holmes himself mentioned in *Study* one test for hemoglobin that was known in 1887. The guaiacum test was "very clumsy and uncertain." There is a modern version of this test called the Hemoccult Test, used to detect blood in fecal specimens. In the Hemoccult Test, filter paper is guaiac-impregnated. The fecal specimen is applied to the paper, and then a few drops of hydrogen peroxide are applied. If blood is present in the specimen, a blue color develops on the filter paper.[2] (A newer version of this test called the HemoQuant Assay has been widely touted recently as *the* Sherlock Holmes Test!) However, neither the Hemoccult Test nor the HemoQuant Assay is the Sherlock Holmes Test.

The Holmes Test, as the text of *Study* clearly indicates, employs blood dissolved in water, the addition of white crystals, and finally the addition of a transparent liquid. All of these substances must be added in a precise order to obtain the dull mahogany color of the liquid and then the brownish dust precipitate.

Raymond McGowan in "Sherlock Holmes and Forensic Chemistry" theorizes that Holmes's knowledge of forensic chemistry far surpassed that of his contemporaries.[3] Mr. McGowan reviewed the existing tests to precipitate blood that were known in Europe between 1800 and 1881. His conclusion was that none of the tests produced the sequence of color and precipitate as described by Watson in *Study* with chemicals added according to the story's description. Earlier, D. A. Redmond, in "Some Chemical Problems in the Canon," wrote that Holmes based his test for hemoglobin on the tests of F. W. Zahn and F. L. Sonnenschein in 1871,[4] which Mr. McGowan subsequently investigated and discarded for very good reasons. The Zahn test used the addition of hydrogen peroxide to water containing blood, resulting in the production of gas bubbles, not a precipitate. The Sonnenschein test did produce a voluminous reddish-brown or chocolate precipitate when a solution of blood was treated with a saturated solution of sodium tungstate acidified with acetic acid. However, Mr. McGowan's experiments clearly established that the sodium tungstate, which *is* a white powder, must first be acidified by being mixed with the acetic acid *prior to* being added to the hemoglobin solution. This procedure effectively disqualifies a promising possibility as the true Holmes Test.[5]

One of the current methods used for the measurement of hemoglobin concentration in blood employs the principle that hemoglobin can be oxidized to methemoglobin and then converted to a stable cyanmethemoglobin, which is green in color. But not only is this color wrong for the Holmes Test, there is no precipitate. The concentration of cyanmethemoglobin is measured by the amount of light that it absorbs, using a spectrophotometer.[6]

THE TRUE HOLMES TEST

A newer method for determining the type of hemoglobin in blood is electrophoresis. The principle of electrophoresis states that certain particles or molecules will move through a medium between positive and negative electrical poles at different rates depending upon their attraction to those poles. This principle was first applied to the study of proteins in 1973.[7] It is currently used to separate the types and determine the concentrations of hemoglobin in human blood.

Remsen Ten Eyck Schenck in "Baker Street Fables" makes

the statement that "Holmes's discovery would certainly be in universal use today were it valid, and it must therefore be concluded that his belief in its specificity for haemoglobin was unfounded. Presumably he discovered on further study that a similar result was obtained with other common substances, or else that it was not due to haemoglobin at all, but rather to some other ingredient in the blood, but not peculiar to it."[8]

In reality, Ten Eyck Schenck was wrong, and Sherlock Holmes was right. The principles of the Holmes Test *are* used today as the *first steps* in preparing blood to quantify the types and concentrations of hemoglobins by electrophoresis. When blood is added to water, the red cells rupture, releasing their contents. If the solution is then made alkaline with a base chemical, the hemoglobin molecule is denatured. With the addition of another chemical, most human hemoglobins are precipitated.[9] Normal adult hemoglobin consists of a majority of hemoglobin A, some hemoglobin A_2, and a very small amount of hemoglobin F (fetal hemoglobin).[10]

The Holmes Test was based on Sherlock Holmes's knowledge of the tests of his time, his knowledge of chemistry, and methods employing trial and error. Indeed, note his surprise in discovering the correct chemicals: "I've found it! I've found it! . . . I have found a re-agent which is precipitated by haemoglobin and nothing else." Holmes's test, we will recall, must consist of a procedure in which blood is added to an amount of water, and white crystals are introduced into this, followed by a transparent liquid. In fact, chemicals introduced by such a procedure and in just such an order *are* used in preparing hemoglobin for electrophoresis.

The elusive chemical substances used in the Holmes Blood Test, at last, can now be named: sodium hydroxide (today delivered in white pellets, but available in white powder or crystalline form in Holmes's day) and a saturated solution of ammonium sulfate, a clear liquid.

The procedure for the Sherlock Holmes Test is as follows:

1) To a test tube containing 7 ml of distilled water add one drop of whole human blood. Mix the contents until a clear reddish transparent fluid is obtained.

2) Add one pellet of sodium hydroxide (which may be crushed to acquire its Holmesian crystalline appearance). Mix

the contents until the crystals are completely dissolved. A dull mahogany-colored liquid appears.

3) Rapidly add 2.5 ml of saturated ammonium sulfate. Mix the contents. Add another 2.5 ml of saturated ammonium sulfate rapidly. Mix the contents. A brownish dust will precipitate to the bottom of the test tube.

To verify that this is indeed the true Holmes Test, it is necessary to employ the procedure to test not only for hemoglobin but also to eliminate those substances that so worried Ten Eyck Schenck and that Holmes himself said his test would differentiate from hemoglobin. Accordingly, this procedure was used to test human blood, dog blood, calf blood, rust, mud, and strawberry juice. As a control, human and animal plasma and serum were used to prove that the brownish precipitate results from hemoglobin and not from other blood proteins present in both serum and plasma. The results:

SUBSTANCE ANALYZED	RESULT
1) human whole blood	brownish dust precipitate
2) human plasma	slightly milky liquid
3) human serum	slightly milky liquid
4) dog whole blood	brownish dust precipitate
5) dog plasma	slightly milky liquid
6) calf whole blood	brownish dust precipitate
7) calf plasma	slightly milky liquid
8) rust in 0.85% saline	brownish liquid
9) rust in water	brownish liquid
10) mud in water	beige liquid
11) strawberry juice in water	light yellow liquid

As can be noted from the procedure, the quantities of chemicals used are not exactly as Holmes described. Much less water is used to dissolve the blood, and much more ammonium sulfate is used. If less than a total of 5 ml of ammonium sulfate is used, it takes much longer for the brownish dust to precipitate. The amount of brownish dust is also proportional to the amount of blood dissolved in the water. The dull mahogany color that Watson describes has less a reddish-brown and more a brown color in this procedure. But this can very easily be explained in any number of ways: the uncertain light of gaslamps in 1881, the lack of purified chemicals of the day, and the simple cleanliness of Holmes's glassware, and so on.

Yet, it is clear that the remarkable scientific fact Holmes discovered in 1881 was that hemoglobin A is denatured by sodium hydroxide and then precipitated with saturated ammonium sulfate. He did not seem to know, as we do now, that hemoglobin F, which is the major hemoglobin of the fetus and the newborn, resists alkaline denaturation and therefore is not precipitated by ammonium sulfate.[11] Additionally, this procedure will not differentiate adult human blood from animal blood. But Holmes never claimed it did. The hemoglobins of all vertebrates are remarkably similar not only in their types of proteins but also in their structure.[12] It was not until 1901 that a method was discovered to differentiate dried human blood stains from animal blood stains.[13]

But aside from our demonstration that the Holmes Test is no fable, it is important to understand that the test has not been hidden for these last one hundred years. It has been in almost daily use in hospitals and research laboratories, as a part of the electrophoretic process, since its rediscovery in the 1930s. How it was lost in the first place and why Holmes never received acknowledgment for it remains a mystery.

Perhaps it is enough, however, to know that in his centennial year Sherlock Holmes has been vindicated as the wisest and best chemist whom it has been our pleasure to know.

—December 1987

1. I am deeply indebted to several individuals who provided valuable assistance in the preparation of this article. Among these are Dr. Roy Alexander, Alan Lipe, Frances Brock, and Walter Becker. My thanks also to Karen L. Johnson who clarified some chemical references in the article, suggested running experimental controls, and provided the animal blood used in the experiment.

2. Norbert W. Tietz, ed., *Fundamentals of Clinical Chemistry*, 2nd ed. (Philadelphia: Saunders, 1976), p. 431.

3. Raymond J. McGowan, "Sherlock Holmes and Forensic Chemistry," BSJ (NS) 37 (1987), 14.

4. D. A. Redmond, "Some Chemical Problems in the Canon," BSJ (NS) 14 (1964), 147.

5. McGowan, op. cit., p. 12.

6. Tietz, op. cit., p. 411.

7. Ibid., pp. 127–28.

8. Remsen Ten Eyck Schenck, "Baker Street Fables," BSJ (NS) 2 (1952), 87–88.

9. Tietz, op. cit., p. 431.

10. John Bernard Henry, M.D., ed., *Clinical Diagnosis and Management* (Philadelphia: Saunders, 1984), p. 674.

11. Tietz, op. cit., p. 431.

12. Vernon M. Ingram, *The Hemoglobins in Genetics and Evolution* (New York: Columbia University Press, 1963), p. 137.

13. Jurgen Thorwald, *The Century of the Detective* (New York: Harcourt, Brace & World, 1965), p. 118.

Throughout the Canon, Holmes refers obliquely to his
monographs and other writings. But what did these rare
and wonderful documents contain?

THE WRITINGS OF MR. SHERLOCK HOLMES

by WALTER KLINEFELTER

WHAT WITH all the to-do being made nowadays to seek out and
appraise the productions in print of everyone—be he notorious, renowned, or otherwise—who has put pen to paper or
tapped at a typewriter with literary intent, one would almost be
inclined to conclude that the works of none of that gentry had
escaped the inquiry of the book critics and the book sleuths.
There is, however, at least one very obvious omission to be
tallied against these searchers of titles and assessors of literary
properties. I refer to their failure to take any note whatsoever
of the writings of Mr. Sherlock Holmes. In view of the notable
significance of his scientific works alone, so glaring an oversight
on their part, if indeed it is an oversight and not a conspiracy of
silence, well nigh surpasses belief. They certainly cannot gloss it
over with protestations to the effect that they have never seen
any works with title-pages alleging authorship by the great consulting detective, much less with expressions of doubt as to
whether Holmes ever actually engaged in literary composition.
Such dodges are of no avail. All the evidence—sound, incontrovertible evidence—is against them. Let these critics and bib-
liographers put aside their mistaken assumptions and their
unfounded beliefs, and let them resolve to make whatever rep-
aration they can for their remissness.

In the meantime, so that they may know what it is that they
are looking for, it is only meet that there should be made available for their guidance the evidence which they seem to have
overlooked, evidence composed of the several scattered references to be found in various passages occurring in the text of
the Sherlockian Canon as indited by the worthy Dr. John H.
Watson of blessed memory. From these references it is possible
to compile, and arrange in an order more or less chronological,

the titles of all the literary works that can now be identified as having come from the pen of Mr. Sherlock Holmes.

1. "The Book of Life."

An article published anonymously in the magazine, unidentified as to title and unplaced as to date, which Dr. Watson picked up and read while impatiently waiting for his breakfast on the memorable morning of 4 March 1881 (*A Study in Scarlet*). An exposition of those practical theories of the science of deduction and analysis that he was to see applied on that very day with such amazing success in the investigation of the "bad business" at 3, Lauriston Gardens, and more or less frequently thereafter for the next thirty-some years with like results, the article struck him as "being a remarkable mixture of shrewdness and absurdity," and "smartly written," but, as he expressed it to Holmes, "ineffable twaddle," and "evidently the theory of some armchair lounger who evolves . . . neat little paradoxes in the seclusion of his own study." The reader will recall that Watson did not proceed very much farther in his critical assay of "The Book of Life" before Holmes claimed authorship of the piece and also made some disclosures that resolved most of the questions which had been troubling his fellow-lodger ever since they had set up in Baker Street some weeks before.

While "The Book of Life" is the first of the detective's writings mentioned in the codex, the bibliographer will probably find that it cannot be accorded first place in any strictly chronological listing of his works. And the fact that Holmes did not sign the article may not only account for much of the fog that obscures him in his *rôle* of author, but also portend many difficulties for his bibliographer, for it permits the entertainment of the supposition that all of his printed works may have been issued unsigned or under a pseudonym.

2. *Upon the Distinction between the Ashes of the Various Tobaccos: An Enumeration of 140 Forms of Cigar, Cigarette, and Pipe Tobacco, with Coloured Plates Illustrating the Difference in the Ash.*

That this work was already in existence, at least in manuscript, if not in book form, by 4 March 1881, when Watson read "The Book of Life," is established by Holmes's own words spoken on the same day: "I have made a special study of cigar ashes—in fact, I have written a monograph upon the subject" (*A Study in Scarlet*). He did not then disclose its actual title; that remained unknown until his biographer gave to the world the story called *The Sign of the Four*, which recounted the adventures incident to their participation in the case of the Sholto murder and the theft of the Agra treasure in September, 1887. At that time, however, after more than six years of close association with Holmes, Watson would appear to have remembered nothing about his reading of the article entitled "The Book of Life," since he expresses himself in *The Sign of the Four* as having been greatly amazed when Holmes made mention of his writings and showed him printed copies of several of his works, among which was the monograph on tobacco. On the face of it, this lapse of memory on Watson's part may seem to be but one of the many inconsistencies and seemingly irreconcilable statements that abound in the Sacred Writings of Dr. Watson just as in all other canonical relations, but in this particular instance the lapse probably was intentional, for reasons which shall appear in due course.

Referred to again by its author in 1889 during his investigation of the murder of Charles McCarthy in Boscombe Valley, *Upon the Distinction between the Ashes of the Various Tobaccos* is the only one of Holmes's works which Watson quotes the detective as mentioning more than once in the Canon. Consequently, it may be inferred that he took more than a little pride in its authorship, probably considering it his most important contribution to what may be termed the minutiæ of scientific detection. The work undoubtedly met with its most appreciative reception from the small number of private detectives who employed methods most like Holmes's own. One may be sure that the more obtuse of the Scotland Yarders regarded it with disdain, and in that attitude they were not alone: the reading public also looked on Holmes's remarks upon the "difference between the black ash of a Trichinopoly and the white fluff of bird's-eye" as so much nonsense. In fact, the general opinion regarding the work seems to have been most aptly stated by the gentleman who made Watson's revelations available to the publishers. "Rather funny, isn't it?" he remarked when a Philadelphia tobacconist wrote to inquire where he could obtain a copy of the monograph.

Since it is known from Holmes's own statement (in *The Sign of the Four*) that in 1887 François le Villard of the French detective service was translating the work into his native language, the bibliographer is also constrained to locate and record a French edition of it presumably published about 1888.

3. Two short monographs upon the variations in the shape of the human ear, not specifically titled, which Holmes in the gruesome case of *The Cardboard Box* declared to be from his pen and to have appeared "in last year's *Anthropological Journal*." Watson does not date *The Cardboard Box*, but according to the chronology of the Holmesian saga established by Mr. H. W. Bell in his *Sherlock Holmes and Dr. Watson*, that adventure took place in 1885, from which it may be presumed that the issue of the *Anthropological Journal* for the year 1884 is indicated. Should the monographs not be found in the volume for that year, it can only be concluded that Mr. Bell has erred in his dating of the case, in which event a wider search through the back files of the *Journal* would be necessary.

4. *On the Dating of Manuscripts*
    A monograph that had appeared in print before the blood-chilling affair of *The Hound of the Baskervilles*, which Mr. Bell places in 1886. If this dating is incorrect, however, it presents for a second time the question of accounting for Watson's amazement at Holmes's mention of his works in September, 1887 (*The Sign of the Four*), as well as the additional

problem of explaining his omission of this particular one from the list of Holmes's writings. From the fact that Holmes assumed Dr. James Mortimer may have read this paper, one deduces that it probably saw publication in some journal which enjoyed a wide circulation among men who followed the scientific professions. If the bibliographer fails to uncover a French edition of this work, he may be inclined to believe that François le Villard never made a translation of it, a conclusion which would seem logical enough in case the original turns out to have been concerned wholly with old English manuscripts.

5. *The Tracing of Footsteps, with Some Remarks upon the Uses of Plaster of Paris as a Preserver of Impresses.*

A monograph that is definitely known to exist in book or pamphlet form, since Holmes showed a copy of it to Watson on 7 September 1887 (*The Sign of the Four*). In all probability there is also an edition in French to be accounted for, since it is mentioned among the works that François le Villard was translating at that time. Apropos of this monograph, it will be recalled that after his solution of the Priory School case in 1901 Holmes had material for an interesting note on the subject of faking the prints made by animals, with special reference to the devices employed by some of the robber Barons of Holdernesse during the Middle Ages to disguise the tracks of their horses.

6. *A Study of the Influence of a Trade upon the Form of the Hand, with Lithotypes of the Hands of Slaters, Sailors, Cork-cutters, Compositors, Weavers, and Diamond-cutters.*

This work appeared either in book or in pamphlet form and was among those being translated by François le Villard in 1887 (*The Sign of the Four*). The subject, Holmes pointed out to Watson, was "of great practical interest to the scientific detective—especially in cases of unclaimed bodies, or in discovering the antecedents of criminals."

7. *On Tattoo Marks.*

This monograph may have appeared as a pamphlet or as an article in some scientific journal, or it may have been published in both forms. Mention of it is found in the adventure of *The Red-Headed League*, which took place in 1890. There can be little doubt, however, that the bibliographer will have occasion to assign the work a much earlier date.

8. *Explorations in Tibet*, by ——Sigerson.

Holmes's account, under a Norwegian pseudonym, of his two years' sojourn in innermost Asia, in the course of which he visited Lhassa and spent some time there with the head lama (*The Empty House*). While it is possible that these remarkable adventures made their first and only bid for readers in book form, the context of the Canon leaves room for the assumption that they may have been reported originally in letters to various London newspapers. This, however, is a question that will have to be resolved by bibliographical research, which, fortunately, need not be expended outside of publications that appeared in the years 1892 and 1893, for Holmes spoke of the adventures as having been printed some while before his return to Baker Street.

9. *Report of a Visit to the Khalifa at Khartoum.*

A paper which Holmes submitted to the Foreign Office in 1893 or early in 1894, probably while he was conducting researches in the coaltar derivatives in a laboratory at Montpellier, before his dramatic return (*The Empty House*). The original manuscript no doubt still lies buried somewhere in the files at Number 10, Downing Street. If the report ever got into print, its title will very likely be found to read *Report of a Visit to the Khalifa at Omdurman*, since Holmes, displaying for once a trait much more characteristic of his Boswell, had had a lapse of memory when he mentioned the paper to Watson, having forgotten that he could not have called upon the Khalifa at Khartoum, which then lay in ruins by that ruler's order, but at Omdurman, the city that he made his capital at the time when the detective visited him.

10. *On the Polyphonic Motets of Lassus.*

A monograph in process of composition in November, 1895, when brother Mycroft brought the case of the Bruce-Partington plans to Sherlock's attention. Completed at some unspecified time after the conclusion of that deplorable business, *On the Polyphonic Motets of Lassus* was printed and distributed privately. And Watson records that experts acclaimed it "the last word upon the subject." Printed as it was for private circulation, it probably will prove to be one of the more elusive of Holmes's productions.

11. *A Study of the Chaldean Roots in the Ancient Cornish Language.*

A piece of philological research which Watson reported Holmes to have begun while vacationing in Cornwall in March, 1897 (*The Devil's Foot*). This work also Holmes had to lay aside for a time because of a professional interruption—in this instance, the Cornish horror, which he considered the strangest case he ever handled. When that mystery had been cleared up, he returned "with a clear conscience" to the development of the thesis that the ancient Cornish tongue "was akin to the Chaldean, and had been largely derived from the Phoenician traders in tin," and in all likelihood he completed it before returning to London—his next recorded case, *Shoscombe Old Place*, opening in Baker Street in May, 1897—but there is nothing in the Canon which would indicate that the results of his research were published. If after protracted quest the bibliographer does not encounter them in printed form, he may have to resign himself to being content with the hope that some day perhaps he will unearth the original manuscript.

12. *Secret Writings: Analyses of 160 Separate Ciphers.*

"I am fairly familiar with all forms of secret writings, and am myself the author of a trifling monograph upon the subject," said Holmes in *The Dancing Men*, " . . . but I confess that this [cipher of the dancing men] is entirely new to me." *The Dancing Men* took place in 1898, a circumstance which accounts for the place assigned *Secret Writings* in this listing but, unfortunately, does not establish definitely, or even approximately, the time of the composition and appearance of that work. Incidentally, *Secret Writings* is the last of the technical publications mentioned in the Canon.

On several occasions, both before and after his self-imposed exile from England, Holmes intimated that he had thoughts of writing papers on other aspects of detective science. Among the subjects he intended to deal with were the typewriter and its relation to crime (*A Case of Identity*, 1888), malingering (*The Dying Detective*, 1889), and the uses of dogs in the work of the detective (*The Creeping Man*, 1903). Though the intentions are duly recorded in the Canon, they cannot be taken too seriously, for there is nothing said about their fulfillment. The same is true of Holmes's proposal, announced in *The Abbey Grange*, 1897, to devote his "declining years to the composition of a textbook, which shall focus the whole art of detection into one volume." That his intentions of undertaking any such work also were not overly serious may be surmised from a statement he made in 1891, when, with Moriarty almost run to earth and retirement in his mind, he said to Watson: "Of late I have been tempted to look into the problems furnished by nature rather than those more superficial ones for which our artificial state of society is responsible" (*The Final Problem*). And when one also considers the subjects he is known to have written about between the date of his exodus from England in 1891 and the time of his retirement to the Sussex Downs, *circa* 1904—namely, his experiences in Tibet, conditions in the Sudan, the polyphonic motets of a mediaeval composer, the origins of the ancient Cornish language—the conclusion that in 1891, and even before that date, he had done with writing on the science of detection is almost inescapable. True, the subjects he wrote on in those years were hardly problems of the kind furnished by nature, his probing of which would have to await his retirement, but at the same time they were not at all related to the science of detection. In fact, it cannot fail to be the earnest conviction of anyone who ponders deeply the problems presented by Holmes the author that not only were the technical writings the direct outgrowth of the special and out-of-the-ordinary studies which he undertook in preparation for his life's work while still at college, and which he continued after he came up to London, but that the composition of the major ones, such as those upon tobacco ashes, the dating of manuscripts, the influence of a trade upon the form of the hand, the tracing of footsteps, secret writings, and perhaps one or two others, was a *fait accompli* when the Baker Street ménage became a reality.

13. *Practical Handbook of Bee Culture, with Some Observations Upon the Segregation of the Queen.*

In print at the time Holmes made his last bow in August, 1914, this work probably had been completed and delivered to the printer prior to his engagement in the job of trapping Von Bork, a piece of counter-espionage that took him two years to carry through to a successful conclusion. It is described as a small blue book, with *Practical Handbook of Bee Culture* in gold lettering on the front cover. Holmes called it "the fruit" of his "leisured ease," "the *magnum opus*" of his "latter years."

14. "The Adventure of the Blanched Soldier."
Published in *The Strand Magazine*, November, 1926, and in *The Case-Book of Sherlock Holmes*, London and New York, 1927.
"Why do you not write them yourself?"
"I will, my dear Watson, I will" (*The Abbey Grange*).
And he did. This is one of them. In its appearances in English this story should present no difficulties for the bibliographer. It is the search for all the translations of it which have been made that he will find a bit exhausting.

15. "The Adventure of the Lion's Mane."
Published in *The Strand Magazine*, December, 1926, and in *The Case-Book of Sherlock Holmes*, London and New York, 1927. The same comment which was made on the preceding story also applies to this one. In connection with these two tales it only remains to add that Watson's literary agent must have been a very persuasive fellow to have prevailed upon Holmes to permit these two pieces to appear in a book along with tales by the good Doctor, whose literary methods the detective so frequently and so unfeelingly deplored.

And speaking of Holmes's opinions of Watson's literary efforts reminds one that to the detective's strictures on the products of his Boswell's pen must undoubtedly be attributed the reason why so disappointingly little is known about most of his own writings. Those well-intentioned critical pronouncements wounded the great and justifiable pride which Watson took in his tales more deeply than the famous discomfitor of criminals ever realized. But even though Watson's feelings always were hurt on such occasions, and though his resentment usually was very bitter, apart from an infrequent outburst of protest, he generally kept his peace, for early in his association with Holmes he had hit upon a way to get even with him for all those verbal barbs.

Never again after he delivered his snap judgment on "The Book of Life" did he openly criticize the writings of his friend. In fact, he went much farther than that: whenever he could do so he said very little about them, and when he could not very well omit mention of them he certainly said a great deal less than he knew. Consequently, his friend's works are comparatively unknown now, while his own are read wherever print serves as a means of communication.

Yet after the bibliographer and the literary critics have done their duty by the great fathomer, who knows but what his works may not some day be as well known as the works of Watson are today?

—October 1946

In this exhaustive treatise, Ms. Stern fills the
bookshelves of 221B Baker Street with the volumes that
we know were owned by Holmes, thus revealing a man
of more than eclectic tastes. . . .

SHERLOCK HOLMES: RARE BOOK COLLECTOR
A Study in Book Detection
by MADELEINE B. STERN

SHERLOCK HOLMES was as canny and secretive in his book-collecting practices as in his methods of detection. Hence, though much has been written about the Baker Street library,[1] the real treasures of 221B have remained concealed until now. Everyone is aware of the nature of Holmes's reference books; he made no attempt to cover up the occupational shelf that contained his copy of *Crockford*,[2] his *Continental Gazetteer*,[3] or his set of *Whitaker's Almanac*.[4] The maps of London,[5] the ordnance map of the Devonshire moor[6] that Stanford's provided, the London telephone directory,[7] and Debrett[8]—all are common knowledge. Holmes needed those books and placed them openly on his shelves or beside the mantelpiece, where any visitor, in however agitated a state, could observe them, and where Watson, if he wished, could browse freely.

Even from Watson, however, Holmes successfully concealed the nature and extent of his bibliographical rarities. On one occasion only—and then in a moment of unguarded enthusiasm to which even the shrewdest collectors are subject—did he reveal the qualities of one of his most precious "finds." Even then he concealed his excitement with an off-hand phrase: "This is a queer old book I picked up at a stall yesterday—*De Jure inter Gentes*—published in Latin at Liège in the Lowlands, in 1642."[9] "A queer old book," indeed! Actually, one of the most extraordinary volumes in the Holmes treasure room!—a book unique both for its contents and its imprint. The *De Jure inter Gentes*, though published anonymously, was really written by Richard

Zouche, 1590–1661, the English civilian. Prior to Holmes's "find," the first edition was thought to have been printed at Oxford in 1650 under the title *Juris et Judicii fecialis, sive Juris inter gentes,* and it was the second part of the title that suggested to Bentham the felicitous phrase "international law." The anonymous edition, bearing the title *De jure inter Gentes,* is rare enough when it carries the Leyden 1651 imprint. But Holmes's copy antedates even the so-called first edition of 1650, and hence is a find of extraordinary magnitude, one of the most desirable books in any legal collection.

Holmes, of course, was aware of this when he emphasized the early date of the Zouche by remarking to Watson, "Charles's head was still firmly on his shoulders when this little brown-backed volume was struck off." His copy was further enhanced by an interesting provenance. "On the flyleaf," Holmes pursued, "in very faded ink, is written 'Ex libris Gulielmi Whyte.' . . . Some pragmatical seventeenth century lawyer, I suppose." As if he did not know that the copy had belonged to the English divine, William White, 1604–78, who had fathered several interesting Latin works under the pseudonym of "Gulielmus Phalerius." Holmes had indeed made a remarkable find that March day in 1881 when he returned from his wanderings among the stalls of Ludgate Hill with a treasure fit to stand beside the first edition of Grotius. In a way, the 1642 Zouche is, because of its remarkable date, an even more interesting volume. Indeed, had Thomas James Wise evinced any interest in international law in the year 1881, one might almost be ready to accuse him of perpetrating the work in question. But such a thought is unworthy. Holmes had tucked a fine treasure under his arm, and had it not been for his unusual powers of self-discipline, he surely could not have laid the Zouche aside to turn to the problems of the Brixton Road affair which Watson subsequently immortalized as *A Study in Scarlet.*

Holmes never again referred, beyond a title or two, to any of his notable finds. Observing that Watson was bent upon publicizing his successes in detection, he kept from his Boswell any clue that might reappear in the popular case-histories and bring to his doorstep a rival collector or a predatory bookseller. He had said more than he should have about the Zouche. Henceforth his lips were sealed. He would find his treasures and enjoy them in solitude. Bibliographically, he would walk alone. He might drop a word about an author in his possession, but he was done with revealing imprints to Watson. Only a determined literary sleuth would be able to detect the true nature of the rarities that gradually found their place on the secret shelves of 221B. For it is certainly not too much to assume that the man who captured the 1642 Zouche continued to add treasures of equal stature to his collection. From the few brief hints that he dropped, it is possible, even at this late day, to follow him on his bibliophilic meanderings and to describe in detail the prizes he carried away. Nearly every aspect of the great detector has been detected. Let us detect now the secret hoard of rare books to which he turned when, weary of his test-tubes and his violin, the great man sat alone in Baker Street.

There are eight fine books, plus a small collection of works on one subject that can be assigned without question to the Holmes bookshelf. Although there is no doubt that it was a first edition, Holmes made no secret of his possession of William Winwood Reade's *The Martyrdom of Man*. In 1887,[10] in the course of his investigation of *The Sign of the Four*, he handed the volume to Watson, recommending it as "one of the most remarkable ever penned," and later, during the same investigation, he returned to a discussion of the book, citing the author's views on individual and aggregate man. Reade, a traveler, novelist, and controversialist, as well as a nephew of Charles Reade, had expressed his atheistical opinions in his *Martyrdom of Man*, and the book became so popular that by 1884 it had reached an eighth edition. Knowing, as we do, that Holmes had in 1881 discovered the unique pre-first of Zouche, we cannot doubt that he owned a copy of the 1872 first edition of Reade. He was not loath to share the book with Watson simply because, though it was a first, it was not a rarity in 1887.

The same situation holds true of Holmes's copy of the Rev. John George Wood's *Out of Doors*. While engaged in his solution of *The Lion's Mane* in 1907, he admitted openly that the garret of his little house in Sussex was "stuffed with books," and, having rummaged through that minor store-house, he emerged with a copy of the volume that revealed the nature of the deadly *Cyanea capillata* which had killed Fitzroy McPherson. Again, there is no question that Holmes's copy of *Out of Doors* was a first of 1874 rather than one of the later editions of the work by the popular nineteenth-century English naturalist. Like the Reade *Martyrdom of Man*, the book was not sufficiently scarce to warrant any secrecy, though there is no doubt that it was a first edition. Incidentally, it is interesting to observe that Wood was also the author of *Bees, Their Habits and Management*, a subject to which Holmes gave no little attention between 1904 and 1912.

By 1889, Holmes had in his possession a volume which he modestly referred to as his "pocket Petrarch." It will be recalled that, on the train to Ross near Boscombe Valley, when in 1889 he was unraveling *The Boscombe Valley Mystery*, he remarked to Watson, "And now here is my pocket Petrarch, and not another word shall I say of this case until we are on the scene of action." While it may excite some wonder that Holmes should have carried with him so delightful a little rarity, there can be no question that the volume to which he referred was any other than the charming *Il Petrarca* printed in italic letter at Lyons in 1550, ruled in red, and adorned with the delicate heart-shaped woodcut medallion showing portraits of Petrarch and Laura by Bernard Salomon. Any doubts about the identity of the edition must be stilled when we recall that in 1881 Holmes had discovered that really unobtainable Zouche. After such a find he could have been satisfied with no other "pocket Petrarch."

We come now to one of the most interesting book references ever made by Holmes. In 1894, while engaged in *The Adventure of the Empty House*, the great detector, it will be remembered, disguised himself as an elderly book dealer. Watson, who "struck against" him and knocked down several of the books he was carrying, thought him "some poor bibliophile, who, either as a trade or as a hobby, was a collector of obscure volumes." As Watson picked up the books, he noticed that the title of one was *The Origin of Tree Worship*. Subsequently, Holmes, still in his disguise, appeared in Watson's study and mentioned three more titles that he was carrying: *British Birds*, Catullus, and *The Holy War*. Before doffing his disguise he remarked that he ran a little bookshop at the corner of Church Street, Kensington.

The question first to be considered is whether Holmes had just selected those books at random from a Church Street bookshop, or whether they had been in his possession previously.

Since Holmes had last seen Watson, he had extricated himself from the Reichenbach Fall and traveled for two years in Tibet. Upon his return to London, he had gone immediately to Baker Street, finding that his brother Mycroft had preserved his rooms and papers exactly as they had always been. It is clear, then, that Holmes had taken the four volumes in question from his own shelves before assuming his disguise. The disguise itself is elucidating, however, for Holmes undoubtedly identified himself with the bookseller who had, at some time prior to 1894, supplied him not only with those volumes, but with several others. The dealer was none other than Alfred B. Clementson, who plied his trade at 73 Church Street, Kensington, W.[11] Just as we know that Holmes obtained his maps from Edward Stanford of Cockspur Street,[12] we can now assure ourselves that he had found several of his more treasured items at Clementson's.

The identification of the four named volumes is less important actually than the identification of the book seller by appointment to Her Majesty, Sherlock Holmes. However, to complete the record, there can be little question that the books which Holmes offered (so safely, it may be added) to his friend Watson included the first Aldine Catullus: *Catullus. Tibullus. Propertius,* printed in italic letter by Aldus at Venice in 1502, with the title-page in the first state, reading Propetius for Propertius—a rare edition though, of course, not, under the circumstances, an incunable. The *British Birds* which Holmes, in the disguises that he planned to drop shortly, could offer with impunity as a bargain, was not a minor nineteenth-century work, but the fine *History of British Birds* with the Bewick wood engravings printed in two volumes at Newcastle in 1797 and 1804. *The Holy War* was obviously a copy of the 1639 first edition of Thomas Fuller's *History of the Holy Warre,* and not one of the numerous reprints of that popular work on the Crusades. Knowing Watson's desire to interest the British public in the exploits of his friend, even occasionally at the expense of accuracy, we may safely assume that what he called *The Origin of Tree Worship* was actually *Der Baumkultus,* written by Boetticher in 1856, a title which Watson, for the sake of his English public, translated a bit too freely.

There is little doubt that the Alfred B. Clementson of Church Street, Kensington, who had originally supplied Holmes with those volumes, also sent him a most interesting selection of books while the detector was resting at Poldhu Bay in 1897. During the spring of that year, Holmes, at the advice of the Harley Street physician Dr. Moore Agar, had gone to a small cottage near Poldhu Bay to rest. While there he naturally became interested in the ancient Cornish language, and had received a "consignment of books upon philology" which he was studying when the problem of "The Cornish Horror" interrupted his researches. It was Holmes's thesis that ancient Cornish was allied to Chaldean and had been "largely derived from the Phoenician traders in tin"—a theory that could be developed only by a study of the philological works which he ordered from Clementson. Among them was surely to be found a copy of Lhuyd's *Archaeologica Britannica* of 1707, a work containing a grammar of the language. There also must have been included in that intriguing "consignment of books" Edward Norris' *Ancient Cornish Drama* printed in Penzance in 1859, to which a "Sketch of Cornish Grammar" is added as an appendix. Nor would the collection have been complete without Jago's *Dialect of Cornwall* printed at Truro in 1882, Williams' *Lexicon Cornu-Britannicum* (Landovery 1865), Bannister's *Glossary of Cornish Names* (Truro 1871), and the Courtney and Couch *Glossary of Words in Use in Cornwall* (Penzance 1880).

With these works at hand, Holmes not only could pride himself upon an extremely interesting group of Cornish imprints, but could work with diligence upon the monolith inscriptions, the Cymric division of Celtic, and the Brythonic dialect that engrossed his attention. It was with the aid of these books that he was attempting to ally cuneiform and monolith inscriptions, and there is little doubt that he would, in time, have arrived at the conclusion that "Chaldee" was a misnomer for the dialect that was really the language of the Southwestern Arameans, had not *The Devil's Foot* taken his mind from the mysteries of Cornish philology to the mystery of the Cornish horror. Indeed, had it not been for the intervention of the Tregennis family, it is clear enough that Holmes would have produced one of the most remarkable treatises on comparative philology, a treatise linking the fragments of Gnostic hymns with ancient Cornish inscriptions. While we must regret that his work is lost to the world, we find contentment in being able to reconstruct with so great a degree of accuracy the philological bookshelf that eventually found its way to Baker Street.

The final work which can be definitely given a Holmes *ex libris* is the "small tract, embellished with a rude engraving of the ancient Manor House" of what Watson called "Birlstone," purchased by the great detector in 1900 for one penny from the local tobacconist. The interesting ephemeron which proved of such aid in connection with *The Valley of Fear* was, of course, a tract on the manor house, not at Birlstone, but, as has been pointed out,[13] at Brambletye, Sussex. It is entitled *Particulars of an important freehold & small part copyhold estate* and consists of nine pages of text with a plan. Printed in London in 1843, it was offered for sale by a tobacconist who in 1900 saw no interest in it and was glad to exchange any of his remaining copies for a penny. Holmes knew its worth—not only in connection with the so-called "Tragedy of Birlstone"—as a fascinating ephemeron fit to join the many rarities already on his shelves.

Law, philosophy, literature, natural history, philology—all are represented by the rare books or first editions definitely known to have belonged to Holmes. For him, no over-specialized collecting. All knowledge was grist to his mill. Had he not declared that "a man should keep his little brain-attic stocked with all the furniture that he is likely to use, and the rest he can put away in the lumber-room of his library, where he can get it if he wants it"?[14] We may be sure that the lumber-room of Holmes's library contained some of the finest furniture, and that when he buried himself among his "old books" they were not only old but rare. The man who detected the 1642 Zouche would have been happy in no other company.

Thus far there is no doubt at all regarding the titles in the Holmes collection. Concerning the following group, however, there is some slight question as to Holmes's ownership. All that can be said with definiteness is that they were *probably* in his possession. The doubt arises because Holmes—like many other wary collectors—mentioned the works but never exhibited or produced them. In all likelihood they were his, and the little element of questionableness simply heightens the desire to make sure.

Who can doubt, for example, that, while Holmes would never have endured a Gaboriau on his shelves ("Lecoq was a miserable bungler. . . . That book made me positively ill"[15]), he must have admitted Poe to his library. Although in 1881, at the time of *A Study in Scarlet,* he considered Dupin "a very inferior fellow," he returned to a discussion of that character six years later when he was investigating the problem of *The Cardboard Box,* stating to Watson, "Some little time ago . . . I read you the passage in one of Poe's sketches in which a close reasoner follows the unspoken thoughts of his companion."[16] It may therefore be assumed that, either prior to 1881, or, more probably, between 1881 and 1887, Holmes acquired a copy of the New York: Wiley and Putnam, 1845 edition of Poe's *Tales,* including both "The Murders in the Rue Morgue," which contained the passage in question, and "The Mystery of Marie Rogêt."

In that same year of 1887, Holmes, engaged in the case of *The Sign of the Four,* twice quoted from Goethe in the original German, and offered a brief but brilliant analysis of Richter, referring to the latter's conception that "man's real greatness lies in his perception of his own smallness." Is it not permissible to conclude that a set of Goethe's *Poetische und prosaische Werke* (Stuttgart & Tübingen 1836–37) stood side by side with Jean Paul's *Herbst-Blumine* (Tübingen 1810–20) on the Holmes bookshelf?[17]

In that fruitful period, during his work on *The Noble Bachelor,* Holmes took occasion to cite Thoreau's remark on circumstantial evidence, which is very strong "as when you find a trout in the milk"—a clear enough sign that he may have owned a copy of Thoreau's *Miscellanies* (Boston 1863), to which Emerson had added a biographical sketch including sentences from the unpublished writings. Among the sentences was, of course, the remark on circumstantial evidence, actually taken from the as-yet-unpublished Journals of Thoreau.

Two years later, Holmes referred to four other authors in a manner suggesting that their works may have adorned his shelves. Having concluded *A Case of Identity,* he quoted to Watson the old Persian saying, "'There is danger for him who taketh

117

the tiger cub, and danger also for whoso snatches a delusion from a woman,'" remarking at the same time, "There is as much sense in Hafiz as in Horace." Since the *Diwân* of the Persian poet, Hafiz, was not translated in its entirety into English prose until 1891, we must assume that Holmes's copy was either of the 1800 Hindley edition of the *Persian Lyrics* printed in Persian and English with verse and prose paraphrases and a catalogue of the Gazels, or of the fine 1875 edition containing a verse rendering of the principal poems by Bicknell. Nor is it too much to assume that a copy of Horace—doubtless, because of Holmes's interest in printing types, the Parma 1791 edition published by Bodoni—also graced the detector's library.

During the affair of *Boscombe Valley* in the same year, wishing to discontinue a discussion of James McCarthy's innocence, Holmes suggested, "And now let us talk about George Meredith, if you please, and we shall leave all minor matters until tomorrow." Having concluded the case, he quoted Baxter with "There, but for the grace of God, goes Sherlock Holmes." May we not infer that Meredith's *Ordeal of Richard Feverel,* in the three-volume 1859 first edition,[18] as well as Baxter's *Saint's Everlasting Rest* in the 1650 first edition were among the choice items in the Holmes treasure room?

While there may be some doubting Thomases who will scoff at the suggestion, it seems clear that Holmes, some time between 1888 and 1900, acquired a fine Bible. It has been pointed out that in 1888, having concluded the problem of *The Crooked Man,* Holmes admitted that his Biblical knowledge was "a trifle rusty," though he thought that the "small affair of Uriah and Bathsheba" could be found "in the first or second of Samuel." By 1900, Holmes could surely have checked the reference, finding it in the "second of Samuel." In that year, when, in connection with *The Valley of Fear,* he was confronted with the problem of deciphering Porlock's coded message which had been based upon a book, Watson mentioned the volumes which Porlock imagined would be in Holmes's possession. Among them was a Bible. Holmes's reply was non-committal: "Good, Watson, good! But not, if I may say so, quite good enough! Even if I accepted the compliment for myself, I could hardly name any volume which would be less likely to lie at the elbow of one of Moriarty's associates. Besides, the editions of Holy

Writ are so numerous that he could hardly suppose that two copies would have the same pagination."

Surely Holmes could have "accepted the compliment for himself." Porlock knew a thing or two about the great detector, although it was natural enough that Holmes did not wish to air one of his most treasured possessions to his frank and open Boswell. Surely, between 1888 and 1900, Holmes had obtained a copy of the Bible—not of any inferior edition, either, but, aware as we are of his philological interests and his preoccupation with "Chaldee," of none other than the celebrated Complutensian Polyglot Bible edited under the auspices of Cardinal Ximenes between 1514 and 1517, and printed in Hebrew, Chaldee, Greek, and Latin—the earliest, indeed, of the great Polyglots. Yes, Holmes had probably acquired a treasure fit to stand beside the incomparable Zouche, a treasure which would not only have proved of no aid in deciphering Porlock's message, but which he was naturally reluctant to reveal to Watson.

The final "probability" among Holmes's fine books may have been welcomed to his shelves by 1890, when, at the successful termination of the adventure of *The Red-Headed League,* he misquoted Flaubert's words to George Sand, *"L'homme c'est rien— l'oeuvre c'est tout,"* and thus implied that he had purchased a copy of the 1884 Paris edition of Flaubert's *Lettres . . . à George Sand* with the introductory study by Maupassant.

Accepting the probabilities as actualities, we may conclude that several rarities in literature, philosophy, and theology had joined shelves already resplendent with the calf- and vellum-bound volumes that definitely bore a Holmes ownership inscription. When both groups are considered together—those that were positively and those that were probably in the Holmes library—we are struck more forcibly than ever by the catholicity of the great detector's collecting tastes. When his "book and pipe lay by his chair," as they so often did, we may safely assume that, though the pipe tobacco may not have appealed to all, the book did. It was almost always a worthy book, and it was almost always in a rare or first edition.

In addition to his fine individual items of general interest, Holmes undoubtedly also acquired several small collections of a more specialized nature. These were the books which he needed at his elbow when he was preparing his well-known monographs and articles, and, like the others, they were often scarce and always interesting.

While it is true that for his article "The Book of Life" Holmes probably relied entirely upon his own observations, for his remaining monographs he needed and undoubtedly purchased the works of other scholars. Thus, for the first of his contributions to learning, "On the Distinction between the Ashes of the Various Tobaccos," Holmes certainly obtained Redi's *Esperienze intorno a diverse cose naturali* (Florence 1686), containing the first scientific tests with nicotine, as well as Philone de Conversationibus' *Venus Rebutee* (Cologne 1722), an account of the various kinds of tobacco raised in Virginia and Germany with a description of the types of ash produced by each. His tobacco collection was not complete without Tiedemann's *Geschichte des Tabaks* (1856), dealing with various smoking mixtures and cake tobacco, cigars, cigarettes, and snuff, nor—though it was not directly related to his studies—could Holmes have resisted the purchase of *Medical Reports, of the Effects of Tobacco* (1788) by Thomas Fowler, who wrote also on the effects of arsenic. It is interesting to note that Holmes's article, written by 1881, probably influenced Gaetano Casoria, whose treatise, *Sulla combustibilità di alcune varietà di tabacchi*, with a chemical analysis of the ash of various tobaccos, appeared the following year.

In March 1886, Holmes produced two short monographs for the *Anthropological Journal*, "On Variations in the Human Ear," and by the next year he had written another article of anatomical interest, "The Influence of a Trade upon the Form of the Hand." There is no question that for his aural researches he obtained a copy of Falloppio's *Observationes anatomicae* (Venice 1561), a work containing the first clear description of the *membrana tympani*, as well as Duverney's *Traité de l'organe de l'ouie* (Paris 1683), the first scientific account of the structure of the ear. For his study of the influence of a trade upon the form of the hand, he must have acquired, for his medico-anatomical shelf, a copy of Ramazzini's *De morbis artificum diatriba* of 1670, the first account of occupational diseases.

At about the same time that he was engaged upon his investigations on the form of the hand, Holmes was also preoccupied with a monograph "On the Tracing of Footsteps, with Some Remarks upon the Uses of Plaster of Paris as a Preserver of Impresses." Holmes's work, completed by 1887, antedates most of the researches in this field. While much attention had been given before that time to fossil footprints, it was not until Holmes led the way that André Frécon in France[19] and Anton Prant in Germany[20] could produce their works on the more modern variety of footprint. Some material on gypsum or plaster of Paris was, however, available to Holmes, who surely acquired for his work a copy of Richard Peters' *Agricultural Enquiries on Plaister of Paris* (Philadelphia 1797) as well as Mathijsen's *Du bandage plâtré* (Liège 1854), a treatise which, incidentally, introduced the modern plaster-of-Paris bandage.

It was not until 1890 that Holmes completed his essay "On Tattoo Marks." In this field, also, most of the works on tattooing, corporal marking, and ethnic mutilation follow rather than precede Holmes. Yet there were one or two books that could have provided him with information, and these he certainly purchased: Lacassagne's *Les Tatouages* (Paris 1881), Robert Fletcher's *Tattooing among Civilized People* (Washington 1883), and A. W. Buckland's *On Tattooing* (London 1888). It was not until after Holmes's article had cleared the ground that the important investigations of Maori and Samoan tattooing were at last undertaken.

By 1897, Holmes completed his treatise "On Secret Writings," and two years later his work "On the Dating of Documents." For the latter study—the art of "diplomatic"—he surely admitted to his shelves such treatises as Mabillon's *De re diplomatica* (Paris 1681) and Madox's *Formulare Anglicanum* (1702). His little collection on ciphers and secret writings was more interesting. It undoubtedly included two fine seventeenth-century works: Falconer's *Cryptomenysis patefacta* (London 1685), on such pertinent subjects as deciphering secret writings, Bacon's cipher, and the systems used by the Turks, as well as that ingenious volume on cryptography, John Wilkins' *Mercury* (London 1694). Eighteenth-century researches in the field were represented among the Holmes sources by John Lockington's edition of Bowles's *New and Complete Book of Cyphers* (1795), illustrated with plates of ciphers. Holmes's shelf undoubtedly also contained the study of Thomas Young, who deciphered the Rosetta Stone: *An Account of some Recent Discoveries in Hieroglyphical Literature* (London 1823) as well as Champollion's *Précis du sys-*

tème hiéroglyphique des anciens Egyptiens (Paris 1828), with its useful plates of hieroglyphic alphabets.

Up to this point, Holmes's researches have all been along lines more or less directly connected with his work as detector. He did not, however, confine himself to those fields. In writing, as well as in collecting, he evinced a catholicity of interest by producing, around 1896, a privately printed monograph on "The Polyphonic Motets of Lassus." The difficulty of writing about the Belgian composer Orlando di Lasso (1530–1594) has been pointed out.[21] The Lasso motets number 510 and, having been intended for voices only, can neither be heard nor played, but only read. There is little doubt, therefore, that Holmes must have acquired the rare first book of Lasso's motets published at Antwerp in 1556, and containing the great motet in honor of Cardinal Pole. It is possible, though by no means certain, that Holmes also indulged in the extravagance of purchasing Lasso's first book of madrigals published in Venice the preceding year.

Holmes's final work indicates, like his monographs on Lassus, the broadness of his interests. His *Practical Handbook of Bee Culture, with some Observations upon the Segregation of the Queen* occupied him between 1904 and 1912, a period during which he must have acquired a remarkably fine apiarian collection. Holmes's shelf on bee culture boasted undoubtedly a copy of Charles Butler's *The Feminin' Monarchi; Or The Histori of Bee's* (Oxford 1634), a volume of interest not only for its useful advice on the subject, but for its introduction of the use of phonetics in English. Close by this curious treatise stood Bazin's lengthy dialogue entitled *Histoire naturelle des abeilles* (Paris 1744) with its finely engraved folding plates. Réaumur's *Natural History of Bees* (London 1744), together with Ruccellai's poem on bees, *Le Api* (Parma 1797), with its observations made by means of a magnifying mirror, were surely included in the Holmes collection. Only two copies of Ruccellai's work were printed on silk, and it is quite possible, though not definite, that the Holmes copy was one of them. Thacher's *Practical Treatise on the Management of Bees* (Boston 1829) probably completed the small but select apiarian collection enhanced by a Holmes provenance.

There is a final group of works, forming a little library in themselves, that doubtless also appeared on Holmes's shelves. These are the books related to his general interests. Here, however, we cannot be on such firm ground as we have been in the past. His interests were many and generalized, and it is impossible to decide with absolute accuracy just which books appealed sufficiently to those interests to have been admitted to his library. All we can do is throw a hint here and there, with the necessary caution that this portion of Holmes's library is purely conjectural.

Watson, listing the limits of Holmes's knowledge and appraising his general interests for readers of *A Study in Scarlet*, advises us in 1881 that the detector's acquaintance with botany was "variable," but that he was "well up in belladonna, opium, and poisons generally." It is probably safe to assume, therefore, that Holmes, being, as we have seen, an avid book collector by that date, owned several important works in those fields. His toxicology collection probably included Santes Ardoyno's *Opus de venenis*, though more likely in the Basle 1562 second edition than in the incunable first edition. To this he may well have added such fine volumes as Mercuriale's *De venenis* (Frankfurt 1584) and Codronchi's *De morbis veneficiis* (Milan 1618). The nineteenth century produced many informative toxicologies which Holmes doubtless purchased from time to time. He was not likely to have passed up Sir Robert Christison's *Treatise on Poisons* (Edinburgh 1829), since Christison had taught medical jurisprudence at Edinburgh and had performed the autopsy on one of the victims in the trial of Burke and Hare.

Another treatise, published the same year, Morgan and Addison's *Essay on the Operation of Poisonous Agents upon the Living Body*, was very possibly added to the Holmes collection, since it was the first book in English on the action of poisons in the living body. Dragendorff, who introduced methods for the detection of poisons in the human body, was more than likely represented on the Holmes shelf by his *Die gerichtlich-chemische Ermittelung von Giften* (St. Petersburg 1868). On the specific subject of opium, Holmes may have acquired Hartmann's *Discursus quidam de opio* (Wittenberg 1658), Young's *Treatise on Opium* (London 1753), and, of course, a first edition of De Quincey.[22]

On the subject of belladonna, Holmes surely purchased Kilmer's treatise, *Belladonna: A Study of its History, Action and Uses in Medicine,* when it appeared in 1894.

Holmes's geological interest in soils, evinced as early as 1881, marks him out as a forerunner in the field. Most soil analyses appeared later than that date, except, for example, Bergman's *Specimen academicum, caussas sterilitatis agrorum exponens* (Upsala 1754), which Holmes very likely acquired. When the works of Sir John Bennet Lawes and Charles Barnard[23] emerged—the former in 1883 and the latter in 1894—Holmes almost certainly added them to his library.

Watson tells us also that Holmes's knowledge of chemistry was "profound." Who can question, then, that, as a book collector, he acquired Giovanni Battista della Porta's *De distillatione* (Rome 1608) with its splendid woodcuts of chemical apparatus, or Lavoisier's *Traité élémentaire de chimie* (Paris 1789), *Lectures on the Elements of Chemistry* (Edinburgh 1803) by Joseph Black, founder of quantitative analysis and pneumatic chemistry, or a first edition of Davy's *Elements of Chemical Philosophy* (London 1812).

"Accurate, but unsystematic" is Watson's description of Holmes's knowledge of anatomy. It is difficult, therefore, to do more than suggest one or two titles that may have appeared on Holmes's shelf, although we have already been able to indicate the works he owned on the anatomy of the ear. Bidloo's *Anatomia* (Amsterdam 1685) probably bore a Holmes *ex libris,* and it is even possible that the detector may have invested in one or two incunables, such as Mondino de' Luzzi's *Anathomia* (Pavia 1478), the first book devoted solely to anatomy. It is difficult to be sure of this, however, though there is little doubt that Holmes acquired later works in the field, notably Sir Charles Bell's *System of Dissections* (Edinburgh 1798–1803).

Holmes's knowledge of sensational literature was, according to Watson, immense. "He appears to know every detail of every horror perpetrated in the century." Though Holmes probably owned *The Newgate Calendar . . . from . . . 1700 to the Present Time* (London [1773]) as well as the later *Newgate Calendar; Containing the Lives . . . of . . . Housebreakers, Highwaymen, etc.* By an Old-Bailey Barrister (London [1840?]), it must be admitted that his "immense" knowledge of the field was based upon his own commonplace books in which, from time to time, he placed his cuttings on crime, pasted extracts, and made out his ever-useful indexes.

The detector, Watson advises us, "is an expert singlestick player, boxer, and swordsman." We know, too, that he was an expert book collector, and so, while we have no actual proof, we may hazard the conjecture that he added to his library books in those fields. On singlestick and swordsmanship, he may have owned the *Practise* (London 1595) of Saviolo, L'Abbat's *Art of Fencing* (Dublin 1734) and, more than likely, *Anti-Pugilism, or the Science of Defence Exemplified in Short and Easy Lessons, for the Practice of the Broad Sword and Single Stick . . . .* By a Highland Officer (London 1790) with four copperplates by Cruikshank. On boxing, he may well have purchased the Mercurialis, *De arte gymnastica* (Venice 1573) with its boxing cuts, Whitehead's *Gymnasiad* (London 1744), the first publication dealing exclusively with boxing in English, *The Art of Boxing* (1789) by the champion, Daniel Mendoza, and other lesser works on the Queensberry rules and "la boxe française."

Concluding his analysis of Holmes, Watson informs us that he "has a good practical knowledge of British law." It is fairly safe, therefore, to suppose that he owned Fritzherbert's *Great Abridgment of the Law* ([London] 1516), the first serious attempt to systematize the law of England, as well as Littleton's *Tenures in English* (London 1583) and a copy of the first edition of Blackstone's *Commentaries* (Oxford 1765–69).

Upon a subsequent occasion, in 1889,[24] Holmes mentions that he has made "some recent researches which have a medico-criminal aspect." Can there be any doubt that those "researches" included visits to the rare and secondhand bookshops of London? There was a wealth of related material from which Holmes could choose, all the way from Codronchi's *Methodus testificandi* (Frankfurt 1597), the first important work on forensic medicine, to the latest researches in that delectable field. Holmes never could have resisted Antoine Louis' *Mémoire sur une question anatomique relative à la jurisprudence* (Paris 1763), in which the author weighed the differential signs of murder and suicide in cases of hanging. The articles of Hunter "On the Uncertainty of the Signs of Murder, in the Case of Bastard Children" (London 1784) and of Gross "On Manual Strangulation" (Cin-

cinnati 1836) must have made an immediate appeal, while Bertillon's great work *Les Signalements anthropométriques* (Paris 1886), which introduced to the world the "Bertillonage" method of identifying persons by selected measurements, must surely have added to the medico-criminal bookshelf of Sherlock Holmes.

Ten years later, in 1899, we find Holmes admitting an interest in printing types: "The detection of types is one of the most elementary branches of knowledge to the . . . expert in crime,"[25] and, we might add, to an expert in book collecting. There is, therefore, little doubt that specimens of Granjon's *civilité*, the Estienne, the Bodoni, Fournier le Jeune, the great Enschedé type-specimen book with its exotic fonts, had all by 1899 found their way to Holmes's library, where they could enthrall Holmes, the book collector, as specimens of the *Leeds Mercury* or the *Western Morning News* enthralled Holmes, the expert in crime.

Toward the end of his active career, in 1914, Watson informs his readers that Holmes is living "in a small farm upon the downs" and dividing his time "between philosophy and agriculture."[26] Without anything more specific to go on, it is impossible to do more than venture a guess at the books that may have facilitated those studies of Holmes's later years. In philosophy, he probably dipped into his first editions of Hume and Kant, Liebniz and Locke, Spinoza, Hobbes, and Berkeley. For agricultural entertainment, he may have turned to his 1560 first edition of Tatti's compendium, *Della Agricultura,* or to such lesser works as Blith's *English Improver, or a new Survey of Husbandry* (1649). It is useless to do more than speculate upon the nature of Holmes's philosophical and agricultural shelves. The man had so many facets to his nature, and the books available were of such an enormous range, that we must satisfy ourselves with what we have, and go no further.

It is supremely tempting, however, to ask ourselves where Holmes obtained his many fine books. As we have seen, his favorite book dealer was almost undoubtedly Alfred B. Clementson, who plied his trade at 73 Church Street, Kensington, and who suggested one of Holmes's many disguises. Close at hand—at 36 Baker Street—he found the newsvendor James Ellis Hawkins, who could dispatch the latest editions of London papers to Holmes's rooms, and for maps he would always find

Edward Stanford of Cockspur Street most reliable. There were other dealers, scores of them, into whose musty shops Holmes surely ventured as he passed through the winding lanes and alleys of his London. The Strand was full of shops, where books towered to the ceiling and spilled over onto the floors as Holmes browsed among them, his expert's eye glancing at a calf or vellum back. Newington Butts could always give him a field day, and who can doubt that he would walk through Camden passage without a visit to Mrs. Susannah Kettle, or through Church Street, Paddington, without a glance at Uriah Maggs's stock? For medical works, he could journey to Wardour Street, where Richard Kimpton plied a specialized trade, but everywhere— on Farringdon Street and New Oxford Street, on Praed Street and Drury Lane—he could, and did, wander through the dimly lighted cellars and the intriguing ante-rooms of one bookseller after another.

There was Framjee Feroza on Camberwell Road; there was William Wright on St. Martin's Lane; there was Mrs. Robenah Boyle on White Horse Street in Stepney—there were dozens upon dozens of dealers from whom he could buy the earliest on opium or the latest on belladonna. For a French treatise, he might patronize Madame Celine Subtil in Prince's Buildings, Coventry Street, although probably for most of his French works Holmes used the services of his translator, François le Villard of Paris, a gentleman who may be identified as the son of Francisque Le Villard, author of works on the Paris Theater.

Some from whom he bought, or tried to buy, still flourish: George Harding, Henry Stevens & Son, Bumpus, Quaritch, Francis Edwards. Most of them have vanished, and with them have gone the records of Holmes's purchases. Some may question, therefore, how Holmes, who once belittled himself as "a poor man,"[27] could possibly have acquired so remarkable a collection of rarities. Books were cheaper in those days, for one. For another, Holmes had a keen eye for "finds" (we must not forget the great Zouche discovery at a London stall). Finally, Holmes was far from "a poor man." Like Mr. Holder, the banker, many of his clients proved "not . . . ungrateful,"[28] and his fees sometimes amounted to five hundred pounds[29] or an emerald pin from Windsor.[30] No, there is no question that Holmes was able and eager to acquire a fine collection of rarities, though the records vanished with the dealers who made the sales. Yet, a loving eye can restore them all—the booksellers of old, the keen-eyed detector who wanders from shop to shop in search of a quarry in calf; even the books themselves, as we brush off the dust of the past, assemble them once again, and restore them to their rightful shelves in the treasure room of Baker Street.

—July 1953

NOTES

1. Notably the chapter "Ex Libris, Sherlock Holmes," in *Profile by Gaslight*, and Julian Wolff, "A Catalogue of 221B Culture," in *To Doctor R.: Essays . . . in honor of . . . Dr. A. S. W. Rosenbach* (Philadelphia 1946).

2. *Crockford's Clerical Dictionary* was on Holmes's shelf by 1898, when he took the name of J. C. Elman from it in connection with *The Retired Colourman*.

3. Holmes used a *Continental Gazetteer*—probably *The Gazetteer of the World* (London 1885 and in progress)—in 1887, when he checked the Andaman Islands in connection with *The Sign of the Four*, and again in 1889 when he looked up Egria, Bohemia, for *A Scandal in Bohemia*.

4. *Whitaker's Almanack* for 1899 and 1900 were in Holmes's possession and provided him with the key to Porlock's cipher in *The Valley of Fear* in 1900.

5. Holmes spread out his big map of London in 1895 in connection with *The Bruce-Partington Plans*.

6. Holmes sent down to Stamford's (i.e., Stanford's—see n. 12) in 1899 for the ordnance map of the Devonshire moor, used in the case of *The Hound of the Baskervilles*.

7. In the 1902 London telephone directory Watson was able to locate N. Garrideb on Little Ryder Street. See *The Three Garridebs*.

8. The "red-covered volume" which in 1887 provided Holmes with genealogical information about Lord Robert Walsingham de Vere St. Simon, in *The Noble Bachelor*, was obviously a Debrett. Another of Holmes's reference books was his so-called *American Encyclopaedia*, used in *The Five Orange Pips* in 1888 when Holmes checked it for the Ku Klux Klan. *The International Cyclopedia* (New York 1885), which contains an article on the Klan, was possibly the work in question.

9. See *A Study in Scarlet*.

10. For this and all other dates referred to, I am indebted to Gavin Brend, *My Dear Holmes* (London 1951) whose Chronological Table, pp. 179–81, has been followed.

11. See *London Post-Office Directory* for 1890.

12. See Ibid., where Stanford is listed as "sole agent for ordnance and geological survey maps in England and Wales."

13. By H. W. Bell, in *Profile by Gaslight*, p. 288.

14. *The Five Orange Pips*.

15. *A Study in Scarlet.*

16. See also *The Resident Patient.*

17. For another Richter work probably in Holmes's library, see no. 22.

18. A. Conan Doyle, a minor contemporary of Holmes's, was also attracted by Meredith, remarking that his "beloved 'Richard Feverel' . . . lurks in yonder corner. What a great book it is, how wise and how witty!" (*Through the Magic Door* [New York 1908], p. 158).

19. André Frécon's *Des Empreintes en général et de leur application dans . . . la médécine judiciaire* appeared in Lyons in 1889.

20. Anton Prant's article "Über das Aufsuchen von Fuss-spuren and Händeabdrucken und ihre Identificirung" was printed in the *Archiv für Kriminal-Anthropologie* (Leipzig 1899).

21. By Harvey Officer, "Sherlock Holmes and Music," in *221B: Studies in Sherlock Holmes,* ed. Vincent Starrett (New York 1940). Holmes's purchase of contemporaneously published music books is briefly considered in Guy Warrack, *Sherlock Holmes and Music* (London [1947]).

22. It is likely that Holmes also owned a copy of the London 1867 edition of De Quincey's *Confessions of an English Opium-Eater,* an edition to which are added *Analects from John Paul Richter.* Among the analects is one on "The Grandeur of Man in His Littleness," a concept to which Holmes referred during his work on *The Sign of the Four.*

23. Sir John Bennett Lawes & others, *The Nitrogen as Nitric Acid in the Soils and Subsoils of . . . Rothamsted* (London 1883), and Charles Barnard, *Talks about the Soil in Its Relation to Plants and Business* (New York 1894).

24. *The Dying Detective.*

25. *The Hound of the Baskervilles.*

26. *His Last Bow,* Preface.

27. *The Priory School.*

28. *The Beryl Coronet.*

29. *His Last Bow.*

30. *The Bruce-Partington Plans.*

*Perhaps the most famous impersonator of Sherlock
Holmes recounts the circumstances of a remarkable
meeting. . . .*

"Daydream"

by Basil Rathbone

I HAD ALWAYS LOVED the county of Sussex. It held for me some
of the happiest memories of my life—my early childhood. Early
in June I had slipped down, for a few days' much-needed rest,
to the little village of Heathfield, to dream again of the past and
to try and shut out, for a brief period at least, both the present
and the future.

A soft spring had ushered in a temperate summer. I walked
a great deal, reread Galsworthy's *Forsyte Saga*, and slept with
merciful regularity and contentment.

The last afternoon of my holiday I was walking back across
the gentle countryside to my lodgings in Heathfield, when I was
rudely stung by a bee. Startled, I grabbed a handful of soft
earth and applied it to the sting: an old-fashioned remedy I had
learned as a child. Suddenly I became aware that the air about
me was swarming with bees. I stood motionless and waited.

It was then that I noticed the small house with a thatched
roof and a well-kept garden, with beehives at one end, that Mrs.
Messenger, my landlady, had so often mentioned. Mrs. Messenger was large, comfortable, and ageless. She rented me a
room "with board." She also loved to chat, which she did with a
ceaseless rhythm reminiscent of a light sea breaking on a sandy
beach. It was not unpleasant so long as one made no effort to
retaliate.

Apparently "he" had come to live in the thatched cottage
many years ago. At first his visits were infrequent. But, as time
passed, he came more often and stayed longer. He called the
place his bee farm. As he bothered no one, no one bothered
him, which is both an old English custom and a good one. Now,
in 1946, he had become almost a legend. He had been "Someone" once, and Mrs. Messenger's father was sure he came from
London and was either a doctor or a lawyer or both.

I saw him now, on this late summer afternoon, seated in his garden, a rug over his knees; reading a book. In spite of his great age he wore no reading glasses; and though he made no movement there was a curious sense of animation in his apparently inanimate body. He had the majestic beauty of a very old tree: his features were sharp, emphasizing a particularly prominent nose. The veins in his hands ran clear blue, like swollen mountain streams, and the transparency of his skin had a shell-like quality.

He was smoking a meerschaum pipe with obvious relish. Suddenly he looked up and our eyes met. It embarrassed me to have been caught staring at him.

"Won't you come in?" he called in a surprisingly firm voice.

"Thank you, sir," I replied, "but I have no right to impose on your privacy."

"If it were an imposition I should not have invited you," he replied.

As I opened the little white wicker gate and went in I felt his eyes searching me.

"Pull up a chair and sit down."

He gave me another quick glance of penetrating comprehension. As I reached for the chair and sat down I had an odd feeling that I was dreaming.

"I'm sorry to see that you have been stung by one of my bees."

Self-consciously I wiped the patch of dirt from my face and smiled: the smile was intended to say that it didn't matter.

"You must forgive the little fellow," he continued; "he's paid for it with his life."

"It seems unfair that he should have had to," I said, hearing my own voice as if it had been someone else's.

"No," mused the old man, "it's a law of nature. 'God moves in a mysterious way His wonders to perform.'"

A thrush began to sing in a hedge near by. The incident—for an incident it had become—was strangely tempered with magic. I felt excited.

"May I order you some tea?"

"Thank you, no," I declined.

"I used to be a prolific coffee drinker myself. I have always found tea an insipid substitute by comparison."

A faint smile hovered about the corners of his mouth.

"Do you live here?" he continued.

"No, sir, I'm on a short holiday."

"Do you come here often?"

"As often as I can. I love Sussex. I was born near here."

"Really!" This time the smile reached up and touched his eyes. "It's a comforting little corner of the earth, isn't it, especially in times like these?"

"Have you lived here all through the war, sir?" I asked.

"Yes." The smile disappeared. Slowly he pulled an old Webley revolver from under the rug which covered his knees. "If 'they' had come, six of them would not have lived to tell the story. . . . I learned to use this thing many years ago. I have never missed my man."

He cradled the gun in his hand, and left me momentarily for that world which to each of us is his own; that little world in which we are born and in which we die, alone. He replaced the gun on his knees and looked at me. There was quite a pause before I had the courage to ask, "Were you in the first World War, sir?"

"Indirectly—and you?"

"I'm an Inspector at Scotland Yard."

"I thought so!" Once again he looked at me with penetrating comprehension and smiled.

At that moment the book in his lap fell to the ground. I reached down, picked it up, and handed it back to him.

"Thank you." He made a sound that closely resembled a chuckle. "And how are things at the Yard these days?"

"Modern science and equipment have done much to help us," I said.

"Yessss." His hand went to a pocket and brought forth an old magnifying glass. "When I was a young man they used things like this. Modern inventions have proved to be great time savers, but they have dulled our natural instincts and made us lazy, most of us at least—press a button here, or pull a lever there, and it all happens, hey presto!" He looked annoyed and a little tired.

"You may be right, sir. But there's no middle course; we either go forward or back."

He put the magnifying glass and revolver back into two voluminous pockets of an old sports jacket, with leather patches at the elbows. Then he took a deep breath and released it in a long-drawn-out sigh.

"I've followed your career very closely, Inspector. The Yard is fortunate in your services."

"That's kind of you, sir."

"Not at all . . . you see, I knew your father quite well at one time."

"You knew my father!" The words tumbled out.

"Yesss. He was a brilliant man, your father. He interested me deeply. His mind was balanced precariously on that thin line between sanity and insanity. Is he still living?"

"No, sir; he died in 1936."

The old man nodded his head reflectively. "These fellows with their newfangled ideas would have found him intensely interesting subject matter. What do you call them? pyscho . . . psychoanalysts!"

"Psychoanalysis can be very helpful if used intelligently, don't you think, sir?"

"No, I don't," he snapped back. "It's a lot of rubbish—PSYCHOANALYSIS!" He spat out the word contemptuously. "It's nothing more than a simple process of deduction by elimination."

We talked of crime and its different ways of detection, both past and present; its motives, and society's responsibility for conditions that foster the criminal, until a cool breeze crossed the garden with its silent warning of the day's departure.

He rose slowly to a full six feet and held out his hand. "I must go in now. It's been pleasant talking with you."

"I am deeply indebted to you, sir." I wanted to say so much more, but felt oddly constrained. He held out the book in his hand.

"Do you know these stories?"

I glanced at the title: *The Adventures of Sherlock Holmes*.

"They are often overdramatized; but they make good reading." Once again the smile crept up from the corners of his mouth, and this time danced in his eyes.

I acknowledged an intimate acquaintance with all the works to which he referred, and he seemed greatly pleased by my references to "The Master." He accompanied me slowly to the little white wicker gate and, on the way, we spoke briefly of S. C. Roberts, and Christopher Morley, and Vincent Starrett.

"The adventures as written by our dear friend Dr. Watson mean a great deal to me at my time of life," he reflected, retaining my hand and shaking it slowly like a pump handle. "As someone once said, 'Remembrance is the only sure immortality we can know.'"

On my return, Mrs. Messenger greeted me with a cup of tea and an urgent telegram from Scotland Yard, requesting my immediate return. I didn't speak to her of my visit to "him." I was afraid she might consider me as childish as the youngsters in Heathfield who still believed "he" was the great Sherlock Holmes.

Which they did, until they reached an age when he was dismissed, together with Santa Claus, Tinkerbell, and all those other worthwhile people who, for a brief and beautiful period, are more real than reality itself.

—October 1947

*If Sherlock Holmes is immortal, then his incarnations
must be many—including models for the Age of
Space. . . .*

The Archetypal Holmes

by Poul Anderson

The work of Carl Gustav Jung does not seem to belong in our era. Some would make it a relic, albeit a fascinating and suggestive one, of an earlier and more credulous stage in human development. Others maintain that our culture has not yet advanced to the right point where we can fully comprehend and use the insights of the late great Swiss psychiatrist.

For whatever it may be worth, which isn't much, I take a middle position. On the one hand, it is difficult for a hard-boiled, physical-science-oriented, show-me positivist to swallow such Jungian notions as the racial unconscious. They don't seem to refer to anything observable. I prefer incontrovertible, understandable realities, such as particles that have no mass, stars which are too big to shine, and, of course, Sherlock Holmes.

On the other hand, no one can deny that Jung performed a great service. He broke free of the rigid Freudian mold, he made a fresh and still valuable classification of personality types, he founded a school of psychoanalysis that helped many people, and on and on. The Jungian concept that should be of special interest to Sherlockians is the archetype.

Webster defines "archetype" as "the original pattern of which all things of the same species are representations or copies; original idea, model, or type." Jung gave it a less strictly Platonic meaning. In his researches he found that certain images recur again and again in the mind, in many different forms but always identifiably the same. He found them not merely in his European patients, but in healthy people of every race and background, in dreams, reveries, fantasies, myths, religions, and mystical experiences. Among these figures he identified the earth mother, the persona, the anima, and the shadow. We have only to think about them to see how fundamental and universal they are.

135

For instance, the earth mother occurs as a thousand different goddesses, from Kwan-Yin in the East to Juno in the West and on to similar figures in the Americas, Africa, and Oceania. She is also a type of woman, the big, strong, patient but indomitable heroine of innumerable novels. Now and then you meet her in some real person. Probably your own mother was the first one who gave you this impression. If you are at all introspective, you will quickly realize how the earth mother likewise pervades your dreams and your day-dreams.

I think we can accept Jung's archetypes without needing his collective unconscious to explain them. They arise out of human experience, the long pilgrimage of mankind as a whole, the subtle interaction of societies and individuals, and the ordinary lives of each one of us—these lives being, after all, very much alike.

In other words, an archetype doesn't spring out fullblown, it evolves. Many influences converge to form it. At last it takes a definite shape. Then the archetype has gained full power. It goes on through the centuries in countless different forms, all of which are traceable back to the first fully developed one. Some of these new forms are mythical, literary, or what have you. Others are real. That is to say, whenever a real person comes along who more or less fits an archetype, we will inevitably think about him in terms of that archetype.

No doubt this sounds abstract. To wit: Sherlock Holmes is an archetype.

That is, the general idea of a Holmesian figure had been slowly evolving for a long time. Its time was ripe in the late nineteenth century, and the elements crystallized in Sherlock Holmes, who gave them their essential eternal shape. It does not matter that he actually existed; he could just as well have been a character in a story. The point is that he expressed certain vital factors in his culture. As a result, the Holmes figure has reappeared in any number of reincarnations already, and seems likely to go on indefinitely.

It is not easy to define the elements of Holmes. In fact, his complexity, the veil that is never lifted between the world and his ultimate self, is part of the image. But we can point to a few obvious traits. The brilliant deductive mind; the intense concentration on any problem; the occasional furious activity; the

136

physical courage and competence; the philosophic musings; the idealism and affection nearly always masked by sardonic reserve; the austere habits of life, relieved by certain minor vices and self-indulgences—but I need not remind you further.

Now, the interesting thing for present purposes is that Holmes-like characters are hard to come by in other civilizations and earlier times. We do have ancient detective stories, like those concerning the prophet Daniel. It is said that the Caliph Haroun al-Rashid often wandered around Baghdad in disguise to learn what people really were doing. Robert van Gulick's stories about Judge Dee, who made shrewd deductions, were adapted from the Chinese. But while all these, and others, contain certain aspects of Sherlock Holmes, they do not approach the totality. Nor do we find anything that suggests him among, say, the Olympian gods. Zeus is wise and powerful, Hermes is clever, Hephaestus is inventive, and so on. But the pieces are scattered, and some are missing altogether.

The most Holmesian figure I can think of, real or imaginary, in the ancient world is Archimedes. He lived in the third century B.C. and is best known popularly for his detective work when he proved that alloy had been substituted for gold in a royal crown. The legend that, when the solution hit him, he leaped from his bath and ran down the streets crying, "Eureka! I have found it!" is quite Holmesian. Not that Sherlock would ever do any such thing, but at least he was careless in his dress. Archimedes was a brilliant mathematician (a hint of Moriarty there?) but also a research scientist, an artificer, a helper of his country in its hour of peril. He is said to have been ascetic and brusque. He was killed when he wouldn't leave the diagram he was studying to go away with the conquering Roman soldiers.

Archimedes might thus have become the seminal figure we are after. But he was too isolated. The decaying Hellenistic world, its intellectually unenterprising Roman successor, had small use for his kind of man. So, if anything, he is especially clear in our minds today because he fits an archetype that has evolved after his death.

It does seem to be one which belongs peculiarly to Western civilization. Our Celtic and Nordic predecessors already show the germ of it. Is Merlin, the magician confidant of King Arthur, not Holmesian in several ways? We think of him as gaunt, enig-

137

matic, possessed of knowledge and intelligence such as are granted no one else. Incidentally, for him too there was just one woman, of dubious associations and dangerous ambitions.

Still more Holmesian is the Northern god Odin, or Wotan if you prefer the operatic name. He is described as both wise and shrewd, benevolent and terrible; he fights the powers of evil with cunning rather than with spear, yet he can wield that well if he desires; he is tall and lean and dignified, though a few comic stories are told about him; he presides over the riotous feasting in Valhalla but does not otherwise join in; he is an inventor of magical techniques, and a linguist who first read the runes; he is the brooding foreknower of the inevitable future.

As European history proceeds, we find men appearing oftener and oftener, in fact and fiction, who look increasingly Holmesian. To name just a few, consider Roger Bacon in the Middle Ages and Francis Bacon in the Elizabethan era. Down south we get personages such as Machiavelli, a much-maligned thinker who was simply a frank realist, and Leonardo da Vinci, who I once suggested might be a collateral ancestor of Sherlock Holmes. The type becomes rare again during the upheavals of the Reformation, but in the Enlightenment it flourishes more luxuriantly than before. Newton and Leibniz are obviously proto-Holmes, as well as Locke, Hume, and above all Voltaire.

The Napoleonic era did not produce many. Those who were around at the time were leftovers from the Enlightenment. Apparently Holmes figures belong to relatively settled and civilized milieus. Hence they are scarce in the earlier nineteenth century, which was dominated by Romanticism. But presently a long, stable peace brought forth this sort of man afresh, and plentifully. Again making a brief random selection, consider Disraeli, T. H. Huxley, Clerk Maxwell, John Stuart Mill, and, inevitably, Dr. Joseph Bell.

Meanwhile, on the literary side, Holmes had been foreshadowed by such as Reynard the Fox in the folk tales, Shakespeare's Hamlet, Voltaire's own Zadig, Mark Twain's Pudd'nhead Wilson and Connecticut Yankee, Poe's Dupin, Stevenson's Prince Florizel, and others. And now we are well into the age of Victoria.

The hour had arrived. The Master came into being. We will pause for a moment in honor.

It would take far more scholarship and patience than are mine to explore the immediate effects of the coalescence of the archetype. Clearly, almost every detective of the classic period is essentially Holmes. Some are good expressions of the basic form, like Hercule Poirot; some are not so good, like Philo Vance. But I need not elaborate for this readership.

It would be interesting to trace the archetype elsewhere. Curiously enough, I don't think you find it in H. G. Wells. He claimed to be a rationalist, but in fact he was too passionate, too much a believer, too little strengthened by Holmes's streak of healthy cynicism. By contrast, in his life even more than in his writings, George Bernard Shaw strikes me as very Holmesian. Kipling employed the archetype several times, notably when he created Strickland and Lurgan Sahib in his stories of India. The Head of the school in *Stalky and Co.* is rather a Sherlockian figure, and so on occasion is the chaplain, whom you will remember as getting the boys to do things that needed doing but were impossible for an adult. To some extent *Stalky* is a Holmesian book told from the viewpoint of The Baker Street Irregulars.

Unfortunately, the Victorian–Edwardian environment did not last, but went out in the catastrophe of the First World War. That was when Western civilization cut its own throat. It has been bleeding to death ever since. We have already remarked that the Holmes archetype feels most at home in a free but essentially orderly society.

An enclave of this remains, to a degree, in the sciences. Hence it is not surprising that many scientists and engineers have much in common with the Master. Their work depends on both intellect and physique; they are devoted, clean-living, but comparatively aloof and eccentric men. To name just one, I might observe that the oceanographer and deep-sea explorer Jacques-Yves Cousteau goes so far as to look like Sherlock Holmes!

On the whole, though, few Victorian adventurers are left. This is yet more obvious in literature than in life. The protagonist—I won't say hero—of the average "serious" novel is a snivelling little neurotic that Lestrade himself wouldn't wipe his feet on. The protagonist of the mystery and suspense story is apt to be a drab organization man, a psychopathic brute, or a grubby and fearful espionage agent. I don't say this is good or bad. No doubt it reflects the reality of our times. But there are those among us who wish the reality were a bit different.

Therefore we turn to sheer fantasy for escape, including that branch of fantasy known as science fiction. And here we find the Holmes archetype enjoying very good health, thank you. Indeed, it dominates the field so thoroughly that other kinds of hero are in danger of becoming extinct.

Take, for instance, J. R. R. Tolkien's *The Lord of the Rings*. Are not Strider and, especially, Gandalf Holmes personalities? For that matter, is Sauron not another Moriarty, and are the hobbits not a multiple John H. Watson? The popularity of this epic, particularly among younger readers, is encouraging. It suggests that man has not altogether abandoned the wish for a sane and decent order of things.

Science fiction in the strict sense is positively loaded with Holmes types. Among so many, I might arbitrarily mention Sir Austin Cardynge, the "lean gray tomcat" of E. E. Smith's Lensman series; or Jay Score, the gentle robot created by Eric Frank Russell; or Susan Calvin, a female version by Isaac Asimov. But mainly, I wish to point out that one science fiction personality, who has seized the mass imagination as no other has ever done, is pure Holmes. I refer to Mr. Spock on the television show "Star Trek."

Tune it in sometime, if you haven't already. Mr. Spock is only second in command of the space-ship *Enterprise,* but it is plain that Captain Kirk depends on him every bit as much as a certain gracious lady did on the Master. Spock exalts the intellect and derides the emotions in the strictest tradition; but, also in that tradition, he obviously has intense feelings that he never ordinarily reveals. He is courteous but distant where women are concerned, except on one or two occasions when he can no longer help himself. He has the cat-like neatness and curiosity of a Holmes (and, incidentally, the super-cats in Clarence Day's little essay, *This Simian World*, are rather Holmesian).

Spock exasperates his less intellectual companions, but usually meets their sarcasms with a ready and biting wit. At the same time, he is athletic, cool, and capable in danger. He is withdrawn, austere, philosophical and, as played by Leonard Nimoy, allowing for the uniform and the pointed ears, presents an excellent physical image of Sherlock Holmes.

One thing he does lack on the show, and that is a Watson. But in real life he has thousands, as devout as any Baker Street Irregular. Some of them publish magazines about him. Though they include both sexes and every age, he has a special attraction for young girls.

When "Star Trek" finally goes off the air, which I hope will not be for a long while, Leonard Nimoy will be looking for a new role. I suggest that he is the perfect successor to Basil Rathbone, and that you write to the networks and movie companies saying so. I further suggest that his popularity is another hopeful sign. The girls who today adore this nearly 200-proof Holmesian archetype will be the mothers of tomorrow. They, their husbands, and their children may well create a new age of Victoria.

—September 1968

*Much has been written with regard to the implausibility
of Holmes's story about what happened in Switzerland
in 1891. In this lucid essay, the Silversteins explicate a
likely version of the truth. . . .*

CONCERNING THE EXTRAORDINARY EVENTS
AT THE REICHENBACH FALLS

by ALBERT SILVERSTEIN *and* MYRNA SILVERSTEIN

"MY DEAR WATSON," said the well-remembered voice, "I owe
you a thousand apologies. I had no idea that you would be so
affected." With these words did Sherlock Holmes preface his
conclusion to the (by now) legendary account of his final meeting with Professor Moriarty at the Reichenbach Falls and of his
own subsequent disappearance. It is a moving and a dramatic
account, and one containing so many incredible features that
no serious Sherlockian can free himself of the haunting suspicion that it is not completely accurate. There have been several
distinguished attempts either to resolve these implausibilities
within the traditional account or to offer a substitute version of
what actually happened, but none of them can adequately
resolve these implausibilities. The truth about the events at
Reichenbach stands today as the central enigma of the Canon.
But the evidence is available for a reconstruction of that truth,
and we hope to marshal it in a manner that will bring us at last
to a complete understanding of that historic confrontation.

First, we shall recapitulate all of the significant implausibilities, both those previously exposed and those that first appeared to us during our investigation. Trivia, such as how it
could be that Holmes could have had a flask of brandy available
to him while he was disguised as an aged bibliophile, will not be
explored. The incredible events under consideration will be
presented in three chronological divisions: Holmes's flight and
Moriarty's pursuit, the confrontation itself, and Holmes's disappearance. Then we shall piece together a theory to account for
the implausibilities that deduction will reveal as an inescapable
conclusion. While we shall present much new material, we are
deeply indebted to the prior researches of Walter Armstrong,[1]

T. S. Blakeney,[2] Anthony Boucher,[3] and Pope Hill, Sr.[4] It was also valuable to have at our disposal Baring-Gould's *Annotated Sherlock Holmes*,[5] which allowed us to grasp all of the perplexing features of the Canonical account within a brief span, along with analyses of many of them.

Three strategic principles have guided our attempt to reconstruct what took place. The first was to remain as faithful to the Canon as our credulity allowed. We have particularly endeavoured never to call into question the honesty of Dr. Watson in making his report. But, while prior evidence and loyalty militate against any suspicion of Dr. Watson's sincerity, we were forced to entertain seriously the possibility that on several issues Watson had been misled or had erred. Second, we have attempted to resolve the greatest number of implausibilities with the smallest number of hypotheses, rather than proliferating special hypotheses to deal with each difficulty. It is possible, indeed, to cover all of the difficulties by the capricious expedient of labelling each one an independent slip on the part of the author. This expedient is, of course, totally gratuitous and allows for no independent support from either logic or fact. By such a line of argument, any plausible segment of the Canonical report might just as easily have been an author's slip that turned out well only by accident. To explain any of the major implausibilities by relegating it to ineptness on the part of the author is no explanation at all. It is an admission of defeat. Our third principle has been drawn directly from the Master and requires no justification: When you have eliminated the impossible, whatever remains, no matter how unlikely it appears, must be the truth. We believe that our reconstruction is the only one to date to satisfy these criteria. While it is tempting to criticise prior theories in detail, space does not permit us to do so. Suffice it to say that those few theories that encompass most of the difficulties parsimoniously (e.g., Holmes and Moriarty were really one man) have done so either by straying undefensibly far from the Canon or by becoming "inherently impossible."

In considering the events leading up to the final confrontation, we find three serious implausibilities in Holmes's behaviour: (1) That Holmes would trouble to disguise himself so capably as an Italian priest for the initial flight from England and then travel with an undisguised Watson whom Moriarty

143

was certain to connect with the great detective (Armstrong). (2) That, once on the Continent, Holmes would travel about in leisurely fashion, without plan or purpose. While such actions were conceivable as long as Holmes believed that the entire Moriarty gang was doomed, the telegram telling Holmes that Moriarty had escaped renders such behaviour ludicrous. It was clear to Holmes that Moriarty was on his heels, and the great detective was certainly the last man to be without any plan at all in an emergency. (3) That Holmes would travel unarmed despite his certainty that his arch foe was stalking him. While Holmes carried a handgun infrequently, he respected Moriarty's deadliness sufficiently to finger a revolver in his dressing gown during the Professor's visit to his Baker Street lodgings.

Let us turn now to Professor Moriarty's behaviour during this pre-confrontation phase of the saga. There are two inconsistencies to be observed here: (4) That Moriarty's trap for Holmes would consist of nothing more than himself, unarmed and hurrying up the path toward Holmes (Hill). As numerous critics have pointed out, Moriarty was not particularly large physically. But his intellect was, according to the Master, unexcelled by anyone in the world. Thus, the Napoleon of crime must have reckoned that Holmes (who was younger, heavier, immensely strong, and both an expert boxer and singlestick player) would have no difficulty in disposing of him in a purely physical contest. In addition, while we are led to believe that Holmes was unarmed, Moriarty could not have known this. (5) That Moriarty would write a note to Watson which almost certainly would not deceive a Holmes on his guard (Armstrong and Hill). Moreover, even if this preposterous note did succeed in drawing Watson back to Meiringen without rousing Holmes to special watchfulness, how could Moriarty be sure that Holmes would not accompany the Doctor in his return to the inn? Indeed, Holmes's remaining alone at the Falls seems like the least probable outcome. Perhaps even more fundamental is the question of why Moriarty should be so keen on separating Holmes and Watson. Both men would have been easy prey in a well-constructed ambush along that narrow path, and it was to the Professor's advantage to leave no historian of his disposal of Holmes. On close consideration, Moriarty's note seems to be one of the two most absurd actions in the whole extraordinary series of events.

The account we read in the Canon of the confrontation itself is no less bizarre than that of the events leading up to it. Considering Holmes's actions again, we are told that (6) the great detective, whose brilliant planning smashed the Moriarty empire of evil, remained in full view at the end of the path to the Falls without any plan until the Professor arrived on the scene (Armstrong and Hill). Yet, in his note to Watson, Holmes admitted that he "was quite convinced that the letter from Meiringen was a hoax, and . . . that some development of this sort would follow." While it is true that this same note reveals Holmes's willingness to end his life if he can be certain of ridding society of Moriarty thereby, there could be no such certainty while standing in that death trap without any advance indication of what sort of trap awaited him. For all Holmes knew, the Professor might have been advancing with a pack of thirteen armed thugs. Once the two men confronted each other, Holmes wrote his note to Watson and then walked to the brink of the Falls, "Moriarty at my heels." This account is supported by Watson's finding two sets of prints leading to the edge of the precipice, and none returning. But would Holmes have trusted the most evil man in creation this way (Hill)? If he had, surely the inevitable outcome would have been that Moriarty would have lunged forward to push the Master over the brink. The entire picture we are given of a chivalrous struggle between two Titans is ineffable twaddle. It is totally inconsistent with the characters we have been given of Holmes and Moriarty, if for no other reason than that neither man could have foretold its possible outcome, nor would have gambled on it. Part of this same preposterous picture is the view of Moriarty (8) hurrying up the path to meet his arch-enemy (Hill) and then (9) allowing him the "courtesy" of writing a farewell note to Watson. Moriarty's only hope of eliminating Holmes rested on his ability to surprise him. This would have been nearly impossible under any circumstances while moving up the path, but that Moriarty should have hurried is totally unthinkable. And if there is any description stronger than that, it must be applied to Moriarty's courtesy in the matter of the note-writing. The only reason for such an apparent courtesy would have been to get Holmes off his guard in preparation for some cunning trick. But surely Holmes would not have risked such an eventuality. And, in any event, we are told that the Professor did not use such duplicity.

Moran's behaviour during this confrontation must now be scrutinized. We do not actually know what the Colonel was doing during his master's struggle with Holmes, but Holmes's conclusion (10) that he was guarding the approach to the path is surely not tenable. If both men were on the scene, and if both were intent upon Holmes's demise, they both would have taken part in the attack upon Holmes. In this context, we must also note the implausibility of (11) Moran's refraining from launching his attack upon Holmes for all the hours during which the great detective clung to his ledge above the path, and then (of all things) throwing rocks at him. As Walter Armstrong has reminded us, Holmes was concerned about air-guns even prior to his flight to the Continent. Is it conceivable that the assassin who made such expert use of Von Herder's fiendish invention would hang back from using it to kill the man who destroyed the Moriarty organisation?

The final implausibilities to be considered are those connected with the events succeeding Moriarty's death. To begin with, we have a number of critics who claim that (12) the timetable of events recounted by Watson is impossible. The core of this contention is that Watson would not have had time to go back and forth twice from the Falls to Meiringen in what remained of that fateful day. Since Holmes and Watson set out in the afternoon, since Watson had to secure Swiss experts to examine the path, and since the sun set at Meiringen at approximately 7:00 P.M. on 4 May, it is argued that Moran's rock-throwing could not have occurred both after the departure of the experts and no later than twilight (Boucher). Other scholars have debated the possibility of the timetable, and Baring-Gould provides us with an excellent summary of this debate.

Of all the inconsistencies we have reviewed, those connected with Holmes's behaviour after he had disposed of Moriarty rival his note for the premier level of absurdity. Holmes claims that (13) he decided to sham his own death because at least three others besides Moriarty had escaped the police net, yet the telegram he received at Strasburg positively asserted that all of the gang except Moriarty had been secured (Armstrong and Blakeney). So we must wonder how Holmes knew that the others were also at large. Then, after taking the initial steps in his plan of disappearance, Holmes is attacked by Moran, who must, thereby, know of Holmes's escape from the watery death that Moriarty had planned for him (14). Nevertheless, Holmes pursues his plan for disappearance, even though the most important person to deceive can no longer be deceived by this plan (Blakeney and Boucher). Nor can it be argued that Holmes had some form of mental lapse which made his plan still seem workable, since he tells Watson (in *The Empty House*) that his old enemies are the only ones besides Mycroft who know he is alive, and that they are watching his rooms for his return. Thus, Holmes knew that his enemies were aware that he was not dead, and yet he disappeared in order to persuade them that he was dead. This tale is so wildly unbelievable in its strict form that no thoughtful reader would swallow it. Then it becomes even more unbelievable that (15) Holmes would tell it to Watson if he knew it to be false. If the truth about Holmes's disappearance had to be concealed (by Holmes, by Watson, or by Doyle), why select such a patently absurd substitute for the truth? Indeed, no writer of decent fiction would ever attempt such an implausible account. Thus, the very absurdity of the Canonical account furnishes additional evidence that Sherlock Holmes and his adventures were not purely fictional!

No review of the events at the Reichenbach would be complete without mention of Boucher's contention that (16) Holmes's personality and behaviour underwent fundamental changes subsequent to his return to his rooms in Baker Street in 1894. "To sum up," writes Boucher, "there disappeared in 1891 an able violinist, addicted to drugs, well-versed in spies, and ready to retire." There returned in 1894 a theoretical musicologist (who does not play the violin), free from narcotic vices, ignorant of spies, and eager to continue the profession of detective."

There are two essential premises upon which our theory of the truth of the Reichenbach episode is based. The first is that Holmes prepared an ingenious counter-trap by which he skillfully lured Professor Moriarty to his death. To Walter Armstrong must go the credit for first elaborating such a theory, but ours differs from Armstrong's in certain critical respects. The second premise is that Holmes's disappearance was indeed planned to convince the remnant of the Moriarty organisation that he was dead and that his continuation with that plan remained the most sensible course of action even after Moran's discovery.

Having spent the most arduous six months of his life in carefully constructing a net in which to snare the Napoleon of crime, Holmes was not likely to have placed all his hopes for the final capture upon the London police. "I might have known it!" Holmes groans upon hearing of Moriarty's escape. "Of course, when I had left the country, there was no one to cope with him." It is certain that Holmes had prepared a plan for this contingency. In the week following receipt of that fateful telegram at Strasburg, Watson tells us that Holmes, in exuberant spirits, again and again reverted to the fact that if he could be assured that society was freed from Professor Moriarty he would cheerfully bring his own career to a conclusion. Our first clue to this brilliant scheme comes after Holmes assures Watson that Moriarty intended a murderous attack upon them had he overtaken them en route to the Channel. Holmes adds, "It is a game, however, at which two may play."

Each of us has felt short-changed at one time or another by Watson's failure to disclose the brilliant means by which Holmes destroyed the Moriarty organisation. But the plan for removing Moriarty himself, should Scotland Yard fail, must have been of equal brilliance; and it is ours to know if we apply Holmes's own methods. Holmes's flight to the Continent and his subsequent travels involved an incredibly delicate balance between allowing Moriarty to know where he was and yet slipping away from his enemy just in time. At the same time, Holmes took great precautions not to let Moriarty divine his intentions. The best example of this is found in implausibility #1, Holmes's elaborate disguise of himself combined with his rendezvous with an undisguised Watson on the boat train. Moriarty just missed catching them there. After hearing of Moriarty's escape, Holmes's pace slowed during that charming week in which he and Watson wandered up the Valley of the Rhône and ultimately came to Meiringen (implausibility #2). Having carefully read his enemy's psychology, Holmes could be certain that Moriarty would attempt to take his vengeance. He must have had means of staying abreast of Moriarty's movements, and determined to leave Meiringen just prior to the Professor's arrival there. He also made no secret of where he and Watson were going from the Englischer Hof. The culmination of Holmes's plan pointed unfailingly to those terrifying Falls at Reichenbach, a spot he must have known well from his prior travels. Naturally, his biographer had to be kept in the dark about this premeditated (but thoroughly justified) homicide. This accounts for Watson's mistaken belief that Holmes was unarmed during this episode (implausibility #3). It is also the reason that Watson was not at the scene of the final encounter. Holmes counted on Moriarty to follow them and secrete himself in a place from which he could easily ambush them as they returned on that tortuous path from the Falls. And it was Holmes himself who wrote that bogus note that was delivered to Watson. Indeed, no one but Holmes could have been certain that such a note would result in Watson's return to Meiringen alone (implausibility #5), because only he could be sure that he would not accompany Watson. Here we have the conclusive evidence of the counter-trap that Holmes laid. For, if Holmes was responsible for Watson's return to Meiringen, the only motive he could have had for promoting this, in the face of his own avowed certainty that Moriarty was close upon them, was to obtain seclusion for his disposal of the Professor. Imagine Moriarty's consternation as he saw Watson return down the path alone and waited in vain for the sight of his hated adversary!

Meanwhile, Holmes walked to the edge of the cliff and then ascended to that perch above the path from which he told Watson that he watched him form his inevitable and totally erroneous conclusions about what had happened there. Thus, instead of an unarmed Moriarty (implausibility #4) hurrying up the path (implausibility #8) to meet a virtually defenseless Holmes (implausibility #6), we have both men armed, hidden and waiting. But Moriarty was confused by the turn of events and ventured forth cautiously, following Holmes's footsteps. These footsteps led him past Holmes's Alpine-stock and to the very brink of the precipice. No doubt they also led past the spot to which Holmes walked backwards in order to begin his ascent to his famous perch. Thus we have two sets of footprints that Watson observed leading to the brink of the Falls (implausibility

#7). From his place of perfect concealment (neither Watson nor the Swiss police noticed it) Holmes had Moriarty completely at his mercy. But to arrest him and return him to England would have involved the grave risk of Moriarty's escape, as well as forcing Holmes to remain in the open. (Recall that Holmes claimed to have known already that at least three others of the Moriarty organisation were still at large.) The only alternative was to bring about Moriarty's demise by Holmes's own hand. But lest we judge Holmes too harshly here, let us remember that Moriarty was placed in that jeopardy only because of his own murderous intentions.

We shall probably never know whether Moriarty's descent into the dreadful chasm was effected by a bullet or a rock, but we can be fairly certain that it served as the signal for Holmes to write his celebrated farewell note to Watson. The note admittedly involved deceit, since Holmes survived the encounter with Moriarty and let Watson believe he did not. The question is, when was the deceit planned? Holmes claimed that the deceit was founded upon his desire to trap the remaining members of Moriarty's organisation, but this reveals a further deceit on Holmes's part. He must have known that these other sinister individuals were at large prior to the time when Watson was lured back to Meiringen by the bogus note, because it is inconceivable that Moriarty would have imparted this intelligence during the final confrontation. Moreover, Holmes could not first have decided to disappear at the time that Moran discovered him, because by that time he had already put the first part of his plan into operation by hiding on the ledge. Yet Holmes never communicated his knowledge of these other surviving members of the Moriarty organisation to Watson (implausibility #13), which can only mean that Holmes had already planned to disappear by the time that he and Watson parted at the Falls. Here we have strong evidence that Holmes was planning a counter-trap for Moriarty, for such a plan would be one of the few motives that Holmes could have for planning a disappearance before actually meeting the evil Professor. His eloquent farewell note, an integral part of his disappearance scheme, was undoubtedly planned prior to his final discussion of those questions which lay between himself and Moriarty, but was executed subsequent to that discussion. The note could not have been left under the cigarette-case prior to the encounter with Moriarty, for then the latter would have been able to read Holmes's scheme in it. Nor can we allow that Holmes wrote it under Moriarty's courteous eye (implausibility #9). Thus, Holmes must have written the note while perched on his ledge subsequent to Moriarty's demise and then lowered it, attached by moisture to his cigarette-case, to the boulder by a string which he slipped off.

Returning momentarily to the problem of how Holmes knew of the freedom of the other members of the Moriarty group, we find three possibilities. Holmes might have read it in the telegram at Strasburg, but lied to Watson; he might have received a second message at some other time; or he might have had information that was not available to the police. It is true that he immediately hurled the telegram into the grate, so that Watson was unable to see it, but a lie about its contents might easily have been discovered by Watson at some later time. Moreover, the almost constant proximity of Holmes and Watson makes a subsequent telegram unlikely. These considerations, coupled with the fact that the police allowed Moran to remain at liberty, make it seem most likely that Moran and his two confederates were unknown to the police in 1891. Very likely they had served in consulting capacities to the Moriarty organisation rather than as regular members on its payroll, and only Holmes knew of their activities.

The most reasonable explanation for Moran's not joining Moriarty in tracking Holmes to the Falls (implausibility #10) is that he was not there. Indeed, there are two excellent reasons for the two criminals' travelling from England separately. First, if it is true that Moran was not wanted by the police, it would have behooved him to remain separate from the Professor. Second, two men scouring the Continent for Holmes stood a far better chance of finding him separately than they did together. Moriarty, having traced Holmes to Meiringen, would have sent a telegram to Moran immediately, and proceeded to the village alone. We have seen that Holmes timed his departure to the Falls to anticipate Moriarty's arrival in Meiringen by a very short time. The intelligence that Holmes would be viewing the Falls was readily available to Moriarty, and must have seemed an irresistible invitation to conclude Holmes's presence on earth single-handedly. Moran, arriving in Meiringen later in the day, may well have made his way to the Falls by following Watson after the good Doctor realised he had been tricked into returning to the village. In order to see what had occurred without showing himself, Moran would have taken the path to the crest of the cliff. From there he could have seen Watson evaluating the false evidence on the path and Holmes secreted on the ledge.

It remains for us to consider the curious incident of the shots from Moran's air-gun, the curious incident being that there were no shots from the air-gun, only hurled rocks (implausibility #11). Unfortunately, our argument here must be largely speculative, since we have no information about the exact relationship of the top of the cliff to the ledge where Holmes lay. According to Messrs. Crawford and Moore[6] there is no ledge today on the east side of the Reichenbach Falls, but there was one in 1891 which fell away as part of the general erosion and rock fall in March 1944. Quite possibly the top of the mountain overhung Holmes's ledge in such a way as to make it impossible for Moran to take effective aim or to fire without exposing himself to Holmes's revolver. Again, we cannot be sure of the effective range of Von Herder's air-gun. Mr. Ralph Ashton's estimate[7] is 50 yards, and this might not have been sufficiently great to reach Holmes. Finally, we must remember that, in the failing light, Moran at the crest of the mountain was much more visible than Holmes down in the gorge. All of these possibilities would have made it more sensible for Moran to attempt Holmes's life with boulders rolled down the face of the cliff, and it is clear that the attempt came perilously close to being successful. Holmes could not, of course, have mentioned being armed, since that would have cast doubt on the first part of his story.

We must now turn our attention to the events that followed Moriarty's richly deserved end. The first implausibility connected with these events is that of the necessary timetable (#12). We believe that one simple, heretofore-ignored possibility will render the Canonical account adequate. That possibility is that the experts whom Watson mentions as having examined the path did not arrive at Reichenbach until the next day. The quote in which the term appears reads merely: "an examination by experts leaves little doubt that," etc. In the narrative dealing with Watson's return to Reichenbach from the village, we read merely: "In a tingle of fear I was already running down the village street, and making for the path which I had so lately descended." While there is no mention of any companion here, Holmes (in *The Empty House*) speaks of "you, my dear Watson, and all your following" investigating the situation. Most likely, in his haste to return to the Falls, Watson secured the company only of the handiest guide available and the village Constable (and an unseen Moran). Holmes's remark must have had a trace of irony in it. Indeed, any sort of expert police officer could not have been closer to Meiringen than half a day's trip. Thus, Watson returned to the Falls but once that day, which can be accommodated easily within the time remaining before sunset. This alternative also accounts for the ease with which Holmes's retreat from the path was kept from observation. It is quite likely that his descent from the ledge was farther down the path than where the experts were concentrating their attentions and that his footprints were easily merged with those of the men who had followed Watson to the Falls on the previous day.

We have already dealt with the problem of how Holmes knew that Moran and two others associated with Moriarty were still at liberty (implausibility #13), and have shown that these men were not likely to be in danger from the police. This brings us directly to the problem of the cause for Holmes's disappearance, a disappearance whose avowed intention was the deception of the one man who knew that Holmes was not dead (implausibility #14). In turn, this leads us to the implausibility of Holmes's telling Watson such a preposterous story if he wished to conceal the truth with it (#15).

Our contention is that Holmes decided to disappear for the reason he stated (but decided so long before Reichenbach), that he maintained the plan after Moran discovered him because it was still a useful one, and that he simply failed to alter his motive in the story he told Watson according to the new contingencies. Let us remember that, after six months of continuous labour to trap the Moriarty gang, followed by a nerve-racking final encounter with Moriarty at the Falls, Holmes must have been close to a state of total collapse. Blakeney reminds us that once

153

before (in *The Reigate Squires*) Holmes had collapsed after a prolonged and intense investigation, and that affair was nothing compared with the effort required to eliminate Moriarty and his influence. Therefore, when Moran's boulders began to rain down upon him, Holmes must have decided to bolt. Very likely he did not reconsider his plans until he was within the comparative safety of Florence. But he was never deluded that Moran believed him to be dead. Note the exact wording in which Holmes related these events to Watson. He concluded by saying that he had "the certainty that no one in the world knew what had *become* [italics ours] of me."

Careful reconsideration of his options must have shown Holmes that his original plan, while not as good as it had been prior to Moran's surprising him, was still the best one that he could develop. Holmes's motive was not fundamentally different than it had been originally: to lie low and save his life from Moran's vengeance while arranging his own trap for the Colonel. In this way the initiative for the final encounter with Moran would rest with Holmes. What else could Holmes have done? In Holmes's own words:

> "So long as he [Moran] was free in London, my life would really not have been worth living. Night and day the shadow would have been over me, and sooner or later his chance must have come. . . . I could not shoot him at sight [in England, that is], or I should myself be in the dock. There was no use appealing to a magistrate. They cannot interfere on the strength of what would appear to them to be a wild suspicion. . . . But I watched the criminal news, knowing that sooner or later I should get him."

But Holmes was an astute psychologist[8] and knew that the only way to convince Moran that his disappearance was permanent was to make the world at large believe that he was dead.

Holmes was relating his story to Watson chronologically and, therefore, was likely to give him the first motive for disappearance early in the story. From Holmes's perspective, the change in motivation was so slight that its omission was trivial. Holmes often omitted minor details from his reconstruction of events, and he simply didn't see this one as anything but minor. Usually the points that Holmes omitted were retained by Watson. But the Reichenbach events constitute one of the rare instances in the Canon in which Watson related a crucial event without

154

himself being present during its occurrence. Remember that Watson had pressed Holmes for the story immediately, while the trap for Moran was being readied. With so little time available, and being so bowled over by Holmes's reappearance, Watson didn't clear up the point for himself until some time later. The narration of *The Empty House*, however, ended that very evening. Ironically, the point that seemed the most deceptive of all the Reichenbach implausibilities involved no deception whatever.

Finally, we must deal with the personality and behaviour changes in Holmes subsequent to his return to Baker Street. Boucher's own theory, that Holmes had also died at the Falls and was replaced by an impostor, is inherently impossible, as Walter Armstrong has ably shown. The idea of any impostor living with Watson undetected boggles the imagination. But it is not at all unlikely that a man of Holmes's openness of mind should return to his former life refreshed and altered after a three-year holiday during which he had first-hand experience with the philosophy of the East. A more reflective, theoretical man, less able to deal with sharp contingencies than before, but more willing to take the law into his own hands, is exactly what one would expect from such a hiatus. And more than one tortured mind has found Oriental philosophy an adequate substitute for drugs. In fact, were it not for the other implausibilities we have dealt with, these personality changes would never have caused so much as a lifted eyebrow. One final change, that Holmes, who always honoured an adversary, jeered at Moran, will be dealt with in a moment.

Was Holmes travelling around the world between 1891 and 1894, or was he secreted in London (as Armstrong contended) the whole time, waiting for Moran to make a false move? And if he travelled, was Irene Adler involved? These questions involve scholarly territories upon which we decline to intrude. The evidence seems too conflicting to allow certainty. We lean toward the story told in the Canon, however, mainly because of the personality changes shown by Holmes upon his reappearance and his evident nervous exhaustion prior to his disappearance. The elements of the trap for Moran (including the plaster bust of Holmes) could have been readied by Mycroft in Holmes's absence. On the other hand, Holmes might well have spent the last few months of the Great Hiatus in London, but omitted this from his narrative. We cannot be sure. But certain we are that Holmes disappeared because he could not abide the prospect of living as a hunted man, and that he waited for the *moment juste* when he could trap Moran as he had previously trapped Moriarty—with himself as the bait. Small wonder that Holmes was unable to restrain himself from taunting the old *shikari* on that fateful night.

—March 1970

NOTES

1. Walter P. Armstrong, Jr., "The Truth about Sherlock Holmes," BSJ (os) 1 (1946), 391–401.

2. T. S. Blakeney, *Sherlock Holmes: Fact or Fiction?* (London: Murray, 1932).

3. Anthony Boucher, "Was the Later Holmes an Impostor?" in *Profile by Gaslight,* pp. 60–70.

4. Pope R. Hill, Sr., "The Final Problem," BSJ (ns) 5 (1955), 149–53.

5. W. S. Baring-Gould, *The Annotated Sherlock Holmes,* II (New York: Potter, 1967).

6. Bryce Crawford and R. C. Moore, "The Final Problem—Where?" in *Exploring Sherlock Holmes,* pp. 82–87.

7. Ralph A. Ashton, "Colonel Moran's Infamous Air Rifle," BSJ (ns) 10 (1960), 155–59.

8. For a discussion of these powers, see "Sherlock Holmes and the Interference Theory of Forgetting," BSJ (ns) 14 (1964), 216–18.

*During his Great Hiatus, Holmes claimed to have
visited both Lhassa in Tibet and the closed city of
Mecca. But did he?*

NOTES ON A JOURNEY TO LHASSA AND MECCA

by DONALD POLLOCK

WHAT HOLMESIAN, when but a fledgling, failed to shed a tear at the untimely demise of the Master at Reichenbach, only to take up the chase once again with the *Return* in *The Empty House*? Yet, a problem lingers. The events of Holmes's life from 23 May 1891 to April 1894 surely remain one of the great unsolved mysteries of our time. There can be little doubt that no one has ever read Holmes's own account without pausing to reflect upon the "confusion and perplexities" involved in that tale.[1]

Theories to account for the Hiatus abound. Indeed, Baring-Gould found it convenient, if not necessary, to categorise them in his introduction to *The Empty House*.[2] In that series of studies we find Holmes in London, America, France, and occasionally, according to some perhaps gullible yet stalwart scholars, in Lhassa, Mecca, Khartoum, etc. Only, of course, if we are still speaking of the same man!

Commentators on the Hiatus opt for one of two of the Master's favourite lessons. One camp, having eliminated as impossible the journey described to our good Doctor, defends improbable hypotheses finding Holmes virtually everywhere *but* in those Canonical places. The other camp takes the same lesson to heart, but defends the possibility of orthodox doctrine. This paper belongs to that second faction, but proceeds with the added caution that theories (as the Master tells us) must be grounded in fact.

Toward this end, and in hopes that the debate has not staled, I propose to submit a small but relevant body of data which will correct what appear to be commonly accepted, though mistaken, beliefs, and to offer a few observations on the possibility of a journey to Lhassa and Mecca.[3]

A history of scholarly laxity begins, regrettably, with Edgar Smith's article on the Hiatus,[4] which constitutes a frequent starting-point for subsequent research. In that paper we find Smith's statement that ". . . no European, Norwegian or otherwise, came anywhere near the forbidden city of Lhassa until 1903. . . ."[5] Therefore neither Holmes nor Sigerson could possibly have visited Lhassa as early as 1891. Even so eclectic an authority as Baring-Gould accepts Smith's scholarship here without question, and quotes no other sources to the contrary— simply noting rival theories likewise based on a dearth of evidence.[6]

Actually Smith's claim is remarkable, and no less so is its unchallenged stand for nearly twenty years. Though it is disputed, the first claimed European entry into Lhassa was made in the early fourteenth century by a Catholic priest, Friar Odoric of Pordenone. The first undisputed European entry into the forbidden city was made in 1661 by the Jesuit Fathers Grueber and D'Orville, who were there for two months. In 1707 two Capuchin priests, d'Ascoli and de Tours, arrived in Lhassa, and shortly after, the Italian priest Ippolito Desideri repeated the feat. The first Englishman to reach Lhassa was Thomas Manning in 1811. After Manning came the French Lazarist priests Huc and Gabet in 1846. To this list should perhaps be added the so-called "pundits," mock-pilgrims who penetrated to the city in a series beginning in 1865, and who supplied the British with much information.

By the time of the Hiatus there was renewed interest in Tibet, and indeed, the whole of the mysterious East captured the British public's imagination. Holmes had, in all probability, read *Narratives of the Mission of George Bogle to Tibet and of the Journey of Thomas Manning to Lhassa* (London, 1876). And though it appeared five years after the *Return*, it is interesting to note the existence of a Capt. F. E. S. Adair's *The Big Game of Baliston and Ladakh: A Summer in High Asia* (Thacker, 1899)— interesting, as it brings to mind Col. Sebastian Moran's *Heavy Game of the Western Himalayas*, purported published in 1881.[7] But the adventure in which this information appears did not reach the public until October 1903,[8] and it is within the bounds of belief that there is a connection between Capt. F. E. S. Adair, our own Ronald Adair, and Col. Moran.

To return to Lhassa: In spite of its inaccuracy, Smith's statement has some intentional value. For though the Chinese agreed in 1865 to the establishment of a British post in Lhassa, passage to the city was forcibly blocked by the Tibetans until 1903, when a British military mission gained entry.

But here again we must proceed with caution, and remember the lesson of the pundits, and Holmes's disguise chest. Far from presenting an insurmountable obstacle, the blockade presents an excellent reason for Holmes's presence in the area.

ON TO MECCA

There have been two major objections to Holmes's claim to have visited Mecca: (a) civil war in the area would have made travel impossible for an English non-Muslim,[9] and (b) the explicit dangers involved in entering the holy city amount to an effective prohibition. The first objection, put forward by Smith, has been ably dealt with by Benson Murray, who also questions the reliability of Smith's sources. It appears that the "war" was in reality little more than a political struggle between the Sharif and the Ottoman administration.[10] To Murray's information we may add that Doughty notes that in 1879 the Sharif of Mecca issued a proclamation stating that any and all Europeans passing through his country should be treated courteously and sent directly to him at El Ta'if.[11]

Murray furthermore notes that a number of non-Muslims have successfully completed the hajj, and many have left their stories in print. Several accounts were available to Holmes in 1891: Buckhardt's *Travels in Arabia* appeared in 1829, Keane's *Six Months in Mecca and My Journey to Medinah* in 1881, and a translation of Hurgonje's *Mekka* in 1889. Perhaps the most useful work was Richard Burton's *Personal Narrative . . .*, which not only comments on the earlier reports, but serves as a handbook of sorts for the next chap who wishes to try.

If I may digress for a moment, I would like to note that there are, besides their pilgrimages, a number of interesting parallels between Holmes's and Burton's lives. Both men were remarkable linguists (Burton spoke over 30 languages); both were masters of disguise; and, Watson's list to the contrary, Holmes shared with Burton an extensive knowledge of literature. Burton was widely travelled, and left records of visits to at least five continents and Iceland. Holmes, if we allow his own account, was also widely travelled, even having visited America. Some minor points are also worth mention: both Burton and Holmes wrote a number of important short monographs. Burton's, particularly those on the bayonet and sword, were neglected for years by the military. Holmes's, on topics ranging from dogs to ears, were by all evidence similarly neglected. Finally, each man experienced a curious lack of British commendation—Holmes by choice (he refused a knighthood, though he accepted foreign honours); Burton in spite of his life-long desire (though many foreign honours were bestowed upon him).

Burton died in 1890. It is far from unlikely that Holmes had in fact met Burton. Is it hard to believe, then, that Holmes's own hajj was in the manner of a testament to the memory of that second most remarkable man? Or that Holmes chose the guise of an explorer on his journey?

It only remains to note that, regardless of the veracity of Holmes's own account of the Hiatus, mounting evidence must convince the reader that it was possible, if not probable. Here, at least, we have no reason to believe that either Holmes or Watson has deceived us.

—June 1975

NOTES

1. Edgar W. Smith, "Sherlock Holmes and the Great Hiatus," BSJ (os) 1 (1946), 278–85.
2. W. S. Baring-Gould, BSJ (ns) 17 (1967), 152–60.
3. And not least of all to make some use of a modest bit of research.
4. Smith, op. cit.
5. Ibid., 279.
6. Baring-Gould, op. cit.
7. *The Empty House.*
8. *The Strand Magazine,* October 1903.
9. Smith, op. cit., pp. 279–80.
10. See Baring-Gould, op. cit., pp. 159–60.
11. Charles Doughty, *Travels in Arabia Deserta* (London, 1931), 337.

Editor's Note: For more on this subject see Evan Wilson's "The Trip That Never Was," BSJ (ns) 20 (1970), 67–73.

*Sherlock Holmes's disappearance after the episode at the
Reichenbach Falls has generated much speculation, not
the least of which is this tale-in-verse about the
"remarkable" Norwegian Sigerson. . . .*

A CANONICAL KIPLING

by THADDEUS HOLT

(Enthusiasts of the verse of Mr. Rudyard Kipling will find of
interest the following poem, unaccountably omitted from the
Barrack-Room Ballads, which has recently come to light under
circumstances for the story of which the world is not yet
prepared.)

SIGERSON

I served the Widow in India for more than thirty years;
I've seen all the tricks of 'oly men an' lamas an' fakirs;
But when it comes to readin' minds, an' piercin' a deep-laid
plan,
Forget your lamas an' 'oly men: a Norsker is your man.

Riley an' me was on sentry-go the night the Norsker came;
'E ups to us from out o' the dark an' says, "Sigerson's my
name;
"I've come all the way from Lhassa town, in the Land of
Eternal Snow;
"You must take me straight to your Colonel, lads, for I've
things that 'e must know."
'E was dressed in rags, with a turbaned 'ead, an' 'is face
was black as soot,
But 'is eyes flashed fire, an' 'e spoke like a gent, an' said,
"'Urry! The game's afoot!"
So we called the Sergeant, 'oo took him in, an' the next
day what do we see
But the same tall chap, in *pukka* kit, with a face as white
as me.
"'E's a Norsker bloke," the Sergeant says, "that the
Colonel seems to know;
"They sat up all night with the Colonel's maps, in the
Colonel's bungalow."

Now those were the days of Mohammed Khan, the
 scourge of the old Frontier;
The regiment went to 'unt 'im out 'alf a dozen times a year.
We'd scour the 'ills an' valleys, the mountains an' the
 plain,
An' find no trace of Mohammed Khan, an' march back
 'ome again.
"There's somethin' rotten in Denmark," the Colour-
 Sergeant would say;
"'Oo tips Mohammed Khan the wink, so 'e knows we're
 on the way?
"Gentlemen, 'ush! an' mark my words! on this you may
 rely:
"We 'ave no bloomin' traitors 'ere; but we've got a
 bloomin' spy!"
Well, Khyber camp was as tight as tight, sewed up like a
 rajah's sleeve;
The Queen 'erself could not ha' got in, without the
 Colonel's leave;
We knowed the Colour-Sergeant was right, but blamed if
 we could see
Just 'ow in the name of the Thousand Gods a thing like
 that could be!
Now, there was a bloke named Krishna Dass, 'oo was one
 of your *fakirs*;
With a rag before, an' a rag be'ind, an' earrings in 'is ears,
An' a pet mongoose, an' a bamboo flute, an' a cobra in
 a jar,
'E roamed the countryside about from 'ere to Buldahar.
'E'd pay the regiment a call, every two months or so,
An' squat on a rug afore the gate, an' give the lads a
 show.
'Is tricks was bloomin' clever, an' 'is visits was a treat;
'E'd walk unshod on livin' coals, an' never warm 'is feet;
'E'd make 'is cobra dance a waltz an' drink a cup of tea;
But most of all 'is pet mongoose was what we loved to see.
She'd stand on 'er 'ead, an' walk on wires, an' fetch an'
 carry 'an run;
We called 'er Little Sally, an' didn't she give us fun!

A fortnight after Sigerson came, old Krishna came
    around,
An' spread 'is rug outside the gate, an' squatted on the
    ground,
An' Sigerson, 'e came along, to see what was about.
'E studied Little Sally, 'ow she'd fetch an' take so neat;
An' when Krishna walked across 'is coals, 'e studied
    Krishna's feet;
An' 'e smiled the smile of the Man 'Oo Knows; an' after
    the show was done,
'E gave two annas to Krishna Dass, an' thanked 'im for
    the fun.
That night the Sergeant says to me: "You an' Riley turn
    out;
"The Colonel wants me two best men, so mind what
    you're about!"
We goes to the Colonel's bungalow, an' settin' there in
    the dark
Is Sigerson an' the Colonel; an' Sigerson says, "Not a
    Spark!
"Not a glimmer o' light! Not a whisper! sit yonder that
    side o' the room!"
So we sets and we waits, like old *shikaris,* there in the
    murk an' gloom.
We sets an' we waits for hours there, till the night is
    nearly through;
Then we 'ears a thumpin' an' scratchin' sound, an' a
    crackle of papers too.
"Now!" says the Norsker sudden, an' 'is dark-lantern
    flashes up.
There on the Colonel's table, big as a mastiff pup,
Is Little Sally, the trained mongoose, the pride of Krishna
    Dass,
An' in 'er jaws is the Colonel's secret map o' the Khyber
    Pass!
"Well, there's your spy," says Sigerson, as Little Sally
    runs out;
"Send these two lads for Krishna Dass, they'll see what 'e's
    about.

"They'll find 'im copyin' out your maps an' plans, as sure
   as sin."
An' that's what Riley an' me did find, an' we brought old
   Krishna in.
"You must wash 'is face," the Norsker says; "'e's as white
   as you or I;
"For this is Van Doncken of Palembang, the secret agent
   an' spy!
"'E's a Dutchman born," says Sigerson, "'oo early turned
   to crime.
"'E robbed the ship *Matilda Briggs* an' fled to a safer
   clime.
"'E lived for years in Sumatra, in the opium trade,
   they say;
"An then 'e started another trade, as a spy in Russian pay."
"But 'ow did you know," the Colonel says, "just 'oo this
   chap would be?"
"Elementary," Sigerson says, "as you will shortly see.
"Beyond the mountains, in Lhassa town, the Great 'Igh
   Lama knows
"Whatever 'appens in the East; for every wind that blows
"Brings tidings to 'is ears, they say; an' 'e told to me a tale
"'E said 'ad come to 'im just now upon a western gale,
"Of 'ow, beyond the Khyber Pass, somewhere near
   Bildahar,
"The Giant Rat of Sumatra was spyin' for the Czar.
"I don't believe in sorcery, an' magic's not my style;
"But I knowed Van Doncken of Palmenbang 'ad been
   missin' for a while.
"So I came 'ot-foot direct to you, an' found you 'ad a spy.
"An' I settled in, an' poked about, an' pondered the 'Ow
   an' Why.
"An' then I saw Little Sally play 'er fetch an' carry game,
"An' I says to myself, there's your giant rat; now, what's
   this Krishna's name?
"Well, I once wrote a book," the Norsker says, "that you
   might someday peruse,
"About the marks left on the feet by sixty kinds of shoes.
"You can dress as you please, Van Doncken me boy, an'
   blacken up your face,

"But you'll 'ave to wear a pair o' boots, if you wants to 'ide
    your race;
"For there upon your ankles plain for the knowin' eye
    to see
"Is the mark of the wooden shoes you wore as a lad by
    the Zuyder Zee!"
"You fiend! You devil!" old Krishna cries, with a string of
    oaths an' such,
An' the Sergeant an' Riley leads 'im away, shoutin' 'is
    wrath in Dutch.

Well, the very next week we marches out, with the
    Colonel lookin' grim,
An' this time we catches Mohammed Khan, an' that's the
    end of 'im!
So that's the tale, an' I tells it straight (for I seed it with
    these two eyes),
Of the Giant Rat of Sumatra, an' Sigerson the Wise!

I served the Widow in India for more than thirty years;
I've seen all the tricks of 'oly men an' lamas an' fakirs;
But when it comes to readin' minds, an' piercin' a deep-laid plan,
Forget your lamas an' 'oly men: a Norsker is your man!

—March 1985

165

The death of Sherlock Holmes has never been reported.
Even The Times *of London admits that. . . .*

Morte de Sherlock

by Stephen A. Kallis

The following is based upon the latter pages of W. S. Baring-Gould's *Sherlock Holmes of Baker Street,* and is presented at his suggestion.

I have considered it very ignoble for the Master to die peacefully on a park bench—or to die at all, if it comes to that. With his British heritage, alternate solutions present themselves, this one being more pleasant to contemplate.

The reading of this account may cause a few raised eyebrows, but I diffidently try to lay the necessary groundwork, so that it may be more understandable. We must understand the ancestral heritage of Sherlock Holmes, a true son of England's past: Richard the Third, the Royal Stuarts, Galahad the Deliverer, and a mightier name—one that, like that of Sherlock Holmes, shall last as long as England endures, and doubtless beyond that. Recall, if you will, the name of the greatest of the ancient kings of England. He is known also as "The Once and Future King," who in the proper time will come forth once more to rule England—"He who will come."

The old man, who had walked at sunset along the cliff path, sat musing upon the bench overlooking the Channel. Sherlock's memories were past, and the trend of his thoughts turned to the present, and, indeed, the future.

One hundred and three years! This extended span, however, would have its end. Yet, in this extended span, how much had been wrought!

The old man on the bench shook his head. It was as well that his fame would rest on his own *Whole Art of Detection,* never on those tales of Watson's.

Well, his work was done now, and well done, on the whole.

166

There were a few cases whose elements had never been satisfactorily resolved, yet the world would long remember the name of Sherlock Holmes.

It had seemed to grow much colder, and very dark.

The old man on the bench drew his caped overcoat still closer about him. The grey eyes closed. The white-maned head fell forward on his breast.

For the last time that night, the thin lips spoke aloud.

"Irene," the old man said. "Irene."

The coldness seemed to wrap around him. He sighed.

Like a blanket of frozen eider-down, the coldness pressed upon him, slipping through his coat like water through a sieve. And yet, nonetheless, there seemed to be a kind of warmth within it. A gentle, cloying, insidiously seductive warmth.

The wind whistled icily, and the surf pounded against the cliffside, but Sherlock Holmes paid no attention. That warmth! That cloying black warmth! It meant something important.

And then it came to him with a flash of insight. Of course . . . that warmth meant something! It was the Ultimate Foe . . . negation.

Hm! The Royal Jelly held the fellow off, but still he persisted. Well, if he had to have his record closed this night, it could not be said that he had lived wholly in vain. He could view his life with equanimity.

And yet . . . there were a few cases that he had never solved. Even with Watson—good old Watson!—he was never to learn what had happened to Mr. James Phillimore, or the cutter *Alicia*; or the duellist Persano and his mysterious worm, or the singular doings of the Hastings Laboratory.

But most galling of all was the irregularity of Watson's passing. Why should the old retired doctor decide to visit Crile Hospital in Cleveland in the United States? Surely, at his age, to travel across an ocean and half-way across a continent! Yet, Watson had some remarkable characteristics of his own.

But . . . that terrible fire and the investigation that followed. He had hurried across to the United States to help, yet there was no trace of Watson. Nobody had any recollection of an aged doctor visiting the hospital on fateful May 15th. Yet, if he did not perish in that dreadful fire of 1929, he must have vanished tracelessly!

167

But that irregularity was most singular. Was Watson claimed by the Ultimate Foe, or had he managed somehow to evade . . . ?

Sherlock's mind raced. The black-magic cult that enmeshed poor Sherrinford! And the destiny . . . the hope Providence assures in the flowers.

It was night now, and cold. The waves smashed against the cliff and brought to mind thoughts of the sea, and thence to the traditions of England.

The old man sprang to his feet, and his grey eyes had the introspective cast of exerting his full powers.

The Ultimate Foe was closing in fast, and solving its problem would be a pretty problem, indeed! Yet, certain elements might yet show the way.

The old man filled his pipe with shag, and paced around the bench. And the night dragged on.

Dawn broke chill and grey when Constable Anderson started his rounds. Leaden clouds hung low overhead, but the air was clear along the ground. Anderson strolled slowly along his route, looking at the sky with grim foreboding, for it seemed to him that a rainfall was inevitable. As he came to the cliff overlooking the Channel, he was amazed to see a figure seated upon a bench, "Coo," said he. "Now who would be sitting out here at this hour of the morning?"

As he approached, he recognized the seated man and smiled. "Oh, it's you, Mr. Holmes. I might have guessed. You always were one for getting about early."

"Oh," said the old man, looking up. "It's you, Anderson. It is good to see you. You have come just in time to help me."

"To help you, Mr. Holmes?" Anderson looked concerned. "You look a bit of poorly, sir. Would you like to take a visit to a doctor?"

"No, it's too late for that." Holmes gasped for breath. "Without help I cannot last an hour. I have deduced the proper course of action that must be taken, but it has proved to be a lengthy task, and in doing so, I fear I have taken almost too much time."

"Coo, sir, are you feeling all right?"

"Anderson, I have little time to talk," said Sherlock hesitatingly. "As a favour to an old friend, I would ask you to do the following for me."

168

Here Sherlock reached into his pockets and withdrew a couple of objects. These he pressed into the hands of Constable Anderson, saying: "Here, then, are my pipe and magnifying glass. Take them from here, and go to the edge of the cliff. Throw them with all your might into the Channel there. Observe what happens, and report the details to me."

"Well, if you say so, Mr. Holmes," said Constable Anderson. And so he departed, but on his way he glanced at the pipe and glass of the old man. He said to himself, "This pipe and this glass are the belongings of the great Holmes, and were I to throw them into the Channel, no good would come of it; only harm and loss."

And therefore did Constable Anderson slip the objects into a voluminous pocket, stand on the edge of the cliff, and simulate a throwing motion. Then he returned to the old man on the bench.

"Quick, Anderson," said Sherlock sharply, "give me your report."

"Well, Mr. Holmes, I threw the objects out towards the sea and they fell with a splash. They disappeared immediately, and I came right back to you."

Holmes glared. "You must not think that I have been living in a home for the weak-minded," he snapped. "I perceive a bulge in your pocket that was not there when you left me. You did not bend down and pick up something, nor did you rock back as far as you would have had you actually thrown objects from your hands. Nor, for that matter, should your report have been what it was had you actually followed my instructions."

Sherlock paused for breath. "I have not much time yet remaining. And yet you seem like a good fellow; you have been friendly to me for a long time. Indeed, it was your father who shared with me the singular adventure I have chronicled as *The Adventure of the Lion's Mane.*

"You are a good man. So go again, humour an old man and do as I bid you, for your long delay has placed me in jeopardy of my life."

Eyes wide with wonder, Anderson backed off, and strode quickly towards the edge of the cliff. Pausing there, he extracted the pipe and the glass and regarded them.

Then, with a shrug, he flung them towards the Channel.

The pipe and the glass flew outwards with spinning motion. They slipped through the air in a graceful arc, separating very little. As they approached the turgid Channel, a strange thing happened. The waves subsided, and the water was suddenly as smooth as a sheet of grey glass. But just before the pipe and glass hit the slick surface an arm arose from out of the waters, and with a cat-quick motion caught both objects. Three times, and then once more, the arm waved around, and then withdrew below the surface.

And Constable Anderson spun and ran back to the bench. Excitedly, he described the happenings to Sherlock Holmes.

"Capital!" said Holmes. "It is as I have deduced."

"But what does it mean, Mr. Holmes?" asked the distracted constable.

"Look about you," said Holmes.

For round about, it was clear no longer; a death-white mist had swept over the Channel and the land. And yet, it was not a mist of chill—of formless dread or of menace; rather was it an exciting mist, as full of adventure as the tread upon the stair at the old flat in Baker Street.

"Coo, Mr. Holmes! What has happened?"

There was a glint in old Sherlock's eye. "It is as I have deduced, and this change is normal. Yet it means that you must help me further, for I am woefully weak. Help me to my feet."

Bewildered, the good constable did so.

"Good," said Sherlock, and walked slowly forward, in the direction of the edge of the cliff.

"Have a care, Mr. Holmes," advised Anderson.

"Do not worry," said Sherlock.

Anderson followed the detective a few steps, then stopped in amazement. For there, at the point where Sherlock Holmes had suddenly stopped was a black hansom cab, ornately decorated.

"Where did that come from, Mr. Holmes?"

A clarion-like woman-voice range out: "Trouble yourself not about that. Sherlock has done well, but it has near taken him too long."

"Forgive me, Morgana," said the detective, softly.

Anderson looked around, then spied the driver of the hansom. To his utter surprise, it was a woman, dressed in flowing black robes, with her head hooded. Her face was not averted, yet

170

Anderson could never describe it afterwards, save to say it was beautiful. She wore a golden crown.

"Help me in, Anderson," said Sherlock Holmes, opening the door of the cab.

The detective clambered aboard, helped by the constable, and settled into the seat. Once he saw that Sherlock was settled, Anderson withdrew.

Then he heard the following conversation between Holmes and the woman he had called Morgana.

"Am I correct, then, in deducing that Watson did not perish at the hospital?"

"The doctor's time was not as yours. He waits, with the Dane, attending the Once and Future King, awaiting your arrival."

"Capital! We must not keep them waiting. Drive on, then, Morgana. I wish to meet Arthur and Ogier and Watson once more. Drive on to Avalon!"

There was the crack of a whip, and the cab lurched forward into the mist. Anderson tried to cry out that the cab was heading towards the edge of the cliff, but the mists swallowed the hansom.

Anderson thought he heard the wind whisper "The game is afoot," but then there was silence.

The mist lifted suddenly, but no trace of the cab could be found; not wheel-tracks, not hoofprints. The sun broke through the leaden overcast, and the world seemed more at peace.

And it is whispered by certain men that on the Isle of Avalon there resides not only the greatest of the kings of England, not only Ogier the Dane, not only Morgan Le Fay, but also one of the greatest Englishmen of any age, waiting with Arthur to come forth once more; waiting with his friend in that isle of eternal youth until the day that England will need them all.

—September 1964

HAIL, SHERLOCK HOLMES!

by EDGAR S. ROSENBERGER

Hail, Sherlock Holmes! Here's to a life
   Of individuality:
A lighthouse in an age that's rife
   With colorless conformity.

No loutishness or boorish ways,
   But gentleness and courtesy;
Misogynist through all your days.
   Yet paragon of chivalry.

Proof positive that man has worth,
   And excellence and dignity;
That there's a place upon this earth
   For kindliness and charity.

Revered defender of the law,
   Of justice and of liberty:
The wicked trembled when they saw
   The bane of their iniquity.

A man of learning, with a flair
   For knowledge and philosophy;
A connoisseur of volumes rare
   And French and German poetry.

A gourmet and an epicure;
   A lover of gastronomy:
Indulgent tippler, to be sure—
   But always with sobriety.

Performer on the violin,
   Expert in musicology,
And dreamily delighted in
   Great Sarasate's melody.

In England and in Europe too,
　A favorite of royalty;
And yet a Briton through and through
　Who spared his Queen no loyalty.

Precise of diction, keen of speech,
　A master of philology;
A dilettante who sought to reach
　The unknown depths of chemistry.

Toward Watson, great and honored friend,
　Sincere and lasting amity;
A kinship that will never end,
　But last into eternity.

Contemptuous of banal talk,
　Averse to sociability;
And yet a man to always walk
　The narrow path of probity.

Disdainful of the pomp and show
　Of wealth and aristocracy,
A man whose joy it was to know
　The virtues of simplicity.

A boxer, wrestler, fencer, too;
　An athlete of agility;
In later years a man who knew
　The wonders of agronomy.

Alas, this senseless craze for speed!
　Alas, this shallow century!
Let's turn the pages and recede
　To Sherlock Holmes—and sanity.

　　　　　　　　　—July 1956

The image of Dr. Watson as a boobus Britannicus *is familiar to generations of film viewers and readers of parodies. In this essay, Mr. Struik sets the record straight.* . . .

THE REAL WATSON

by DIRK J. STRUIK

A RECENT FIND among the old papers of Sir Arthur Conan Doyle has again raised the question of the position which Dr. Watson occupies in the Holmes–Watson team. It will be recalled that Holmes played no rôle whatsoever in the original version of *A Study in Scarlet,* and that he was brought in as an afterthought. This remarkable discovery suggests that Watson was, after all, a more important figure than appears from the published documents. Is it possible to find a better estimate of the merits of Dr. Watson than we have so far deduced from the texts?

Questions like this are bound to arise wherever two persons appear simultaneously before the public eye and one of them stands out more prominently than the other. Boswell, in his life of Johnson, has so effaced himself that we are surprised to find him an interesting and capable person in his own right. Polton stayed so modestly in the shadow of Thorndyke that R. Austin Freeman had to write a special book to establish him as a person of considerable independent merits. Are we justified in forgetting the self-effacing Bergen because of the brilliance of Charlie McCarthy or the rustic witlessness of Mortimer Snerd? How many men in positions of influence are only the vigorous externalization of a powerful Mrs.? The *fidus Achates* has a personal life of his own which the faithful historian must not forget.

Let us not forget that practically all our information concerning Sherlock Holmes is derived from Watson. We know little of Holmes through his own writings. There are two stories in the Canon written by Holmes himself, but they reveal very little which we did not know before, except that the great detective was a storyteller of indifferent merits. All the other writings of Holmes, his book on bees, his monographs on cigar ashes,

174

on the motets of Orlando de Lassus, on the characteristics of hands, are bibliographical rarities of such a transcendental kind that it is hard to find anybody who has actually laid hand on one of them. The only direct information concerning these books comes directly from Watson, who has even given us an occasional quotation. In short, we have to face the bitter fact that Holmes stands to us in the same position as Zeno of Elea or Demsoritus of Abdera, whose deeds have become known to us only through the writings of others, from whom we also have received some few direct quotations.

The analogy to classics is suggestive. The lively figure of Socrates has been preserved to us exclusively through other authors, notably through Plato. But we all know that Plato's Socrates was—well, was Plato's Socrates, and not the original one. True, there is a similarity between Xenophon's Socrates and Plato's, but the Socrates of Aristophanes cuts an entirely different figure. Plato's Socrates did not suspend himself in a basket from the ceiling and study the proboscis of gnats, as did the Socrates of Aristophanes. Can it be that we have in Watson's Holmes but a modern version of Plato's Socrates? Would a modern Aristophanes have drawn an entirely different picture of Holmes, perhaps showing him as a henpecked husband, a quasi-Oriental Yogi, or the bespectacled director of a nudist colony?

We have said that the two stories written by Sherlock Holmes himself do not shed much new light on the real Holmes. Yet, there is a passage in *The Adventure of the Blanched Soldier* which gives food for serious thought. Holmes describes his relation to Watson, and, to tell the cruel truth, is downright nasty about his friend. Moreover, he is nasty without provocation—he is just plain nasty. Now, why should he go out of his way to emphasize that Watson was an absolute ass? Only one reason comes to mind. He was afraid the public would see through an elaborate smoke screen, and conclude that Watson had effaced himself for the glory of Holmes. In other words, Holmes functioned under a complex, an inferiority complex. To counteract it, he did what people with such a complex usually do: he shifted to an opposite position, and endeavored to assert his own masterful superiority. No other conclusion seems possible.

One conclusion leads to another. Watson, for reasons of his

own, must have placed in Holmes's mouth and in Holmes's actions several words and moves which were really his own. An accomplished storyteller, he understood that the public wanted a man with extraordinary abilities, a master-mind, a superman. The present comic books show the same Watsonian understanding of the taste of the reading public. They provide us with Captain Marvel, the Bat Man, the Shadow, Captain Midnight, Superman, and *tutti quanti*. We all love these figures, and spend unforgettable hours listening to their exploits on the radio and reading about them in corners where our friends and children cannot see us, probably because they are doing the same thing in other corners. It may also be that Watson was modest, too modest, and shunned for himself a position of publicity accruing to Holmes for his extraordinary abilities. Whatever it may have been, it is permissible to believe that many a bright idea ascribed to Holmes was really Watson's own.

Even in the published texts, Watson emerges in final analysis as a much better man than he seems to give himself credit for being. When, for instance, did Watson write all these wonderful stories? In these tales, when he is not trailing behind Holmes, he is invariably occupied in loafing, fostering his mysterious wound, or half-heartedly pursuing his medical profession. Here we trap him in some serious understatement of his own abilities. This extraordinary storyteller must have had, moreover, a wonderful memory. How did he remember, often years after the events, the most minute actions of his friend? How was he able to reproduce the subtle reasonings of Holmes? Was he, like a modern war correspondent, always on the job with pencil and notebook? If so, how did he achieve that nice balance between data and deeds when thrown into a situation where he had to shoot it out? Is it not far more likely that Watson did some of his subtle reasoning himself, and that much of the sleuthing which he ascribed to his friend was actually his own?

Here and there this aspect of the truth appears even in the pages of the Canon. In *The Retired Colourman*, Holmes praises Watson's memory for faces. Obviously the truth had here to be told because Watson in this instance was unable to ascribe all things wonderful to Holmes. In some of the other stories Watson contributes substantially to the sleuthing—*vide The Hound of the Baskervilles*—though Watson often allows Holmes to deny that

176

it has contributed to the solution. Careful and critical reading of the text, however, convinces us that Watson's work was an important factor, even in the matter of *The Disappearance of Lady Frances Carfax*. And in other places the same truth obtrudes itself in other forms. It has already been observed by one keen critic that Watson's descriptions of Holmes's shooting ability show clearly that it was not Holmes, but Watson, who was the crack shot. Why, after all, did Holmes insist that Watson should accompany him? Holmes's own explanation, that he burdened himself with Watson's companionship because each development came to him as a perpetual surprise, is very thin, to say the least. The true explanation is, of course, that Holmes needed the additional support of Watson's brains and courage.

Other remarkable things, which have struck Holmesian scholars, can now be seen in their proper light. There exists an abortive theory, promoted by Rex Stout, that Watson was a woman. This theory has been universally rejected, and rightly so. But just the same, the scintillating scholarship of Mr. Stout unearthed some weighty evidence. He based his theory mainly, as will be remembered, on the deep affection which Watson showed for Holmes. Mr. Stout explained it as the affection of a wife for a husband or a sweetheart. Is it not rather the affection of a father for a beloved child? Watson had built up Holmes with the self-effacement of a Sorrel papa; he had helped him along, given him publicity and fame, fed the barbarian with quotations from Horace and Hafiz, protected that poor shot with his own gun, and attributed his own excellent ideas to that already masterful mind. No wonder Watson loved that brilliant but pampered child of his! Let us not forget that when Watson left Holmes near the Reichenbach Fall for a while entirely to his own wits, the poor devil messed up everything and had to disappear from the public eye for three years. It has been observed how eagerly, and how clumsily, Watson tried to clear up the mess Holmes made in that adventure near the fateful Fall. All this points to the existence of a far better Watson than he depicts himself to be, and to Holmes as a prima donna of undoubted talents, basking in the unusually brilliant sunshine artificially produced by an able publicity director.

In order to discover another hint of the real Watson we must search for that spot in the man's character where his own vanity is so strong, his ego so deeply affected, that he simply refuses to yield any of his own merits to another man, be it even his best friend. Such a spot in a man's character is usually his relation to women. And, indeed, on this subject Watson is far from self-effacing. He actually boasts of an experience of women which extends over many nations and three separate continents—no mean achievement indeed. He not only allows Holmes to tell him that women are his—Watson's—domain, but even takes pleasure in relating how Holmes's wits were no match against those of the charming Adler girl. Here he reveals no meek inferiority, but rather a decided cockiness.

And so we see gradually emerging, through the artificial fog, the real Watson: the stalwart veteran warrior and crack shot, the able physician who immediately detects an aortic aneurism, the well-read theoretician, who even knows Dr. Trevelyan's monograph on obscure nervous lesions, the industrious and accomplished storyteller, the brilliant analyst, the congenial companion of Holmes, and the dashing gallant, hero of Sabatini proportions, to boot.

We have little doubt that this estimate of Dr. Watson's merits will be amply confirmed, when objective scholarship at last gains access to the original files of the Sherlockian adventures, even now anxiously guarded in the grim vaults of Cox's Bank at Charing Cross.

—January 1947

Watson, too, had "art in the blood"—the rare ability to
conjure lasting images for his devoted readers. . . .

JOHN H. WATSON—WORD-PAINTER

by H. C. POTTER

JOHN H. WATSON, M.D., has been the subject of countless disser-
tations in The Writings about the Writings. We know him well,
from the tip of his badly-brushed bowler to the soles of his
mud-marred boots, The Good Companion; the loyal friend;
the oft-times obtuse but good-natured bulldog; the perfect
alter ego for The Master.

To my knowledge, however—and yet I cannot help hearing
Holmes's cynical whisper, "It has all been done before"—there
is a facet to The Compleat Watson which has never been given
its just due. I refer to his great skill as "a word-painter" (to bor-
row Mr. D. Martin Dakin's happy phrase[1]).

Let me exclude—without gainsaying—his depiction of grip-
ping action, his deft characterisations (always excepting Americans, white or black), his ability to create turn-of-the-screw
suspense and mounting tension. I limit this study to his considerable skill as a pictorialist and scenic designer; his ability
to word-paint the vivid and memorable *mise en scène* for each
Adventure.

Watson understood the imperative of the master scenic designer; it is not enough to mount the story in an acceptable setting. When the curtain rises the set must instantly evoke the
mood of the play—before a word is said. What Jo Mielziner
achieves time after time in the theatre, so does Watson in
the Saga.

Every devotee of the Canon has in his memory a gallery of
Watson's word-paintings. Unlike the collector of conventional
art, the owner of an authentic Watson is all the more pleased to
know that vast numbers of his *confrères* have the very same picture hanging in their own galleries. Stroll with me through

179

mine, and let me point out some of my favourites. Some of them—indeed, I hope, all of them—will be yours also.

To begin with, here are three of Watson's quick sketches. Time was short and the tempo of the action permitted no prolonged interruption. The effect must be immediate. The label under the first reads:

A STUDY IN SCARLET

"Number 3, Lauriston Gardens wore an ill-omened and minatory look. . . . [It] looked out with three tiers of vacant melancholy windows, which were blank and dreary, save that here and there a 'To Let' sign had developed like a cataract upon the bleared panes."

Succinct and deft, is it not? Hanging next to it:

THE SPECKLED BAND

"The old mansion . . . was of grey, lichen-blotched stone, with a high central portion, and two curving wings like the jaws of a crab. . . ."

An artful simile, reflecting the house's evil, tenacious proprietor. The third sketch is from:

A SCANDAL IN BOHEMIA

Irene Adler's villa in St. John's Wood is evoked in *one word*: " . . . a bijou of a villa."

As Watson sets it down the word is Holmes's, not his own. But I believe the truth of the matter to be that Holmes's original estimate of the villa was a blunt "small," revised by Watson to "bijou" when he had seen it for himself later that day.

We move on to the larger canvases. Much frustration has been experienced by scholars in trying to run down the actual locales of the Adventures. The usual reason for failure is accepted as Watson's desire to "protect his sources." I believe that it is also Watson's irresistible urge to enhance the mood of his setting, rather than just photograph it. If he felt he must forgo verisimilitude, like any good painter he never hesitated. No Andy Warhol's 1000%-accurate Tomato Soup Can for him.

Watson would have painted us a soup can with "the wrong look," a can to set us to brooding, puzzled and suspicious.

The first full-size canvas in my collection is:

THE MAN WITH THE TWISTED LIP

" . . . a long, low room, thick and heavy with the brown opium smoke, and terraced with wooden berths, like the forecastle of an emigrant ship.

"Through the gloom one could dimly catch a glimpse of bodies lying in strange fantastic poses, bowed shoulders, bent knees, heads thrown back and chins pointing upwards, with here and there a dark, lack-lustre eye turned upon the new-comer. Out of the black shadows there glimmered little red circles of light, now bright, now faint, as the burning poison waxed and waned in the bowls of the metal pipes."

Scholars, it is no matter that there was no opium den in Upper Swandam Lane—no Upper Swandam Lane, either. London's East End is all the better for Watson's enhancement: is now, and ever more shall be.

THE GREEK INTERPRETER

The interior of The Myrtles, Beckenham, calls for ominous mystery. Watson obliges, enhancing Mr. Melas' original account, I am sure:

" . . . a coloured gas-lamp . . . turned so low that I could see little save that the hall was of some size and hung with pictures. [The room] appeared to be very richly furnished, but again the only light was afforded by a single lamp, half-way turned down. The chamber was certainly large . . . my feet sank into the car-pet. . . . I caught glimpses of velvet chairs, a high white marble mantelpiece, what seemed to be a suit of Japanese armour at one side of it. There was a chair just under the lamp. . . ."

THE SIGN OF THE FOUR

Two paintings. The first: Thaddeus Sholto's sybaritic living room:

"In that sorry house it looked as out of place as a diamond of the first water in a setting of tarnished brass. The richest and glossiest of curtains and tapestries draped the walls, looped back here and there to expose some richly mounted painting or Oriental vase. The carpet was amber and black, so soft and so thick that the foot sank pleasantly into it, like a bed of moss. Two great tiger skins thrown athwart it increased the suggestion of Eastern luxury as did a huge hookah on a mat in the corner. A lamp in the fashion of a silver dove was hung from an almost invisible wire in the centre of the room. As it burned it filled the air with a subtle and aromatic odour."

The second is a Whistleresque Thames-side landscape, as seen from the police boat:

"As we passed the City, the last rays of the sun were gilding the cross upon the dome of St. Paul's."

Watson's word-painting must surely have been the inspiration for Mr. G. F. Allen's magnificent photograph, reproduced in *The Annotated Sherlock Holmes.*[2]

THE HOUND OF THE BASKERVILLES

I have two. In a sense they are both "motion pictures." In the first the camera is mounted on the wagonette as it "leaves the fertile country behind and beneath us" and gives Watson and young Baskerville their first view of "that forbidding moor."

" . . . in front of us rose the huge expanse of the moor, mottled with gnarled and craggy cairns and tors. A cold wind swept down from it and set us shivering. . . . the grim suggestiveness of the barren waste, the chilling wind, and the darkling sky. . . .

" . . . The road . . . grew bleaker and wilder over huge russet and olive slopes, sprinkled with giant boulders. . . . Suddenly we looked down into a cup-like depression, patched with stunted oaks and firs which had been twisted and bent by the fury of years of storm. Two high, narrow towers rose over the trees. The driver pointed with his whip.

"'Baskerville Hall,' said he.

"Its master had risen and was staring with flushed cheek and shining eyes. A few minutes later we had reached the lodge-gates, a maze of fantastic tracery in wrought iron, with weather-bitten pillars on either side, blotched with lichens. . . . The lodge was a ruin of black granite and bared ribs of rafters. . . .

" . . . we passed into the avenue, where the wheels were hushed amid the leaves, and the old trees shot their branches in a sombre tunnel over our heads. Baskerville shuddered as he looked up the long drive to where the house glimmered like a ghost at the farther end."

The other is a landscape by moonlight. The camera is fixed. The only movement is that of the heavy fog as it advances on Stapleton's cottage from Grimpen Mire.

"It was drifting slowly in our direction, and banked itself up like a wall on that side of us, low, but thick and well defined. The moon shone on it, and it looked like a great shimmering ice-field, with the heads of the distant tors as rocks borne upon its surface. . . . Every minute that white wooly plain which covered one-half of the moor was drifting closer and closer to the house. Already the first thin whisps of it were curling across the golden square of the lighted window. The farther wall of the orchard was already invisible, and the trees were standing out of a swirl of white vapour. As we watched it the fog-wreaths came crawling around both corners of the house and rolled slowly into one dense bank, on which the upper floor and the roof floated like a strange ship upon a shadowy sea."

Move on with me now to what I consider Watson's best single setting:

THE REICHENBACH FALLS

Although he had, of course, the actual falls for a model, the many photographs and the reams of reports from faithful pilgrims attest the fact that Watson indeed transcended the impressive-enough reality.

"It is indeed a fearsome place. The torrent . . . plunges into a tremendous abyss, from which the spray rolls up like the smoke from a burning house. The shaft into which the river hurls itself is an immense cavern, lined with glistening, coal-black rock and narrowing into a creaming, boiling pit of incalculable depth. . . . The long sweep of green water roaring forever down, and the thick flickering curtain of spray hissing forever upwards, turn a man giddy."

Very possibly "the Reichenbach Falls" occupies the pre-eminent position in the galleries of all Holmesian enthusiasts.

A rash statement perhaps, but I believe it will resist serious challenge.

There are others in my collection—notably "The Manor House at Birlstone,"[3] "Poldhu Bay and the Cornish Moors,"[4] and "The Crypt at Shoscombe Old Place." Good as these are, to me they have lesser impact. Actually, after *The Final Problem* the word-paintings begin to dwindle until in *The Case Book* there is none worth memorialising. I find this most interesting in the light of serious doubts that have been raised by revered Canonical scholars who question the Canonicity of *The Case Book* in its entirety. Might not the lack, in this collection, of *any* of Watson's word-paintings be another spoke in that wheel?

Another oddity: We have no complete word-painting for the setting we all know and love the best, 221B Baker Street! Watson is content to give us the (sometimes contradictory) details of the suite in driblets scattered throughout the Saga. But exactly what it looked like as a whole—indeed, exactly where it was!— is still somewhat theoretical. Baring-Gould's charming chapter in *The Annotated* is in fact only a compendium of Canonical controversy, hedged with many "we thinks," "might-have-beens," and "may-have-beens," and "assumings." The only comfortable attitude to take would seem to be Pirandello's: Right You Are if You Think You Are. To each his own picture, let that suffice.

At the far end of my gallery hangs my favourite, a perfect example of what I choose to call Instant Mood. Although this word-painting has really nothing to do with the Adventure[5] it introduces, I will wager that when the name of Sherlock Holmes is mentioned something of this particular picture will come to mind—even if only subconsciously. Of all the beginnings of all the Adventures, this is the perfect overture:

"It was a wild, tempestuous night towards the close of November. Holmes and I sat together in silence all evening, he engaged with a powerful lens deciphering the remains of the original inscription upon a palimpsest, I deep in a recent treatise upon surgery. Outside the wind howled down Baker Street, while the rain beat fiercely against the windows. It was strange there, in the very depths of town, with ten miles of man's handiwork on every side of us, to feel the iron grip of Nature, and to be conscious that to the huge elemental forces all London was no more than the molehills that dot the fields. I walked to the window and looked out on the deserted street. The occasional lamps gleamed on the expanse of muddy road and shining pavement. A single cab was splashing its way from the Oxford Street end."

—June 1976

NOTES

1. *The Annotated Sherlock Holmes*, ed. W. S. Baring-Gould, II, 690 n.
2. I, 665.
3. *The Valley of Fear.*
4. *The Devil's Foot.*
5. *The Golden Pince-Nez.*

Were it not for the subtle inconsistencies and errors in the Sherlockian Canon, there never would have been Baker Street Irregulars outside of the pages of the Holmes stories. Were such errors the merest accident— or could they have been deliberate?

DON'T BLAME WATSON

by W. S. HALL

HAVING FINISHED, last night, all that was left of a bottle of Oude Geneva, I found myself in a good mood for brooding. And having at the same time finished reading for, I believe, the twelfth time *A Study in Scarlet*, I started brooding about that and the succeeding stories authored by John H. Watson, M.D. I was wondering how really to account for the long succession of inconsistencies, anachronisms, and contradictions in the stories on the part of an author as clear-thinking, as sane, stolid, and orderly as Dr. Watson. And then it came to me. All this confusion was not accident, but well-considered design. And of this confusion, Dr. Watson was *not* the author.

The first edition of *A Study in Scarlet* proclaims it to be "a reprint from the reminiscences of John H. Watson, M.D., late of the Army Medical Department." No copy of the original appearance of these reminiscences is known to exist, and it is safe to assume that they never saw print. No publisher would have them, apparently, for, in the first place, the author was young and unknown—too young, in fact, to have accumulated any reminiscences worth while—and on top of that the entire opus was altogether too long and wordy. It is well known that about this time, fortunately for him, Watson made the acquaintance of another struggling medico named Arthur Conan Doyle, who added to his meagre income by playing around the fringes of the publishing world as a literary agent. Watson spoke to Doyle about his lack of success with his initial effort in the written word, and Doyle, in true literary-agent fashion, demanded to see the "reminiscences" at once. Watson accordingly turned over his dog-eared manuscript to Doyle, who lost no time in abstracting from it the only portion that failed to put him to sleep—namely, the short story entitled *A Study in Scarlet*.

The appearance of this fragment in *Beeton's Christmas Annual* for 1887 hardly shook the literary marketplace to its foundations, and seemed to prove that perhaps the world was not yet prepared for anything further from the same author. Nevertheless, the one pound sterling, representing his 20% commission, whetted Dr. Doyle's appetite for more. More came, and then more and more still, and the audience and the downpayments and the royalties and the commissions all grew beyond the wildest dreams of the two collaborators.

I use the term collaborators advisedly, but I think it is plain enough now what happened to each succeeding manuscript. As he wrote the final word of each story, Watson, with lessening zeal and exhausted by his effort, took a deep breath, and, posting the pages to Doyle, returned briefly to his neglected practice of medicine. Doyle himself set about reading each new Sherlock Holmes adventure, and we may suppose that he took the liberty of touching it up with a bit of editing.

By this time Doyle had become a well-established author in his own right, and in the field of his own choosing, and his earnings, plus his fees as Watson's agent, made the future look bright indeed. But what about this future? Watson had no children, and seemed unable to take money matters very seriously. But there were three little Doyles, a girl and two physically vigorous lads who as yet gave no evidence of being able to make ends meet later on in life. How to make assurance doubly sure, not only with respect to his own books and short stories, but also with regard to these Sherlock Holmes trifles which Watson was being difficult about? How perpetuate them; how keep them going year after year when he and Watson would no longer be around to worry about them or about anything else?

It occurred to Dr. Doyle—and one must admire the man's shrewdness and uncanny ability to peer into the future—that if certain changes could be made in Watson's stories—slight, hardly noticeable changes—they would pass muster with the proof-readers, but, if properly done, they would puzzle certain avid readers of the future. Thence would follow letters to the press, acrimonious expressions of opinion, and, inevitably, the formation of one or more societies, say like the Browning groups, who would meet and spread, and, in spreading, nourish the demand for the stories. The sales would increase and double, and the royalties—ah, the royalties would go on and on, gloriously!

And so it came about that a wound moved about in Watson's anatomy, that his name changed from John to James and back again, that two brothers of Moriarty of evil fame had the same Christian name, and that Watson got all tangled up in his dates, his places, and his wives. Yes, thought Dr. Doyle, with his pencil poised over his friend's latest effort, I can see these little groups springing up all over the world—in London, in New York, in Chicago, Sydney, and Copenhagen—in fact wherever Holmes is selling. Verily "I hear of Sherlock everywhere." They won't have any trouble finding names for themselves—"The Baker Street Irregulars," or something like that—or maybe they will take their names from the titles of the stories themselves.

Years later, Sir Arthur Conan Doyle began to look even more seriously than ever into the future; in fact for the closing years of his long life nothing else seemed to concern him. He had not seen Holmes or Watson for years, and the stories of the adventures, with which he had so much to do, concerned him even less. He convinced himself, and he convinced others, that he would still be with us after, as it is called, death.

If that is so, then—remembering the part he played in the Irregulars' coming into being—let us bid him welcome!

—April 1953

*We know that Dr. Watson had an experience of women
that spanned three continents. That he appreciated the
ladies' infinite sartorial variety as well becomes
apparent in this little tour de force by Christopher
Morley writing in the persona of Jane Nightwork. . . .*

WATSON À LA MODE

by JANE NIGHTWORK

WATSON WAS COUTURIER at heart. I don't need to remind you
that he was first attracted to Mary Morstan because she was
"dainty, well gloved, and dressed in the most perfect taste."
What he admired about her neat tailleur of grayish beige was
that it was "untrimmed and unbraided." He so approved the
small turban "relieved by a suspicion of white feather in the side"
that he watched it from the window as Miss Morstan went down
Baker Street. It was not until a later occasion, when Mary sat
under the lamplight in the basket chair, dressed in what the Rev.
Herrick would have called her "tiffany," that Watson learned she
did the dressmaking in Mrs. Forrester's household. Shyly he
praised the "white diaphanous material, with a little touch of
scarlet at the neck and waist." She replied "I made it myself,"
and what more surely enlists a prudent man's enthusiasm?

Watson's detailed description of Miss Mary Sutherland, in the
Case of Identity, was of course because he was so horrified by
her *mauvaise tenue*. The hat was "preposterous," slate-colored
straw with a huge red feather; the black jacket was beaded and
fringed and had purple plush at the neck and sleeves; the fur
boa and muff[1] were undoubtedly scraggly. The gray gloves
were worn through. The dress (above the unmated shoes) was a
"brown darker than coffee." Darker than Mrs. Hudson's coffee,
does that mean, implying that it was not brewed strong enough
for Watson's taste? Anyhow, poor Miss Sutherland's costume
horrified Watson's taste in millinery and mode. It was a taste
keenly trained at that time, for he had not long been married.

As far back as *Silver Blaze* (1881) Watson became aware of the
financial possibilities of the dressmaking business. He made no
special comment at the time on Mme. Lesurier's bill, which included an item of 22 guineas for a single costume, the "dove-
colored silk with ostrich feather trimming" for Straker's fancy

189

lady, but we may be sure he made a mental note. In the early cases we hear little of falbalas and fanfreluches; even poor Helen Stoner's frill of black lace was not mentioned as glamour, but because it hid the five livid bruises on her wrist. But see, after the meeting with Mary Morstan, how much more technical, realistic (even carnal) the Doctor's female observations become. Just for the fun of parallel columns, let us compare a few of Watson's comments with Holmes's more delicate and spiritual remarks about the same clients:

HOLMES	WATSON
(Irene Adler)	
The daintiest thing under a bonnet. A lovely woman, with a face that a man might die for.	Her superb figure outlined against the lights.
(Mrs. Neville St. Clair)	
This dear little woman.	A little blonde woman . . . clad in light mousseline de soie, with a touch of fluffy pink chiffon at her neck and wrists . . . her figure outlined against the flood of light.
(Violet Smith)	
There is a spirituality about the face.	Young and beautiful, tall, graceful, and queenly.
(Anna Coram)	
Attired like a lady.	At the best she could have never been handsome.
(Lady Hilda Trelawney Hope)	
The fair sex is your department.	The most lovely woman in London . . . subtle delicate charm, beautiful coloring of that exquisite head . . . white gloves . . . framed for an instant in the open door . . . dwindling frou-frou of skirts.

Characteristic of Holmes's comments is his description of Violet de Merville: "a snow image on a mountain; beautiful with ethereal other-world beauty." Typical of Watson is his note on Grace Dunbar: "a brunette, tall, with a noble figure." He liked them framed in doorways, and preferably lit from behind. Certainly Watson would not so often have said "I have seldom seen," or "One of the most lovely I have ever seen," unless it was feminine contour that preoccupied him. At the Abbey Grange, Lady Brackenstall elicited his double instinct for both form and garb:—

> I have seldom seen so graceful a figure, so womanly a presence, and
> so beautiful a face—blonde, golden-haired, blue-eyed . . . a loose dress-
> ing gown of blue and silver . . . a black sequin-covered dinner dress.

These boudoir details filled Watson's mind so that he apparently gave no medical attention to the hideous plum-colored
swelling over one blue eye.

Watson's cotquean regard for galloons and trimmings was
more discreet in his own home. Of his wife's friend Mrs. Isa
Whitney he only remarks that she was "clad in some dark-
coloured stuff." How much livelier when off on the road with
Holmes! See Miss Turner of Boscombe Valley: "One of the
most lovely young women that I have ever seen in my life . . .
violet eyes shining, pink flush, her natural reserve lost." There
were moments perhaps when Watson thought that loss of natural female reserve an excellent thing. And was not his special
sympathy for bright freckle-faced Violet Hunter because of the
unpleasant electric-blue dress (again "a sort of beige") she had
to wear?

Watson's silences are sometimes as revealing as anything he
says. He was too shrewd to argue against Holmes's frequent
foolish complaints that women's motives are inscrutable. The
behavior of the woman at Margate who had no powder on
her nose (v. *The Second Stain*) would have been no surprise to
Watson. If the Doctor had written the story of the Lion's Mane
we would surely have seen beautiful Maud Bellamy in clearer
circumstance. She had "the soft freshness of the Downlands in
her delicate coloring," writes Holmes (in the new vein of sentiment that bees and Sussex inspired), but if only Watson had
been there we might at least have seen "a touch of white at the
neck and wrists."

Am I too fanciful to think that good old John Hamish Watson
was the first Victorian to do justice to the earliest white-collar
girls? Do you remember Laura Lyons of Coombe Tracy whose
fingers "played nervously over the stops of her Remington
typewriter"?[2] Her cheeks were "flushed with the exquisite bloom
of the brunette, the dainty pink which lurks at the heart of the
sulphur rose." Watson never made more candid confession
than then: "I was simply conscious that I was in the presence of
a very handsome woman." It was a consciousness warmly and
widely diffused, and always double, for the creature herself and

for her covering. He spoke with equal enthusiasm, at the same time, of Beryl Stapleton "with her perfect figure and elegant dress."

There are other passages, but I have said enough to remind students of Watson's specific interest in miladiana, "over many nations and three separate continents," a theme which few but Mr. Elmer Davis[3] have ever examined candidly, and which is so murky that it has even led to the gruesome suggestion of Mr. Rex Stout in his atrocious venture "Watson Was a Woman."[4] It has glowwormed others into the uxorious theory that Watson was thrice married. My own notion is offered only as a speculum into the unknowable.

Mary Morstan, a clever dressmaker, found time on her hands after she and Watson moved into the house in Paddington. The medical practice was not lucrative (we know that their slavey Mary Jane was of a very humble order), there were no children, and John Hamish ("James") kept up his frequent sorties with Holmes. Watson, with his special interest in dressmaking, encouraged Mary in her ambition to start a little business of her own. The Agra pearls were sufficient capital. Mrs. Cecil Forrester and friends were sure customers, and the business spread. What else was the needlework which Mrs. Watson laid down that evening when her husband, giving his first yawn, heard Kate Whitney at the bell? Begun at home, by '89 or '90 the business needed seamstress help and an atelier. Watson would not wish his friends to know that his wife had gone into trade, so for her business style she adopted some name of fantasy which has not yet been identified. A business directory of London in the early '90s would undoubtedly shew some Mme. Agra, or Mme. Boulangère, or Mme. Medico, or Morstan Styles, *confections de dames,* doing business a little west of the haute couture. The bills were not as steep perhaps as those of Lesurier on Bond Street, but it was a sound middle-class connection. And Watson, though he had countenanced this, was horribly ashamed.

What else would account for the Doctor's contradictory and baffling references? Mary was properly fond of him, but she had her own life to live, without benefit of Sherlock. The "sad bereavement" to which Watson referred when Holmes came back in '94 was not bereavement by death, but the fact that

Mary and he had separated. Divorce, even if desired, was socially impossible in the holy deadlock of those days. Watson, I have pointed out before ("Dr. Watson's Secret," in *221B*), had a sly ("pawky") camouflage of his own. As time and success went on, Mary wearied of giving her whole time to dressmaking; and Watson, at the age of 50, even grew a little fatigued with Holmes. Watson's so-called second marriage was when he and Mary decided to resume mutual bed and board. So Watson's second wife was actually his first wife; and there never was a third.

Holmes was too genuine a philosopher to have called Watson's first marriage "selfish." He knew it was part of the destiny of average mankind. He did think it selfish when, after ten years of separation, Watson and his wife decided to make a second try. So when John and Mary set up housekeeping afresh in Queen Anne Street about the autumn of 1902, Holmes began looking for property on the Sussex Downs. Mary farmed out the dressmaking business and said she had always wanted to write. Her first (and last) attempt was *The Mazarin Stone*.

Mary Morstan's influence on women's wear was not lost. Morstan Styles (or whatever the trade name was) became a limited company and she and John still drew dividends. In 1914 the Doctor, long relieved of money anxieties, was "still the same blithe boy."[5] The business spread to the U.S. after the First War. How else do you account for *Morstyle Frocks, Inc.,* in the Manhattan telephone book; or *Morston Textiles* (Morstan & Watson), ibid.

—January 1946

NOTES

1. Is not H. W. Bell in error (*Sherlock Holmes and Dr. Watson*, p. 63) in calling them feather boa and feather muff?
2. *The Hound of the Baskervilles.*
3. "The Emotional Geology of Baker Street," in *221B*.
4. In *Profile by Gaslight*.
5. *His Last Bow.*

*Among A. Conan Doyle's most famous and effective
works is* The Hound of the Baskervilles. *Taking a
more customary literary critical tack than is common
among* JOURNAL *contributors, Mr. Watt explains
why. . . .*

THE LITERARY CRAFT OF
THE HOUND OF THE BASKERVILLES

by DONALD J. WATT

DOYLE'S BEST-KNOWN piece of longer fiction, *The Hound of the
Baskervilles,* is a particularly good example of careful literary
craftsmanship in a popular story. Unlike the work of pioneer-
ing British novelists writing at the same time as Doyle, the masterpiece of Sherlock Holmes's creator contains no startlingly
new subject matter, no revolutionary approaches to narration,
no manifesto of art for art's sake. *The Hound of the Baskervilles* is
not concerned with the mythic determinism of Thomas Hardy's
Tess of the D'Urbervilles, the psychological impressionism of
Joseph Conrad's *Lord Jim,* or the hedonistic aestheticism of Oscar
Wilde's *The Picture of Dorian Gray.* Instead, Doyle's book offers a
ripping good yarn which is related by means of some astutely
manipulated conventional literary devices. *The Hound of the Baskervilles* makes effective use of at least three important aspects
of literature: structure, mood, and metaphor. It is Doyle's
achievement in the book that he knits these three literary features closely together to present a narrative that is both mobile
and unified.

The structure of *The Hound* is a tripartite one which stems
from Doyle's use of Watson as a foil as well as a companion for
Holmes. Doyle's uses of Watson in the Holmes repertoire have
been discussed in earlier pages of this JOURNAL and need not
concern us here. What does concern us, though, is the fact that
Doyle establishes Watson's position at the outset of the book
and, at the same time, anticipates the overriding form of his
presentation. In the opening chapter of his story Doyle, with
typical economy, sets up the contrast between Holmes and
Watson. Examining the stick left behind by Mortimer, Holmes

invites Watson to deduce what he can about its owner. Holmes then proceeds to deflate Watson by extending and adjusting his inferences in a series of remarkable observations. Holmes's analysis is corroborated shortly by the appearance of Mortimer, at the end of the chapter, to seek assistance in the Baskerville mystery.

Doyle's first chapter thereby anticipates the process of the entire novel. Chapters 1–5 introduce the subject of the investigation (the mystery of Baskerville Hall); Chapters 6–11 bring Watson to Devonshire to learn what he can of the mystery; and Chapters 12–15 find Holmes on the scene to hone the truth out of Watson's uneven judgment of the case and to bring about his own unerring solution. In this sense, then, Doyle's first chapter gives us a miniature mystery—the mystery of Mortimer's cane—which is a microcosmic reflection of the process he uses in resolving the far larger issue, the mystery of Baskerville Hall.

Yet Doyle's structure is more subtle than this. Having impressed the reader by Holmes's ability with the cane, Doyle must now suggest the prowess of his opponent. Doyle accomplishes this in the first third of the book, especially in Chapters 4 and 5, by creating another mystery, the mystery of the stranger in London, which Holmes *fails* to solve. Holmes realises that someone is following Sir Henry and attempts to discover the tracker's identity. He tries to pursue three lines or threads, three leads—the possibility that the bearded man is Barrymore, Cartwright's search of London hotels for cut sheets of *The Times*, and John Clayton's description of his spying fare. Doyle concludes his chapter on "Three Broken Threads" with Holmes's tribute to "a foeman who is worthy of our steel" and with his apprehensions about sending Watson into a thoroughly dangerous situation in Devonshire. This chapter is the last one in the London section of the novel. Hence the first major structural division of Doyle's book gives us two mysteries which serve together as an introduction for the third, the generating mystery of the tale.

At this point we can begin to consider the way Doyle weaves mood into his carefully patterned novel. The major contrast in setting for the book is, of course, the contrast between comfortable, civilised, orderly London and the wild, savage, unruly moors. Doyle's structuring of the book allows him to make full use of this contrast by severing the vulnerable Watson from Holmes. One thing which adds measurably to the reader's suspense as Watson approaches Devonshire is the realisation that we are now in the wilderness, on the home ground of the cunning opponent. As the wagonette carrying Watson, Mortimer, and Sir Henry tops a rise, Doyle describes "the huge expanse of the moor, mottled with gnarled and craggy cairns and tors." They have just been informed that the vicious murderer, Selden, is lurking on that "desolate plain," "hiding in a burrow like a wild beast, his heart full of malignancy against the whole race which had cast him out." Doyle writes: "It needed but this to complete the grim suggestiveness of the barren waste, the chilling wind, and the darkling sky. Even Baskerville fell silent and pulled his overcoat more closely around him." One is reminded of the foreboding moors of Hardy and of Emily Brontë, and, though Sir Henry is a product of that mastering landscape, Watson is not; we are led to wonder how Holmes's assistant can possibly survive in such a hostile environment.

Doyle accordingly exploits a mood which was much in vogue in British literature toward the close of the nineteenth century. The threat of a possible reversion to primitivism was a key notion in England during Doyle's middle years. Extending as far as Charles Pearson's sociological study, *English National Life and Character: A Forecast,* the *fin de siècle* idea of the twilight of rational, civilised humanity appears, with various emphases, in works as diverse as Hardy's *Jude the Obscure,* Stevenson's *Dr. Jekyll and Mr. Hyde,* and H. G. Wells's *The War of the Worlds.* When Watson makes his first report to Holmes from Baskerville Hall, Doyle strums a dark chord in the mind of the late Victorian reading public: "The longer one stays here, the more does the spirit of the moor sink into one's soul, its vastness, and also its grim charm. When you are once out upon its bosom you have left all traces of modern England behind you, but, on the other hand, you are conscious everywhere of the homes and work of the prehistoric people." This prehistoric setting, filled with "huge monoliths" and "grey stone huts," threatens to render Watson's ethical value system invalid. Watson is schooled in Holmes's scientific method, but the reader senses, with much apprehension, that the inscrutable moor will defy any intrusion by modern man. T. H. Huxley, some few years before *The Hound of the Baskervilles* was published, delivered a well-known lecture called "Evolution and Ethics," wherein he argued that man's puny, artificial ethical process was merely a temporary protective bulwark against the supreme powers of the cosmic process, and the reader responds with dismay to Watson's precarious situation.

Thus, when Holmes finally appears on the moor at the end of Chapter 11 (the beginning of the book's third, and last, major division), it is most appropriate that we see him as the ordering principle of the story. Doyle does not describe Holmes as such in so many words, but rather he alludes to a pattern of metaphors which further illustrates the economy of his craft. In brief, Doyle derives one of his most effective figures from the very moor on which he places his characters, and then juxtaposes that figure against one which is a favourite of Holmes's. Miss Stapleton intercepts Watson as he returns from Merripit House in Chapter 7. As Watson questions her about her concern for Sir Henry, he exclaims: "Please, please be frank with me, Miss Stapleton, for ever since I have been here I have been conscious of shadows all round me. Life has become like that great Grimpen Mire, with little green patches everywhere into which one may sink and with no guide to point the track." The bogs of the moor impress Watson deeply as emblems of the murkey, ominous enigma of the Baskerville case. Watson is plainly out of his element, floundering, stumbling in the dark. Later, in his second report to Holmes, Watson thinks he has discovered the reason for Stapleton's opposition to Henry's interest in Beryl. Watson accepts at face value Stapleton's explanation to Henry that he was too attached to his sister to consider him as a suitor. "So there is one of our small mysteries cleared up," Watson proudly writes to Holmes. "It is something to have touched bottom anywhere in this bog in which we are floundering." But Watson is, of course, in error, just as he was earlier mistaken about the initials on Mortimer's cane. In effect, Watson is incapable of confronting the mire. Unaided, he would be as helpless as the doomed pony of Chapter 7.

When Holmes appears, then, in the climactic part of the

story, Doyle equips him with a figure by which he resists the amorphous bog. In that same passage where he claims to have "touched bottom," Watson exultantly passes on "to another thread which I have extricated out of the tangled skein." Watson is echoing Holmes's figure earlier, when Holmes finds himself in London with three broken threads. By the time Holmes makes his appearance on the moor, though, he has more than a collection of threads. He has a net. Watson senses the presence of Holmes in a net metaphor even before Holmes reveals himself in the hut: "Always there was this feeling of an unseen force, a fine net drawn round us with infinite skill and delicacy, holding us so lightly that it was only at some supreme moment that one realized that one was indeed entangled in its meshes." The net becomes Holmes's figure, the way he envisions his pursuit and entrapment of Stapleton. Holmes tells Watson in Chapter 12 that "My nets are closing upon him, even as his are upon Sir Henry. . . ." Stapleton has used the impenetrable bog as a refuge while hunting Sir Henry. Stapleton is as deceptively dangerous as the mire, and he threatens to pull Sir Henry under. But now Holmes is "fixing the nets" to ensnare Stapleton and to resolve the fen-like enigma of Baskerville Hall. "We have him, Watson, we have him," Holmes declares in Chapter 13, "and I dare swear that before to-morrow night he will be fluttering in our net as helpless as one of his own butterflies. . . . The nets are all in place, and the drag is about to begin." Appropriately, Stapleton eludes Holmes's net only to be caught, it seems, in the swamp of his own evil cunning. The net figure suggests Holmes's superiority over the bogs of crime, his ordering power over the dark, moor-like regions of men's felonious minds. It is indeed fitting that Doyle, at the close, returns to the Baker Street world of logic and civility.

Doyle thereby weaves the fabric of his story as carefully as Holmes puts together his cases. It is too easy to forget that the man who creates Holmes is the same man who, with Watson's narrative assistance, relates the tales. In *The Hound of the Baskervilles* Doyle presents a fully developed yarn. The structuring of the plot carries the reader smoothly from Mortimer's cane to Stapleton's bog. The contrasting environments of sophisticated London and the primeval moor intensify the threat of lurking evil most effectively. And the figures of the mire and the net reinforce Doyle's theme tellingly at crucial junctures of the story line. Doyle's literary craft in *The Hound of the Baskervilles* reminds us that, in the select world of high-quality detective fiction, he is himself "a foeman who is worthy of our steel."

—December 1972

If the story of the Baskerville Hound sometimes has the sound of epic verse, there is a very good reason for it, argues Ms. Herzog. . . .

THE CENTO OF THE BASKERVILLES

edited by EVELYN A. HERZOG

THIS ARTICLE is a contribution to the study of John Hamish Watson, novelist and poet. Until recently, serious scholarship has concentrated on Watson's prose compositions: not without reason, since they are his only published works. At this time, however, it has become possible to uncover and present for further study fragments of a hitherto unknown poetic work by Watson, the verse epyllion,[1] *The Hound of the Baskervilles*. As my researches show, it is beyond doubt that Watson originally intended to cast the story of the hound in this dramatic verse form.

The verse *Hound* was never published, however; perhaps never even finished. The reason for this cannot as yet be stated with certainty: it may have been caused by Holmes's disapproval[2] of so aesthetic a treatment of this important professional case, or caused by the discouragement of Watson's literary agent, in doubt of the work's reception by the public; it may have been simply that Watson's muse deserted him.

Nonetheless, certain sections of the poem had been completed before the project was abandoned, and Watson was evidently loath to let them disappear entirely. The story of the Baskerville mystery had to be given to the public eventually; when it was, it was in the form of a short novel. With his earlier drafts at hand, Watson lifted phrases, lines, even groups of lines from the poetry and worked them into the prose. Naturally, it is difficult to identify individual phrases as having passed from poetry to prose and that demanding task has not been attempted in this preliminary work. Entire lines, on the other hand, are more easily located. A considerable number of these lines of blank verse have been found in the prose *Hound*. These have been examined carefully and regrouped in the dramatic passages which they must originally have formed.[3]

200

In this edition not one word that Watson penned has been moved from its place in its line, although punctuation has necessarily been realtered to conform to the original. Every student of the *Hound* will recognise the familiar lines, some of which have found places in the final prose version far different from those for which they had originally been composed. For those who fail to recognise every line, a list of the pages (in the Doubleday one-volume edition) on which each line can be found is supplied in the right-hand margin.

The work of Holmesian and Watsonian scholarship on this poem has just begun. The present work does not claim to be complete, the compiler realising only too well how much of the narrative remains unre-created. The rest of the Canon remains to be explored for other fragments from the pen of the poet Watson. Further studies will certainly focus on Watson's skill as a poet. Even at this early point in reconstruction it can be seen that his prosody is not faultless; the originality of conception of a detective story in verse outweighs this defect, however, at least in the present editor's mind.

In its present state, the reconstructed verse *Hound* consists, besides a fragmentary preface, of the last part of the story: the confrontation with the hound, the hunt for Stapleton, and the recapitulation at Baker Street. Identification of the speakers is made in the left-hand margin. These include: SH—Sherlock Holmes; JW—Watson as character in the drama; Narr.— Watson as narrator of the tale; HB—Henry Baskerville; JM— James Mortimer; BS—Beryl Stapleton. Without further introduction, then, the cento version of *The Hound of the Baskervilles*:

INTRODUCTORY SECTION

Narr.:	If I have set it down, it is because	675
	that which is clearly known hath less terror	675
	than that which is but hinted at and guessed:	675
	but I will tell you all and you shall judge.	716

ON THE MOOR. HOLMES, WATSON, BASKERVILLE.

Narr.:	The young heir glanced round with a gloomy face.	702
	That lonely walk upon the ill-omened moor	755
	was weighing heavily upon his mind.	755

201

HB:	"I tell you straight, sir, that I don't like it.	731
	Look at the noises on the moor at night:	732
	there's not a man would cross it after sundown.	732
	Glad I shall be to be quit of it all."	732
SH:	Said Holmes, "The rest of our work must be done	758
	and every moment is of importance.	758
	It is essential that you should do it."	751
Narr.:	Sir Henry put his hand upon my shoulder.	718
	I may say that I was his personal friend.	673
HB:	"Give me another mouthful of that brandy	758
	and I shall be ready for anything."	758
Narr.:	The stars shone cold and bright, while a half-moon	756
	bathed the whole scene in a soft, uncertain light,	756
	like some fantastic landscape in a dream.	700
	The barren scene, the sense of loneliness,	738
	the mystery and urgency of my task,	738
	the heavy silence of the windless night:	743
	my nerves thrilled with anticipation.	754
JW:	"The fact is that our friend the baronet,	713
	poor fellow, has enough to fight against	728
	without my putting more upon his track.	728
	The exact nature of the problem is . . . ?"	673
SH:	"It seems to me that I have spoken quite	688
	enough about the little that I know.	688
	We may expect great changes to begin,	717
	but I'm not easy in my mind about it."	698
JW:	"Are you sure of this, Holmes? How do you know?"	742
SH:	"You don't believe it, do you, Watson?"	
JW:	"No.	724
	I have no means of checking you," said I.[4]	671
	"A spectral hound which leaves material footmarks?	727
	It is incredible, impossible!"	727
SH:	"Twice I have with my own ears heard the sound,	727
	from miles away, over yonder, I think."	724
JW:	"And yet it would be hardly possible . . . ."	762
Narr.:	But when I came to think the matter over	718
	it became increasingly plain to me.	678
JW:	"But where could such a hound lie concealed, where	727
	did it get its food, where did it come from,	727
	how was it that no one saw it by day?"	727
Narr.:	A long deep mutter, then a rising howl,	724
	the whole air throbbing with it, strident, wild!	724
	Then the sad moan in which it died away.	724
JW:	"What was it? What, in Heaven's name, was it?"	757
Narr.:	We stood straining our ears, but nothing came.	724
	There is an opening between two trees:	717
	there stood a foul thing, a great black beast,	675

shaped like a hound, yet larger than any hound	675
that ever mortal eye has rested on;	675
the small, deep-set, cruel eyes were ringed with fire.	757
Grasping my pistol, my mind paralyzed,	756
I was too far away to be of use.	718
Blindly we ran through the gloom, blundering	743
against boulders, forcing our way through gorse,	743
hard upon the footsteps of our friend.	757
In front of us as we flew up the track	757
ran mute behind such a hound of hell	675
as God forbid should ever be at my heels:	675
the frightful thing which was hunting him down.	757
Then Holmes and I both fired together, and	757
the creature gave a hideous howl which showed	757
the giant hound was dead. Sir Henry lay	757
insensible where he had fallen. We	757
saw that there was no sign of a wound and	757
he was still ghastly pale and trembling,	758
his face white in the moonlight, his hands raised.	757

HB:	"God bless you, sir, and thank you from my heart!"	728
JW:	"I shall be very glad to have you back	698
	under the care of Dr. Mortimer."	759

ENTER JAMES MORTIMER

Narr.:	"Halloa!" cried Dr. Mortimer. "What is this?	701
	What would you advise me to do with him?"	681
SH:	"Go to your room, you two, and we shall talk	723
	further about this matter in the morning;	723
	the matter is a very private one."	735
JM:	"We'll sit up in my room to-night and wait."	717
Narr.:	On the advice of Dr. Mortimer	763
	he was told by the latter all details.	763
	The restoration of his shattered nerves	761
	was simple and direct, although to us	761
	it all appeared exceedingly complex.	761
SH:	"I feared that some disaster might occur!	706
	This man has disappeared!"	
JW:	"And has escaped?	764
	Where is he? He shall answer for this deed!"	744
SH:	"We have betrayed ourselves and lost our man."	691
JW:	"I fail to see how you could have done more."	691
SH:	"But that is no use to us for the moment."	691
JW:	"Who was the man? I have not an idea."	690
SH:	"Mr. Stapleton, the 'naturalist'—	678
	no other supposition could explain	764
	our case, and now we only want our man.	758

	Another day shall not have passed before	732
	I have done all that man can do to reach	732
	a complete knowledge of the whole business!	765
	I tell you, Watson, this time we have got	698
	a foeman who is worthy of our steel,	698
	a foil as quick and supple as my own.	697
	If I could lay my hands upon that man . . . !"	727

ENTER BERYL STAPLETON

Narr.:	Two frightened eyes were looking up at us,	757
	I gazed with interest and some surprise.	749
SH:	"But, first of all, I must keep you in touch:	713
	the lady is his wife and not his sister."	742
JW:	"Then we may find the lady of service." [5]	742
Narr.:	"You bear him no good will, madam," said Holmes.	759
	"Tell us, then, where we shall find him. If you	759
	have ever aided him in evil, help us."	759
BS:	"He frightened me into remaining silent."	753
SH:	"Quite so. But you had your suspicions?"	753
BS:	"Well, sir, I thought no good could come of it;	729
	there was a lurking devil in his eyes.	749
	There is but one place where he can have fled:	759
	the stone huts where the old folk used to live."	732
JW:	"What deep and earnest purpose can he have	732
	to go into so horrible a place?"	708
SH:	"We cannot doubt, from what we know of him	766
	like most clever criminals, he may be	747
	too confident in his own cleverness.	747
	I am inclined to think that Stapleton	764
	would risk his life alone upon the moor."	744
BS:	"How can he see the guiding wands to-night?	759
	We planted them together, he and I.	759
	If I could only have plucked them out to-day,	759
	indeed you would have had him at your mercy.	759
	You should not go alone upon the moor;	718
	no practical good could result from it;	678
	misfortune will befall you if you do!"	699
JW:	"Bring home the guilt to the real murderer!"	762
Narr.:	But the shadows were thick upon the moor	743
	which tapered out into the widespread bog	759
	and nothing moved upon its dreary face	743
	of the man who called himself Stapleton.	761
	Over the wide expanse there was no sound.	738
SH:	"That is the great Grimpen Mire," said he.	707

	"Watson, what do you think of this new light?	729
	He may find his way in, but never out.	759
	No chance of finding footsteps in the mire.	760
	Stapleton never reached that island of	760
	refuge towards which he struggled through the fog.	760
	Down in the foul slime of the huge morass	760
	there is this naturalist Stapleton."	699

EPILOGUE. HOLMES, WATSON.

JW:	Safe and sound in Baker Street once more,	698
	I had a mind to speak to him about it.	717
	I took the chance to ask him a few questions.	731
JW:	"What is the crime and how was it committed?	684
	It all appeared exceedingly complex."	761
SH:	"It would be treating you unfairly not	729
	to tell you all that I know about the	729
	clear case against this very wily man,	754
	wary and cunning to the last degree;	744
	without referring to my notes, I can.	766
	At least it is not difficult to find out	671
	a few particulars about the man.	671
	My inquiries show beyond all question that	761
	the family portrait did not lie, and that	761
	this fellow was indeed a Baskerville,	761
	and found that only two lives intervened	762
	between him and a valuable estate,	762
	for whose sake he has done all that he has.	723
	What further inferences may we draw?	760
	Do none suggest themselves? You know my methods."	670
JW:	"I don't profess to understand it yet."	693
SH:	"The fact is that our friend the baronet	713
	himself told him about the family hound[6]	762
	(natural that the subject should come up)	761
	and he was ready to use any tool.	762
	A flash of genius upon his part:	762
	that huge black creature, with its flaming jaws.	763
	He brought it down by the North Devon line	762
	(it must indeed have been a dreadful sight)	763
	and so prepared the way for his own death.	762
	There was a circle of the old stone huts;	738
	in one of these a staple and a chain	760
	showed where the animal had been confined.	760
	Of course, so far as his concealment goes,	713
	he dared not leave her[7] long out of his sight	763
	and only used the hut upon the moor	765

when it was necessary to be near	765
a safe hiding-place for the creature here.	762
It was for this reason that he took her	763
some article of Sir Henry's attire—	764
the means of setting him upon his track.	764
With these two facts in my possession,	732
for one or two other reasons as well,	731
I felt that either my intelligence	732–3
or my courage must be deficient if	733
I could not throw some further light upon	733
an atmosphere of mystery and of gloom.	704
I was exceedingly preoccupied	677
and I walked far upon the sodden moor,	730
convinced at the time that the matter was	678
among the stone huts upon the hillside;	732
that, then should be the centre of my search.	736
I had my own experience for a guide	736
that I had not come upon a false scent	738
and knew at last exactly how I stood.	765
My hardships were not so great as you imagined:	765
trifling details must never interfere	765
with the investigation of a case.	765
We've laid the family ghost once and forever—	757
and end of our investigation."	684

—March 1975

NOTES

1. Epyllion: a small epic; see *The Oxford Classical Dictionary* (Oxford, 1949), s.v. Watson's *Hound* was composed in iambic pentameter, the metre of Shakespeare, to name but the greatest of his compatriot poets. Each reader will have his or her own favourite epyllion, from Catullus' *Peleus and Thetis* to Pope's mock epic, *The Rape of the Lock*.

2. Holmes's criticisms of the romanticism he detected in Watson's prose (*The Sign of the Four*, somewhat modified in *The Copper Beeches*) will be remembered. Since the *Hound* was finally published at a time when Watson believed Holmes dead, it may be easily imagined that he was unwilling to ignore the express wishes of a friend with whom he could no longer debate the matter.

3. Hence the word "cento" in this article's title, signifying a poem constructed from a series of scattered lines. See *The Reader's Encyclopedia*, 2nd ed. (New York, 1965), s.v. "cento"; cf. *A Whimsey Anthology*, ed. Carolyn Wells (New York, 1963), 136–41.

4. An instance of agnosticism on Watson's part; as in similar cases in *A Study in Scarlet* (Chapter 2) and *A Case of Identity*, the story goes on to show that Holmes was right.

5. An uncharacteristic statement by Watson; one might have expected him to demonstrate both greater gallantry and less grasp of the situation.

6. Contrary to fact, unless Holmes here refers to the late baronet, Sir Charles, referring to him as "our friend" in a fit of macabre jocularity at the successful completion of the case. Cf. "Well, I've had a good day, and no mistake" (p. 697), which undoubtedly was originally written as one of Holmes's lines.

7. The hound was a female; "him" in the sixth line following refers to Stapleton.

Editor's Note: Evelyn Herzog's theory is reinforced by "A Ramble in Dartmoor," by Evoe (E. V. Knox), which appeared in *Punch*, 21 January 1948. In it the author attempts to demonstrate that *The Hound of the Baskervilles* was originally written in verse and quotes several fine passages as proof, including:

"The night was clear and fine above us
   The stars shone cold and bright,
While a half-moon bathed the whole scene
   In a soft uncertain light."

and: "I stooped and pressed my pistol
   To the dreadful shimmering head,
But it was useless to press the trigger.
   The giant hound was dead."

And Evoe concludes: " . . . I can only hope that we may one day discover the manuscript of the original poem, ballad, or libretto from which the story has been reduced down into workaday prose."

The Adventure of the Empty Cupboard

by Vincent Starrett

The burglary occurred, it can be shown,
Some time between the hours of four and six.
The Hubbard woman, while a bit prolix,
Is certain of the times. The stolen bone,
Which, at the stroke of four, was plainly seen,
At six o'clock had vanished from its place;
Thus, it is clear, a prima facie case
Rests against someone in the hours between.

That is our problem. Let us now assume
Some of the data to have been suppressed.
This was an inside job, as you have guessed—
There was no strange intruder in the room.
In the bare cupboard certain prints were found:
They were the footprints of a gigantic hound!

—April 1948

In Holmes's day, the number 221 did not exist in Baker Street. Clearly, then, Holmes's and Watson's lodgings were concealed by another Baker Street address. But what?

THE PROBLEM OF NUMBER 221

by WILLIAM S. BARING-GOULD

CERTAINLY there have been few more fertile fields for Sherlockian scholarship than the true location on Baker Street of No. 221.

Let us begin this re-examination of the problem by noting that the rooms shared for so many years by Holmes and Watson were positively *not* in the house which, until recently, bore the number 221.[1] Nor, in Holmes's and Watson's day, could *any* house in Baker Street proper have possibly been numbered 221.

The facts are these:

1. In 1881, Baker Street proper "was barely a quarter of a mile long and consisted of about seventy four-storey terrace buildings of generous proportions. At the southern end, the roadway passed along one side of Portman Square and continued as Orchard Street—a name which it still bears—to Oxford Street. Northwards, past the crossing of Dorset Street, it was named York Place, and beyond the next crossing at Marylebone Road it was Upper Baker Street" (Shearn, art. cit., p. 53). *The numbers ended at 85.*
2. In January, 1921, York Place was incorporated with Baker Street.
3. In 1930 Upper Baker Street was merged in Baker Street and numbered on the west side (which, as we shall see, is the side that concerns us) from 185 to 247. *For the first time there was a No. 221.*

Had the quarters of 1881 been in the vicinity of the present Abbey House, then Holmes would have had to *anticipate* that Upper Baker Street, where he lived, would some day be merged into Baker Street proper, and that his house, after renumbering, would become 221—which is precisely what he did do, if we are to accept the suggestion put forward by Mr. Shearn ("It is the writer's considered opinion that notwithstanding other claims, Sherlock Holmes's real address was none other than this house which later became known as 221 Baker Street").

If, on the other hand, we choose to disregard this suggestion, we must ask ourselves what house on Baker Street proper or beyond, Watson in 1881 masked as No. "221."

Our single most important piece of Canonical evidence is the route taken by Holmes and Watson in *The Empty House*—from Cavendish Square into Manchester Street and so to Blandford Street, then down a narrow passage.

This narrow passage must be one of two: Kendall Mews, leading south, or Blandford Mews, leading north.

If Holmes and Watson turned *south* into Kendall Mews,[2] then "221" Baker Street, which stood opposite "Camden House," was on the *west* side of Baker Street, between George Street and Blandford Street, among the *present* Nos. 19–35.

No. 19—"I think it is clear that our rooms were in South Baker Street, and yet if I can trust your estimate of distances we were at least 200 yards from the Oxford Street end. Personally, I would put it a little less than that. My estimate would be that our quarters were somewhere between George Street and Blandford Street, on the left-hand (west) side going North. . . . (Probably) No. 19, first house after George Street, on the left-hand side going North."—James T. Hyslop, "The Master Adds a Postscript," BSJ (os) 2 (1947), 118.

No. 27—This house was suggested by Dr. Maurice Campbell in "Sherlock Holmes and Dr. Watson: A Medical Digression."

Despite Watson's "*down*" a narrow passage, Gavin Brend, among others, is convinced that Holmes and Watson did *not* turn south into Kendall Mews: "It is unlikely that they turned into [Kendall Mews], for they had started from Cavendish Square which is to the south. Coming from Cavendish Square therefore they would have made an unnecessary detour when they turned into Manchester Street instead of continuing on into George Street. Holmes knew his London far too well to lose time and distance in that way" (*My Dear Holmes*, p. 51).

Mr. Brend further contends that *The Hound of the Baskervilles* provides additional evidence that 221 was *north* of Blandford

Street. This evidence he summarizes in a letter as follows: " . . . there is one further argument which I have not previously put forward. . . . It is that if the arguments which I have put forward as 'Stage #2' [in *My Dear Holmes*], i.e. (A) that both cabs were in the same block; (B) that there was at least 50 yards between them; (C) that 'halfway down the street' means halfway between 221B and the nearest side street behind the cab; and (D) that neither cab stopped at a street corner—that if all these are accepted, then it follows that Dorset Street–Blandford Street must be the correct site since there is none other long enough in the whole length of the street."

Let us assume, with Mr. Brend, that Holmes and Watson turned *north* into Blandford Mews. "221" Baker Street would then be on the *west* side of Baker Street, between Blandford Street and Dorset Street, among the *present* Nos. 45–67.

No. 49—"Reliable local authority has informed us that No. 49 is accepted in that district as being upon the site." T. S. Blakeney, *Sherlock Holmes: Fact or Fiction?*, p. 50.

No. 61—"As between [the three numbers 59, 61, and 63][3] there is little to choose, and we are not justified in eliminating any of them, but if anything, the advantage is slightly in favor of No. 61."—Brend, op. cit.

No. 66—This house, we are told, once satisfied Vincent Starrett's "occult sense of rightness" as the dwelling place of Mr. Sherlock Holmes. (But this number would be on the *east* side of the road and therefore could not have been opposite Camden House, also on the east.)

Nos. 59–67A inclusive—"If one were to retrace the route followed . . . one would be in the block of Nos. 59–67A." —Paul McPharlin, "221B Baker Street: Certain Physical Details," BSJ (os) 2 (1947), 181.

We must now note that Holmes and Watson, turning north into Blandford Mews, *might* have continued north along the route sketched by H. W. Bell (*Sherlock Holmes and Dr. Watson: The Chronology of Their Adventures*, pp. 76–77): "[In this case] Holmes and Watson must have gone the length of Blandford Mews, crossed Dorset Street, kept on through Kenrick Place, and at Paddington Street have turned to the right into East Street, and then to the left into Portman Mansions, in order to reach York Mews North, in the rear of Camden House. (York Mews South—

known since 1936 as Sherlock Mews, W. 1—which is entered from Paddington Street opposite the north end of Kenrick Place, is a blind alley, having no communication with York Mews North.)" "221" would then be on the *west* side of Baker Street, between Dorset Street and the Marylebone Road.

No. 109—"Necessarily one of half a dozen houses on the opposite side of the road (the western side) must be Number 221B .... The present numbers 109 or 111 single themselves out as likely, being the central houses in the block. Our own choice is 109. Here is the colourless brick front. Here, too, are the three first-floor windows and the chimney pots, just as Dr. Watson described them. . . . If further proof is needed in favour of Number 109, consider the opposite side of the roadway, and note the yellow-faced front of 114 Baker Street. Watson drew special attention to the glare of the sunlight upon the yellow brickwork of 'the house opposite' in his record of the strange case of Miss Susan Cushing (*The Cardboard Box*)."—Ernest H. Short, "From the Editor's Commonplace Book," BSJ (os) 4 (1949), 51–52.

James Edward Holroyd is another who is said to have proved to his own satisfaction that 221 Baker Street is the present No. 109. See "Red-Headed League Reviewed," SHJ, 2 No. 1, 32.

No. 111—"Spending a part of his summer vacation in London, a few years ago, Dr. Gray Chandler Briggs of St. Louis, the well-known roentgenologist, mapped Baker Street from end to end. . . . Like Holmes himself, he had . . . turned into a narrow alley and passed through a wooden gate into a yard, to find himself at the back door which had admitted the detective. Looking in, he saw the long, straight hall extending through the house to a front door of solid wood, above which was a fan-shaped transom. Conclusive, all of it, for already over the door in front he had read the surviving placard—*Camden House*. . . . The deduction that followed this discovery was, obviously, elementary. Since Camden House stood opposite the famous lodgings, the rooms of Sherlock

Holmes in Baker Street were, of necessity, those upon the second story of the building numbered 111."—Vincent Starrett, *The Private Life of Sherlock Holmes,* pp. 60–61.

No. 121—"Of houses still standing the one nearest in look and character is the dwelling that has been absorbed into a branch of Barclay's Bank at 121."—Christopher Morley, "Clinical Notes by a Resident Patient," BSJ (os) 3 (1948), 169.

It seems clear beyond all possible doubt that 221 was on the *west* side of Baker Street, despite Watson's statement in *The Cardboard Box* that the sunlight, which must have been *morning* sunlight, glared on the yellow brickwork of the house opposite. Mr. Brend notes, in this connection, that the shop opposite No. 61 (Hardy & Sons, shoes) "may have had bricks [in our period] but it is completely stucco now." The restaurant opposite No. 59, Richoux, noted for its cream cakes, *does* have yellow bricks, "mainly near the top. Lower down they seem to be darker in colour." Reverting once more to Hardy & Sons, opposite No. 61, he adds: "You may recall that Colonel Moran's whist four was completed by Ronald Adair, Mr. Murray, and Sir John Hardy. Do you think that perhaps Sir John lent the empty house to the Colonel?"

But the question remains—was "221" (1) south of Blandford Street; (2) between Blandford Street and Dorset Street, or (3) north of Dorset Street?

A strong point in favor of the North-of-Dorset-Street school is the fact that, until recent years, No. 118 Baker Street *was* Camden House—Camden House School, a well-known preparatory school, now removed to Gloucester Place.

Against the North-of-Dorset-Street point of view, however, there is the fact, as noted above, that at the time of Holmes's adventures, the modern No. 111—and the the other numbers mentioned directly above—*were not in Baker Street at all.*

As Mr. Bell (op. cit.) has said: "The insuperable objection . . . is the fact that until January 1st, 1921, the northernmost portion of the present Baker Street, between Crawford and Paddington Streets on the south and the Marylebone Road on the north, bore a different name, York Place. In fact, during the entire active career of Sherlock Holmes, and for many years afterwards, the present No. 111 was not in Baker Street at all, and was known as No. 30, York Place."

Against the North-of-Dorset-Street view there is also the evidence of:

1. *The Red-Headed League.* "'You [Watson] walked briskly across [Hyde Park] from your home . . . to meet me [Holmes] promptly at ten for that dramatic end to the plans of the Red-Headed League. You left on the stroke of 9:15, and I doubt if there is a man alive who could have reached No. 111 Baker Street on foot in that time."—Hyslop, art. cit., pp. 117–18.

2. *The Blue Carbuncle.* Assuming, as most commentators have, that Commissionaire Peterson lived at or very near 221 Baker Street, identifying No. 221 as the modern No. 111 "would place us on the left-hand side [of Baker Street] going north, somewhere between York Street and Marylebone, or well towards the main-line railway station at Marylebone. But that theory becomes untenable when you consider the route which our good commissionaire Peterson took to get home after his Christmas jollification. . . . One glance at the map will convince you that no man in his right senses would try to reach 111 by such a route, but that it was, on the other hand, a natural direction for a man bound for any point in Baker Street between Blandford and the Oxford Street end."— Hyslop, op. cit., p. 116.

In this same adventure, Watson tells us that his footfalls and Holmes's "rang out crisply and loudly as we swung through the doctors' quarter, Wimpole Street, Harley Street, and so through Wigmore Street into Oxford Street." "It is as clear as day that [the] path was that of men who lived in the southern part of Baker Street."—Hyslop, art. cit., p. 117.

3. *The Beryl Coronet.* "A further objection to . . . No. 111 . . . is that [it is] much too close to Baker Street Underground Station. . . . A passenger from the Underground [would not] take a cab to visit Holmes. He would no sooner have got into the cab than he would have to get out again."—Brend, op. cit., p. 47.

To summarize: The evidence of *The Empty House, The Hound of the Baskervilles, The Red-Headed League, The Blue Carbuncle,* and *The Beryl Coronet* would seem to indicate that "221" Baker Street was a house on the west side (or left side going north) of Baker Street, *below* Dorset Street, and most probably *between* Blandford and Dorset Streets.

It would not be fair to leave this problem, however, without considering a theory recently put forward independently by Messrs. Russell McLauchlin and Robert G. Harris:

"If . . . we are unable to place Mrs. Hudson's house at [any] of the fatally discordant locations chosen by conflicting scholarships in the past, 'what remains' is that her house was not in Baker Street at all. . . . I submit that the partners lived in Gloucester Place; which is one street west of Baker Street and also runs from Portman Square to the Marylebone Road. . . . 221B, or 111, or whatever Baker Street number you may choose, was merely an 'accommodation' address."—McLauchlin, "What Price Baker Street," BSJ (NS) 2 (1952), 55–70.

"Obviously Gloucester Place is not Gloucester Place at all, but Baker Street; or, if you prefer it, Baker Street was never Baker Street at all, but Gloucester Place."—Harris, "A Confirmation of Mr. McLauchlin's Thesis Independently Arrived At," BSJ (NS) 2 (1952), 71.

—April 1958

NOTES

1. "The house . . . no longer exists. Along with it neighbours it was demolished during the 1930's to make way for the head offices of the Abbey National Building Society. It is now no more than part of the site of Abbey House." A. L. Shearn, "The Street and the Detective," BSJ (XA) 2 (1957), 54.

2. The text reads: "*down* a narrow passage." Had they gone north, Watson might better have said "up a narrow passage."

3. Mr. Brend believes that, in 1881, these numbers "(north to south) would be 56, 57, 58 and 59 very roughly. (There was some overlapping.)" Today No. 61, like Mr. Blakeney's No. 49, which went down in the blitz, is no more: "The northern half of the block [which existed when Mr. Brend wrote *My Dear Holmes*] has now been demolished. . . . Now, there has arisen over the whole area a large block of offices. . . . Architecturally it is probably the most impressive building in Baker Street, though, alas, it can hardly be regarded as Sherlockian."

Editor's Note: Mr. Baring-Gould throughout this essay has referred to the putative house-number as "221" and not "221B" because the "B" in the common term is assumed by all cognoscenti to designate the flat on the first floor, which is to say at the top of the seventeen steps.

*Having permitted the reader to choose a location for
221B Baker Street, Mr. Baring-Gould kindly allows
him a look within those fabled rooms. . . .*

MRS. HUDSON'S INHERITANCE

by WILLIAM S. BARING-GOULD

DURING RECENT YEARS many Sherlockians, here and in Great Britain, have seconded the brilliant identification put forward by Mr. Bernard Davies in the Winter 1959 issue of *The Sherlock Holmes Journal* that the present No. 31 Baker Street is the address we know as No. 221. In October 1963 the present writer was fortunate enough to be able to visit and explore No. 31 in company with Mr. Davies and Mr. Anthony D. Howlett, then the Chairman of the Sherlock Holmes Society of London.

From outside there is little to set No. 31 apart from its neighbours; it is a flat-fronted structure rising four storeys above the pavement. Inside, too, it conforms architecturally to dozens of other houses of its period. But enough of No. 31 as it stands today; let us look instead at No. 31 as it must have been in the late eighties of the preceding century. It is not, unhappily, virgin ground that we are treading here: pioneers like Dr. Julian Wolff and Mr. Frank A. Waters and the late Paul McPharlin[1] (among others who shall be mentioned) have anticipated us in the attempt to re-create the passageways and rooms in which Sherlock Holmes and Dr. John H. Watson walked and talked, supped and slept, relaxed and adventured. The most that we can hope to do here is to add to the picture a few trifling details.

We like to think that the late Mr. Hudson—Martha Hudson's lamented husband—was a small but prospering shopkeeper; that on his death he was able to leave to his widow his modest savings plus a thriving business that she in turn could sell and so realise a tidy profit. The proceeds of this sale Mrs. Hudson invested in a house in Baker Street; this, then, was her inheritance—a good stout roof over her own head and rooms to spare that she could rent out to lodgers at prices which would ensure her a comfortable living for years and years ahead. Well

216

No. 31 (originally No. 72) Baker Street, the only house on the west side which, in 1894, fulfilled the requirements for "221B," photographed from the ground floor window of No. 34, the only house which fulfilled the requirements for "The Empty House." It has recently been taken over by Messrs. Druce & Co., the old-established Baker Street store.

See: "The Back Yards of Baker Street," *The Sherlock Holmes Journal,* Vol. 4, No. 3 (1959).—BERNARD DAVIES

we know what lodgers Mrs. Hudson found for her rooms in Baker Street.

It must have been late in the year 1880 that young Mr. Sherlock Holmes—he was then only 26—first opened the front door of No. 221 (with its semicircular fanlight) to climb the seventeen steps to the (English) first (American second) storey and inspect the "suite in Baker Street," the suite known as 221B Baker Street.

And now, having turned back the clock a good 86 years, let us follow him. Ahead of us, down a short and narrow passage, is a door leading to the stairs to the basement floor. In Mrs. Hudson's time this floor was lighted, to some extent at least, by area windows, long since paved over. It would accommodate the kitchen, a store-room, a corner for the page-boy, perhaps, and a waiting-room for callers, although, for this last, we have only the doubtful authority of *The Mazarin Stone.*

We picture the basement as a warm and cheerful place, even though it was underground and generally lit by artificial light. It would be furnished with deal tables and a dresser, chairs for meals, and perhaps a couple of Windsor armchairs for Mrs. Hudson's leisure moments with her cronies. There would be a huge range fitted with ovens and broilers, and it would consume enormous quantities of coal, stored in a wooden shed in the back yard, under the plane tree. Batteries of iron or copper sauce-pans would reflect its flames, and with these would hang frying-pans, skillets, skimmers, and sieves of varying fineness. In the early days, Mrs. Hudson herself would have done all the cooking,[2] but we are told in *Thor Bridge* that 221 Baker Street had a *new* cook, and a new cook implies an *old* one, perhaps hired by Mrs. Hudson when Holmes's payments for her lodgings became "princely" (*The Dying Detective*) in 1887. The cook would expect to be supplied with numerous fancy moulds for puddings, jellies, and aspics, as well as with preserving pans, bread tins, milk bowls, and many other utensils.

Returning to the ground-floor passage, we would find, to our right on entering, a shop or office, the former dining room and pantry of the house in which Mrs. Hudson invested. The presence of Commissionaire Peterson, in *The Blue Carbuncle*, suggests an *office* rather than a shop. To our left are two flights of steps, seventeen in all, leading to the first floor. At the head of the staircase we shall find (perhaps) two doors: the first we pass leads into Holmes's bedroom (if, again, we may trust *The Mazarin Stone*); the second is the door to the famous sitting-room itself. At the west end of this passageway another flight of stairs climbs to the (English) *second* (American *third*) storey.

Entering the sitting-room, we see it as Watson saw it on that day late in 1880 or early in 1881: It is a "large airy" room, about thirty feet long, twenty-five feet wide and ten feet high, "cheerfully furnished and illuminated by two broad windows."

Mr. Michael Harrison has written (in *In the Footsteps of Sherlock Holmes*) that "the reference to broad windows is curious: for all the windows of the Baker Street houses are of the same width: it is in their *height* that they vary."

And these windows are curious in more than their breadth; it is curious, for example, that Watson should speak of *two* windows, for Baker Street houses of this period almost uniformly boast *three* broad windows looking out into Baker Street (certainly No. 31 does). Perhaps what Watson *meant* to say is that the sitting-room had two broad windows flanking a third window, a *bow-window*, for he mentions "the bow-window" on more than one occasion.

And let us pause here for a moment to try to remove some of the confusion that may exist in the minds of many of us between a *bow*-window and a *bay*-window, for they are two very different things. (No house in Baker Street had or has a *bay*-window, but *bow*-windows, in Holmes's and Watson's day, were plentiful.)

Mr. Ronald R. Weaver has made the distinction between these two "interesting details of the late Gothic school of architecture" remarkably clear in his essay "Bow Window in Baker Street,"[3] in which he says:

> The bay-window is a structural affair, composed of plane or curved sections, projecting from the building elevation proper, with flat or curved glass conforming to the structural sections of the bay. But the bow-window is merely a curve or rounded glass, set in a suitable frame. It can be incorporated in a bay, but it does not require such a structure. On the contrary, it is—or was—far more commonly installed in plane elevations, thereby affording an enlarged view. It was quite fashionable in the Victorian era, but its popularity waned because it was relatively fragile, and difficult and expensive to replace. The window in question, as appears by the Canon, was specifically a bow-window. Therefore, no further time need be lost in looking for a bay, or evidence that such a device once existed, or has been removed, anywhere in Baker Street.

Mr. Weaver suggested that the bow-window was shattered in the very first adventure shared by Holmes and Watson—*A Study in Scarlet*—during the frenzied efforts by which Mr. Jefferson Hope attempted to escape the clutches of Messrs. Holmes, Lestrade, Gregson, and Watson.

It was certainly replaced by another window of the bow type, for Holmes, at the time of *The Hound of the Baskervilles*, first spied Dr. Mortimer on his doorstep from "the *recess* of the window." Again, in *The Beryl Coronet,* Watson stood in the bow-window and watched the unhappy Mr. Holder stagger down Baker Street.

It is probable that the bow-window was shattered again by the firemen who put out the conflagration in 221B set off by the Moriarty gang in April 1891—and it may have been shattered for the third time in April 1894, by the expanding air-gun bullet fired by Colonel Moran (*The Empty House*).

Facing east, as they did, these windows would of course receive the morning sun ("Holmes held up the paper so that the sunlight shone full upon it"—*The Dancing Men*). They were equipped with blinds, and—although Watson does not mention it—they were probably hung with Nottingham lace curtains between the blinds and the heavier serge, damask, or velvet drapes.

The floor of the room, as Mr. Waters has noted, would be wide boards of good old English oak, painted or stained a dark brown. These would be covered, no doubt, with a well-worn carpet, leaving bare only a foot or so around the edge of the room.

The wallpaper, like the carpet, would be heavily patterned in damask or floral designs. Dark reds, greens, and blues were the favourite colours in those days, and these would be repeated in the long thick drapes at the windows.

One wall would be marred, of course, by the patriotic "V. R." punctured out by Holmes with a "hair-trigger revolver and a box of Boxer cartridges" (*The Musgrave Ritual*). This, as Mr. Robert Keith Leavitt has convincingly demonstrated in "Annie Oakley in Baker Street,"[4] would be the script V. R. with crown, and the wall that it disfigured, or adorned, would be the *south* wall, opposite the fireplace, which was centered in the *north* wall of the room.

We know, from *The Noble Bachelor* and later references, that a clock hung someplace on a wall of the room.

Gas fixtures would be strategically placed on the walls to provide illumination ("Our gas was lit"—*The Copper Beeches*). But gas, in Holmes's and Watson's day, was not laid on casually; it was expensive, and was confined to the main rooms. Oil lamps would be used, both for economy and for additional lighting. These gave a soft, clear light, very restful to the eyes, but they involved a great deal of work in cleaning and filling. It is probable that a hanging lamp for mineral oil and candles was suspended from the middle of the ceiling. At 221, as in most Victorian homes, a row of candlesticks would be placed on a hall table every night, and as each person retired, he would take one with him, and by its feeble light undress and go to bed.

There was, of course, no central heating at 221 Baker Street at this time, so the fireplace with its cheery blaze of sea-coals would be the sitting-room's only source of warmth and its chief attraction on a cold winter's day. "Generally, . . . one thinks, the life of the detective went on around the fireplace," Vincent Starrett wrote in his *The Private Life of Sherlock Holmes*; "It follows that everything he might require would be within his reach; certainly it would be so by evening, on any day that he remained at home."

I think we are all agreed that the fireplace was of black marble, with a mantel of wood. Holmes's unanswered correspondence was transfixed by a jack-knife in the very centre of this mantel; in one corner stood his cocaine bottle, and "all the plugs and dottles left from his smokes of the day before" were "carefully dried and collected on the corner of the mantelpiece" (*The Engineer's Thumb*). A looking-glass hung above the fireplace, as we know from *The Beryl Coronet*.

Before the fireplace, we must place the famous bearskin hearth-rug (*The Priory School*). The coal-scuttle, containing Holmes's cigars,[5] stood to the left of the fireplace, we think, and the poker and the other fireplace instruments in their customary place to the right.

Handy, too, would be the Persian slipper stuffed with shag tobacco. It most probably hung by means of a ring to a hook on the wall to the left of the fireplace. This, too, was in all likelihood a custom introduced to Holmes by his good friend Watson *via* Edinburgh. Says Keddie, Senior: In Edinburgh "even unto this day single Persian slippers may be purchased for the selfsame purpose. . . . The slippers so far as I know were never sold in pairs. They were made of soft Persian leather and were without heels. The tobacco was stuffed into the forward, or toe part, of the slipper." (The slipper would not have made a very good humidor, however; the tobacco would surely dry out and become covered with dust, in spite of the rate at which Holmes consumed it.)

The bell-pull, which Watson, on one occasion at least, rang rather petulantly, would presumably hang in a convenient place, perhaps just to the right of the fireplace.

To each side of the fireplace stood an armchair—one Holmes's, the other Watson's. We all, it would seem, prefer to give the *west* armchair (low and velvet-lined) to Holmes. This would allow him to sit adjacent to his coal-scuttle humidor and convenient to his chemicals.[6]

Watson in the east armchair would be well-placed to "put the pearl in the safe and get out the papers of the Conk-Singleton forgery case" (*The Six Napoleons*), as well as for manoeuvres with the poker (*The Three Gables*).

To the far right of the fireplace stood a breakfront bookcase (*The Noble Bachelor, The Sussex Vampire*). Here Holmes kept his maps and his many reference books (Whitaker's Almanack, the

American encyclopedia, the Continental Gazetteer, a Crockford, and a Bradshaw), his toxicology collection, soil analyses, chemistry texts, anatomical guides, factual writings about the misdeeds of criminals and fictional writings about the triumphs of detectives, volumes on singlestick playing, boxing and swordsmanship, law books. Here, too, we would find Hafiz and Horace, Tacitus, Flaubert and George Sand, Thoreau, Goethe, Carlyle, Meredith, and Winwood Reade. Certainly a place of honour would be given to Holmes's own monographs. On the lowest, tallest shelves, we imagine, stood the commonplace books, all neatly lettered on their buckram backs in the precise and clerkly hand of Sherlock Holmes.

The major furnishings of the room—what Watson in *The Noble Bachelor* called "our humble lodging-house mahogany"— would be for the most part heavily carved, highly polished early Victorian. Some of them, perhaps, were of rosewood.

Opposite the fireplace, against the south wall, beneath Holmes's patriotic "V. R.," would stand that piece of furniture variously referred to as a couch, sofa, or settee. It was done, we think, in a worn and faded green, and it was covered with several large cushions. These Holmes sometimes threw on the floor to sit upon. Holmes's violin, when it did not stand in its accustomed corner, frequently lay carelessly upon the sofa. Handy to the sofa stood a small table (the "side-table" of *The Resident Patient*), marred, no doubt, by cigarette burns, and upon this table stood the pipe-rack.

To one side of the sofa stood Holmes's desk and, on the other side, Watson's. Holmes kept his desk locked (at least he did in early 1883, as we know from *The Speckled Band*), and he kept his "small case-book" in one of its drawers. Holmes's diary (*The Blanched Soldier*) was probably kept in that same locked desk, although the "case-book" and the "diary" may have been one and the same.

Another very important piece of furniture was the sideboard. Mr. McPharlin has placed it, correctly, we think, against the west wall. Holmes and Watson kept their sideboard littered with tumblers, cigar boxes, odds and ends of cold food, and, of course, the spirit-case and the gasogene. ·

To the left of the sideboard, as we face it, is the door to Holmes's bedroom; to *its* left is the door to the passageway.

Whether this hall-door hinged to the left or to the right is something of a problem, as Mr. James Edward Holroyd has pointed out in his delightful book, *Baker Street Byways*: "perhaps it achieves its greatest individuality in *A Case of Identity* in which it consecutively opened inwards, hinged left; inwards, hinged right; outwards, hinged left!" On the room side of this door were the pegs for hats and coats. Here hung Holmes's deerstalker and cape-backed overcoat, Watson's top-hat and bowler, his stethoscope and his greatcoat. Between the doors, we think, stood the cane-rack, mentioned in *The Red-Headed League*.

In the centre of the room was a table, undoubtedly the dropleaf kind to save room. On its white cloth the china and silver glimmered in the lamplight (*The Copper Beeches*), and here stood the student lamp which burned low until Holmes and Watson returned from an adventure and turned it up (*Charles Augustus Milverton*).

We will have to scatter around the room one or more wooden chairs, one of which served as a study-rack for a seedy hat (*The Blue Carbuncle*). There was also a basket chair, which Dr. Wolff and Mr. McPharlin agreed should go to the east of the centre table.[7] We also must agree with this: Lady Hilda Trelawney Hope had to "manoeuvre" to reach the basket chair and so place the light at her back (*The Second Stain*). The frequently-mentioned visitor's chair—"the vacant chair upon which a newcomer must sit" (*The Five Orange Pips*)—was probably a low, velvet-covered, brass-nail-edged, antimacassar-protected seat, "calculated to ease the innocent and terrify the guilty," as Mr. McPharlin wrote; it faced the light, and must therefore have stood to the west of the centre table.

We know that a stool stood at Holmes's chemical table, but we may be sure that one or more of the chairs was also equipped with a footstool, for Holmes "squatted down upon a stool" in *The Musgrave Ritual*.

We must also provide the room with a small bookcase for Watson's "medical shelf" (*The Hound of the Baskervilles*). Prominent on the shelf would be his own works: a small brochure with the somewhat fantastic title of *A Study in Scarlet* and that other volume called *The Sign of the Four* are specifically mentioned in the Canon (*The Sign of the Four, The Cardboard Box*). Watson also kept a scrapbook into which he pasted clippings about Holmes's cases (*The Sign of the Four*) and a notebook in which he jotted his none-too-accurate observations (*Wisteria Lodge*). But the good doctor had other interests: On stormy evenings he liked to read one of Clark Russell's fine sea stories (*The Five Orange Pips*); at other times Henri Murger's *Vie de Bohème* attracted him (*A Study in Scarlet*); and he would often sit up late nodding over a yellow-backed novel (*The Boscombe Valley Mystery*).

Watson's books, we are told in *The Cardboard Box*, stood beneath a framed portrait of General Gordon and an unframed portrait of Henry Ward Beecher. The framed portrait is generally accepted as having been a picture of Charles George ("Chinese") Gordon, the hero of Khartoum, 1833–1885. Still, Watson's thoughts when he looked at it soon turned to the Civil War, and this raises the question—might the picture have been that of John Brown Gordon, 1832–1904, Confederate general, senator, and onetime Governor of Georgia?[8]

Finally, it may be observed that a telephone had been installed by 1898 (*The Retired Colourman*), although the use of it, particularly by Watson, seems to have been half-hearted, and Holmes himself remained largely faithful to his telegrams.

"That the chamber was perennially untidy is one of the soundest of our certainties," Mr. Vincent Starrett wrote in "The Singular Adventures of Martha Hudson" (*Baker Street Studies*). "One fancies Watson as making shift to keep the place in order, but there is a clear record of his dispair. The principal duty of the maid, then, upstairs, it may be ventured, was making up the beds." Mr. Starrett, as always, is correct. Fresh editions of every paper were supplied by the news agent, as we are told in *Silver Blaze,* and Watson writes in *The Musgrave Ritual* that "month after month [Holmes's] papers accumulated, until every corner of the room was stacked with bundles of manuscript." Holmes's female clients, in the gowns of the 1880s and 1890s, must often have found it difficult to steer their way about the overcrowded room without knocking something over; fortunately for them, the art of graceful walking was included in the education of young women.

We know, by many references,[9] that Holmes's bedroom connected with the sitting-room. There are, however, two puzzling references in *The Beryl Coronet*; here Holmes "hurried to his chamber and was *down* again in a few minutes," and later in the same afternoon "hastened *upstairs*" from the sitting-room [italics ours]. "In spite of these apparently unambiguous statements," Mr. G. B. Newton wrote in "This Desirable Residence" (*Sherlock Holmes Journal* 3 No. 2 [1956], 12–14), the theory that Holmes had even temporarily betaken himself to the top floor is, I feel, untenable. It is noticeable that while on other occasions Watson deliberately alluded to Holmes's "bedroom" this time he refers to his "chamber"—the word bedroom is not mentioned. It is also noticeable that Holmes used it for the purpose of getting into and out of one of his disguises. By this time he must have accumulated a considerable variety of disguises and other impedimenta and may well have used one of the [lumber] rooms upstairs as a kind of dressing room and store for this purpose. The use of the word "chamber" may be a little odd but Watson who was pedantic enough to refer to one of his own works, *A Study in Scarlet*, as a "brochure" was quite capable of applying the term "chamber" to almost any sort of apartment. We remain convinced that Holmes was firmly rooted to his first-floor bedroom throughout his years at Baker Street.

The bedroom, as we know, had two doors, one opening into the sitting-room, the second into the first-floor passageway, but it is difficult, indeed impossible, to see how a door from the bedroom could possibly lead behind the curtain of the bow-window, as we are told that it did in *The Mazarin Stone*.

Our best description of Holmes's bedroom comes to us in *The Dying Detective*.[10] Here we learn that the bedroom, like the sitting-room, had a fireplace, with a clock on the mantel and a litter of "pipes, tobacco pouches, penknives, revolver cartridges and other débris." Its "every wall" was adorned with pictures of famous criminals. There was a "closet," more probably a wardrobe of oak or mahogany, out of which came many of Holmes's varied disguises before he took possession of the lumber room upstairs. The bed was a large one, and had a high, solid head, for the portly Watson was able to squeeze behind it to later confront a chagrined Culverton Smith. There was a large tin box in the corner, which Holmes once dragged into the sitting-room (*The Musgrave Ritual*).

Its other furnishings were probably sparse. We would add a bedside table, complete with candlestick, a marble-topped washstand with a jug and basin of plain or flowered china, a chest of drawers and a dressing mirror, a simple chair. These are the minimum requirements of an English bedroom.

There has hitherto been some discussion as to whether or not a bathroom opened off Holmes's bedroom (or any other bedroom at 221 Baker Street). In *A Scandal in Bohemia* Watson tells us that Holmes returned to the Baker Street sitting-room in his character of "a drunken groom, ill-kempt and side-whiskered with an inflamed face and disreputable clothes." "With a nod he vanished into the bedroom, whence he emerged in five minutes tweed-suited and respectable, as of old." But Holmes of course used his washstand to remove his make-up, not a bathroom. Bathrooms, with hot water laid on, were not common until the very end of the nineteenth century. Where a room was reserved for bathing, it was usually an ordinary small room converted for the purpose, containing a fireplace, a wood-rimmed metal bath, and sometimes a shower-bath of a sort. The water was heated by the kitchen fire. When Holmes or Watson took a bath (and we know that Watson took a bath at least once—in *The Sign of the Four*) he would have done so in his bedroom, in a hip bath with a high back, or in a flat shallow pan of metal painted to look like wood. This was kept, when not in use, in the maid's closet or under the bed. When wanted it was set before the fire, with large towels spread under it to protect the carpet from splashes. It was filled with hot water brought up from the basement in metal cans, and in it the bather sat soaking and warming himself in comfort, without having to worry about keeping others waiting if he dallied too long. A screen, or covered towel-horse, behind the bather protected him from draughts; and, when he was ready to get out, there were towels already warming before the fire in which to wrap himself. Other essential facilities for comfort and sanitation were provided by commodes, kept usually in the washstand.

And now let us climb the stairs to the English *second,* American *third* floor of the house. Here we will find Watson's bedroom[11] (at the back) and Mrs. Hudson's bedroom (at the front). (The maid, we think, slept on the top—English *third*, American *fourth*—floor, with the two lumber rooms.) It will be remembered that Watson in *A Study in Scarlet* heard both the landlady and the maid preceding him up as he was awaiting Holmes's return one night in the sitting-room.

Watson's bedroom has four ascertainable features: a view of a plane tree in the backyard (*Thor Bridge*); a shaving mirror (*The Boscombe Valley Mystery*); a clock on the mantel, and therefore a fireplace (*The Speckled Band*, *The Abbey Grange*). Surely it was always very neat and tidy, as befitted an ex-army officer.

Watson's bedroom was also the "spare" bedroom. It was available to Percy Phelps at the time of *The Naval Treaty*, for Watson was not living at 221 Baker Street at that time. Some years later, however, when Watson was back in residence (*The Golden Pince-Nez*), Inspector Stanley Hopkins of Scotland Yard had to make do on the sofa in the sitting-room, drawn up before the fire.

This, then, was 221 Baker Street. For Holmes and Watson, in every way, it was indeed "a most desirable residence."

—March 1967

NOTES

1. Wolff: "'I Have My Eye on a Suite in Baker Street,'" BSJ (os) 1 (1946), 296–99.

Waters: "The Rooms in Baker Street," *The Best of the Pips*, pp. 15–20, 1955.

McPharlin: "221b Baker Street: Certain Physical Details," BSJ (os) 2 (1947), 180–94.

2. Holmes, in *The Naval Treaty*, says: "Her cuisine is a little limited, but she has as good an idea of breakfast as a Scotchwoman."

3. BSJ (ns) 5 (1955), 93–95.

4. *Profile by Gaslight*, pp. 230–42.

5. The cigars may have been Holmes's, but the coal-scuttle may well have been Watson's, if he was (as many students think) of Scots descent and a member, for a time, of the Medical College at the University of Edinburgh. As the late James Keddie, Sr., wrote in "Gasogene, Coal Box, Persian Slipper" (*The Second Cab*, pp. 15–17, 1947): "In Edinburgh the coal box was an ornament, and in it were stored such details of fireside comfort as slippers, unread magazines, and so forth. Why not cigars?" Scottish Sir James M. Barrie, in fact, kept both his cigars and his telephone in his coal-scuttle. The scuttle is usually pictured as a metal vessel, but Mr. Waters has suggested that it "was a square box made of wood."

6. The famous reconstruction of the Baker Street sitting-room created for the Sherlock Holmes Exhibition at the Festival of Britain placed Holmes's chemical corner, with its acid-stained, deal-topped table and its formidable array of bottles, retorts, and test-tubes, in the northeast corner of the room. We feel, however, that there is better evidence for placing it in the *northwest*

corner, with a tall stool in front of it. "Scientific charts" hung above it; one of them, surely, was a periodic table of the elements.

7. "Few Americans," the late Christopher Morley wrote in "The Blue Carbuncle, or the Season of Forgiveness," "know what is a basket chair (Minty's Varsity Chair) invented (at Oxford?) to help students fall asleep beside the fireplace." This suggests that the basket chair may have been contributed to the Baker Street ménage by Holmes, as a relic of his student days at Oxford.

8. Mr. Holroyd has called attention to an article in the January 1893 issue of *The Strand Magazine* in which it is stated that a Mr. Ed Clifford "was the only English artist General Gordon ever sat to." If Watson's newly-framed picture showed "Chinese" Gordon, then, it was most probably a reproduction of Mr. Clifford's painting.

9. "He went to his bedroom, from which he returned presently pulling a large tin box behind him"—*The Musgrave Ritual.* "Sherlock Holmes sprang to his feet . . . and rushed into his room"—*A Study in Scarlet.* "With a nod he vanished into the bedroom"—*Charles Augustus Milverton.*

10. Dr. Wolff disagrees: He believes the room described in *The Dying Detective* to be "the sitting-room converted to a sick room." Our view would seem to be borne out, however, by Watson's statement that he heard "the opening and closing of the bedroom door."

11. By many references: "Sherlock Holmes was already at breakfast when I came down"—*The Five Orange Pips.* "I . . . was ready in a few minutes to accompany my friend down to the sitting-room"—*The Speckled Band.* "When I came down to breakfast in the morning . . ."—*The Beryl Coronet.* "I descended to breakfast . . ."—*Thor Bridge.*

*If Mrs. Hudson—Sherlock Holmes's long-suffering
landlady at 221B Baker Street—were given the
opportunity to state her case, what might she say?
Herein, Ms. Wright postulates. . . .*

Mrs. Hudson Speaks

by Lee Wright

I HAVE WRITTEN on a previous occasion that Mr. Sherlock
Holmes was not a man given to easy friendships. As I reflect
upon this remark, I realize that it is an understatement.

Yet, Mr. Holmes's friendships have caused a great deal of
speculation, as is only natural in a world where people are curious in an almost vulgar way, and where information about the
private lives of famous people seems to afford so much excitement and pleasure.

In the early days of my association with Mr. Holmes there
was a much more decent and dignified distance maintained between the individual and his fellowmen. This reserve and reti-
cence was due in some part, no doubt, to the influence of the
Queen, and also to the whole character and temper of the English people, among whom Mr. Holmes first became famous.
Of course, when that fame spread across the Atlantic to America, the situation became quite different. The few Colonials I
have met seem to me rather extraordinary people, with absolutely no regard for the natural reserves with which a gentleman wishes to surround himself. I must admit, in fact, that
their forwardness has always frightened me a bit, and indeed I
am very grateful that none of them has ever thought really to
be interested in my private life. It was very fortunate that they
turned the great white light of their curiosity upon my lodger,
Mr. Holmes.

But I wander from my subject. I had begun this with the wish
to tell a little of what I knew of Mr. Holmes and his friendships.
Possibly I digressed because there is so little to be told.

Of course, there was always, and most importantly, his friendship with Dr. Watson. In this connection I may say that he was
more sinned against than sinning, so to speak. If Dr. Watson

had not been so insistent, so pertinacious, and so willing to accept rebuffs, this remarkable friendship would, I am sure, have been very short-lived.

It is my sincere belief, as I have said previously, that Mr. Holmes undertook to share the rooms in my house only because he was intrigued with its little mystery, and could not himself at that time afford to ask Dr. Watson to leave as soon as his own financial situation had been remedied. He had such profound faith in his powers—always justified by events, I may say—that I am sure he expected to rid himself of Dr. Watson in a very few months. Let me confess it. He always underrated Dr. Watson. Not his brain, mind you, but his character and his tenacity. Mr. Holmes was the most romantic occurrence in Dr. Watson's otherwise rather commonplace life, and I always knew that he had no intention of letting it go without a struggle. The world must indeed be thankful for this tenacity on the Doctor's part, since undoubtedly it was the reason for the stories of Mr. Holmes's cases that he wrote. Originally, I am sure, he began them as an excuse to accompany Mr. Holmes on his investigations and as a further excuse to remain with him at 221B Baker Street. All his time and energy were at Mr. Holmes's disposal.

It was my good fortune to enjoy excellent health during the time Dr. Watson was my lodger, so that I cannot of my own experience express an opinion of his skill as a medical practitioner. Nevertheless, I may be forgiven a guess that he did not keep up with the newest discoveries in medical science as he should have, because he was so obviously much more interested in Mr. Holmes's cases than in his own. Perhaps, after all, Dr. Watson's claim to medical fame is best represented by the tales he wrote, as witnessed by the many letters of thanks he received from convalescents whose bed-ridden hours he had lightened by the fruits of his literary labor.

Certainly it took the strong compulsion of a tender romance to make him abandon the joys of his companionship with Mr. Holmes, and I always had the feeling that marriage and connubial bliss never quite compensated him for his sacrifice. With his marriage, he was forced into a more orderly pursuit of his profession; yet there was never a time that he would not come flying to Mr. Holmes's side when, as the Great Man so melodramatically stated, "the game was afoot."

I never enjoyed sufficient intimacy with Mary Watson to discover how she felt about these diversions from duty, but from what I saw of her before the marriage, and from what I know of all women, I am certain that she did not take them wholly in good part. The Doctor may have been so fortunate as to be called to the bedside only of people not suffering from very dangerous maladies, or rather, I should say the patients were fortunate, if that were the case. It is my opinion that the kind-hearted and dutiful Dr. Watson would without a twinge of conscience have abandoned a hospital full of patients in the last stages of fatal disease sooner than disappoint Mr. Holmes. Ah, well, that was his very slim hold on the affections of that fascinating and self-sufficient man, and I would be the last to blame him for giving up everything before that. One had only to see him during the time he thought Mr. Holmes was dead to realize that a great part of his own life had been extinguished at the Reichenbach Fall. And all the world knows of his untrammeled joy when Mr. Holmes was returned to us, alive and well and in his usual sardonic spirits.

As for other acquaintances, there were only a few, and those of a most fleeting and unimportant nature. I think Mr. Holmes had a rather contemptuous affection for Mr. Lestrade, as one does have towards many human beings whose stupidity is so perfect a foil for one's own brilliance. Mr. Gregson he accepted with no particular show of any emotion. He seemed to have some affection for the urchins who were known as the Baker Street Irregulars, but I am convinced that he did not really know one from the other of them. After all, small boys of a certain age do resemble each other mightily, and Mr. Holmes seldom had time for the sentimental observations which form the basis for all profound human relationships.

I think I may state without fear of contradiction that I have had the best opportunity to know him well. His interest in me was deep at our first meeting, and remained so until the day when he spoke of me as Mrs. Turner, and later offered me a greatly increased stipend for his rooms. Until then he had been professionally interested in my situation, but after that—when he thought he had gotten to the bottom of it to his own satisfaction—we maintained the most conventional landlady–lodger relations. It was understood that he and his habits were a per-

231

manent fixture at 221B, and I was expected to become used to his vagaries. He did not know, nor, I am sure, did he care, how long it took me to become so accustomed. There were many days in the early years when a sight of his room and its indescribable litter would fill me with a really intense despair. I have always been a very orderly person, and untidiness is almost a physical misery to me, but this view of things passed, and I became so accustomed to Mr. Holmes's habits that even the sound of revolver shots above my head—on the occasion when he used the wall for target practice—caused no more than a few regretful shakes of the head from me. I may say that I did insist the next morning on calling in the plasterer, since I feared lest Mr. Holmes's marksmanship had undermined the foundations of the building, and so the ceiling might come down upon his head. He grumbled a bit on this occasion, but he was truly indifferent to his surroundings, and yielded with good grace whenever I felt that things had gone too far and had to be remedied. He took it for granted that he could rely on me for discretion, for meals whenever he wished them, and altogether for attention to his creature comforts. I, in turn, relied upon him for the occasional excitements his affairs brought into my respectable existence. In the days before I knew Mr. Holmes, unconventional incidents had been more frequent and more personally exciting. However, my increased security was a satisfactory substitute.

The greatest speculation has been occasioned by his brief connection with Irene Adler. Dr. Watson recorded that Mr. Holmes spoke of her as *the* woman, and so this appellation has gone down through the years. Undoubtedly what Mr. Holmes actually said was: "She is the woman who is mixed up in this affair." Dr. Watson, who, as I have said, was an incurable romantic at heart, supplied the italics and omitted the balance of the sentence, thus placing an entirely different and meaningful interpretation on Mr. Holmes's casual remark.

It is certainly beyond the realm of my imagination that Mr. Holmes ever accorded this rather notorious adventuress more than a passing thought. Her charms must have been of the rather obvious type, as could not have attracted his interest for more than a moment. Dr. Watson, needless to say, would have been an easy prey for such a woman, and it is clear that since he himself could not write with perfect frankness of her effect upon him—he was at this time married and in no position to do so—he took upon himself the liberty that many writers do, to indicate his own feelings by putting words in the mouth of another person.

After all, who should know better than I whether or not Mr. Holmes felt a romantic attachment for this woman? I can only conclude by stating firmly that, if he had, I of all people in the world would have known it.

—January 1946

Of all the Scotland Yard detectives associated with Sherlock Holmes, it is Lestrade who is most widely known. But who is the man behind the well-known name?

INSPECTOR G. LESTRADE

by L. S. HOLSTEIN

PROBABLY EVERY ADDICT of Sherlockian lore has, at one time or another, bemoaned the dearth of information concerning the characters who move through the tales as recounted by Dr. Watson—some to reappear; some to disappear forever. There are gentlemen, and there are scoundrels; worried wives and maidens in distress; high-born aristocrats; middle classers, and scum from the streets of London.

Search as you will, it is impossible to find biographies or even minor references to those personages with whom Holmes lived and worked, or tracked down; although some later-day research has identified a character or two who, it is evident, were deliberately disguised in the text. True, there are a few thumbnail sketches that throw a glimmer, as in the case of Lord Robert St. Simon, Colonel Sebastian Moran, Dr. James Mortimer, Dr. Huxtable of the unique given name, and Miss Irene Adler—but they are incomplete and unsatisfying.

If one made an accounting of the personalities, aside from Watson and Holmes, who intrigue the student, we would find Mrs. Hudson, Mycroft Holmes, Lestrade, Mary Morstan, young Stamford, the Moriartys, various Violets, John Clay, and a parade of others. Really, there is little choice; every one raises our curiosity, that we may know them more intimately and determine their influences on the life and actions of Holmes himself.

Of all the characters, excepting perhaps Watson and Mrs. Hudson, none seems to have had a more intimate or longer-lasting contact with Holmes than Inspector G. Lestrade of Scotland Yard. He was associated with Holmes in more of the recorded cases than any other member of the Metropolitan Police. That association extended from the early days of Holmes's practice, when he was located on Montague Street, to shortly before his retirement to the Sussex Downs. But even in Lestrade's case, the external records of the man are non-existent, or are at best a few meagre newspaper references. The Yard files, which should be revealing, are not available for public scrutiny.

The non-discriminating reading public generally regard Lestrade with a certain amount of scorn, as inept and bungling; is this a true and faithful picture?

To learn what manner of man this G. Lestrade was, we must, then, in the absence of other data, turn to the saga itself. Therein is found a considerable fund of revealing information, not completely adequate but sufficient to form some fair measure of the man.

We find him active in twelve of Dr. Watson's writings as well as a reference to him in the text of *The Three Garridebs*. He was one of the early callers at 221B, presumably in connection with a forgery case which got him into a fog. We may infer that he had, on occasion, visited Holmes at the rooms in Montague Street. From *A Study in Scarlet* to *The Disappearance of Lady Frances Carfax*, a span of twenty years, we have some record of Lestrade.

Of his forebears, we find no inkling, although to this writer there is some suspicion of a touch of the Gallic in his name and in his oft-times quick actions; but the better likenesses of him do not confirm this suspicion. His Christian name is unknown to us, but the only letter extant, written to Holmes after the arrest of Jim Browner, the seafarer with a penchant for severing ears, is signed "G. Lestrade." One can speculate on the denotation of that tantalizing "G" from George to Gouverneur without success. There is no clue, and without a shred of evidence I lean toward Gustave as a name that fits the subject.

On his early education there are no definite data. That one letter is fairly well composed, and a rather complete schooling without advanced study can be inferred. We know he was able to take Jefferson Hope's recital of his story in shorthand, probably following the Pitman method since the Gregg system did not come into vogue until about 1888.

As to Lestrade's age there is some measure, for in 1881 he says the Drebber murder beats anything he had seen and "I am no chicken." Later he admits that in spite of twenty years' experience, the sight he first witnessed at Halliday's Private Hotel made him feel "sickish." If we make the generous assumption that he joined the Metropolitan Police at the age of twenty-one, he would have been on the high side of forty at the time of the Drebber affair, and we know he was still active in 1903, for in September of that year he appears with a warrant for the arrest of Holy Peters. We may draw the conclusion from all this that Lestrade was Holmes's senior by some ten or twelve years, and served on the force more than forty years.

At the outset, he may have pounded a beat as did John Rance and Harry Murcher, but because of his lack of stature, it is more likely that he came up through the records bureau, and not as a constable. By the time of the *Study*, he already had earned a reputation, for when Holmes discloses his profession to Watson, he refers to Lestrade as a "well known detective," and Watson's account of the pending affair calls him "inspector" (small i). The newspapers at that time designate him as a well-known officer and Scotland Yard official. In 1889 (*The Second Stain*), we find him an Inspector with a capital I—possibly an indication of first rank, but more likely merely a typographical digression. In *The Cardboard Box* (1891), Holmes tells Watson that Lestrade's "tenacity has brought him to the top at Scotland Yard," which surely means that when the Yard was expanded and took up its new quarters on the Thames Embankment, Lestrade came into his own, the change in status having been consummated while Holmes was on his hegira to Tibet and points East.

Now, what of G. Lestrade's appearance? In the *Study*, Watson describes him as "little, rat-faced, sallow, dark-eyed," and later as "lean and ferret-like" with beady eyes—not a very enticing description—but we are told he had an assurance and jauntiness that "marked his demeanor and dress." Still lean and ferret-like, furtive and sly-looking, he appears in 1889 (*The Boscombe Valley Mystery*) dressed in light-brown dust coat and leather leggings, "retained" by Miss Alice Turner. Some have pounced on that word "retained" as used by Holmes to conclude that Lestrade had gone into private practice for a period, but that judgment is not necessarily warranted, for it was not uncommon for Scotland Yarders to aid the provincial police, and Holmes's use of the word was purely conversational. We learn too, in the Boscombe Valley tragedy, that Lestrade's left foot turns in; an insignificant fact, but it does give a clue to his gait. A few years later—in *The Second Stain* and *The Cardboard Box*— Watson is using the terms "bulldog features" as well as wiry, dapper, and ferret-like to describe him, and in 1897 (*The Hound of the Baskervilles*) it is "a small, wiry, bulldog of a man." I am of the belief that this last phrase, along with dapper and cocky, best fit our subect.

Of course, we find no photographs to confirm our ideas of Lestrade's appearance, but sketches by D. H. Friston and George Hutchinson depict him as small, so along with Watson's repeated use of the word, it must be accepted as a fact that he was not tall, and we will settle for a height of about five feet six or seven. It is this lack of stature that leads one to believe he entered the service in the records bureau, rather than in the foot patrol. It is my personal view that the drawings of Robert Fawcett, which illustrate some of the fables published in a national magazine[1] in which Holmes and Lestrade appear, are the best portrayals of Lestrade in his later years when he had put on a bit of weight—short, somewhat paunchy, and with a mustache and bushy eyebrows, a bowler on the back of his head, rather loud suit and spats, and a generally cocky appearance: truly British. Any thought of the Gallic must be erased.

What of Lestrade as a detective; as a man; and what of his attitude towards Holmes—what qualities did he possess? As a detective, we could not expect even "one of the smartest of our detective officers," as the *Daily Chronicle* referred to him, to be in a class with Holmes, and it is apparent almost from the start that Lestrade considered Holmes his superior—although loath to admit it even to himself.

From the contempt and resentment which he showed in *A Study in Scarlet*; from the derision of Holmes's methods, "the deductions and the inferences," we find him gradually assuming a more deferential attitude. As early as 1894 (*The Norwood Builder*), he openly acknowledges Holmes's help to the Yard, and in 1902 (*The Six Napoleons*) he pays homage in as magnanimous a statement as one could hope to hear. It is worth quoting in full, since

237

it reveals one facet of our subject's character: "I've seen you handle a good many cases, Mr. Holmes, but I don't know that I ever knew a more workmanlike one than that. We're not jealous of you at Scotland Yard. No, sir, we are very proud of you, and if you come down tomorrow, there's not a man, from the oldest inspector to the youngest constable, who wouldn't be glad to shake you by the hand." That is not the utterance of a narrow, jealous person!

Lestrade's respect may be revealed in part by the fact that, in the early days, Holmes and he generally addressed each other by their bare surnames, except in occasional outbursts of sarcasm, which you can almost hear in Lestrade's "Mr. Sherlock Holmes" after his discovery of "RACHE"; and on his leave-taking of 221B after the display of Miss Doran's articles found in the Serpentine. As time progressed, Lestrade usually used the term "Mr. Holmes," with an exception now and then, as when he rebukes Holmes for what he believes to be false hopes raised in Holmes's conversation with Miss Alice Turner in *The Boscombe Valley Mystery*.

No one would be rash enough to claim that Lestrade was a brilliant theorist, but he was practical, energetic, and courageous. These qualities were frequently of help to Holmes as, for example, when Lestrade turned up the note from "F.H.M." in Hattie Doran's wedding gown, fished out of the Serpentine. Without that note Holmes would have been without a starting point, and the case might have been prolonged for days. And again, the discovery of the thumb-print of John Hector McFarlane gave Holmes the clincher he needed to smoke out Jonas Oldacre. These are examples of the legwork that was characteristic of Lestrade, even though his deductions from the evidence were not always of the finest.

His physical courage was never lacking, as typified in his arrests of such substantial prisoners as Jefferson Hope, Colonel Moran, and Beppo. He also stood up to Holmes, and did not hesitate to point out that there was a practical side to an investigation; that hard-headed British juries had to be convinced, and that he believed in hard work—a remark that Holmes later on privately admitted had merit. Holmes himself paid unspoken tribute to Lestrade's courage when, on the return to

Inspector G. Lestrade as depicted by George Hutchinson in *A Study in Scarlet* (London: Ward, Lock, Bowden & Company, 1891).

London, he chose Lestrade as the one to help capture the notorious colonel in the Empty House.

There seems to have been a softening of feeling on both sides as the years went by. Holmes even compliments the Scotland Yarder in 1895 for his theorizing as to the lack of a ticket in Cadogan West's pocket in *The Bruce-Partington Plans*: "Good, Lestrade, very good"—one of the few times Holmes acknowledged that Lestrade was worth listening to. We learn, too, that Lestrade would drop in on Holmes and Watson of an evening to smoke a cigar and swap information in a friendly chat.

Summarizing, we picture Inspector G. Lestrade as an asset to the solution of crime in London and thereabouts; as a brave officer, an energetic if not brilliant detective; a man ready to fight for his opinions and equally ready to concede defeat; one who was able to give praise when due; a good leg-man; a friendly, human sort of person; dapper and a bit cocky in manner but a solid official always ready to perform his duty. In short, G. Lestrade was an important and influential adjunct in the life and career of Sherlock Holmes, and he deserves the respect of every student of the lore.

—April 1958

NOTE
1. Not to be confused with Dr. Watson's true accounts.

When Sherlock Holmes said that his brother Mycroft
sometimes was *the British government, he meant it.*
And here we discover why. . . .

MYCROFT AND HER MAJESTY'S INVISIBLE
GOVERNMENT

by J. S. CALLAWAY

IN A MASTERFUL PAPER entitled "The Armchair Still Misplaced,"[1]
Mr. D. A. Redmond has reminded us of a significant failure of
Sherlockian scholarship. That failure is the lack of attention
which has been given to the enigma of Mycroft's position under
Her Majesty's government. Mr. Redmond has himself done
much to correct this lamentable shortcoming by putting forward the closely reasoned hypothesis that Mycroft was an inter-
departmental security agent responsible for the security of
England's state secrets.

To the length that it goes, such a theory covers the facts.
However, there remain cogent indications that Mycroft's relations with the British government struck much deeper than Mr.
Redmond's theory suggests. Though "The Armchair Still Misplaced" must ever commend itself on the grounds of sound
scholarship, the popular motion picture *The Private Life of Sherlock Holmes*[2] may, ironically, come nearer the truth by casting
Mycroft in the role of the chief of Her Majesty's Secret Intelligence Service.

Before criticising too sternly those who have sidestepped the
Mycroft enigma, it must be remembered that this is an area of
extreme difficulty to research. Except for the guarded accounts
of Dr. Watson, Mycroft's name is conspicuous by its absence
from both public and private records of the day. Further, his
only known employer, the British government, disclaims any
knowledge of such a person. Small wonder, in the face of such
official opposition, that scholars have approached the problem
with reluctance and caution. Yet the question remains: What
was Mycroft doing that his country still wishes to conceal? This

MYCROFT HOLMES

From a drawing by the Editor of the JOURNAL to illustrate "A Lauriston
Garden of Verses."

is the crux of the enigma, and to solve it we must push through
the breach Mr. Redmond has opened for us.

Based on Sherlock's statement that his brother "audits the
books in some of the government departments,"[3] Mr. Redmond
has constructed his theory that Mycroft "was ordered to . . .
make an inventory of the books in various departmental libraries and offices" for security purposes and that the information
thus acquired allowed him to "be invaluable to a Minister in
search of facts."[4] As far as this isolated piece of information is
concerned, such an explanation covers the facts, yet it dis-
regards the more comprehensive statement, made in great confidence by Sherlock in *The Bruce-Partington Plans.*

By virtue of this statement we know many of the details of
Mycroft's work. For instance, we know it involved high matters
of state and that it was extremely influential due to its control

over information. We also know that it permitted no public recognition (which would seem to contradict Mr. Redmond), was decisive in the governmental decision-making process ("indispensable" was the word Sherlock used), was unique and of Mycroft's own making.[5]

Although these facts do not exclude the possibility that security of state secrets was among Mycroft's responsibilities,[6] they strongly suggest that he was more than a simple security agent. According to Cadogan West, the British were "lax" in matters of security,[7] so it is most unlikely that a person who specialised in that field would ever have the influence over British policy that Sherlock claims for his brother. Neither would we expect to see a person as conscientious as Mycroft handing out state secrets up and down the length of Whitehall if it was his duty to prevent the disclosure of those very secrets.

But the most telling point against the theory that Mycroft was only a counter-intelligence agent is the peculiar behaviour of England's public-relations men in this matter. But England's P.R. men have done nothing at all in this matter. *That* is their peculiar behaviour. If Mycroft did nothing but protect his Queen's secrets, why does her government harbour such qualms about acknowledging such commendable service? No, it is to the end of the intelligence spectrum opposite security and counter-intelligence that we must look for the answer to the Mycroft enigma—and thus we come to the Secret Intelligence Service.[8]

Ever since Sir Francis Walsingham sent his spies forth to inform his Queen, Elizabeth I, of the intentions of her royal adversaries abroad and the plots of treacherous subjects at home, British statesmen have relied on the information provided by Secret Service to guide their policy decisions. Playing the "Great Game" in the power centres of Europe and around the periphery of the Empire, its agents are often the only men (and women) who can accurately estimate the capabilities and learn the intentions of rivals, neutrals, and even friends. How deeply had the Russians burrowed into the fabric of Afghanistan politics? What ambitions had Germany for its Berlin-to-Baghdad railroad? Would Italy adhere to the Triple Alliance? How far would the Americans go to uphold their Monroe Doctrine? Would France fight to stay in Siam? These were the questions vital to the British diplomacy of Mycroft's day, and the ones the S.I.S. was called upon to answer.

Clearly, the man who controlled the organisation that provided the answers held British policy in a stranglehold—it would be no exaggeration to say that he was, at times, the British government. But if, as the evidence indicates, Mycroft was Her Majesty's minister for secret services, what of Sherlock's statement that his brother's position was unique and that "he has made it for himself"?[9] In espionage-riddled Europe chiefs of intelligence were nothing if not plentiful, and Mycroft could hardly claim to have made for himself a profession that had existed since the sixteenth century.

The answer is to be found in the proliferation of intelligence-gathering agencies that occurred in the last quarter of the nineteenth century. This phenomenon was engendered by the rampant technology of the times that was rapidly transforming the general arts of war (diplomacy by other means) into specialised sciences. Conversely, this obliged those who collected information (i.e., intelligence) about the ability of other governments to conduct their diplomacy by "other means" likewise to become technical specialists. Thus ended forever the era when a single intellect could master both the art of the soldier and the craft of the diplomat.

In England the dawn of the new era manifested itself in the establishment of the Naval Intelligence Division in 1885 under the Admiralty and the Military Intelligence Division the following year under the War Office. While the S.I.S. continued to report to the Foreign Office on the political intentions of the various governments, the N.I.D. and the M.I.D. reported to their parent services on the naval and military forces available to implement those intentions.

Specialisation was the only way the challenge of technology could be met, but the compartmented structure of England's "invisible government"[10] that resulted encouraged the specialists to regard themselves as individuals working on isolated problems rather than as a team striving to master a complex whole. The N.I.D. might, for example, be reporting to the Admiralty that a new class of French torpedo-boats which could be broken down and transported by rail lines between Marseilles and the Channel coast was being improved. Neither Admiralty

"'Come in,' said he, blandly."
Mycroft Holmes in *The Greek Interpreter,* drawn by Sidney Paget
(*The Strand Magazine,* September 1893, p. 304)

nor War Office might learn of the other's intelligence or that
the S.I.S. had informed the F.O. that a new French war plan
called for a rapid concentration of a torpedo-craft in the Channel while the French battle fleet mustered in the Mediterranean
for assaults against Gibraltar and Malta. Such a failure of intelligence could well cost England her naval mastery of the Mediterranean and her empire east of Suez.

What was needed was a man who specialised in omniscience
to coordinate the findings of all of Her Majesty's intelligence
services, analyse the data, and pass them on to the proper
people for action. Such a man would be more powerful than
the chief of any single intelligence service, even the S.I.S., and
the most indispensable man in the country. Also his position
would be unique: never before had the need for such an "intelligence broker" existed, and, if Mycroft as head of the senior
intelligence service convinced (or coerced) the junior services to
coordinate their activities through him, it would be equally true
that he had made the position for himself.

Within the context of the times and the nature of the British government structure, the theory of "intelligence broker" is the most appropriate solution of the Mycroft enigma. It is only to be regretted that Her Majesty's government wishes to conceal Mycroft's rôle in England's secret history. But, considering the power Mycroft exercised in a country devoted to open government by duly appointed officials, it is to be expected that its public government would seek to conceal the existence of the man who *was* Her Majesty's invisible government.

—June 1974

NOTES

1. BSJ (NS) 22 (1972), 78–80.
2. *The Private Life of Sherlock Holmes*, 1970—not to be confused with Vincent Starrett's book.
3. *The Greek Interpreter*.
4. Redmond, op. cit.
5. *The Bruce-Partington Plans*.
6. It is altogether possible that the Special Branch of Scotland Yard, which handles counter-espionage, was party to Mycroft's intelligence consortium. This speculation is based on the list of foreign agents provided to Sherlock by Mycroft in *The Bruce-Partington Plans* and a similar list utilised by Sherlock in *The Second Stain*. Sherlock does not identify the origin of the *The Second Stain* list, but the indications are that it came from Mycroft, who was in touch with British counter-espionage.
7. *The Bruce-Partington Plans*.
8. For information on the modern British Secret Service (MI 6) and the care it takes to conceal its existence and the identity of its chief, see D. Wise and T. B. Rose, *The Espionage Establishment*, Chapter III.
9. *The Bruce-Partington Plans*.
10. The phrase "invisible Government" was coined by Wise and Rose in the title of their book on the American intelligence community to stand for the multiplicity of intelligence-related agencies that attempt to operate out of public view.

IDENTIFYING THE DIOGENES CLUB: AN ARMCHAIR EXERCISE

by S. TUPPER BIGELOW

" . . . from an armchair I will return you an excellent expert opinion."—Mycroft Holmes

IN THE Winter 1964 issue of *The Sherlock Holmes Journal,* C. O. Merriman attempts to identify the Diogenes Club as the Athenaeum, largely on the strength of the fact that, as he had found out, Sir Arthur Conan Doyle had been elected a member of the Athenaeum in 1901. But on page 126 in the June 1965 issue of THE BAKER STREET JOURNAL, its erudite editor, Dr. Julian Wolff, seems to make out a better case for The Travellers', based on a book review of *Leather Armchairs: A Guide to the Great Clubs of London* which appeared in *The New York Times* of 30 November 1964, which quotes the author, Charles Graves, anent the Travellers': "The chief tradition of The Travellers' is that members do not speak to each other."

Oddly enough, these two references are the only ones in the writings upon the Writings that deal with the matter of the identification of the Diogenes Club, and it seems somewhat remarkable to me that it would take until 1964 before any Sherlockian made any attempt to identify this haven of "the most unsociable and unclubable men in town."

Now, it seems to me—although this may possibly be regarded as the height of effrontery, as I have never been in England, much less in London—that a more or less creditable effort can be made to identify the Diogenes Club when one is equipped only with *Whitaker's Almanack* of 1889 (since Baring-Gould's *Chronology,* which I have no hesitation in accepting as the outstanding authority, places the action of *The Greek Interpreter* in September 1888), *Leather Armchairs,* and, of course, any old copy of *The Greek Interpreter,* as any textual differences in the various editions of the Canon will mean nothing so far as this study is concerned.

We know, first of all, that the Diogenes is in Pall Mall. Whitaker lists 14 clubs located in Pall Mall in order, with the street-address numbers assigned to them by Whitaker. They were:

Army & Navy, 36
Athenaeum, 107
Carlton, 94
Guards, 70
Junior Carlton, Pall Mall (no number)
Marlborough, 52
N. Conservative, 9
New Athenaeum, Pall Mall W. (no number)
Oxford and Cambridge University, 71
Reform, 104
Royal Water Color [*sic*], 5A
Travellers', 106
United Service, 116 and 117
Unionist, 68

As Mycroft was a civil servant, we can at once throw out the political clubs. In the 1889 *Almanack,* the political clubs are mentioned in the column entitled "Remarks." This is what it says:

Carlton: Conservative;
Junior Carlton: Strictly Conservative;
N. Conservative: Conservative;
Reform: Strictly Liberal;
Unionist: Unionist.

Now, what the difference can be between "Strictly Conservative" and "Conservative," I'm sure I don't know, but I do know, or at all events feel certain, that it would be highly improper for a civil servant to be a member of any club that was either political or strictly political.

As for the N. Conservative Club, one presumes that the "N." stands for "National"; Whitaker just didn't have room to put in "National." But there was and still is a National Liberal Club, although no National Labour Club. Maybe the Labourites are not "clubable" types.

247

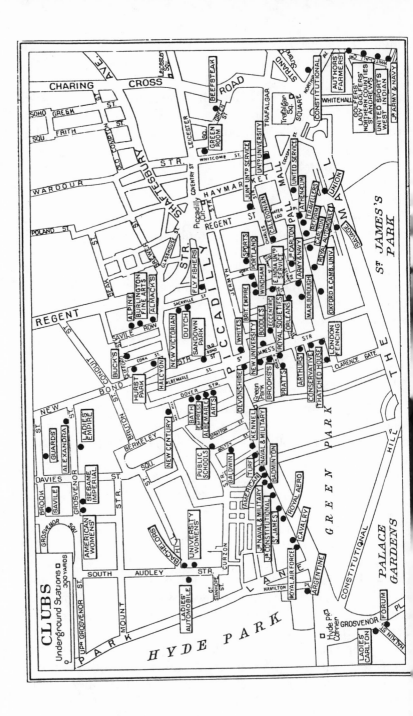

248

The Unionist Club is not mentioned in Mr. Graves's excellent work, and one might be tempted to confuse it with the Union Club, if one were an ignorant colonial such as I am, but research pays off. In Whitaker's remarks, as will be seen above, the members were "Unionist," and that sends us to the *Shorter Oxford English Dictionary*. There, "Unionist" is defined as: *"British politics*: A member of the political party which advocated or supported maintenance of the parliamentary union between Great Britain and Ireland, formed by coalition between Conservatives and Liberal Unionists in 1886 [that's near enough], and later known indifferently as 'Unionist' or 'Conservative.'" In any case, the Unionist was obviously a political club, so it can be knocked out of contention.

The Army and Navy Club comprised officers of the Army and Navy; the Guards, officers of the Guards regiments; and the United Service (it seems to me that that should be "Services," but let's not quibble with Whitaker), senior officers only. Mycroft was none of these; or if he was, we have no evidence in the Canon that he was. So these three clubs can be thrown out of our calculations.

We can, I think, readily throw out the Oxford and Cambridge University Club. While the Oxford or Cambridge debate about the university at which Mycroft's illustrious brother attended, if either or both, may go on until the end of time, there is no evidence in the Canon that Mycroft attended either.

And this leaves us with only five possibles:

Athenaeum
Marlborough
New Athenaeum
Royal Water Color [*sic*]
Travellers'.

I think we can safely throw out The Royal Water Color Club to start off with, as, although the Holmes family may have had "art in the blood," there is nothing in the Sherlockian saga to indicate that Mycroft had any interest in the purposes of The Royal Water Color Club, which, according to Whitaker, were "Art Conversazioni, &c."

According to Mr. Graves, the Marlborough, of which he says little, and the New Anthenaeum, of which he says nothing, have long since disappeared into the mists of time. They are, indeed, beneath Mr. Graves's notice. If they are beneath his notice, they should be beneath ours, and, *a fortiori,* Mycroft's as well. Lacking any data that Mycroft's brother was so insistent upon having on so many occasions—well, two, anyway—we will simply ignore those two fly-by-night clubs and get on with the business at hand.

And that leaves us with the two we started with: the Athenaeum and the Travellers'.

Mr. Graves's description of the Athenaeum might fit any men's club in England or on the North American continent. It has no "Stranger's Room," nor, for that matter, has the Travellers'. Guests waiting for member–hosts in the Athenaeum must, however, sit at the far end of the entrance hall. There is not the slightest hint that its members are unsociable or unclubable; whatever hard feelings may exist in the club's members about other members seem to be a resentment that too many bishops are members (30) and too many archbishops, likewise (6). A tale is told of a member who lost his umbrella in the club. He said: "That's what comes of admitting all those confounded bishops."

Misanthropy of a very mild sort, it seems to me.

As for glass panelling in the entrance hall, there is none in either club, judging from Mr. Graves's description of both clubs—whatever glass panelling is, come to think of it.

"A door some little distance from the Carlton" would admittedly fit either the Anthenaeum or the Travellers', as the Carlton was at 94, Pall Mall; the Anthenaeum, 107; and the Travellers', 106.

We go back to the opening line in Mr. Graves's description of the Travellers': "The chief tradition of the Travellers' is that members do not speak to each other." That should really be enough.

But it gets worse:

> The Travelers' maintains its non-speaking reputation even at luncheon and dinner when members come in with books, newspapers or magazines in their hands, practically daring anyone to talk to them. Neither talk nor guests are tolerated in the library. There is occasionally some furtive conversation in the mezzanine bar, but most members only learn to know each other on Sundays or in August when they are allowed to use the Garrick. For there, anyone who comes to the luncheon table with a book or newspaper has it firmly removed from him by the re-

doubtable Barker, the Chief Steward, with the words, "Excuse me, Sir; it isn't done at the Garrick."

And the Travellers' must have the world's record for black-balling illustrious citizens. Graves doesn't tell us how many black-balls kept a candidate for membership out of the club, but my guess would be one. Among others who were blackballed at the Travellers' were Cecil Rhodes, Lord Rosebery, Lord Randolph Churchill, Sir Edwin Landseer, Lord Crewe, and Lord Lytton.

At the moment, 20% of the members of the Travellers' are in the Foreign Office. Such a club would have an undeniable attraction for Mycroft.

Mycroft's screw,[1] it will be recalled, was £450 per year, or $2200, give or take a buck or two, in 1888. Less a few pence income tax. Not too bad, in those days, but even today, at the Travellers', they do rather well in the "quick luncheon room." We would call it a snack bar, I suppose. A paltry 6s. will buy meat, veg. and pudding, sweets or cheese; or soup and cheese with all the trimmings, like biscuits,[2] butter, tea, &c., are only 2s. 6d., the same as Mr. Francis Moulton paid for breakfast at "one of the most expensive hotels" in London in 1886.[3] With what some writers have called Mycroft's attenuated salary (although it does not seem so to me), he would have appreciated the charges at the Travellers'; I'm sure they didn't and don't do their members that well at the Athenaeum. Mr. Graves doesn't tell us.

And now I can hear some querulous reader saying, "Just one thing you've overlooked: Don't you remember Sherlock Holmes said, speaking of the Diogenes Club, 'My brother was one of the founders . . .'? I have a *Whitaker,* too; the Athenaeum was founded in 1824, and the Travellers' was founded in 1819. So how about that?"

My readers, being intelligent students of the Canon, know very well that the various editions have been cursed with misprints, particularly the American editions. Some U.S. editor, unfamiliar with English usages, changed the text to make it more realistic, as he thought, even although the text was sometimes changed back in The Limited Editions Club and Heritage editions. I could give countless examples of this, but that is not my purpose in this monograph.

Let us go back to *The Greek Interpreter,* when Sherlock Holmes said to Watson: "When I say, therefore, that Mycroft has better powers of observation than I, you may take it that I am speaking the exact and literal truth."

"Is he your junior?"

"Seven years my senior."

There was the error or misprint, whatever you want to call it. What Sherlock Holmes actually said was:

"Seventy years my senior."

Sherlock Holmes, having been born in 1854, was therefore 34 years of age in 1888, and Mycroft was 104 years of age in the same year. This should not occasion any surprise, as the Holmes family has long been renowned for its longevity. Is not Sherlock Holmes today now approaching (at the time of this writing) 114 years of age?

Sherlock and Mycroft, therefore, were half-brothers, and there is nothing in the Canon to disprove this statement. All of us know cases where half-brothers with the same surname refer to each other as brothers, rather than half-brothers. They had the same father, of course, and like all the other Holmeses of whom we know, the old man must have lived for a long time to father two sons 70 years apart in age, but *The Guinness Book of Records* is full of even more astonishing statistics; the thing is a long way from impossible.

Colin Prestige, the learned and erudite Honorary Secretary of The Sherlock Holmes Society of London, buttressed the half-brother theory rather well in an address he made at a meeting of the Society as long ago as 13 September 1951, when he said:

> Mycroft and Sherlock were not brothers at all, but half-brothers. . . .
> Both brothers were six feet tall, and they would inherit their height
> from their father. But it is not unfanciful to suppose that Mycroft
> would inherit his corpulence from his mother and Sherlock his lean,
> spare, gaunt figure from *his* mother. Again, Sherlock had a thin, sharp,
> eager face and sharp features, whereas Mycroft's face was massive and
> "had preserved something of the sharpness of expression which was so
> remarkable in that of his brother." Sherlock's hands were long, thin and
> sensitive like a surgeon's; Mycroft's were broad and flat, like the flippers
> of a seal. Both had grey eyes."

So when the Travellers' was founded, in 1819, Mycroft was 35 years of age; just the right age to think about founding a club of the kind that the Travellers' was and still is, to this day.

Do I hear my querulous friend asking what evidence there is in the Canon about Mycroft's doing any travelling? Perhaps he wants to remind me of Sherlock Holmes's words: "Mycroft lodges in Pall Mall, and he walks round the corner into White-hall every morning and back every evening. From year's end to year's end he takes no other exercise, and is seen nowhere else, except only in the Diogenes Club, which is just opposite his rooms."

Remember, he was 104 years of age! When you are 104, dear reader, let us hope that you will be able to do as well.

In the Travellers', the only requirement for candidates for membership, so far as travelling is concerned, is that they must have travelled at one time or another at least 500 miles in a direct line from England. By the time Mycroft was 35, he must have got around a bit. Even in 1819, it was no great trick to travel 500 miles out of England. And, as a founder, he must have been responsible for either making this rule or at least approving it, so that it must be assumed that he was eligible on that footing.

I think that I have made my point that the only possible candidate for the Diogenes Club is the Travellers'. For general ornery cussedness[4] and misanthropy, I don't think it can be beaten in the western or civilised world.

—June 1968

NOTES

1. Salary to you, Buster.
2. Crackers in American.
3. Chronology by Baring-Gould.
4. An American expression I picked up somewhere.

Watson noted that there was something positively
inhuman about Sherlock Holmes at times. Could the
same be said of Mycroft?

MYCROFT RECOMPUTED

by LYTTLETON FOX

"BY THE WAY, do you know what Mycroft is?" Out of a sky that was anything but clear, and getting murkier by the minute, Sherlock, as you'll remember, propounded this portentous question to Watson in *The Bruce-Partington Plans*.

Watson's answer showed that after all those years he still hadn't begun to have a complete or accurate conception of what Mycroft was. All he knew about Mycroft was what Sherlock had chosen to tell him some years before at the time of *The Greek Interpreter*. And even the scanty disclosure made on that earlier occasion represented a dramatic relaxation of Sherlock's policy of treating any and all information about Mycroft as a tiptop secret. He had theretofore kept the very existence of Mycroft hidden from his closest, most trusted friend. It now appeared that on the earlier occasion Sherlock had not told Watson much. It was evident that where Mycroft was concerned Sherlock had virtually been restricting Watson to a need-to-know basis.

"You told me," Watson now recalled, "that he had some small office under the British Government."

Holmes chuckled. "I didn't know you quite so well in those days," he remarked. "One has to be discreet when one talks of high matters of state."

Now, after many more years of intensely intimate association and the closest and most confidential collaboration with Watson in delicate and vastly important matters of detection, Sherlock ventured to allow himself to go a little further in lifting for Watson's benefit the security veil that obscured the truth about the nature and occupation of Mycroft.

But, as I shall try to show, Sherlock did not even now feel that the time was quite ripe to put Watson fully in the know about the Mycroft secret. He was still holding out on him. Indeed, that question, "Do you know what Mycroft is?" has not been answered in depth, satisfactorily, thoroughly, authoritatively, incontrovertibly, and *in toto* until now. Such an answer, I make bold to assert, is given for the first time in this paper.

By the way, if that declaration seems to bespeak a somewhat flagrant lack of modesty on my part, I'll remind you that in avoiding the restraining influence of modesty I'm merely following one of the cardinal intellectual doctrines of the Master himself. He did not, as he emphatically explained, count modesty among the virtues. Hence he conscientiously abstained from it. He felt that this so-called virtue was inimical to objectivity and hence to truth itself. It follows that if I were to differ with the Master on this point I would be guilty of nothing less than Canonical heresy. Luckily, as you can see, this form of Canonical heresy is not one of my weaknesses.

Let us now review the description of Mycroft's character and *raison d'être* as set forth by Sherlock in *The Bruce-Partington Plans*. It was a fair enough exposition as far as it went—which, as we shall see, was not very far.

"You are right in thinking that he is under the British Government," observed Sherlock. Then came the astounding, albeit only partial, eye-opener. "You would also be right . . . if you said that occasionally he *is* the British Government."

Noting Watson's bewildered astonishment at this remark, Holmes said, "I thought I might surprise you." He then gave a summary of Mycroft's unique position at Whitehall. "He has the tidiest and most orderly brain, with the greatest capacity for storing facts, of any man living," stated Sherlock.

Now it seems to me that this capacity of Mycroft's, exceeding that of any human being, for storage of facts is extremely significant. It almost makes one think of a computer, does it not? We are all quite aware that no one has ever lived who could hope to approach the ability of a computer to preserve within its small chilly viscera of microfilm and memory drums millions and millions of information items for instant recall.

At this stage of our inquiry it would, of course, be utterly premature to jump to any conclusive inferences about the superhuman ability, common to Mycroft and the computer, for seemingly effortless retention and recollection of vastly voluminous data. It is suggested, however, that this point be kept in mind as possibly having a real bearing on the question we are re-examining, namely, "Do you know what Mycroft is?"

In that same conversation Sherlock threw some further light on the nature of Mycroft's work for the Government. "The conclusions of every department are passed to him," Sherlock revealed, "and he is the central exchange, the clearing-house, which makes out the balance."

Let's ponder those words: "The conclusions of every department are passed to him." There may be an important clue here to just how Mycroft works—or *is* worked. This passing on of conclusions from government departments to Mycroft is what is known in computer technology as "input," is it not? In other words, Mycroft's *modus operandi* involves being fed a prodigious input of data in the form of departmental conclusions. Mycroft, then, does seem to have certain attributes of a computer. It would be utterly superficial, however, to conclude from this that he *is* a computer. At this stage I do not ask you to accept any such conclusion, but rather to suspend all conclusions until this recomputation is complete.

We must consider some further evidence. What else did Sherlock tell Watson that morning? You will remember, of course, that it was in the third week of November 1895, and Holmes and Watson had just pushed back their breakfast dishes in the Baker Street apartment, which was enveloped in a dense yellow fog.

By the way, before anyone objects that this dense yellow fog, which had settled down upon London and stayed at least four days, could hardly have penetrated inside the Baker Street rooms, I would be inclined to take the opposite view on the basis of my own London experience. It happens that I once lived through one of those dense yellow fogs. One evening in the middle of the fog I went to the theatre to get away from it—the theatre of escape, so to speak. Well, to my flabbergasted consternation I found that this outrageous fog, which was indeed of a dense yellow, had made its way to a certain extent inside the theatre itself, and partly obscured the stage. As this theatre was only a few blocks from Baker Street, I have no doubt whatsoever that the dank, fuliginous atmosphere had passed through the bow window or other fenestral apertures and perhaps had appreciably reduced the visibility in their sitting-room. But, needless to say, there was no fog in Sherlock's brain that morning—any more than any other—and he went on lucidly with his description of Mycroft.

"We will suppose," he said, "that a Minister needs information as to a point which involves the Navy, India, Canada, and the bi-metallic question. . . . Only Mycroft can focus them all and say offhand how each factor would affect the other. . . . In that great brain of his everything is pigeon-holed and can be handed out in an instant."

Here we have a fruitful hint about what is done with this prodigious input contained in Mycroft's massive frame. Here is where the minister needing information comes in. It is superfluous to point out that this minister is a programmer. He tells Mycroft by means of punch-cards, word of mouth, or other device that Sherlock did not bother to specify, just what he needs to know. Thus programmed, Mycroft consults his voluminous stored-up input and out comes the answer lickety split.

By the way, with your indulgence, I can't help digressing for a moment and pointing out that whether you are dealing with Mycroft or an ordinary computer the answer you get will depend to an extent that might be positively frightening on the personality and predispositions of the programmer. Suppose, for example, the programmer wanted to find out this about the bi-metallic question: Whether a currency based on a combined gold and silver standard, with one of those precious metals convertible freely into the other on a fixed ratio of weight, would work out successfully as a medium of exchange in the Navy, India, and Canada? Let's suppose further that this question was asked—or programmed—by two different public figures, each with definite ideas about the bi-metallic question. I refer to Gresham, the much quoted economist, and that more bi-metallic politician–statesman, William Jennings Bryan, who flourished in the 1890s when this conversation about Mycroft took place.

I think that regardless of whether the question was put to Mycroft or a conventional computer the answer would have depended on which of the two, Gresham or Bryan, was the programmer. If Gresham had asked the bimetallism question in his way the instant reply would have been: "The cheaper money drives the dearer out of circulation." If Bryan had put the question in his way, with carefully controlled manipulation of the program cards, the reply from either Mycroft or the standard machine would unquestionably have been: "You shall not crucify mankind upon this cross of gold."

Returning now to the main point, we can now plainly see two provocative parallels between Mycroft and the conventional computer. Both require input. Both have to be programmed. Are there other points of similarity, besides input and programming? My answer to that is: There sure enough are. Just wait and I'll show you.

A computer must have some means of reading or scanning the punch-cards, magnetic tape, or other program media, referring them to its memory drum, microfilm—I'll come back to this subject of microfilm very shortly—or other input memoranda in order to figure out its answer in the limited time (usually about a millionth of a second) allotted to it for the entire job. Did Mycroft have such a reading or scanning device? Let's look at the evidence. As everyone know, one of the reliable, tried and true mechanisms in general use today for looking over punch-cards and enabling the computer to make up its tidy mind is the photo-electric cell. Even if you don't own a computer you've seen those photo-electric cells thousands of times in supermarkets where they open the door for you as you walk out. (For some reason or other they refuse to give you any assistance when you walk *in*.)

Well, was Mycroft equipped with a photo-electric cell? (I'm not alluding to the door-opening type, needless to say, but to such a one as might have been suitable for examining punch-cards, tape, film, and the like.)

Yes, it seems to me uncontrovertible that Mycroft was so equipped. Consider, if you will, the following sentence of Watson's from *The Greek Interpreter*. On seeing Mycroft then for the first time, the astonished Watson observed: "His eyes, which were of a peculiarly light watery grey, seemed to always retain that far-away introspective look. . . ."

This description of Mycroft's "eyes" seems to constitute evidence whose importance to this inquiry—or recomputation—cannot be exaggerated. I ask you to face the question unflinchingly. Were *these* really eyes at all? Who ever saw eyes, real eyes, on a natural human being that were of a peculiarly light watery grey? No, there never were such odd eyes. Now, bearing this undeniable point in mind, will you close your own eyes, such as they are, for a moment, so to speak, and concentrate your memory down hard on those photo-electric eyes, or cells, on the door of your supermarket. Are they not of a peculiarly light watery grey, with a far-away introspective look? Of course they are. The inescapable fact is that Mycroft's so-called eyes were photo-electric cells. They were no doubt used primarily for scanning and correlating input, program, and memory data.

I honestly think now that the evidence already considered is of such weight and cogency as to justify the tentative conclusion that Mycroft, although undeniably human in some respects, was not, strictly speaking, human at all. After all, that's nothing very serious against him, is it? Besides, in some respects, he was clearly superhuman, which I'm sure Mycroft himself, if given the choice, would have preferred to being merely human.

What was—or rather, what *is*—Mycroft, then?

He is an anthropomorphic model of a somewhat old style of computer. I say he's old style, bearing in mind that at this writing (1968) Sherlock is 114 years old, and therefore Mycroft, whom we know to be seven years his senior, is now 121. A computer 121 years old wouldn't exactly be *le dernier cri*.

All right, then we have still to consider whether Mycroft is analogue or digital. Clearly he's analogue, because he can be shown beyond question not to be digital.

How can that be shown? Quite simply. Referring once again to the occasion described in *The Greek Interpreter* when Watson had the unsurpassable thrill of seeing Mycroft for the first time, he made this profoundly significant observation about the formation of Mycroft's hands: "I am glad to meet you, sir," Mycroft said to Watson, putting out *a broad flat hand like the flipper of a seal.*

There you are. The outstanding and distinguishing characteristic of the flipper of a seal is that it is one big undifferentiated paddle—without anything resembling fingers or toes. In other words, no digits. Ergo, being without digits, Mycroft couldn't be a digital computer. Ergo, he's analogue, because all computers, unless they are hybrids, are either digital or analogue.

By the way, how did Mycroft store his input? What data storage medium did he use? While we can't answer this with absolute certitude, the evidence leads one to the belief that he favoured microfilm. What evidence? Why, the very name Mycroft is evidence enough. Or isn't it? Does not Mycroft sound like an abbreviation or nickname for microfilm? If that leaves the "t" in Mycroft unaccounted for, maybe "t" stands for type—thus the name Microfilm Type, which is a handy abbreviation of the particular model. I do not insist on this point, however.

If Mycroft was a computer, did he have any special-purpose adaptions? There is reason to believe he had two. He had a cheque-writing attachment which was used to issue regularly the cheques to Mrs. Hudson to pay the Baker Street rent during the years of Sherlock's disappearance. Probably Mrs. Hudson never noticed the magnetic numerals at the foot of the cheques.

Was there another special adaption? I strongly believe so. What, then?

There is strong evidence that Mycroft was adaptable for use as an automatic pilot. Consider the facts. There are two principal types of automatic pilot in common use. One, of course, is the aeronautical, with which, manifestly, we are not concerned here. The other and older mechanism of this kind is used for steering ships. It could probably be used for other purposes, I dare say, with a few simple adjustments. Now, this variety of steering or guidance mechanism is known as the "Iron Mike."

Well, although I can't prove it beyond a scintilla of doubt, I'm convinced that it was an Iron Mike, not a human coachman, that drove the brougham that took Watson on that fateful day through the streets of London, past many lurking enemies, to join Holmes at Victoria Station for the blood-curdling trip to the Continent that ended up at that fearful place, the Reichenbach Falls. Yes, it was an Iron Mike that drove that brougham, and that Iron Mike was Mycroft.

Now for my Final Problem I am about to throw some much-needed light on that utterly *sui generis* institution, the Diogenes Club, with special reference to the exact nature of Mycroft's relationship to it. The clarifications here presented are based not so much on grubby research—which my doctor told me to avoid when I explained that it always gave me a splitting headache—but are, rather, the products of that pellucid, high-level ratiocination to which we Sherlockian scholars are peculiarly partial.

First of all, I must make bold to take exception with the Master—something which no Sherlockian would ever do without the gravest reflection. I question his appraisal of the Diogenes Club as the queerest club in London.

It was indeed a mighty queer club, and no questions asked. Nevertheless, I cling insistently to the view that it was only the second queerest.

In my opinion, the queerest club in London, far and away beyond any reasonable dispute, was the club to which that amiable gander, Mr. Henry Baker, belonged—the Goose Club at the Alpha Inn. You won't find an organisation like that once in a blue carbuncle. It seems to have been a kind of ornithological predecessor of the modern Christmas club in which geese of a feather painstakingly deposit their money regularly, receiving no visible advantage that they could not have achieved on their own, with a modicum of character, without the club.

In passing it is worth noting that the Goose Club at the Alpha Inn differed sharply from the Diogenes Club in respect to their conception of the value of silence. Although conversation was forbidden at the Diogenes Club under pain of expulsion for the third offense, it is understood that in the clubrooms at the Alpha Inn there was no restriction on honking.

I must now lay aside any air of levity that may have slipped into these remarks. I want to consider with intense seriousness what the origin, functions, and character of the Diogenes Club really were. It is, after all, quite irrational to accept the glib explanation, given out to the public, that it's a social club. In the first place, there is nothing even faintly social about the outfit. We must look deeper.

In one of those blinding flashes of insight that, happily, are vouchsafed generously to us Sherlockians from time to time, it came to me that the so-called Diogenes Club is in reality, to give it its more descriptive name, the Diogenes Foundation.

As you all know, Diogenes' quest for an honest man was not brought to successful fruition in his lifetime. Every day he went out searching with his lantern. (Since he worked in daylight it could just as well have been a dark lantern, for all the use it would have been to him.) But every night the old World Cynic No. 1 returned to his tub empty-handed. No honest man. Realising that his search for an embodiment of virtue might not be completed in his lifetime, what could have been more natural than to establish the Diogenes Foundation to carry on the pursuit after his death? He probably was able to endow the foundation generously by turning over to it all the money he saved on rent by living in a tub.

At last, after some 2,200 years, the Diogenes Foundation came upon Mycroft. They discovered that he never told a lie. His answers, which is to say, his output, were always meticulously faithful to his input. With cries of "Eureka," which Diogenes would probably not have recognised as an Anglicisation of *Eureke,* the Foundation brought Mycroft into its headquarters building. He was the only permanent occupant. The mysterious other clubhouse figures, scanning newspapers silently in their cubicles, were not members, as Holmes and Watson supposed. Undoubtedly they were various special-purpose adaptors for Mycroft.

Mycroft actually had the place all to himself, and he deserved it. Diogenes, through his testamentary foundation, had found his honest man.

—March 1969

The infamous Professor Moriarty, the nemesis of
Sherlock Holmes: how much of the career of such a
secretive one as he can we reconstruct?

MORIARTY: A LIFE STUDY

by PHILIP A. SHREFFLER

MY PAPER "The Dark Dynasty: A Djinn Genealogy" appeared in the March 1971 issue of this JOURNAL, and in it I presented some preliminary remarks concerning the parentage of Professor James Moriarty, as well as what I now believe to be some erroneous conclusions. New evidence, however, has come to light which should permit us finally to put to rest a number of mysteries which currently surround this man who may well have been one of the world's foremost mathematical theorists.

Briefly, my earlier article identified one Barnardo Eagle, a travelling conjurer, who was patronised by George IV, William IV, and Victoria, as the father of Professor Moriarty. The magician was suggestively referred to as "The Napoleon of Wizards," and putting that into juxtaposition with Baring-Gould's suggested birth date for Moriarty—31 October 1846—I hastily reached a conclusion which now seems rather amiss. I persist in thinking, however, that Barnardo Eagle is a credible starting point in Professor Moriarty's history for entirely different reasons, which I shall outline later. I realise that the false start of my previous article casts a shadow of a doubt over my own credibility in this matter, but I trust that the rather remarkable evidence presented here will allay any extant scepticism.

The Moriarty family, or O'Moriarty, from the Irish Ó Muircheartaigh, resided chiefly on both sides of the Castlemaine Harbour in Ireland. Even today statistics show that ninety per cent of the births registered in the name of Moriarty occur in County Kerry. Historically, the Moriartys were an interesting lot. The Most Reverend David Moriarty (1814–1877) "was remarkable for his opposition not only to the Fenians but to Home Rule" (indicating that there was more than one unpopular Moriarty). Reverend Patrick Eugene Moriarty (1804–1875),

263

born in County Kerry, later became famous as Augustinian Superior in the United States. And Henry Augustus Moriarty made his name in 1866 by recovering a broken Atlantic cable in mid-ocean. There seems to be another branch of the Moriarty family, too, in the Midlands, where Ó Muircheartaigh has survived in modern times as Murtagh. (It is significant to note that the Scottish form of Murtagh is Murdoch, a fact of which we shall make use later.)[1] It should, at any rate, suffice to say that the Moriarty family was an exemplary one for both its determination and its intelligence.

Since I have not had access to any British parish records, it is well nigh impossible to name the man who was Barnardo Eagle or to fix a definite birth date for Professor Moriarty. If we accept the proposition that he was born in 1846 or thereabouts (which I am rather inclined to do), we will understand the sense of Sherlock Holmes's remark in Chapter I of *The Valley of Fear* to the effect that Moriarty came from "a west of England family." During the turbulent years of the potato famine a great tide of emigrants fled Ireland. County Kerry, being not only a marine but also a farming district, did not escape this disaster. Although Barnardo Eagle, alias Moriarty, was described in a publicity poster as being a celebrated conjurer in 1845, we may assume that he was shuttling between Ireland and England as early as the 1820s during the reign of George IV. When the tragedy of the famine struck with full force in 1846, Eagle's possibilities for life in his homeland were shut off. Undoubtedly he settled in Liverpool where there were, and still are, great concentrations of Irish. So was established the "west of England family" from which sprang Professor James Moriarty.

The publicity poster for Barnardo Eagle mentions only a daughter named Georgiana as the offspring of the wizard (probably so named in appreciation of the patronage of the King). Since that poster is dated January of 1847, we may certainly assume that the three James Moriartys were born after mid-1846. We find also that Eagle was on the road with his show in early December of 1846, so that if Professor Moriarty was born in 1846, we may fix the date as some time prior to December, on the assumption that Eagle would wish to be with the baby before setting out again. If his birth date must be in 1846, but before early December, we may consider the end of October or the beginning of November. This satisfies Baring-Gould's intuition that Hallowe'en of 1846 was the date in question.

So young James (the *first* James, our Professor) spent the early years of his life travelling about England with his show-man father, since it would have been unlikely for him to have remained in Liverpool with his mother. Given the hereditary intelligence of the Moriarty family and the cleverness of his father, it is little wonder that James should have been attracted to mathematics, for all its concreteness one of the most abstract and intellectual of human endeavours. But the future Professor Moriarty was not alone in his pursuits. The Moriartys of Liverpool produced *two* mathematicians, as we shall see.

By the time he was twenty-one, James Moriarty had written his treatise on the binomial theorem. Since it is unlikely that he had any formal education, he certainly produced this work through his own studies. In point of fact, the binomial theorem was not new to the world of 1867. Although it became popular in Victorian times, it had been developed by Sir Isaac Newton as an algebraic short cut for raising a binomial to any power.

The theorem had something of a vogue in the later nineteenth century (it is even mentioned in "the Major-General's Song," in Gilbert and Sullivan's *Pirates of Penzance*), and Moriarty's monograph on the subject attracted some attention. On the strength of the paper, and no doubt due to the fact that his father had been patronised by several crowned heads, James was appointed to the mathematics chair at what Holmes described in *The Valley of Fear* as "one of our smaller universities."

Given this information, it is not difficult to identify Moriarty's university. Prior to 1880, there existed no more than four English universities: Cambridge, Oxford, London, and Durham. We may rule out the universities in Scotland and Wales because Holmes says one of "our" universities (presumably meaning English). Then, too, we learn from Holmes that when Moriarty was forced to resign his chair, he came *down* to London. So we find that Moriarty could not have come down to London from London, and Oxford and Cambridge were definitely not "smaller universities." When we eliminate all the other possibilities, the truth that Durham was the Professor's university remains.

The University at Durham was chartered in 1832 with funds from a church grant and was devoted primarily to ecclesiastical education. No doubt it would have remained so had it not been for the radical changes brought about by the Industrial Revolution. The increased demand for technological instruction was probably the cause of an opening in the faculty which allowed James Moriarty to become a professor. But it is no mystery that in the isolated, small town of Durham and in a parochial university those "dark rumours" which surrounded Moriarty should precipitate his dismissal from his post. But before we deal with Moriarty's resignation, there are a few other avenues to explore.[2]

I wrote in my earlier essay that Sherlock Holmes must have known of the Professor's existence and even his lineal descent in referring to him as "The Napoleon of Crime" well before *The Valley of Fear* and *The Final Problem*. Now there is evidence to support this. Ironically, it was Dr. Watson who recorded Holmes's sidelong allusions to Moriarty in *A Study in Scarlet,* years before Watson had ever even heard of the man. The first of these occurs in Chapter IV where Holmes remarks: "You know a conjuror gets no credit once he has explained his trick. . . ." The suggestion here is that Holmes always knew that he was at odds with Moriarty, son of the conjurer, and that he is making an apt metaphor. But if this is not enough, there is one of the most perplexing Canonical puzzles which is explained by Holmes's knowledge of Moriarty—Holmes on astronomy. Why should Holmes have become irritable at the mention of the Copernican system? Clearly, he must have known of Moriarty's treatise, *The Dynamics of an Asteroid,* and was unable to control his anger, even toward his roommate. This, incidentally, dates both the treatise and Moriarty's entry into the world of crime some time between 1867 and 1881.

Parenthetically, we must note that *The Dynamics of an Asteroid,* "a book which ascends to such rarefied heights of pure mathematics . . . that there [was] no man in the scientific press capable of criticising it," came at a time when little was known about asteroid movement and its mathematics. But we can only understand that Moriarty had picked up where Karl Friedrich Gauss (1777–1855) had left off. One of the greatest mathematicians of all time, Gauss had made astounding investigations into the dynamics of asteroid movement, and had done work with binomial equations! Thus, we may well have been underestimating Moriarty's mathematical achievements. To say that he ranked with Gauss is to say that he was one of the four greatest mathematicians in history.[3]

What was it, then, that caused the dismissal of this genius from the faculty of Durham University? Was Holmes correct about Moriarty's connection with the case of the vengeful Scowrers? And how was it that Holmes had so harried the Professor before 4 May 1891 that a fatal contest ensued?

We know from *The Valley of Fear* that Holmes is aware of "a master hand" as the planning agent in the murder of Birdy Edwards. We have always assumed it was Moriarty, but we need assume nothing when there is proof. Obviously the murder was well planned, from beginning to end, even down to the hotel reservations for Ted Baldwin—and the name of the hotel was the Eagle Commercial! It was the perfect touch for a man with a bit of the theatrical in his blood. And if the reason for Barnardo Eagle's alias and the choice of the Eagle Commercial Hotel is not obvious by now, we have but to consider the arms of the only Moriarty family listed in *Burke*: "Moriarty (Ireland). Argent, an eagle displayed, sable. Crest: an arm embowed in armour, holding a dagger, the blade environed with a serpent." Nothing more need be added. In taking this liberty, Moriarty had "made a trip—only a little, little trip—but it was more than he could afford."[4]

Nathan Bengis has broken with most chronologists and has dated *The Valley of Fear* on 7 and 8 January 1891,[5] and I am in agreement with him. For the events which follow the Scowrer's murder were quick and terrible, characterised by viciousness and subterfuge on all sides—and ended in death.

For the sake of brevity, I shall dispense with quotation marks and footnotes in telling the story. For those interested, the information all comes from the beginning of *The Valley of Fear* and *The Final Problem*.

As late as early January of 1891, according to Holmes, Professor Moriarty still held his chair at Durham University for which he received £700 per annum. And, according to both Holmes and Inspector MacDonald, Moriarty maintained a study in which hung a valuable Greuze. Since it is not likely that he would keep a painting of great value in a study in London and teach at the other end of the country, we may infer that the study was in Durham, and that Moriarty, in his best tradition, administered his criminal activities in London through Moran, while he himself was far, far away. We can imagine Holmes making three separate trips to the north in an attempt to gain entry to the study, while MacDonald, a Scot, probably stopped by on Holmes's advice while on a rail journey to visit relatives in Scotland.

But after the outrage of *The Valley of Fear* (which, remember, I date in 1891), Holmes decided to take action to stop Moriarty forever. Knowing the nature of parochial institutions and of small towns in general, Holmes realised it would take little to cast aspersions on the Professor's reputation. So, according to Moriarty's own memorandum book, Holmes crossed his path on the 7th of January in the Douglas murder. (See *The Annotated Sherlock Holmes*, II, 305, to account for this discrepancy.) On the 23rd of January Holmes visited the administration of Durham University with evidence of Moriarty's criminal involvements. This seemed to have little effect, so Holmes enlisted the aid of an agent to spread malicious gossip about the Professor around the town. And Holmes was later to remark about his success: In *The Copper Beeches* he asserted that "the pressure of public opinion can do in the town what the law cannot accomplish." By the middle of February this manoeuvre had seriously inconvenienced Moriarty until at the end of March he was hampered in his plans to the point where he was forced by the university to resign. He hastily moved to London where he set up as an army coach, probably through the aid of his brother Colonel Moriarty, and Colonel Moran. His career there, however, was to last only about a month. At the close of April he visited Holmes in Baker Street to warn the detective of the danger of his continual persecution. And persecution was just the appropriate term. Moriarty had been hounded by Holmes to the point where, like a wounded animal, he was forced to turn and spring.

The rest of the story is familiar—the chase over the continent, and the finale at the Reichenbach. With the death of Moriarty and the capture of Moran, Holmes felt that he could breathe a great deal easier. And yet there was one other problem in the case, one that was by no means final. No mention is ever made of what became of Colonel James Moriarty. Apparently, Holmes thought he had little to fear from him since no steps were taken to apprehend him, and we never hear of him again. But this military man, probably the youngest of the three Moriarty brothers, and probably no more than forty years old at the time (having been born certainly no earlier than 1850), swore to dog Holmes's tracks to the end of his days, waiting for the proper moment. We see him at least once more in the Canon, living near Holmes on the Sussex Downs years after Holmes's retirement. He appears in *The Lion's Mane* as Ian Murdoch, the mathematics coach at Harold Stackhurst's academy, The Gables, and he is described as "a tall, dark, thin man, so taciturn and aloof that none can be said to have been his friend. He seemed to live in some high, abstract region of surds and conic sections with little to connect him with ordinary life." Little, that is, except Mr. Sherlock Holmes. Murdoch's physical description, intellectual prowess, and temperamental disposition are enough to link him with Professor Moriarty. But there is one further point: Murdoch, as we have noted, is the Scottish variant of Moriarty!

—June 1973

A MORIARTY CHRONOLOGY

1210	O'Moriarty, Chief of the Name, marries daughter of a leading Fitzgerald
1653	Father Thady MacMoriarty martyred under the Penal Code
1714	Four priests named Moriarty proscribed under the Penal Code
late 1820s	Barnardo Eagle (Moriarty) first patronised by King George IV
1835	Birth of Georgiana Moriarty
early 1846	The Barnardo Eagle family emigrates to Liverpool, England
31 October 1846	Birth of Professor James Moriarty
1847–1860	The younger James Moriarty born during this period
1855	Karl Friedrich Gauss dies
1866	Henry Augustus Moriarty recovers broken Atlantic cable
1867	Oldest James Moriarty writes paper on binomial theorem and wins mathematics chair at Durham University
1867–1881	Professor Moriarty enters life of crime and writes *The Dynamics of an Asteroid* during this period

7–8 January 1891	*The Valley of Fear*
23 January 1891	Sherlock Holmes calls on administration of Durham regarding Moriarty
End of March 1891	Professor Moriarty moves to London after dismissal from faculty at Durham
24 April–4 May 1891	*The Final Problem*; death of Professor Moriarty
1909	Colonel James Moriarty living at The Gables under the name Ian Murdoch

NOTES

1. Information on the Moriarty family is from *Irish Families: Their Names, Arms, and Origins,* by Edward MacLysaght (Dublin: Hodges Figgis, 1957), p. 230.

2. Information on the English universities is from *England: 1870–1914,* by Sir Robert Ensor (Oxford: Clarendon Press, 1936), pp. 147–48 and 321; and *The Age of Reform: 1815–1870,* by Sir Llewellyn Woodward (Oxford: Clarendon Press, 1962), pp. 492–93.

3. The other three giants in the field would be Archimedes, Newton, and Gauss. Physical theorists like Democritus and mystical renegades like Pythagoras cannot, of course, be included in this number.

4. *The Final Problem.*

5. "What Was the Month?" BSJ (NS) 7 (1957), 204–14.

MACAVITY: THE MYSTERY CAT

by T. S. ELIOT

Macavity's a Mystery Cat: he's called the Hidden Paw—
For he's the master criminal who can defy the Law.
He's the bafflement of Scotland Yard, the Flying Squad's
    despair:
For when they reach the scene of crime—*Macavity's not
    there*!

Macavity, Macavity, there's no one like Macavity,
He's broken every human law, he breaks the law of gravity.
His powers of levitation would make a fakir stare,
And when you reach the scene of crime—*Macavity's not
    there*!

You may seek him in the basement, you may look up in
    the air—
But I tell you once and once again, *Macavity's not there*!

Macavity's a ginger cat, he's very tall and thin;[1]
You would know him if you saw him, for his eyes are
    sunken in.[2]
His brow is deeply lined with thought, his head is highly
    domed;[3]
His coat is dusty from neglect, his whiskers are
    uncombed.
He sways his head from side to side, with movements like
    a snake;[4]
And when you think he's half asleep, he's always wide
    awake.

Macavity, Macavity, there's no one like Macavity,
For he's a fiend in feline shape, a monster of depravity.
You may meet him in a by-street, you may see him in the
    square—
But when a crime's discovered, then *Macavity's not there!*

He's outwardly respectable. (They say he cheats at cards.)
And his footprints are not found in any file of Scotland
    Yard's.
And when the larder's looted, or the jewel-case is rifled,
Or when the milk is missing, or another Peke's been
    stifled,
Or the greenhouse glass is broken, and the trellis past
    repair—
Ay, there's the wonder of the thing! [5] *Macavity's not there!*

And when the Foreign Office find a Treaty's gone astray,
Or the Admiralty lose some plans and drawings by
    the way, [6]
There may be a scrap of paper in the hall or on the
    stair—
But it's useless to investigate—*Macavity's not there!*

And when the loss has been disclosed, the Secret Service
    say:
"It *must* have been Macavity!"—but he's a mile away.
You'll be sure to find him resting, or a-licking of his
    thumbs,
Or engaged in doing complicated long division sums. [7]

Macavity, Macavity, there's no one like Macavity,
There never was a Cat of such deceitfulness and suavity.
He always has an alibi, and one or two to spare:
At whatever time the deed took place—MACAVITY WASN'T
    THERE!

And they say that all the Cats whose wicked deeds are
    widely known
(I might mention Mungojerrie, I might mention
    Griddlebone)
Are nothing more than agents for the Cat who all the
    time
Just controls their operations: the Napoleon of Crime![8]

—October 1954

NOTES

[By H. T. Webster and H. W. Starr]

1. "He is extremely tall and thin . . ." (*The Final Problem*).

2. ". . . and his two eyes are deeply sunken in his head" (Ibid.).

3. ". . . and his forehead domes out in a white curve" (Ibid.).

4. ". . . and his face . . . is forever slowly oscillating from side to side in a curiously reptilian fashion" (Ibid.).

5. "Ay, there's the genius and the wonder of the thing" (Ibid.).

6. Possibly Mr. Eliot feels that Moriarty was the man behind Mr. Joseph Harrison and Herr Hugo Oberstein.

7. ". . . endowed by nature with a phenomenal mathematical faculty . . . he wrote a treatise on the binomial theorem" (Ibid.).

8. "He is the Napoleon of crime, Watson" (Ibid.); ". . . this Napoleon-gone-wrong . . ." (*The Valley of Fear*).

*Why should the genius Moriarty have devoted himself
to the study of an issue so mathematically pedestrian as
the binomial theorem? As Poul Anderson suggests, there
was nothing pedestrian about it. . . .*

A Treatise on the Binomial Theorem

by Poul Anderson

PSYCHOLOGISTS HAVE OBSERVED that the correlation between
mathematical and linguistic ability is very small. This is not to
say that a mathematician can learn no foreign languages or that
a linguist cannot master algebra, but that the flair for the original, creative thinking in one field, as distinguished from a mere
power of learning by rote, usually precludes such creativity in
the other. Though the statistical establishment of this finding is
recent, we see it as clearly and profoundly illustrated in the
Canon as all other facets of human experience. Dr. Watson was
not only an inspired reporter; he must have been one of the
greatest intuitive psychologists of all time. It would be interesting to know what he thought of the work of his contemporary,
Sigmund Freud.

Sherlock Holmes's linguistic genius was unsurpassed—not
only was he able to impersonate English types from the rough-
est stable-hand to the mildest Nonconformist clergyman,[1] with
all the variations of dialect and slang implied, but he traveled
widely and seems to have had no language difficulties whatsoever. In Tibet he conversed with the head lama as the Norwegian Sigerson; he "looked in at Mecca," which he could only
have done by passing himself off as a Moslem, probably an
Arab, and "paid a short but interesting visit to the Khalifa at
Khartoum, the results of which [he] communicated to the Foreign Office"—again, doubtless, getting access to secret information by posing as a native; thereafter he lived in the south of
France, where his research in the coal-tar derivatives proves
him to have been fluent not only in every-day but in technical
French.[2] His studies on Chaldean elements in the Cornish language[3] were possible only because he was thoroughly conver-
sant with both ancient and modern tongues. One need not mul-

274

tiply examples to see that he was one of the lucky few who can learn perfectly a foreign speech, no matter how alien, in the course of days. Doubtless his acute musical ear was of value in this.

At the same time, he is not a theoretical scientist in any degree. His knowledge of philosophy and astronomy is nil; of botany, variable, concentrating on poisonous plants; of geology, practical but limited; of anatomy, accurate but unsystematic.[4] While he was perhaps spoofing Watson when he professed ignorance as to whether the earth goes around the sun or vice versa, his indifference to the question is godlike. His knowledge of chemistry may or may not have been "profound," but in all events it must be remembered that at this time chemistry, and particularly the organic chemistry in which he specialized, was very much cut-and-try. Kekulé had discovered the benzene-ring structure in 1866, and Mendeleef the periodic table in 1869, but the firm mathematical basis of crystal and quantum theory was still lacking.

We must conclude that Holmes was a laboratory man, content to get results that worked and not to question why they worked. His acquaintance with the physical and chemical properties of the organics was more than casual, but he probably lacked any system—thus, the fact that water has a high boiling point and specific heat would be enough for him, without troubling why this should be so when its molecular weight is only 18.

His titanic adversary James Moriarty was, of course, precisely the opposite type. It is not known to what extent the professor was a linguist—doubtless he spoke several European languages, including the classic Latin and Greek required of any educated man—but his knowledge stops there, without the slightest sign of interest in more exotic tongues. He was the planner of international crime, laying his schemes and organization at the disposal of anyone who would pay, but probably English was always spoken at such negotiations, and it is known that Moriarty avoided personal action as much as possible. It might have led to an encounter with German irregular verbs!

On the other hand, Moriarty was *the* great mathematician of an age which held many brilliant researchers in this field. He was "the celebrated author of *The Dynamics of an Asteroid,* a

275

book which ascends to such rarefied heights of pure mathematics that it is said there was no man in the scientific press capable of criticizing it."[5] And "at the age of twenty-one he wrote a treatise upon the binomial theorem, which has had a European vogue . . . he won the mathematical chair at one of our smaller universities." "He is a genius, a philosopher, an abstract thinker."[6] Nevertheless, like most of the scientific great, he was a first-rate teacher, for even Inspector MacDonald could grasp his lucid explanation of eclipses in a minute.[7] One envies his students. Could the knowledge and inspiration he gave them be in part responsible for the stupendous flowering of physics in quantum theory, relativity, and wave mechanics during the following decades? If so, Professor Moriarty's ghost must be enjoying a sardonic chuckle as he contemplates the atomic and hydrogen bombs of today.

At this point I must take issue with Mr. A. Carson Simpson, whose "The Curious Incident of the Missing Corpse"[8] suggests that Moriarty had developed an atomic accelerator which shrank the size of objects to zero by way of the Lorenz–Fitzgerald contraction effect. Although Mr. Simpson's theory is ingenious, and does seem to account for numerous peculiar disappearances, including that of Moriarty's own body, I fear the laws of nature will simply not support it.

The theory overlooks one basic item: that in order to accelerate mass, and so shrink it, energy must be applied. A shrinkage of one-half through velocity would require an energy equivalent to the original mass. Thus, to reduce, let us say, a 6-foot, 170-pound man to three feet, an energy of 170 pounds must be applied. Now a mass of one gram is equivalent to 9×10^{20} ergs, sufficient to raise a 30,000-ton ship more than 19 miles into the air. Mass-energy to the amount of 170 pounds, necessarily applied to Moriarty's body through the law of equal and opposite reaction, would not only have destroyed the Reichenbach Falls in one annihilating blow, but probably would have left a large hole in place of the entire Republic of Switzerland. Mr. Simpson goes yet further: postulating that objects were shrunk to nearly zero size. In order to do this, Moriarty would have had to convert the entire sidereal universe into energy, a project somewhat too large even for his ambitious nature.

Moreover, any form of laboratory work would have ill accorded with the professor's character. He, like Albert Einstein, was pre-eminently a thinker, a theoretician, leaving to others the burden of experimental proof. Nowhere in the Canon is there the least indication that Moriarty's scientific tools were anything but paper, pencil, and his own magnificent brain.

No, whatever subtle and diabolical methods Moriarty used, his technology was Victoria's. It is the more credit to his satanic genius that he could achieve such results with no more apparatus than anyone else possessed.

But what, then, *was* his contribution to science?

Mr. Robert Bloch has proposed that *The Dynamics of an Asteroid* foreshadowed the space station now being talked of, and laid much of the theoretical groundwork therefor.[9] This idea seems entirely plausible, but we must remember that the pure mathematician has no time to waste on practical, engineering details. Moriarty's suggestion was doubtless only tossed off *en passant*, casually mentioned, perhaps as a specific example of the use of his equations. His own interest would be in more basic questions.

To the mathematical astronomer, an asteroid is a heavenly body so small that its perturbing effects on the major planets can be neglected. But these same planets can make the asteroid's orbit a wild and wonderful thing. Halley's Comet, for example, has occasionally appeared days off schedule, presumably because some planet's gravitational pull got it away from the computed path.

I suggest that Moriarty developed a *general solution* for the orbit of an asteroid; a set of equations applicable to any such object. The magnitude of his achievement can be appreciated by reflecting that there are nine known major planets, all influencing the asteroid simultaneously, and that no general solution has yet been found even for the three-body problem. (Given the positions, masses, and velocities of three bodies acting under gravitation, find their orbits for all past time and all time to come.) Had Moriarty lived, he would surely have gone on to solve this, and even proceeded to the n-body problem.

Exactly what his treatise on the binomial theorem may have been is harder to say. Obviously it must have been original and important to have had a European vogue; but what new development did it involve?

The theorem itself is simply the expansion of the binomial (a + b) raised to the nth power, where n is any number:

$$(a + b)^n = a^n + na^{n-1}b + \frac{n(n-1)}{1 \cdot 2} a^{n-2}b^2 + \ldots$$

$$+ \frac{n(n-1) \ldots (n-r+1)}{r!} a^{n-r} b^r \ldots + \ldots b^n$$

It vexed mathematicians for many centuries. The Hindus and the Arabs knew something of it. Newton discovered it about 1665, and an exposition is found in a letter dated 1676, but no real proof is given. Bernoulli and Euler sought the proof, but it remained for the Norwegian Niels Henrik Abel (1802–1829) to demonstrate it rigorously for all n. This having been done before Moriarty's time, what remained for him?

A glance at the contemporary state of mathematics permits an informed guess. The nineteenth century was a period of revolution. Lobachevsky, Bolyai, and Riemann created non-Euclidean geometry; Peano's epochal work on number was being developed—the century was one in which it was realized that traditional logic, geometry, and mathematics represented only special cases, and which set itself to develop the most general system: an effort leading in the twentieth century to Whitehead and Russell's *Principia Mathematica,* Gödel's astonishing theorem, and heaven knows what else in years to come.

It seems probable, then, that Moriarty was working on the basic idea of number itself, and that he developed a general binomial theorem applicable to other algebras than the one we know. If he could do this at the three-cornered age of 21, it is obvious that in his case, as in the Master's, genius flowered early.

—January 1955

1. *A Scandal in Bohemia.*
2. *The Empty House.*
3. *The Devil's Foot.*
4. *A Study in Scarlet.*
5. *The Valley of Fear.*
6. *The Final Problem.*
7. *The Valley of Fear.*
8. BSJ (NS) 4 (1954), 24.
9. "The Dynamics of an Asteroid," BSJ (NS) 3 (1953), 225.

With his ill-gotten wealth, Professor Moriarty
collected—or speculated in—the visual arts. Here Mr.
Tracy reveals just which famous painting Moriarty
acquired. . . .

THE PORTALIS SALE OF 1865

by JACK TRACY

THE NAME OF Jean Étienne Marie Portalis (1746–1807) has some
claim to permanence in European history, for the man himself
gained much renown in French legal circles and was the principal author of the Code Napoléon. His son, Joseph Marie Portalis (1778–1858), was also a much-respected jurist of his day.

These facts have significance for the second chapter of *The
Valley of Fear*. They do not, however, nor does anyone by the
name of Portalis, having anything to do with any art sale in
1865 or any other year.

When Watson finally wrote up the Birlstone case 25 years
after its occurrence, no doubt from hurriedly-scribbled notes,
he wrote "Portalis" because the name probably was familiar to
him from the common-knowledge history of his own century.
What Holmes had said on that day at the end of the 'eighties,
though, was not "Portalis" but "Pourtalès."

The one name is reasonably well-known, the other obscure,
and the misspelling has created one of the more tangled cases
of identity in all the Canon—one which is all the more fascinating because there really was a Pourtalès in Paris in 1865.

The Pourtalès were French Protestants living originally in
the Cévennes mountain region of southern France before flee-
ing the country when religious freedoms were revoked in 1685.
One branch of the family established itself around 1720 in what
is now the French-speaking Swiss canton of Neuchâtel in the
person of Jérémie Pourtalès (1701–1784), a merchant. His son
Jacques-Louis (1722–1814) built the business into a diversified
financial empire composed of manufacturing, retailing, and
banking, with outlets in every major city of Europe. He ener-
getically amassed a huge fortune for himself and his heirs, said
to amount to no less than 100,000,000 francs at the time of his

death, and he had no little influence at the Prussian court. His three sons, Louis, James-Alexandre, and Frédéric, were ennobled as counts of Prussia in 1815. It was James-Alexandre who established the Pourtalès Gallery of Art in Paris.

That which today is the canton of Neuchâtel was for two centuries the independent principality of Neuenburg, ruled after 1707 by the royal house of Prussia. Long associated with the Swiss Confederacy, Neuchâtel in 1815 formally became a canton of Switzerland, but its local government remained a monarchy under the Prussian king. When the anti-monarchical uprisings convulsed Europe in 1848, and King Frederick William IV was preoccupied with the larger issues of Prussia and greater Germany, the people of Neuchâtel overthrew his representatives and proclaimed a republican form of government. Frederick William could not retake his principality without technically invading Switzerland, of whose perpetual neutrality Prussia herself was a guarantor by the terms of the Congress of Vienna, and so had to resign himself to the loss of the territory. In 1856 a royalist counter-revolution was put down by Swiss federal troops, and the next year Frederick William renounced all claim to Neuchâtel.

Thus the sons of Jacques-Louis Pourtalès were created Prussian counts in 1815, at a time when, even as Swiss citizens, they owed allegiance to the King of Prussia. Legal successions to the titles were valid until the renunciation of 1857.

By these ennoblements the family was divided into three distinct branches. The main family line, to be called Pourtalès-Steiger, continued through the elder brother Louis (1773–1848), who was active in the military and in Swiss politics. One of his sons commanded part of the federal troops which suppressed the royalist insurrection of 1856, and a grandson was Louis-François de Pourtalès (1823–1880), the famous Swiss-American naturalist. A grand-nephew was Guy de Pourtalès (1881–1941), the French Shakespearian scholar.

The youngest brother, Frédéric, Comte de Pourtalès-Castelane (1779–1861), devoted himself to Prussian government service. His son was Prussian minister to Constantinople and to Paris, and a grandnephew was the German ambassador at St. Petersburg upon the outbreak of World War I in 1914.

The Pourtalès Gallery was founded by the middle brother, James-Alexandre, Comte de Pourtalès-Gorgier (1776–1855), who spurned government service, sold his rights as a nobleman in 1831, and lived his life as an amateur artist and a collector of paintings and antique sculpture in Paris. He spent fifty years and 1,500,000 francs in gathering the treasures which he kept on display in his private mansion in the rue Tronchet. It was considered remarkably complete for a private collection, composed as it was of pictures, sculptures, coins, medals, antique gems, and "almost every variety" of pottery, ivories, and glassware.

"The following anecdote . . . gives one a charming idea of the man himself," wrote Anthony B. North Peat, Paris correspondent to the London *Morning Star*: "The Count's attention was attracted to the works of a young artist, exhibited for the first time at the Salon; the name was then unknown, and it was with some difficulty the Count procured his address. He wrote to request the young aspirant to bring one of the pictures to his house, which request was at once acceded to.

"'I would like to add your picture to my collection, sir,' he said. 'Might I ask its price?'

"'Two thousand francs,' ventured the young man, afraid he had asked for too much.

"'Ten thousand francs!' exclaimed the kindly Pourtalès, feigning deafness, 'Oh, very well, then. I'll pay.'

"True to anecdotal tradition, the struggling painter was as honest as he was poor. He tried to explain that the Count had misunderstood, but he was quickly interrupted.

"'I beg your pardon,' the Count said stiffly. 'I do not bargain.'"

His great collection, "the pride and pleasure of his life," occupied his thoughts even in death. His will specified that it should not be sold or dispersed until he had been dead for ten years. No one knew why he gave such instructions—whether it was a dread of eager collectors beginning to gather before his bones were cold, or "an instance of sagacious foresight," as one commentator put it, or merely a whim—but ten years' expectations and a heightened interest in works of art late in the Second Empire made the decade's delay more than worth while. The Comte de Pourtalès-Gorgier died in Paris on 24 March 1855.[1] During February and March 1865 the collection was auctioned and brought for his heirs a total of nearly 3,000,000 francs.

The objects offered filled a catalogue of 500 pages, and the sale, it was reported, "was attended by the representatives of every considerable museum and collection in Europe." The collection was sold by "departments"—bronzes and terra cottas (150,000 fr.), gems and glassware (46,000 fr.), coins and medals (18,500 fr.), sculptures in wood and ivory, marbles, enamels, stained glass armoirs etc. (500,000 fr.), and finally, commencing on 27 March, the pictures and paintings (over 2,000,000 fr.) to crown the event—and, while almost all the prices received were prodigiously high for the times, the returns fetched by the pictures were truly phenomenal.

More than 400 works, ranging from the renaissance masters to "an élite of the French modern school," went on the block. Titian, Da Vinci, Murillo, Velasquez, Rembrandt, Delaroche, and scores of others were represented.[2] The highest price was commanded by a 1475 portrait of a man by Antonella de Messina, which epitomised the growth in value of the Pourtalès taste. Originally purchased in Florence for 1500 francs, the Antonella was appraised in 1855 at 20,000 francs and at the auction brought 111,250 francs. A Velasquez, purchased by the National Gallery in London for only 37,000 francs, was considered a major triumph in English art circles.

A picture by Greuze, Holmes told Inspector MacDonald, entitled La Jeune Fille à l'Agneau, "fetched one million and two hundred thousand francs—more than forty thousand pounds—at the Portalis sale." In later British editions this was altered to "not less than four thousand pounds," and for good reason. The Greuze sold at the Pourtalès auction brought the second-highest single price of the sale—100,200 francs, or £4000.

The title of the Pourtalès Greuze, Lot No. 264 in the souvenir catalogue, was not La Jeune Fille à l'Agneau; it was Innocence. Nonetheless it did depict a young girl holding a lamb, a favourite subject with Greuze.[3] It was purchased by one Van Cryck, who is believed to have been an agent acting for a number of collectors. It reappeared on the art market in the 1920s, having been the subject of a lawsuit in 1918 upon the occasion of its sale

Innocence by Jean Baptiste Greuze. A picture identical in composition was sold for £4000 at the Pourtalès sale of 1865, but is now believed to be a copy.

from the collection of the Vicomtesse de Curel; its authenticity was called into question at that time, and the work is no longer considered to be genuine. According to the authorities at the Wallace Collection in London, the de Curel picture, as it is now known, is thought today to have been a copy of the Greuze Innocence now in that gallery's possession.[4] In 1951 the copy was owned by J. O. Leegenhock, of Paris, who is known subsequently to have parted with it. Its present whereabouts is unknown.

—March 1976

BIBLIOGRAPHY

The American Annual Cyclopaedia and Register of Important Events for the Year 1865. New York: Appleton, 1866.

Dictionnaire Historique & Biographique de la Suisse (Neuchâtel), 7 vols., 1921–1933.

The Eclectic Magazine (New York), 2:382 (new series), September 1865.

La Grande Encyclopédie (Paris), 31 vols., 1886–1902.

"The London Art Season," *Blackwood's Edinburgh Magazine* (Edinburgh), 98:249, August 1865.

North Peat, Anthony B., *Gossip from Paris during the Second Empire*, selected and arranged by A. R. Waller. New York: Appleton, 1903.

"The Pourtalès Family," *Springfield Museum of Fine Arts Bulletin* (Springfield, Mass.), 23:1–4, December 1956.

"The Pourtalès Gallery of Art," *Month* (London), 2:210–33, March 1865.

The Times (London), February–April 1865.

NOTES

1. The date of the Comte de Pourtalès-Gorgier's death is given in the British Museum catalogue and elsewhere as 1865; this is an error.

2. Two pictures by Holmes's ancestor, Horace Vernet, brought 35,200 fr. and 4000 fr., and one by Horace's grandfather, Claude Vernet, sold for 1100 fr.

3. Professor Moriarty's owning a Greuze, like Enoch Drebber's possession of a copy of Boccaccio's bawdy *Decameron*, is a subtle device pointing up the man's baser tastes. The late Victorians considered Greuze's works to be highly sensual, and thoroughly disapproved of his penchant for depicting pubescent girls *en déshabillé*.

4. Letters dated 30 October and 21 November 1974, from R. A. Cecil, Assistant to the Director of the Wallace Collection, London.

Editor's Note: for more about the sale—and illustrations of Greuze's work—see The Editor's Gas-Lamp, "*Re* Greuze," BSJ (NS) 12 (1962), 195–97; Thomas L. Stix, "Who's Afraid of the Big Bad Moriarty?" BSJ (NS) 12 (1962) 200, 243; illustration on p. 9 of the March 1966 BSJ.

*Irene Adler is famous as the woman who bested
Sherlock Holmes. But records do not show an Irene
Adler born in New Jersey in 1858. Who, then, was she
in reality?*

The Adventuress of Sherlock Holmes
Some Observations Upon the Identification of Irene

by JULIAN WOLFF, M.D.

IT IS QUITE OBVIOUS that Dr. Watson has purposely concealed
the identities of the more prominent persons involved in the
cases of Sherlock Holmes. Much of the recent research has
concerned itself with efforts to discover the hidden names. Fortunately, in nearly every case, Dr. Watson's very efforts at concealment provide the astute investigator with the clues necessary for the solution of the problem. Thus, Mr. Rolfe Boswell
has been able to demonstrate Professor Moriarty's close connection with a famous English mathematician, formerly best
known as a writer of nonsense for children.[1] Mr. Edgar Smith
has made a most notable contribution with his identification of
the King of Bohemia,[2] discovering at the same time the identity
of the illustrious client and of "one of the highest, noblest, most
exalted names in England."

Strangely enough, there seems to have been little effort to
learn the real name of *the* woman known as Irene Adler. A survey of the literature leads to the conclusion that no serious
claims have been set forth on behalf of any of the possible aspi-
rants to this distinction. The theory that there is some connection with New York's own Polly Adler does not even deserve serious consideration. There has been some vague mention of
Lola Montez, the Irish dancer who had a European vogue, and
who once caused a King of Bavaria to lose his throne. This romantic entanglement with European royalty of Germanic descent has been offered as circumstantial evidence, but circumstantial evidence is a tricky thing when the point of view is
shifted. After all, the King of Bohemia, unlike his present-day
grandson, distinctly did not choose to give up his throne for *the*
woman *he* loved. Besides, the first entry after the name of Lola

The [New?] Jersey Lily

Montez in any biographical dictionary reads, "Born 1818, died 1861"—thus eliminating her from any further consideration, and once again showing the danger of reasoning with insufficient data.

Of course, the nineteenth century, or, for that matter, any other century, did not suffer from a shortage of professional beauties who achieved distinction by causing anxiety in high places. In fact, the list is so long that it is not practicable to investigate every name thoroughly. Fortunately for the purposes of this investigation, the necessary point of departure is furnished by Mr. Smith's identification of the royal boy friend. With this knowledge available, the points in favor of one of these eligible ladies can be carefully considered.

The biography of the lady in question may be found in a standard cyclopedia of reference, sandwiched in between that of an English prelate and that of an American poet who wrote a monograph on music. There, from a discreetly worded statement worthy of Dr. Watson himself, it is ascertained that her beauty "attracted the attention" of the Prince of Wales. (No less an authority than Sherlock Holmes once remarked that Irene was "the daintiest thing under a bonnet on this planet.") The same encyclopedia states that she was born in 1852 and married in 1889.[3] These dates can easily be accommodated to the conditions imposed by the Writings. The variation is well within the limits of tolerance allowed the chronicler, who gives the date of

Irene's birth as 1858, and of her marriage as 1888. In this connection it may be recalled that Mr. Smith has shown that the gentleman in the case practiced a similar harmless deception in regard to his age.

According to her own statement, in a note reproduced by Dr. Watson, Irene Adler had been trained as an actress and was quite at home in male costume. That is readily understood when it is learned that our candidate was an actress of note whose favorite role was Rosalind in *As You Like It*. Furthermore, certain other significant points of agreement appear when her memoirs are compared with the Writings. In these memoirs (which apparently reveal only the less interesting half of her activities, since they were published under the title *The Days I Knew*) there is a passage indicating that His Bohemian Majesty was not *the* King to her—no matter what she may have been to him and to Sherlock Holmes. It reads: "I also had photographs of the Danish King and Queen, but I regret to say that they have been lost or appropriated, as were many other photographs and letters I received from celebrities from time to time." This agrees very well with the remarks of the King of Bohemia, describing his attempt to retrieve the compromising photograph, "Twice burglars in my pay ransacked her house. Once we diverted her luggage when she travelled. Twice she has been waylaid." (Probably an understatement.)

Now the real woman is beginning to appear out of the fog. Dr. Watson came closest to revealing her true identity when he wrote that she was born in New Jersey. For, while to Sherlock Holmes and to a host of other admirers, Irregular as well as Bohemian, she is always *the* woman, our heroine, distinguished from all other lilies of the field, is known to the world as the Jersey Lily.

—January 1957

NOTES

1. "In Uffish Thought," BSJ (os) 1 (1946), 21.
2. "A Scandal in Identity," in *Profile by Gaslight*.
3. These are the dates given in *The Columbia Encyclopedia*. In *The Encyclopaedia Britannica* the date of her marriage has been changed to 1899—probably because of influence exerted by a certain gracious lady who wished to avoid a family scandal in Bohemia.

While Dr. Wolff identifies Irene Adler as Lillie Langtry, William Jenkins has compelling reasons to think that the woman who bested Holmes was really another. . . .

"WE WERE BOTH IN THE PHOTOGRAPHS":
I. ADLER AND ADAH I.

by WILLIAM D. JENKINS

"SHE has the face of the most beautiful of women, and the mind of the most resolute of men." The King of Bohemia thus characterized Irene Adler. And in the eyes of Sherlock Holmes she "eclipses and predominates the whole of her sex."

"Miss Menken had the keenest mind I ever encountered in a member of her sex. Indeed, few men were her mental equals, and she could discourse fluently on matters pertaining to literature, the sciences and the latest news of the world in which we live. She was a learned theologian, and I have heard her hold long erudite talks with Dr. Henry Ward Beecher, the Rev. Jonathan Flaherty and other divines of note, in which she more than held up her end of the conversation. Her erudition, coupled with her great beauty, made her the rarest of her sex."[1] Robert Henry Newell, editor of the New York *Sunday Mercury*, thus characterized Adah Isaacs Menken, an American, an actress, and an adventuress if there ever was one.

(Dr. John H. Watson was a great admirer of Henry Ward Beecher.[2] Did Watson know that a young woman named Adah Isaac Menken was capable of discussing theology with Beecher?)

She was born Adah B. Theodore in New Orleans in 1835, of uncertain ancestry which she claimed to be Spanish-Jewish. The claim may have been inspired by her marriage to Alexander Isaac Menken, a Jewish musician, in 1856. In any case the Sephardic touch lent glamour to her background and the young actress continued to avow Judaism even after her rabbinical divorce in 1858. She even retained her ex-husband's middle name with an added letter "s."

289

(In Sherlock Holmes's index, Irene Adler's biography followed that of "a Hebrew rabbi.")

But Alexander Menken instituted civil divorce proceedings in 1859, calling Adah "an adventuress." Adah's love affair with John C. Heenan, the American heavyweight boxer, was certainly adventurous, perhaps bigamous, since she married him before the civil decree was final. In the event, Heenan decided he was not married after all and deserted Adah in New York to sail for England where he won the World's Heavyweight Championship.

(He was never a great boxer, but he was a heavyweight champion and John Heenan's career was known in minute detail to Arthur Conan Doyle, whose knowledge of prize-fighting was encyclopedic. As he says in the five pages of his autobiography devoted to the sport: "My own experience in boxing and my very large acquaintance with the history of the prize-ring found their scope when I wrote *Rodney Stone*. No one but a fighting man would ever, I think, quite understand or appreciate some of the detail."[3])

The ultra-Bohemian scandal made Adah notorious, but it did nothing to help her theatrical career, and she was reduced to playing cheap music halls. Adah's biographer, Mankowitz, notes that "the humiliation of the coarse audience's jeering drove her from the place after a few performances. . . . She left for Jersey City. There in Jersey, in a cheap wretched room Menken set herself to compose a statement." It was a pseudo-suicide note of five paragraphs dated 29 December 1859. The closing paragraph reads:

"My worthless life has long since left me and gone to dwell in the breast of the man, who by foul suspicion of my love and truth for him, has thus ushered me up the bar of the Almighty, where I shall pray for his forgiveness for the cruel and wrong he has done the weak and defenceless being whose sin is her love for him, as my death proves. *God bless him*, and pity me."

The newly-crowned King of the Heavyweights had deserted Adah. Mankowitz comments further:

"Adah thus carefully constructed her suicide scene. . . . From her ashes would arise two new and powerful female phoenixes; one of them a poetess who, like her mentor and model Whitman, cared nothing at all for the barbarians who had destroyed her

Adah, the overwhelming female, nevertheless played many male roles as an actress. Here she is, a slim youth in her walking clothes, as *The French Spy,* a play second in popularity only to *Mazeppa* in her repertory. She also played William the Sailor Boy in *Black-Eyed Susan,* Pip in *Great Expectations,* and *Little Jack Horner.* As a contralto, Irene Adler might have sung such transvestite roles as Prince Orlofsky in *Die Fledermaus,* Niklaus in *The Tales of Hoffmann,* and possibly Cherubino in *The Marriage of Figaro,* although the latter role is usually sung by a soprano. (*Harvard Theatre Collection.*)

frailer self; the other, a self-confessed theatrical Bohemian, determinedly voluptuous, fatal and flashy, temperamental, tempestuous and a terror to all men."[4]

(So Adah the "theatrical Bohemian" was born again in New Jersey in the year 1859. Irene Adler was "born in New Jersey in the year 1858." The closing paragraph of her letter to Sherlock Holmes reads in part: "The King may do what he will without hindrance from one whom he has cruelly wronged.")

Her courage regained, Adah returned to New York, found herself a new theatrical manager, and achieved increasing success. Her place in theatrical history was finally assured in June 1861 when she opened in Albany in the title role of an adaptation of Byron's epic poem *Mazeppa*. The part required the actress to cross the stage naked tied to the back of a spirited horse. Mazeppa was supposedly a heroic Tartar chieftain, and Adah looked decidedly unmasculine in a flesh-colored body stocking. Convincing or not, the star was a spectacular hit and her show soon opened on Broadway where she played to the proverbial packed houses.

There she was seen and loved by the literary intellectual Robert Henry Newell who became her third husband in 1862. Newell (a.k.a. Orpheus C. Kerr) loved Adah not for physical beauty alone but for her beauty of soul and intellect as well. Under the personal tutelage of Walt Whitman she had become a poetess with a score or more of published verses to her credit. Newell thought *Mazeppa* unworthy of Adah's talents, and after the marriage he took her to his home in, of all places, Jersey City. There he tried to persuade her to renounce the stage and to devote her future exclusively to poetry and philosophy. Adah renounced Jersey City instead. She had been re-born in New Jersey once, and once was enough. She returned to the free Bohemian life of New York.

But the rest of the world was waiting to see *Mazeppa*, and Adah went on tour. In San Francisco she terminated her marriage with Newell and took up with the poet Joaquin Miller, whose fringed buckskin persona was almost as flamboyant as that of Adah herself. On one occasion on leaving the beach in Miller's company, Adah threw her handkerchief into the sea crying, "Goodby, gray old grandfather, good-bye." The impressionable Miller may not have known that a similar poetic figure had been used by Swinburne.[5]

In San Francisco Adah also renewed an interest which had attracted her in New York—Spiritualism. She visited a well-known medium named Emma Hardinge whom she helped to spread the faith with generous financial support and to whom she dedicated a poem. At one séance the medium established communication with Adah's mother.

(Arthur Conan Doyle warmly admired Emma Hardinge. In his last authoritative work, *The History of Spiritualism*, he called her "the female St. Paul of the movement. She was a young Englishwoman who had gone to New York with a theatrical company and had then remained in America."[6] Emma Hardinge published at least eight books and pamphlets on Spiritualism, and Conan Doyle, at some time in his life, probably read them all, recommending especially *Modern American Spiritualism*, 1869, and *Nineteenth Century Miracles*, 1883. According to Higham,[7] Conan Doyle attended his first séance in 1879. In his autobiography,[8] Sir Arthur notes that he began the serious investigation of psychic phenomena in 1886, five years before writing *A Scandal in Bohemia*.)

Adah moved on to Nevada with *Mazeppa* in 1863, winning rave notices. The critic for the Virginia City *Territorial Enterprise*, Mark Twain, enthused over her beauty and intelligence, adding "she's a literary cuss herself." After other engagements La Menken departed for Britain in April 1864, and enjoyed a ship-board romance with a handsome American professional gambler named James Barkley.

In London's Astley Theatre *Mazeppa* had the most successful run ever. After playing almost a year in London, Adah, still accompanied by Barkley, toured Britain to popular acclaim but sometimes to genteel disapprobation. Among the unappreciative was *The Albion* of Liverpool, which grumbled:

"America has sent us many things for which we have had little reason to thank her—Spiritualism, Mormonism, Barnumism, Davenportism, and a host of outrageously bad actors, but *La Menken* surpasses and transcends all in utter worthlessness."

(The Davenport brothers, William and Ira, were pioneers in the public demonstration of psychic phenomena such as spirit writing and luminosity. In London their séances attracted interested friends including Adah Isaacs Menken. But in the provinces they were frequently denounced as frauds. In Liverpool the press created such hostility that the audience rioted. In his *History of Spiritualism* Conan Doyle relates these events in indignant detail, devoting many pages to a vigorous defense of the Davenports as genuine mediums.)

In her fashionable salon in London Adah continued her discreet love affair with Barkley who eventually resented her flirtations with other gentlemen and returned to New York in a jealous rage. Adah followed him shortly thereafter, and in August 1866 she agreed to marry him for a very good reason. She was pregnant. Barkley was her fourth and last husband.

As might have been expected, marriage with Barkley was unsuccessful. Her latest husband had no interest in matters spiritual or intellectual. He wanted a meal ticket so he could gamble in the United States where he felt at home, and he demanded that Adah cancel a planned season in Paris. Three days after the wedding Mrs. Barkley was aboard ship bound for France.

There in the City of Light, Adah Isaacs Menken naturally gravitated to the most kindred of spirits, the free-living, free-loving, male-costume-wearing, cigar-smoking Baroness Amandine Aurore Dudevant, better known as George Sand. The French literary lioness became the protectress and confidante of the expectant mother, and the first words of practical wisdom imparted to the protégée were to this effect: Adah was not really Jewish after all. In France of the Second Empire it was better not to be born a Jew. So the little boy born to Adah was christened Louis Dudevant Victor Emmanuel Barkley; and George Sand, wearing female garments as the godmother, Baroness Dudevant, was present in the cathedral.

("'Good-night, Mister Sherlock Holmes.' . . . the greeting appeared to come from a slim youth in an ulster who had hurried by. . . . 'Male costume is nothing new to me. I often take advantage of the freedom which it gives. . . . my walking clothes.'" So wrote Irene Adler to Sherlock Holmes. *A Scandal in Bohemia* appeared in *The Strand Magazine* for July 1891. The second *Strand* story followed immediately in August 1891. That was *The Red-Headed League* which concludes with a quotation in French:

"'L'homme c'est rien—L'oeuvre c'est tout,' as Gustave Flaubert wrote to George Sand.")

Jew or Christian, little Louis Barkley looked upon France only a few months. He died in the summer of 1867.

Meanwhile Adah had performed on the Paris stage in a vehicle written especially for her talents which had won the warmest admiration of Royalty. The German princeling, King Charles of Württemberg, had allied his troops with Austria against Prussia in the War of 1866, and after his defeat had retired to Paris to recuperate. His Majesty established his entire Court at the Grand Hôtel and there he was graciously pleased to receive La Menken, in his splendid full-dress uniform replete with decorations, and no doubt sometimes less formally attired as well. For many months she was seen in public so frequently in the King's company that society gossiped about a secret morganatic marriage.

("During a lengthy visit to Warsaw" the King of Bohemia "made the acquaintance of the well-known adventuress, Irene Adler." " . . . 'Prima donna Imperial Opera of Warsaw— yes!' . . . 'Was there a secret marriage?' 'None.' . . . 'My photograph' . . . 'We were both in the photograph.'")

Perhaps the King of Württemberg never committed the indiscretion of being photographed with Adah. Or perhaps burglars in his pay recovered the evidence. In either case, Mankowitz observes:

"Menken was one of the first actresses in the history of the theatre to realize the importance of photography in star-making. Wherever she went she sought out the best local photographers and held long sessions with them, resulting in the circulation of hundreds of cartes de visite, photographic reproductions, roughly 2½ inches by 3¾, sold or given away. She had first organised such photographic sessions in 1859, and since then conducted them in any city she was in where she could find a half-way good photographer. Several thousand photographs were made of her in the ten years of her career, and when she died she was the world's most photographed woman."[9]

Whether the King tired of La Menken or vice versa, there is no doubt that Adah next loved and was loved by a better man

Copies of the many scandalous photographs for which La belle Menken posed with Alexandre Dumas were widely distributed by both subjects as well as by the photographer who sold them for publication all over the world. The most sensational of the lot provoked ridicule. "Can M. Dumas be her father?" jeered one Paris newspaper. Dumas tried to get a court injunction against further publication but his petition was denied until it was too late to mean anything. (*Harvard Theatre Collection.*)

than he. The superior lover may have been as fat and old as Falstaff, but he was one of the world's most popular novelists, Alexandre Dumas, père. The Old Musketeer was the son of a black Dominican mother, and Adah may have felt a special bond of sympathy because of her own vague Creole lineage. Whatever the reason, they were both eager for the liaison and they were photographed several times.

In October 1867 Adah was again in London, scene of a great theatrical triumph and what was to be a scene of her last and most interesting amorous triumph. The principal reason for the visit was to arrange for the publication of a volume of her collected poems, for which she chose the title *Infelicia*. The unhappy title was happily reminiscent of "Felise" and of "Dolores," both poems by Algernon Charles Swinburne. Adah quoted four lines from "Dolores" as an epigraph for her book, but she dedicated it to Charles Dickens, who graciously accepted the dedication.

Dickens soon departed for his long tour of the United States, but Swinburne, whom Adah had long esteemed, was available in London. The affair between Adah Isaacs Menken and Algernon Charles Swinburne, one of the greatest English lyric poets of all time, was arranged by his friends, Dante Gabriel Rosetti and Sir Richard Burton, partly as a joke and partly as a sincere attempt to wean Swinburne away from his notorious addiction to flagellation.[10] The poet was taken to see *Mazeppa* at Astley's and thereupon expressed an eager desire to meet Adah. The psychotherapy began with a surprise nocturnal visit by the lady to Swinburne's rooms.[11] The flattered lyricist rhapsodized to his friends about his conquest, although La Menken confided later that she could not "get him up to scratch. . . . I can't make him understand that biting's no use."

If Adah's ministrations did Swinburne no good, neither did they work any harm. The poet's hopeless sexual perversion had become apparent even in much of his verse. For example, "Dolores: Our Lady of Pain. . . . the raptures and rose of vice." And "Felise: Mutable loves and loves perverse . . . So sweet, so wicked, but my verse / Can dream of worse."

(Despite his frail physique Swinburne retained his sensitive intellect until his death in 1909. Among his later literary enthusiasms was Sherlock Holmes.[12] One suspects that the aged poet

To Algernon Charles Swinburne she was always *the* woman. The little poet crowed lustily to all his friends about his conquest of Adah. He distributed so many copies of their photograph that it became an article of commerce, sold as a postcard in London stationery shops. Swinburne pretended to protest, but in his case it was good publicity to let it be thought that he indulged in anything so normal as keeping a mistress. (*Theatre Museum of London.*)

read the story of the American adventuress, the German King, and the scandalous photograph with some feeling of *déjà vu*.)

It seems somehow fitting that toward the end of her tempestuous career Adah should win two indisputably great men as successive lovers. Dumas was deservedly famous; Swinburne was deservedly both more famous and more notorious. Perhaps Adah, though still a young woman, had no more worlds to conquer.

An offer came to Paris to star in another new play. To Paris, then, she returned, and while the new vehicle was still under revision, she began to rehearse a revival. After the first week she collapsed on the stage and had to remain in bed for more than a week. She returned for two more days, collapsed once more, and never appeared on stage again.

Henry Wadsworth Longfellow happened to be passing through Paris at that time and spent most of one day at Adah's bedside composing twelve lines of verse for her album. She died in August 1868, probably of cancer. Adah Isaacs Menken was buried with Jewish rites in the Jewish section of the Père Lachaise cemetery in Paris. Her collection of poems, *Infelicia*, was published in London a week after her death.

(*A Scandal in Bohemia* was published in London in 1891 at which time Watson refers to "the late Irene Adler of dubious and questionable memory." If she had died the same year, Irene Adler would have been 33 years old. Adah Isaacs Menken died 1868, aged 33 years.)

Of Adah's four husbands only the third, Newell, seems to have valued her appropriately. Her other three husbands, and probably most of her lovers, were mediocre personalities. But consider the extraordinary number of literary figures who knew and admired her in varying degrees: Walt Whitman, Henry Ward Beecher, Mark Twain, Bret Harte, Joaquin Miller, Artemus Ward, Henry Wadsworth Longfellow, Charles Dickens, Dante Gabriel Rossetti, Sir Richard Burton, Théophile Gautier, George Sand.

Arthur Conan Doyle was only nine years old when Adah Isaacs Menken died. But she was still remembered as a glamorous legend during his adolescence. However much or little the mature Conan Doyle may have known about her life, it was certainly enough to suggest that only a woman with such a wit could have beaten the best plans of Mr. Sherlock Holmes. Only such a woman could have been *the* woman.

—March 1986

NOTES

1. Quoted in Wolf Mankowitz, *Mazeppa: The Lives, Loves and Legends of Adah Isaacs Menken* (New York: Stein and Day, 1982), p. 85. Unless otherwise indicated, all biographical details concerning Menken are from this book. Special thanks are due Mr. Mankowitz for his well-wrought index which has eliminated the necessity for repetitious "ibids" in these footnotes.

2. *The Cardboard Box.*

3. Arthur Conan Doyle, *Memories and Adventures* (Boston: Little, Brown, 1924), pp. 265–69.

4. Mankowitz, pp. 75–76.

5. Algernon Charles Swinburne, "The Triumph of Time": "I will go back to the great sweet mother / Mother and lover of men, the sea."

6. Arthur Conan Doyle, *The History of Spiritualism* (London: Cassell, 1926), I, 140–42.

7. Charles Higham, *The Adventures of Conan Doyle* (New York: Norton, 1976), p. 61.

8. Conan Doyle, *Memories and Adventures*, p. 79.

9. Mankowitz, p. 175.

10. Swinburne frequented a flagellation brothel located in St. John's Wood.

11. By an odd coincidence, Swinburne occupied rooms at 22A Dorset Street, just off Baker Street.

12. Mollie Painter-Downes, *At The Pines: Swinburne, Watts-Dunton and Putney* (Boston: Gambit, 1971).

Beloved Irregular James Montgomery one day made a
shocking discovery: that his own Aunt Clara Stephens
was in fact Irene Adler. This is her lurid story. . . .

AUNT CLARA

by JAMES MONTGOMERY

(It was Jim Montgomery who discovered that his Aunt Clara
was really Irene Adler, *the* woman, and added an entirely new
annexe to the Canon. As a result he undoubtedly contributed
more to our enjoyment than any other Sherlockian has ever
done.—J.W.)

We never mention Aunt Clara,
Her picture is turned to the wall;
Though she lives on the French Riviera,
Mother says that she's dead to us all.

She used to sing hymns in the old village choir,
She used to teach Sunday School class;
Of playing the organ she never would tire—
Those dear days are over, alas!
At church on the organ she'd practice and play,
The Preacher would pump up and down,
His wife caught them back of the organ one day,
And that's why Aunt Clara left town.——CHORUS

With presents he tempted and lured her to sin,
Her innocent virtue to smirch,
But her honor was strong and she only gave in
When he gave her the deed to the church.
They said no one cared if she never came back,
When she left us her fortune to seek,
But the boys at the fire-house draped it in black,
And the ball team wore mourning that week.——CHORUS

They told her she'd toil by night and by day,
She'd have to scrub floors for her bread;
But inside of a week she discovered a way
To earn her board lying in bed.
They told her that no man would make her his bride;
They prophesied children of shame.
But she married four counts and a Baron beside,
And she hasn't a child to her name.——CHORUS

They told her the wages of sinners was death,
But she said since she had to be dead,
She'd just as soon die with champagne on her breath,
And pink satin sheets on her bed.
The good things of life always go to the pure,
The Sunday School lessons all teach,
But I wonder, when I see a rotogravure
Of her eighty-room shack on the beach.——CHORUS

They say that Hell fires will punish her sin,
She'll burn for her carryings on,
But at least for the present she's toasting her skin
In the sunshine of Deauville and Cannes.
They say that to garments of sackcloth she'll sink,
With ashes to cover her head,
But just at the moment it's ermine and mink,
And a diamond tiara instead.——CHORUS

They told her she'd live in the muck and the mud,
Yet the paper just published a snap
Of Aunt Clara at Nice with a Prince of the Blood,
And a Bishop asleep in her lap.
They say that she's sunken, they say that she fell
From the narrow and virtuous path,
But her formal French gardens are sunken as well,
And so is her pink marble bath.——CHORUS

My dear Mother's life has been pious and meek,
She drives in a second-hand Ford,
Aunt Clara received for her birthday last week
A Rolls-Royce, a Stutz, and a Cord.
My Mother does all of the housework alone,
She washes and scrubs for her board,
I've reached the conclusion that virtue's its own
And also its ONLY reward.

We never mention Aunt Clara,
But when I grow up big and tall,
I shall go to the French Riviera,
And let Mother turn me to the wall.

—March 1968

Establishing the actual dates on which Holmes's adventures occurred has been called the purest form of Sherlockian writing. Here Ernest B. Zeisler, one of the field's great chronologists, demonstrates the process. . . .

CONCERNING *THE VALLEY OF FEAR*

by ERNEST B. ZEISLER

MR. ANTHONY BOUCHER, the acknowledged world's leading authority on *The Valley of Fear,* has dated this case as in 1897, and considers the year 1888, at which I have arrived, to be impossible. His argument is, briefly, as follows:

The Scowrers were arrested in 1875. Those who were not executed could not have begun their prison terms until the second half of 1875, and since they served a full term of ten years it must have been as late as the second half of 1885—and was probably not before 1886—when Birdy and Ettie Edwards were forced to flee Chicago; hence it was not before 1886 that Edwards, now as Douglas, met Barker in California. That meeting "dates back not less than eleven years," as stated by Inspector MacDonald, Barker concurring; hence the tragedy at Birlstone cannot have occurred before 1897, a year which accords with Watson's statement (at the close of Part I) that it was "some twenty years" after the events of Vermissa Valley.

Watson did say that it was "at the end of the '80's," but in view of his calligraphy it could well have been near the end of the '90s, as Mr. Boucher believes. The year 1898 can be excluded because in that year there was a near-full moon in the sky at the time of the tragedy on January 6th and at the time of the vigil on January 8th, which does not fit with the darkness of which we are informed. The year 1899 can be excluded because on January 8th of that year the temperature in London, which is almost the same as that in Tunbridge Wells, varied between 44° and 54° F., certainly not cold enough for the description we are given. But in 1897 both moon and temperature are consistent with the requirements. Hence the only two possible years are 1897, Mr. Boucher's year, and 1888, the year at which I have arrived.

Mr. Boucher's argument, a strong one, rests largely on the final paragraph of the last chapter of the chronicle:

> And yet, as he had guessed, the game was not over yet. There was another hand to be played, and yet another and another. Ted Baldwin, for one, had escaped the scaffold; so had the Willabys; so had several others of the fiercest spirits of the gang. For ten years they were out of the world, and then came a day when they were free once more—a day which Edwards, who knew his men, was very sure would be an end of his life of peace. They had sworn an oath on all that they thought holy to have his blood as a vengeance for their comrades. And well they strove to keep their vow! From Chicago he was chased, after two attempts so near success that it was sure that the third would get him. From Chicago he went under a changed name to California, and it was there that the light went for a time out of his life when Ettie Edwards died. Once again he was nearly killed, and once again under the name of Douglas he worked in a lonely canyon, where with an English partner named Barker he amassed a fortune. . . .

From this it seems to follow that Edwards was chased from Chicago after the end of the ten-year prison term of Baldwin and others, so that 1888 seems quite impossible. But let us examine the matter more carefully.

Two paragraphs earlier we are told that after the trial the Scowrers were "broken and scattered," which implies that not all of them were either executed or imprisoned. McGinty and eight others were hanged; Baldwin, the Willabys and "several others of the fiercest spirits of the gang" were imprisoned and "were out of the world" for ten years. "Fifty-odd had various degrees of imprisonment." Hence more than forty had various terms of less than ten years; some may have had short terms, and others presumably were acquitted and "scattered." Hence it would have been both possible and likely that an attempt could and would have been made on Edwards' life as soon as he could be found in Chicago, which could readily have been in 1876, so that Edwards, under the name of Douglas, could have met Barker in California in 1876 without in the least stretching the facts; a little more than eleven years later could, therefore, have been in January of 1888. Were it not for the apparently clear implication in the final paragraph (quoted above) that Edwards was chased from Chicago after the end of the ten-year prison term there would be no difficulty at all in accepting 1888 as the year of the Birlstone tragedy.

It is noteworthy that for the first American edition Watson divided the final paragraph into *two* paragraphs, the second beginning with "From Chicago he was chased . . . ." This latter version allows for an interpretation in which the attempts on Edwards' life in Chicago occurred much earlier than at the end of the ten years in prison. This very fact is doubtless what led Watson to divide the final paragraph in this way, for he either had himself noticed or had it called to his attention that the first version was misleading. When Watson says

> For ten years they were out of the world, and then came a day when they were free once more—a day which Edwards, who knew his men, was very sure would be an end of his life of peace.

this can very well refer to the life of peace at *Birlstone*, where Douglas, knowing the length of the ten-year sentence and the date of its beginning, would have been awaiting the end of that term with misgivings. Indeed, *it is most unlikely that Edwards could have led a life of peace in Chicago for all those ten years,* for at least forty-odd of the Scowrers would have been free before the end of that period. One may object that the use of the name "Edwards" in the above sentence implies that it was in reference to the Chicago period when he still went under that name, but this may be disallowed in consideration of Watson's saying that "Ettie Edwards died" in California, for at the time she died she was living under a different name. Thus the year 1888 is entirely consistent with the chronicle as given in the first American edition.

But the year 1888 is not only consistent with the chronicle; it is much more likely than 1897. In the first place, with the latter year it would have taken Baldwin more than eleven years after his release to trace Edwards, whereas with 1888 it would have taken him the much more reasonable time of between one and two years. Furthermore, with the later year, one must assume that Baldwin made three unsuccessful attempts on Edwards' life—two in Chicago and one in California. From what we know of Baldwin this is not easy to believe. Nor is it easy to believe that after tracing and following Edwards to California, Baldwin would have been unable to find him again for more than eleven years.

But the crucial test, of course, is that Professor Moriarty and Colonel Moran were both alive and at liberty at the time of the Birlstone tragedy, whereas Professor Moriarty was killed in 1891 and Colonel Moran was probably still in prison in 1897, which was only two and a half years after his conviction and imprisonment for attempted murder in 1894.

—July 1954

THE ADVENTURE OF THE VEILED AUTHOR

by EDGAR W. SMITH

IN AUGUST, 1917, when the cold and bitter wind from the east had been blowing on England for three long years, Dr. John H. Watson was just turning sixty-five. He had offered himself gallantly to his king and country when the blast had risen,[1] and despite his old wound and the ripeness to which he had attained, it is quite possible that he was still, as the humor of the times had it, doing his bit. For Watson was a rugged soldier; a veteran who had won renown in another campaign long ago, and who had fought a valiant fight in the private war that he and Sherlock Holmes had waged together, through all the years between, against the forces of evil within the kingdom. And Britain, in her hour of peril, had need of men like that.

We shall never know, perhaps, just what it was that Watson did during those first three years of the First World War. It may indeed have been his duties in the army that preoccupied him; or it may have been the somnolent enjoyment of some retreat where he had gone to contemplate his latest honors and achievement. It may even be—perish the thought!—that he had become a casualty again, nursing the twinges of a third wound suffered somewhere between Mons and Ypres and somewhere between the subclavian artery and the tendo Achillis. Whatever it was that kept him from the world that knew him, the fact remains that he was no longer a part of that world. It is a matter of simple statistical record that more than three years had gone by since he had given his eager public a new adventure of Sherlock Holmes.

Holmes himself had retired from active practice, of course, in the autumn of 1903; but long after that, and until the war broke out, Watson's tales had kept on coming. Of the 47 stories he wrote before "that most terrible August in the history of the world," a full twenty appeared in the pages of *The Strand Magazine* after the rooms in Baker Street were abandoned. His most recent short story, *The Dying Detective,* had come out in the issue of December 1913; and *The Valley of Fear,* which appeared serially from September 1914 to May 1915, was the product of the early summer of 1914. Both of these stories related to episodes which had occurred a quarter of a century before, and the tin dispatch box in the vaults of Cox & Co. was still available for recourse, surely, if Watson had been inclined to seek out the treasures in its depths. But sadly enough none of the waiting jewels came forth, and a fateful silence fell upon the scene—a silence that endured through all those war-torn days when Britons and Americans alike would gratefully have turned an ear to listen to a well-beloved voice.

And then, in the month of August 1917, when the air was full of grimmer sounds, the September issue of *The Strand* came upon the streets. Oh frabjous day! Callooh! Callay! There, in their familiar setting for all the world to see, and shouting themselves above the din of the guns in Flanders, were spread the epic words: "HIS LAST BOW: THE WAR SERVICE OF SHERLOCK HOLMES"! Watson had spoken at last: the sweet singer had come out of limbo with a contribution to the national welfare far richer than any he could possibly have made by virtue merely of wearing his country's uniform. . . .

But no—a closer examination of the happy pages revealed that this new tale of spy and counter-spy was *not* by Watson. It bore the marks of placement in the magazine by the literary agent through whose medium the doctor had always worked; but this story, the forty-eighth about the great detective to appear in print, was otherwise anonymous.

A quick perusal of the account set forth of Holmes's trapping of the notorious Von Bork, to the confusion of the plans of the German military and naval strategists generally, convinced many readers that Watson was, in fact, the author, but that the record had cagily been written as if by some third person in order that the suspense demanded by the plot might be sustained. It would, admittedly, have been difficult to conceal the identity of "Altamont," and to give the drama its proper and timely dénouement, if the story had been told from the vantage-point of the chauffeur's seat in which Watson actually entered the scene. Resort to the subterfuge suggested would be natural and excusable in the circumstances, and the theory of Watson's duplicity in the matter of authorship is, therefore, a dangerously plausible one. But in the light of a closer analysis of all the facts involved, it is a theory that is wholly inadequate.

We are confronted first of all by the historical datum that five more years were to go by, on top of the three that had already passed, before Watson came to publish a story in his own name.[2] His acknowledged contributions to the *Strand*, beginning again with *Thor Bridge* in February and March 1922, were fairly frequent if somewhat sporadic: no year went by, up to 1927, without at least one offering. It is surely significant, in the light of Watson's well-merited reputation for reliability, that there was a lapse of eight years, after 1914, during which *no* stories bearing his signature appeared. And it is stretching credulity a little too far to suggest that he chose, as his single offering during this interval, a tale which demanded by its content the suppression of his sponsorship. Whatever the circumstances may have been that led to his long silence, the persistence of those circumstances uninterruptedly for eight years is a much more likely eventuality than the alternative possibility that *two* such sets of circumstances arose, one of which endured for three years and the other immediately thereafter for five. The miracle of resurrection is seldom so transient and evanescent a thing as this.

We must grant, then, that strong argument can be advanced, on the historical record as it stands, in support of the contention that Watson did not actually come back to life again in 1917 as many have supposed he did. This in itself should be enough; but the evidence from internal sources tending to deny his authorship of the *Last Bow* is more convincing still. The style is not his; the method of treatment is at wide variance with the method Watson invariably employed; and the facts set forth as essential ingredients in the tale could not possibly have been within the compass of his knowledge.

The question of style need not be dwelt upon here: there are weaknesses and strengths, descents to colloquialisms and banality, and flights to rare poetic heights, that mark it as distinct from anything that Watson ever wrote. Nor need we take account at this juncture of the care, or lack of care, that charac-

310

terizes the telling of the tale itself: more will be said of that as our examination proceeds. The salient feature, for this present consideration, is the revelation throughout the text of an intimate familiarity with the high statecraft of the realm, and an equally intimate familiarity with the recent doings of Sherlock Holmes. And on neither count was Watson qualified to speak.

It will be recalled, to the latter point, that when the two adventurers had settled down together in Von Bork's study over the bottle of Imperial Tokay, Holmes turned affectionately to his friend and said: "But you, Watson . . . I've hardly seen you in the light yet. How have the years used you? You look the same blithe boy as ever." And then a little later, as they stood upon the terrace with Von Bork crammed into the back seat of the car like a dressed fowl, the great detective uttered these portentous words: "This may be the last quiet talk we shall ever have. . . ."

Here is the token of a long separation, only recently repaired and soon to be resumed. It marks a situation in which Watson would have found it impossible to gain a coherent knowledge of the developments leading up to Holmes's long sojourn in America and Ireland, or of the real significance of the swiftly moving adventure in which he found himself engaged. Watson had obviously been dragged into the drama at the last moment, and just for old times' sake: it all had to be explained to him in a breath—and he was, we must admit, notoriously slow on the uptake. There was not to be, this time, the leisurely review and analysis of the case back in the rooms in Baker Street, and, in the very nature of things, no documentation would be forthcoming of the sort upon which Watson traditionally relied. Against the meagre background he possessed, the telling of the tale as it is told was surely quite beyond him.

For even had he known of Holmes and Holmes's doings during those critical years before 1914, what could he hope to know of the deep and complex pattern of events in which the Master was enmeshed? How could a humble medical officer, even if he had entered active service again, speak with meaning and authority of the activities of a German spy who was engaged in plotting the downfall of the British Empire? It is stated categorically by the author of the tale that Von Bork had perched himself on the chalk cliffs overlooking Harwich "four years before"; that he was a man "who could hardly be matched among all the devoted agents of the Kaiser"; that it was the peculiar talents he possessed "which had first recommended him for the English mission." These were all facts of which a few men in the secret places of the kingdom were aware; but they were not facts, in all conscience, of which Watson was aware.

No; it was not the old remembered pen which wrote this tale of high diplomacy and political intrigue. It was not the pen of any amateur in world affairs, or of a man who had long been absent from the hurrying scene. It was, we must believe, the pen of one who had the pregnant facts before him as he wrote; who knew the inner meaning of the drama that unfolded—and who knew, besides, the crucial part in its unfolding that Sherlock Holmes had long been called upon to play.

Who was it, then, if it was not Watson, who set this story down to celebrate great Sherlock's triumph in a new and most exacting area of endeavor? Who was it who had dared intrude himself into a field of writing that had been sacred, until that moment, to the one familiar Boswell? It was no rank outsider, patently; for neither the British Government nor Sherlock Holmes himself would have tolerated such impertinence. Nor was it Sherlock Holmes who wrote the piece: a knowledge of the facts recited was conceivably within his grasp, but the style in which the tale is couched is not the feeble style we know to be the master's own[3]—it was, as we have noted, vigorous and well-disposed for all its faults, with passages of genuine poetic beauty. And, to cite a last speculation, it was not the literary agent himself who wrote the tale, for this man, highly capable though he was, had dedicated himself deliberately and as a matter of stated preference to the field of the historical romance—and he was, besides, heavily occupied at the time with questions of psychic research.

We may well ask ourselves, in seeking to determine the authorship of this tale, what specifications can be set down as tending to establish the identification. Much has already been suggested that seems significant in this regard. The author must have known in fine detail, as we have seen, the part that Sherlock Holmes had played, for two long years, in preparing himself for the masterful blow he struck in England's name. And he must have had as well an intimate knowledge and understanding of the confidential policy and procedure of the British Foreign Office in those days of growing crisis. The first of these specifications calls for someone who was very close to Holmes in mind and spirit and body—someone closer, even, than the man who shared, as Watson did, every tie that links two men together save only that of common blood. And the second calls for someone who had associations with the British Government; someone who was a part of the British Government; someone, we are tempted to suggest, of whom it might be said that occasionally he *was* the British Government.

There was only one such man. In the light of all the evidence that has been adduced, we are led irresistibly to the conclusion that that man, the veiled author of *His Last Bow*, was Mycroft Holmes, statesman, recluse, philosopher, whose specialism in Government was omniscience, and who knew his brother as he knew himself. It was Mycroft who for years had drawn together the threads of diplomacy and power-politics which were spun by his better-known associates at Whitehall; it was Mycroft who had been party to the secret of Sherlock's hegira more than two decades before, when both Dr. Watson and Mrs. Hudson had believed him dead. He is the perfect solvent in the colloidal chemistry of a tale involving both secular and canonical mysteries that none but he could fathom.

There are many incidental arguments that suggest themselves in support of the attribution to Mycroft Holmes of the authorship of this tale. He was, it is universally acknowledged, a genius; and only a genius would have interlarded what is otherwise a lucid and moving recital with stupid and inexcusable omissions and confusions. There is, as a case in point, the reference to Martha, the dear ruddy-faced old lady who had been planted in Von Bork's household to keep an eye on things until the hour struck. Was she or was she not Mrs. Hudson, as most of us have supposed? The plodding, earth-bound Watson would have told us; but Mycroft, from the rarer heights of his intellect, left the question in the air. And then there is the little matter of the labels on the pigeonholes in Von Bork's safe. We find, in contrast to the others, which are clear enough in meaning, that one was marked "Fords." What, from the standpoint of military significance, could possibly be meant by that? We ask; but Mycroft the genius gives no answer. And if the argument needed clinching, we have the final evidence of the rendition given to the American slang which Altamont allegedly spoke. Here is genius at its loftiest peak; here we see the hallmarks of a mind which clearly lacked the common touch, and to which all but the speech of Whitehall was a foreign tongue.

We may be sure, on many counts, that it was Mycroft Holmes who wrote this tale. He shared, no doubt, the family prejudice against ranking modesty among the virtues, and he would therefore be prepared, and even eager, to glorify his brother's deeds on this unique occasion when he, and he alone, could do it. But in giving the story to the public, that all might hail the name of Holmes again, he would be moved, as any man would be who occupied so exalted a place, to temper pride with wise restraint. A lesser light, if there could have been one capable of writing such a tale, might boldly put his name upon the page, knowing he could not be held accountable for what he said. But Mycroft, in the revelation of these high arcana, was talking shop; and every instinct of his being would prompt him, however much it may have hurt, to hide his light beneath a bushel. Concealment of his own identity was the natural and inevitable result, and it is this very stamp of anonymity that spreads his signature across the page.

And so the veil is torn aside, and there he stands for all the world to see—Mycroft Holmes, habitué of the Strangers' Room at the Diogenes Club; inheritor with his brother of the queer artistic tendencies of the Vernet blood; a mental giant, with unparalleled powers of observation and an unlimited capacity for storing facts; a man whose word again and again had decided the national policy—and author, we may believe, of this *Last Bow* of Sherlock Holmes.

—April 1946

314

1. Cf. *His Last Bow*: "As to you, Watson, you are joining us [up?] with your old service, as I understand. . . ."

2. *The Mazarin Stone*, in *The Strand* for October 1921, was also anonymous. It was almost certainly by some other writer than either Dr. Watson *or* the author of *His Last Bow*. Miss Jane Nightwork, "Watson à la Mode," has advanced the speculation that it was written by Mary Watson. [Reprinted in the present volume.]

3. In 1926, when he was 72, Holmes published two distinctly inferior stories in *The Strand Magazine*: *The Blanched Soldier* (November) and *The Lion's Mane* (December). It may be unfair to judge him by these senile efforts, but the writings in question are, except for his highly technical book on bee culture, the only ones from his pen which have survived the years.

The extant manuscripts of the Holmes adventures are
known to be in the handwriting of one A. Conan Doyle.
But if that is true, then whose handwriting intrudes
into the manuscript of The Second Stain?

THE SECOND HAND IN *THE SECOND STAIN*

by RICHARD LUMAN

THE MANUSCRIPT OF *The Adventure of the Second Stain,* "the one
supreme example of the international influence which he has
exercised,"[1] reposes in the vault of the James P. Magill Library
of Haverford College, the gem of an extensive collection given
by the College's distinguished alumnus Christopher Morley,
'10. The manuscript contains 9900 words, and is written, on
thirty-one pages, in a vellum-bound notebook measuring 33.3
cm. × 19.2 cm.[2] Pages 1–23 and 29–31 are in the well-known
neat fair hand of the Literary Agent, Sir Arthur Conan Doyle.[3]
The remaining pages are in a second hand, quite unlike that of
the Literary Agent. It is to the question of the identity of the
second hand that this essay is directed.

Yet, even in the section of the MS which is certainly the work
of Dr. Doyle, there are some interesting, and perhaps unexpected, events which might be noted. One does not often see
studies of the manuscripts of the Master's cases. It may be true
here, as so often elsewhere, that large issues may be found to
arise from very small considerations.

For example, on page four, dialogue has been stricken ruth-
lessly from the text. Following the sentence "Holmes considered for some little time," still standing, there originally appeared this exchange:

> "Your discovery was made early, sir" he remarked.
> "Yes, Mr. Holmes, before I dressed."
> "So I gathered from the fact that you have cut yourself twice in
> shaving."

Again, on page eight, introduced into the text over a caret, is
the well-known line "The situation is desperate but not hopeless." Further down that same page, we observe Edward Lucas
transmogrified into Eduardo, hence becoming more foreign,

and surely much more sinister. This happy inspiration seems to have come in the very process of composition, since only three lines later, "Eduardo" stands original ("Is that Eduardo Lucas of Godolphin Street?"). Pages ten and eleven reveal a number of alterations in the description of the visit of Lady Hilda Trelawney Hope to 221B Baker Street, none of them significant.

Perhaps the most astonishing, and in its small way disquieting, of these textual changes occurs at the very bottom of page twelve. Lady Hilda Trelawney Hope has just taken a distraught departure, and Holmes turns, as is his wont, to the good doctor for insight into the mind behind "that beautiful haunted face, the startled eyes and the drawn mouth," because, as he says to his companion, "Now Watson, the fair sex is your department."[4] This is surely one remark regarded by everyone who reads the Canon as quintessentially Holmesian.[5] It has been subjected to endless subtle exegisis in order to understand the character both of Dr. Watson and of the relationship between the doctor and the detective. Yet, as one casts one's eye down the twelfth page of the manuscript, one finds that what Holmes in fact said was something quite different: "Now Watson, what's the meaning of that?" The original remark is lined through and the more famous version written above it in the same hand:

" Nay, madame, there again you ask me more than
an possibly answer."

"Then I will take up no more of your time. I cannot
[me] you, Mr Holmes, for having refused to speak more [freely], and
on your side will not, I am sure, think the worse of me because
Once more I beg that you will say nothing of my visit.
[desire], even against his will, to share [my husband's] anxieties." She looked
                                                            ^
[at us] from the door and I had a last impression of that beautiful
[muted] face, the startled eyes and the drawn mouth. Then she was
[gone].

                    the fair sex is your department " said
" Now, Watson, ~~what's the meaning of that~~ ! " asked Holmes,

And so is born the wit of the master from the ambiguity of afterthought.

The only other change of interest in what we may call the "Doyle hand" appears on page 21, where "We were shown into her own boudoir" is more modestly restated as "We were shown into the morning room." Though the whole number of changes in the manuscript cannot amount to many more than a hundred words, they do raise both specific questions and a general question. Scholars of the Canon have long disputed about difficulties in the events of this case of the Master, and its relation to what appear to be two other cases which Watson, who seems to have been very pleased with the title, also called "the second stain."[6] But few have troubled to see the serious situation in the manuscript itself. Even this review of pages 1–23 and 29–31 must raise one deeply disturbing problem in the mind of any scholar: just what is the historical status of remarks which seem to be afterthoughts of an amanuensis or literary agent?

If the MSS are mere transcriptions of Dr. Watson's own versions of Holmes's little problems, how *dare the copyist substitute his own phrases*? For we surely are not willing to assume that the transcriber was so conscientious (or so dense?) as to copy both the canceled original text *and its replacement* in a text intended for final production. On the contrary, he would simply have recorded the final version in a fair hand. Were, then, these last-minute thoughts (or "more correct reminiscences," since they occur in dialogue) incorporated by Dr. Watson himself? No, for the hand is the same. Should we then picture the good Doctor (whose own medical hand is thought by many to have been unreadable even by himself) leaning over the shoulder of his scribe, making corrections as he wrote? Surely not. One is led, therefore, to the unsettling thought that some of the most famous lines in the Canon are not Dr. Watson's at all, but "improvements" devised by the supposedly passive Literary Agent. Since these passages often occur in dialogue, moreover, the printed text thus *may not contain* the *ipsissima verba* of Holmes at all![7] Far from being presented with an historically faithful transcript of those famous conversations, we may have been offered mere works of fiction. Consider what a devastating effect on our whole conception of Jesus and the early Church there would be were we to have one of the original MSS of the Gospels with obviously reworked *logia*! At the very least, if the manuscript text reflects the true state of affairs, Sherlock Holmes was much less a sparkling conversationalist than we have been led to believe.

Were that the only problem to be posed by the manuscript of *The Second Stain,* it would be burden enough. But there is more. Pages 24 through 29 are written in a completely different hand (with the exception of a few lines inserted here and there in the "Doyle hand") from that in the rest of the text. It is a large, straggling, even sprawling hand, difficult to read, in striking contrast to the small, neat, extremely legible "Doyle hand." To whom does this second hand belong? How came it in the manuscript? Christopher Morley commented on the matter himself. A short letter on his own notepaper, enclosed now within the bound manuscript, calls the attention of his brother Felix to the existence of the second hand, which he says is "evidently in the hand of an amanuensis." He thinks it might be worth a "possible footnote." Later scholars seem not to have moved beyond this conjecture. It is possible, naturally, that such is indeed the solution of the puzzle, but it would seem that a ready acceptance of so easy a conclusion would constitute a premature abandonment of the intellectual quest, unSherlockian and unscholarly. In addition, there are reasons for a modest skepticism. The "second hand" seems hardly designed by Nature for the production of fair copy for a printer or even a typist; and it is certainly *not* the writing of a trained, professional secretary. Who could be this extraordinary amanuensis, who writes with the delicacy of a bear?

The last resort of the critical scholar in dealing with the manifold inconsistencies and chronological problems in the Canon has been Dr. Watson's handwriting. It is assumed to have been execrable, on the *a priori* grounds that the handwriting of all physicians is execrable.[8] That the doctor's hand was unreadable is regarded as self-evident by all who work in the matter, an assumption needing no proof or demonstration. Thus, the misunderstanding of his text by others, or of his notes by himself, has been the allegedly solid foundation for vast and intricate structures of textual emendation, speculation, and chronological manipulation. The script of literature's second most-beloved physician[9] has thus been burdened with the responsibility (no doubt viewed as *opportunity* by critics) for all sorts of egregious errors, confusions, misdatings, chronological impossibilities, and critical re-writings of his reminiscences.[10] It is surely not too much to say that the Doctor's hand has been one of the great

319

"It was a letter of mine, Mr. Holmes—
an indiscreet letter [written before my marriage]— a foolish letter,
a letter of an impulsive loving
girl. I meant no harm, & yet he would
have thought it criminal. Had he read
that letter his confidence would have
been for ever destroyed. It is years
since I wrote it. I had thought that
the whole matter was forgotten. Then
at last I heard from this man Lucas
that it had passed into his hands and
that he would lay it before my husband.
I implored his mercy. He said that
he would return my letter, if I would
bring him a certain document which
he described in my husbands despatch
box. He assured me that no harm
could come to my husband. Put
yourself in my position Mr Holmes!
What was I to do?"

"Take your husband into your confidence"

The Second Stain, MS p. 26. The last line is in the "Doyle hand."

critical tools in the mining and rebuilding of the texts, in the quest for the historical Sherlock.

It is perhaps cruel to point out that this is but an assumption, unproved, and, in the nature of things, unsusceptible of demonstration: for we have *no certain exemplar of Dr. Watson's handwriting*. Dorothy L. Sayers writes:

> The only document we possess, purporting to be in the handwriting of Dr. Watson, is the sketch-map which illustrates the adventure of *The Priory School*. It bears his name in block letters at the right-hand bottom corner, and presents at first sight an aspect of authenticity.[11]

But the "aspect of authenticity" agrees no more with the evidence from other plans in the Canon than it does with Miss Sayer's conviction that Watson wrote badly, or the need, for her critical theories, that he be shown to have written badly. So, she concludes, "Watson . . . had it [his purported signature] excised from the block as a tacit admission that neither sketch nor writing was from his hand." She has a fall-back position: even should it be shown beyond cavil that the hand is that of Dr. Watson, it would still signify nothing, for "whoever executed this wording would, of course, be taking particular pains to make it legible and suitable for reproduction as a line-block, and it probably is very unlike the same person's hand when writing ordinary MS or notes."[12] Her argument seems to me, however, to be conclusive: we have no authentic note, not a scrap, not an *alpha* or an *omega*, a ℞, which comes uncontestably from the hand of Holmes's friend and biographer.

What has all this to do with the manuscript of *The Second Stain*? Just this: might the second hand not be that of Dr. Watson? It would confirm all critical suspicions concerning his hand, and without egregious assumptions about the noble art of medicine and its practitioners: Dr. Watson's poor calligraphy would be his own, not an inadmissible deduction from his profession—after all, many people write badly without professional training. It would also account for the anomaly of an anonymous second hand in a MS presumably prepared only by the Doctor or the Literary Agent. It rests on at least as solid a foundation as all the other speculations concerning the good Doctor's writing, and would have the added advantage of giving an admittedly involutionary but nevertheless substantial assistance to the analysis of questions otherwise difficult to resolve. There are no doubt problems which are insoluble even with this aid: Dr. Watson's migrating Jezail bullet wound cannot be ascribed to his inept manipulation of the pen; no doubt there are difficulties with the identification, but the balance of probabilities might be perceived to lie in that direction.

—September 1978

NOTES

1. The astute reader will note the divergence of the MS at this point from the *editio princeps* (*The Strand Magazine*, 18 [December 1904]), which has a

reading not attested in the MS at all: "The most important international case which he has ever been called upon to handle." All subsequent published versions I have seen have followed the *Strand* text.

2. The description of the MS and the publication of examples of the two hands are made with the kind permission of the Magill Library and its distinguished Director, Dr. Edwin B. Bronner. The staff member who works most closely with the Morley Collection is Mr. David A. Fraser, Associate Librarian. Reference: Misc. Coll. Box 800.5.

3. In none of the discussions of the execrable medical handwriting of Dr. John H. Watson does the extraordinary clarity and neatness of the handwriting of *Dr.* Doyle seem ever to be noticed: but surely it is relevant evidence if one seeks a meaningful generalization. The "first hand" is certainly that of Dr. Doyle. I have compared it with texts known to be written by Doyle.

4. It is perhaps worthy of note that the fictional detective Nero Wolfe has a similar conviction concerning the penetrating insight of his assistant, Archie Goodwin, into the feminine heart. In works of fiction, of course, one may exaggerate such matters as much as one likes. In any case, Wolfe is clearly modeled on Mycroft, about whom we know next to nothing.

5. It is, of course, the title of an essay in Baring-Gould's *Annotated Sherlock Holmes,* and is a line quoted in dictionaries of quotations—e.g., *The Oxford Dictionary of Quotations* (2nd ed., 1955), p. 188.

6. See *The Yellow Face* and *The Naval Treaty* where other cases are mentioned under the same title. See also D. Martin Dakin, *A Sherlock Holmes Commentary,* pp. 98, 129, 203, and H. W. Bell, *Sherlock Holmes and Dr. Watson: The Chronology of Their Adventures.*

7. Unless one is willing to see Holmes overseeing the copying and directing the inserting of what he really said, or, what he thought afterwards he would like to have said, which is surely going too far! The course assumed by the texts and the scholars is as follows: Watson's notes → Watson's MS → a copy by the Literary Agent → print; apparently it was only at this last stage that the Master himself saw the work.

8. I shall not attempt to answer this assumption, or rather canard: I will merely observe that I know well several students of medicine who write most legibly. It may, however, be useful to select a remark from those thought authoritative on the matter: "Watson was a doctor, and his handwriting was therefore probably illegible at the best of times; moreover, he may have written his dates in a contracted form and used, in addition, a J pen in a poor state of repair" (Dorothy L. Sayers, "The Dates in *The Red-Headed League,*" *Unpopular Opinions,* p. 171). Note the piling up of conjectures: not a solid fact in the lot. Comments from other authorities could be quoted; but Miss Sayers states it as clearly and succinctly (in a sense, as outrageously) as any.

9. Even the most fanatic devotee would surely continue to allow pride of place to St. Luke.

10. It is true that there have been those who have argued that the confusion of dates, notes, and tongues in the Canon was deliberate and not accidental, designed as part of a systematic deception intended to prevent the penetration of real identities of persons and places, and of real dates. See, for example, Ian McQueen's *Sherlock Holmes Detected*. Surely it is better to assume this than to accept casually the picture of our beloved Watson built up by critics. *Congruence* may not be a strong argument in theology but it surely is so in Watsonology. Is it fitting to see Watson as: careless in keeping notes, in recording dates, in reading proofs; possessed of a memory defective in the extreme; possessed of poor hearing, an unreadable handwriting, and a derisory intelligence? Can that be aught but unmitigated bleat and ineffable twaddle? A general practitioner of limited experience, yes: but a nincompoop, surely not! How can we trust the rest of his accounts of the Master if in all these crucial matters he is shown to be inept or worse?

11. Dorothy L. Sayers, "Note on Dr. Watson's Handwriting" attached to "The Dates in *The Red-Headed League*" in *Unpopular Opinions*, p. 176.

12. Ibid., pp. 178 (the excision occurred in the 1928 "Omnibus" edition), 177.

In this pair of letters, Irregulars Jon Lellenberg and John Nieminski not only add important data to the argument advanced by Richard Luman in "The Second Hand in The Second Stain," *but they also raise a fundamental question regarding the extent to which objective fact may affect Sherlockian Higher Criticism. . . .*

THE MYSTERY OF THE SECOND HAND: A MUNDANE SOLUTION

From Jon L. Lellenberg ("Rodger Prescott"), a co-editor of *Baker Street Miscellanea*, the BSJ's hated rival on the Surrey shore:

> Richard Luman's article in the September 1978 BSJ on the second handwriting in the *Second Stain* manuscript was certainly a clever and entertaining approach to the problem of the identity of the person who wrote that passage. Unfortunately, his speculation that it was none other than Dr. John H. Watson must be denied. In investigating the question, I employed the simple advice of asking the Literary Agent's surviving child, Dame Jean Conan Doyle (Lady Bromet), whether she recognized the handwriting. She did: it was her mother's, who at the time of the story's writing was still Jean Leckie. Dame Jean was able to produce samples of her mother's handwriting which were identical to that in the MS, and speculates that her father was more likely to have allowed her mother to write the passage herself, to involve her in his work, than to have dictated it to her. In this regard, the fact that the passage deals with Lady Hilda's feminine reactions to being blackmailed is interesting and possibly suggestive.
>
> An article about this discovery was published in the December 1978 *Baker Street Miscellanea* by the editors, reproducing the handwriting samples. And so the search for Dr. Watson's elusive handwriting must continue.

From John Nieminski ("Abe Slaney") *another* co-editor of *Baker Street Miscellanea*, of Chicago, Illinois:

> There is much grist for the commentary mill among the contents of the September 1978 BSJ, but two points especially may be of interest to readers: (1) the mystery of the second hand in *The Second Stain* has, alas, a more mundane solution than that proposed by Dr. Luman in his well-wrought analysis of the MS. The identity of the "extraordinary amanuensis" is revealed in an article in the December 1978 *Baker Street Miscellanea* (Advt.), supported by fairly indisputable collateral evidence. And (2) the theory of a deutero-Watson had even earlier exposure in

print than the 1944 essay, "What Son Was Watson?," mentioned by Mr. Bliss Austin in his letter commenting on the piece by Mrs. Shulamit Saltzman in your March issue. It seems to have been first propounded by Mr. J. S. Coltart in a curiously little-known and seldom consulted article in *The Cornhill Magazine* for November 1934, titled "This Watson"— a nicely done commentary which *BSM* hopes to reprint in an upcoming issue. Taken in tandem, the Coltart, Austin, and Saltzman arguments make a strong case indeed for two biographers, and offer the ambitious student much of the data needed to support Mr. Austin's call for a multiple-Watson theory.

Editorial Observation [by John M. Linsenmeyer]: The Lellenberg–Nieminski solution to the "second-hand" mystery is, let me say, entirely persuasive. It suggests, moreover, a philosophical question of some interest: viz., is it cricket to let objective facts intrude into the Higher Criticism? I recall a controversy on the subject, provoked by a debate between Dorothy L. Sayers and Sir Sidney Roberts concerning Holmes's university. Sayers had tentatively identified Sherlock Holmes with T. S. Holmes, of Sidney Sussex College, Cambridge, and observed that "even if Holmes is not to be identified with the Sidney Sussex man identified in the 1874 Tripos' list" other factors support the choice of that as Sherlock's college ("Holmes's College Career," in her *Unpopular Opinions* [London, 1946], pp. 134–47, esp. p. 145). Sir Sidney called Sayers' identification "unfortunate," pointing out that her "T. S. Holmes became Chancellor of Wells Cathedral" (*Holmes and Watson—A Miscellany* [London, 1953], p. 10 n. 1). Sir Sidney later agreed with the position that "This uncalled-for intrusion of facts into Sherlockian scholarship was a trifle unchivalrous" (Trevor H. Hall, *Sherlock Holmes—Ten Literary Studies* [London, 1969], p. 77). This is, then, perhaps the best exemplar upon which to focus the question of whether the intrusion of extraneous facts (e.g., the putative Holmes's later career) does or does not tend to spoil Sherlockian scholarship. For whatever it is worth, I feel that it does not; the rules of serious scholarship can in no way preclude resort to any objective and extra-Canonical factual material. The application of any such exclusionary principle would, it moreover seems to me, call for an almost impossible degree of discrimination as to what is or is not admissible. Also on the subject of Mr. Nieminski's letter, *kudos* to him for finding that absolute jewel of an article in the 1934 *Cornhill*. Those interested in the archaeology of

Sherlockian criticism will find this worthwhile (and strangely unknown) item from the Golden Age of Knox, Roberts, Milne, Bell, and Starrett most interesting. Our deep thanks to him for unearthing it. Finally, on the subject of Holmes's college, the DeWaal bibliography (items 2957–72) indicates that the majority of writers favour Oxford (five, including Gavin Brend, but *not* including our Founding Father R. A. Knox, who is not indexed), slightly fewer favour Cambridge (four, including Sayers, Morley, and Hall), or London (one), with some indication of support for the Baring-Gould theorem that he attended both Oxford and Cambridge. Actually, your editor has compelling evidence that they are all wrong—a demonstration which will be made in due season, i.e., as soon as (i) I get the time to write the paper and (ii) I can publish the paper without being lynched by disgruntled occupants of the BSJ backlog.

—March 1979

Does the title of The Solitary Cyclist *refer to the pursuer or to the pursued? Here is an old Canonical mystery solved. . . .*

THE SOLITARY MAN-USCRIPT

by ANDREW J. PECK

THE PROBLEM of whether the term "solitary cyclist" refers to Violet Smith or Bob Carruthers has long been a point of contention among Sherlockian scholars. The term itself appears only twice in the story (and, of course, in the title). The two relevant passages are: 1. "I will now lay before the reader the facts connected with Miss Violet Smith, the solitary cyclist of Charlington, and the curious sequel of our investigation, which culminated in unexpected tragedy." 2. "'That's the man!' I [Watson] gasped. A solitary cyclist was coming towards us. His head was down. . . ."

Who your candidate for the solitary cyclist is determines which of those two sentences you stress and which you try to explain away.

Those who favour Miss Smith rely on the first quoted sentence. For example, Mr. Vernon Goslin has said: "I cannot subscribe to the Carruthers school of thought, as the words 'the solitary cyclist' follow immediately after Miss Violet Smith's name in the opening paragraph." [1] Some of Miss Smith's more generous supporters admit that Carruthers is described as "A solitary cyclist," but still insist that "*the* solitary cyclist" is Miss Smith.

Supporters of Bob Carruthers point to the second quotation, where the term "A solitary cyclist" definitely refers to him. They do not feel that the use of the indefinite article matters. They feel that the advocates of Miss Smith have misinterpreted the first reference. As D. Martin Dakin says:

" . . . the solitary cyclist of Charlington" can equally well refer to him [Carruthers], if it is taken, not as a description of Violet Smith, but as a second item in Watson's list: i.e., (a) Miss Violet Smith (b) the solitary cyclist (Carruthers) and (c) the curious sequel. . . . The only point against this interpretation is the comma after "Charlington"; but I

327

doubt if Watson was particular enough about the niceties of punctuation to make this a relevant argument.[2]

So, as it would appear that the answer depends greatly on grammar (the indefinite article vs. the definite article, and a comma vs. no comma), it would seem that nothing new could be added, and that, as often occurs in Sherlockian realms, the problem would be deadlocked, with two equally possible answers. Fortunately, in this case that will not be so. Evidence has been uncovered that gives a definite, incontrovertible answer to the question. This evidence is the original manuscript of the story.

While not trying to be melodramatic by delaying the presentation of my evidence, I think that a short aside would not be too much out of place. I learned of the whereabouts of the manuscript a short time ago when I received a letter from Peter Blau (who has done much research on the locations of the manuscripts, and who has published a "trifling monograph"[3] setting down the locations of all those that have been tracked down) saying that he had found information which led him to believe that the manuscript of *The Solitary Cyclist* might be in Olin Library at Cornell University. So I soon found myself in the Rare Book Room, holding an original Doyle manuscript in my hand, but not quite believing that they were actually going to let me read through the manuscript in order to collate it with the printed version as it appears in *The Annotated Sherlock Holmes*. There were one or two interesting differences in the two versions (which may some day be written up in a letter to the editor), but there were two changes that gave definite proof that, as far as Doyle and Watson were concerned, the term "the solitary cyclist" referred to Bob Carruthers and *not* to Violet Smith. These changes occurred in two of the three places where the term "solitary cyclist" appears—that is, in the title and in the first paragraph (which, it will be noted, are used for evidence that Miss Smith is the solitary cyclist). In the manuscript, that first quotation reads: "I will now lay before the reader the facts connected with Miss Violet Smith, the solitary man [*sic*] of Charlington, and the curious sequel . . . ." "Man" is crossed out, and the correction, "cyclist," appears above it. The same change occurs in the title on the first page. From this I think it can be

The Return of Sherlock Holmes

III

The Adventure of the Solitary ~~Man~~ Cyclist.

now lay before the reader the facts connected with Miss Violet
Smith, the solitary ~~man~~ cyclist of Charlington ~~Common~~, and the
~~tragedy which~~ curious sequel of our investigation, w u.
culminated in unexpected tragedy.

On referring to my note book for the year 1895 I find
that it was upon the Saturday the 23rd of April ~~that that~~ that we first
heard of Miss Violet Smith. Her visit was I remember extremely
unwelcome to Holmes for he was immersed at the moment in a very
abstruse and complicated problem concerning the peculiar persecution
to which John Vincent Harden, the well known tobacco millionaire,
had been subjected. My friend, who loved above all things
precision and concentration of thought, resented anything which
distracted his attention from the matter in hand. And yet without
a harshness which was foreign to his nature it was impossible to
refuse to listen to the story of the young and beautiful woman,
tall, graceful, and queenly, who presented herself at Baker
Street late in the evening and implored his assistance and
advice. It was vain to urge that his time was already fully
occupied for the young lady had come with the determination to

Heading of page 1 and complete page 2 of the original manuscript. Reproduced by courtesy of Cornell University Library.

seen that the identity of the solitary cyclist is finally proved to be Bob Carruthers.

—June 1972

NOTES

1. "In the Footsteps of Sherlock Holmes Quiz," SHJ 9 (Winter 1968), 29–33 at 30.

2. "Cyclists and Snowmen" (letter to the editor), SHJ 9 (Summer 1969), 71.

3. *A Brief Census of the Manuscripts of the Canon* (Pittsfield: The Spermaceti Press, 1971).

*The great Dutch Sherlockian uncovers the undeniable
truth about the source of the most famous cipher to be
found in the adventures of Sherlock Holmes. . . .*

THE TRUE STORY OF THE DANCING MEN

by CORNELIUS HELLING

THE YEAR 1953 saw many important events in the Sherlockian
world, but what to say about the world-shaking discoveries regarding the secret writing in *The Dancing Men*! But let us proceed with order and method, as the Master himself would say.

In the October and December 1952 issues of *Coming Events in
Britain* (publication of the British Travel and Holidays Association) appeared a very interesting article, in two parts, by Mr.
Gavin Brend, author of *My Dear Holmes*, about "The Haunts of
Sherlock Holmes." The author mentions several places in and
outside London, marked by some Holmesian adventure. The
accompanying photographs are well chosen, and would do very
well in a book on the same subject, if ever a Sherlockian would
be ambitious enough to write it. Mr. Brend notably wrote as
follows:

> Perhaps the most interesting landmark of all is Hill House Hotel at
> Happisburgh, near Norwich. Conan Doyle stayed there in 1903 at a time
> when this Norfolk hotel was kept by a family named Cubitt. The pro-
> prietor's son used to amuse himself by writing his signature in dancing
> men. Doyle, then and there, set to work on the story of *The Dancing Men*
> and, when he left, his room was littered with drawings of the dancers. It
> will be recalled that Hilton Cubitt is the name of the central character in
> this tale. Similarly, Ridling[1] Thorpe in the story is a combination of two
> nearby villages, Ridlington and Edingthorpe. Mr. G. J. Cubitt, the origi-
> nal inventor of the dancing men, lives today in Aylesbury, Bucking-
> hamshire. Hill House Hotel can still be visited, but the dancing men
> will, I fear, by now have danced their way into the distant past.

Naturally, I jumped upon the occasion to have information
from Mr. Cubitt, whose namesake in the Holmes case was shot
by the Chicago crook Abe Slaney. By the courtesy of the British
Post Office, my letter from my home in Holland reached Mr.
Cubitt's address, and he very amiably answered my questions.

He even sent to me a very accurate facsimile of his name and former address in dancing men!

It transpired from his letter that Dr. Watson's ability for rendering a case even more romantic and interesting than it actually was (much to Holmes's unfeigned dislike!) was even more developed than scholars have supposed until now.

Mr. Cubitt wrote me:

> The facts are somewhat distorted [in Mr. Brend's article]. I did not invent secret writing or amuse myself by writing my signature in dancing men. My girl cousin requested my mother to ask Sir Arthur to write something in her autograph album, in which I previously, at the age of about seven, had written my name and address in the form of the dancing men. Sir Arthur frequently stayed with us after the Boer War, where [sic] he had financed and run a hospital and medical service. The album gave birth to the idea and he left many drawings about, evidently working out his code and messages. You will recall that at that time he was writing a tale a month for the *Strand Magazine*. The Hill House is seven miles from North Walsham and way station, G. E. R., passing through Edenthorpe [sic] and Ridlington. . . .

It is quite evident that both Mr. Brend and Mr. Cubitt, like so many others, are under the impression that the celebrated writer of historical romances, Sir Arthur Conan Doyle, actually wrote the accounts of Holmes's exploits. They apparently are not aware of the fact that he merely was Dr. Watson's confidant and literary agent, and that he now and again advised him as to the actual redaction of the narratives. This is surely what happened in the case of *The Dancing Men*. Sir Arthur discovered the tiny men, in a somewhat primitive form, in the album, and he immediately saw the possibility of developing them into a very fine cipher. He spoke about this project to Dr. Watson, at their next meeting, and it at once struck fire with the latter. He actually had in his *portfolio* (see Dr. Watson's Preface to *His Last Bow*) the rough draft of an account, in which secret writing played a prominent part. This cipher, however, was not a very original one, perhaps even a quite trivial one. The case being one of Holmes's very best, however, he decided to make use of Mr. Cubitt's dancing men, which much appealed to his imagination, for he was, and perhaps still is, a very competent storyteller. So, the narrative at last appeared in *The Strand,* with the fully developed and analysed cipher of the dancing men.

It is just possible, of course, that Dr. Watson and the agent worked on it in close collaboration. Who shall tell? But, at all events, it will now be perfectly clear that Elsie Patrick's father, of evil memory, was *not* the inventor of the writing, which *would pass as a child's scrawl.*

More than once, it has been pointed out that Dr. Watson's writings are not always reliable, as to details. In Watson's character underlies certainly a very marked streak, not only of pawky humour, but also of *cunning,* and his friend Sherlock Holmes was every now and then brought up against it in a rather unexpected way. "I never get your limits, Watson. There are unexplained possibilities about you," Holmes would remark; or, again: "Your native cunning. . . ." Holmes evidently spoke in a humorous vein, on these occasions, but none the less . . . Watson, too, was often somewhat vague in certain details (*The Second Stain*), and offered fictive names for Holmes's clients and the localities where the events actually happened. Thus "Hilton Cubitt" in the account of *The Dancing Men* is evidently *not* the name of Elsie Patrick's unhappy husband. Watson merely in this way was desirous to render honour to the man who inspired the brilliant idea of the Dancing Men cipher.

—July 1954

NOTE

1. In the U.S. editions the name is "Riding Thorpe."

Baker Street Irregular Rex Stout was the creator of
detective Nero Wolfe, and Mr. Stout never fully denied
the following theory about Wolfe's father that was
bandied among the Irregulars. . . .

SOME NOTES RELATING TO A PRELIMINARY
INVESTIGATION INTO THE PATERNITY OF
NERO WOLFE

by JOHN D. CLARK

IN A RECENT SCHOLARLY ARTICLE[1] a noted historian has demolished the always dubious hypothesis that Nero Wolfe is the son of Mycroft Holmes, and has at the same time demonstrated that he must have been born in the United States at some time between 1 January 1892 and 1 January 1896. Unfortunately, while the author of this article has pointed out the noticeable lack of candor exhibited by Wolfe upon the occasions when he referred to his early life, he has been able to cast no light whatsoever upon the question as to the actual identity of the subject's parents. It is the purpose of this paper to furnish the answer, with a high degree of probability, to this interesting question, and to indicate the most profitable direction of future research into this important matter.

Part of Wolfe's lack of frankness as to his history and parentage may be attributed to his natural bent toward contrariness; but it may well be that he wishes, for reasons of his own, to conceal the identity of his parents. It is of course inconceivable that a detective of Wolfe's perspicacity could be ignorant of the facts himself.

In order to penetrate a bit more deeply into the mystery it is necessary to go back to the last years of the nineteenth century. Although DeVoto has proved that Wolfe was born in the United States some time between the years 1892 and 1895, he has demonstrated nothing whatsoever regarding the geographical location of his conception, but *has* located it in time somewhere between March 1891 and March 1895. These dates should be noted with some care, since in them lies the key to the question under examination.

In the 1890s Montenegro was an isolated and almost inaccessible principality. No railroads passed through, the border was crossed by little except goat trails in the mountain passes, and the little port of Antivari was practically the only entrance to the country. The port could be reached by one of the ships of the "Puglia" steamship line, sailing, infrequently, from Bari on the Italian coast, and a precipitous carriage road connected the port with Rieka and the capital, Cettigne. Cettigne had perhaps three thousand inhabitants, and was the site of the governmental offices, such as they were, of the new palace housing the somewhat Ruritanian court of Prince Nicholas, and of a theatre-cum-opera house.[2]

Cettigne was a city where a man who had reason to believe that he was hunted might find a reasonable degree of security. With a few tribesmen as allies (which would not be expensive) he could rest assured that no enemy could approach unseen, and could easily ensure that none would arrive. (All male Montenegrins carried arms at that time, and the ambush was a highly developed art-form in the mountainous terrain.)

When Sherlock Holmes had his final discussion with Professor Moriarty at the Reichenbach Fall at the beginning of May 1891,[3] we know that he escaped through Italy. We are ignorant of the course of his travels beyond Florence, but it appears not improbable that he traveled by railway to Bari (he had plenty of money, of course, since he was in touch with Mycroft, presumably by cable), and he may well have boarded a "Puglia" steamer there and proceeded to Antivari and thence to Cettigne. He must have remained there for several months. He could easily keep in touch with Mycroft by the telegraph line to Belgrade and Vienna, and by a little discreet bribery, could ensure that no news of his presence would reach the outside world.

Irene Adler was married to a young lawyer, Godfrey Norton, in 1888.[4] As to the course of the marriage, the primary authorities say nothing. It contained within itself, however, the seeds of instability. Norton was a conventional member of a respectable profession in a conformist age. Furthermore, he was of an excitable disposition. It is not unlikely that he was possessed of the high blood pressure that so frequently accompanies such a temperament, and the shock of learning, as he must eventually have done, of his wife's previous career may easily have had fatal results. Whether the marriage ended in his death, in divorce, or in desertion, it can hardly have lasted longer than two or three years.

Irene must then have been left a widow, *de jure* or *de facto*, with very scant means. She was, however, an operatic contralto, apparently of considerable merit, and a return to the stage would not seem too difficult. La Scala would be impossible, as would the Warsaw opera, since she had been retired for some time, but one of the smaller companies that toured through Eastern Europe would give her security as well as a chance to return eventually to the big time, or if not, to capture an affluent and noble (if provincial) protector.

In the course of its travels the company must have come to the opera house in Cettigne. Holmes was a devotee of the opera, and it is inevitable that he must have met Irene Adler again. Her admiration for him compared with his for her,[5] and, although Watson has stated that Holmes was completely devoid of the softer emotions, Holmes was not always completely candid with his friend, and was enough of an actor to be able to dissemble his emotions. Whether Irene was still a member of the company, or whether she had, by that time, come under the protection of one of the local nobility, cannot be determined, but the latter, for reasons which will appear later, seems to be more likely. Whatever the case, Holmes and Miss Adler must have seen much of each other, and when to their mutual admiration was added the fact that they were the only people in the town speaking anything but Montenegrin, Slovene, Servian, Croatian, Turkish, or bad German, an affair was inevitable.

When Irene became pregnant it must have taken really royal bribery plus all of Holmes's ingenuity to get her aboard one of the Italian steamers at Antivari, whence she sailed for Bari and on to the United States, presumably to join her parents in New Jersey. She may well have been disguised as a peasant boy when she boarded the Bari steamer, since the sackcloth costume worn by the peasantry could conceal not only her identity but her condition. Holmes could not accompany her for some reason—presumably because he remained behind to draw off the pursuit by the retainers of her outraged protector.

Nero Wolfe was born in New Jersey (the exact location can unfortunately not be traced) in late 1892 or early 1893, some six months after his mother had left Montenegro. It is clear that she did not long remain with her parents, having outworn her welcome as a returned and widowed daughter, but returned with her son to Central Europe, either in order to resume her career or to visit relatives living in Budapest. She must have married again, and settled in Buda, where she had at least one other child, which accounts for the niece or nephew mentioned by Wolfe at one time. She did *not* return to Montenegro, where the institution of the blood feud was still very much alive, and never came closer than Zagreb, which is some 240 miles from the border of the principality.

The route by which Holmes left Montenegro is uncertain, but it appears from an examination of the terrain that he must have struck east across the mountains into Albania (he was an excellent mountaineer[6]) through the passes into Serbia, and found himself on the railroad at Skoplye. On the railroad he traveled north to Nish, then east to Constantinople, and then south by way of Turkey into the Hedjaz, where he "looked in" at Mecca. From that point on his travels during his exile are as he detailed them to Watson in April of 1894.

Holmes's account of his travels in Tibet and through Persia are the purest invention on his part, produced to account for the time without shocking his good friend Watson. The mention of the "Norwegian traveller Sigerson" is cleverly designed to lead to a degree of confusion in Watson's mind between the mythical Norwegian and the very real Sven Hedin who was at that time starting his Central Asian researches. The visit to the Khalifa at Khartoum is, of course, quite real, since the results are a matter of record in the archives of the Foreign Office. The researches in Montpelier upon the coal-tar derivatives, too, can be confirmed through reference to the contemporary chemical journals.

Whether Holmes ever again communicated with Irene Adler, or with his son, is so far unknown. If he did not, his reasons must remain in the realm of conjecture, since it has never been easy to read the mind of that remarkable man.

Wolfe must have grown up in Budapest, with occasional visits to Zagreb, in the protectorate of Bosnia and Herzegovina. There he must have met his first and oldest friend Marco Vucic. But there is no evidence, not even hearsay, that he ever stepped

337

HIGH MEADOW
BREWSTER
NEW YORK
June 14 1955

Editor of the Baker Street Journal
221B Baker Street
RFD 1
Morristown   New Jersey

Dear Sir:

I return herewith the ms. by John D. Clark of some notes regarding the paternity of Nero Wolfe.

I am obliged to you for sending me the ms. for perusal, and I admire the finesse of your suggestion that "censorship" by me might be desirable and acceptable. As the literary agent of Archie Goodwin I am of course privy to many details of Nero Wolfe's past which to the general public, and even to scholars of Clark's standing, must remain moot for some time. If and when it becomes permissible for me to disclose any of those details, your distinguished journal would be a most appropriate medium for the disclosure. The constraint of my loyalty to my client makes it impossible for me to say more now.

With my best respects,

Sincerely,

Rex Stout

within the actual boundaries of Montenegro. Vucic may have been a Montenegrin—Wolfe, with his talent for confusion, may have claimed to be one—but nationality has not yet been defined on the basis of the geographical location of conception!

It is probable that Wolfe's stepfather secured for him the original position in the Austro-Hungarian civil service which led to his eventual enrolment in the intelligence service of the old Empire. His career in that service is difficult to trace—not only because it is one of the functions of intelligence operatives to make their careers difficult to trace, but because Wolfe himself has added deliberately to the confusion. When he states that he joined the Montenegrin army in 1916, the statement is patently ridiculous, since that army was completely destroyed during the previous autumn. Nor can he have been an Austrian agent when he was (he says) jailed in Bulgaria in 1916, since at that moment Bulgaria had already joined Austria against Serbia. It appears more likely, from the historical background, that Wolfe switched loyalty from Austria to Montenegro at least as early as 1914 or 1915, when he was in Albania; was jailed in Sofia early in 1915, and escaped or was released soon enough to join the Serbian-Montenegrin army before the battles of October and November which destroyed them.[7] How he escaped from the debacle is doubtful, but it seems likely that he was with the refugee remnant of an army that struggled down the Adriatic coast from San Giovanni de Medua and was eventually evacuated to Corfu and then transferred to Saloniki.

The reasons for Wolfe's desertion of Austria can only be speculated upon. It may have been the result of an emotional shock (Wolfe was 22 in 1915) conceivably the result of an insulting remark by an irritated officer about his Montenegrin origin. Or he may have been involved in one of the many minority independence movements that harassed the Empire. The name he carries—obviously a conspiratorial pseudonym—suggests this explanation. But until Wolfe feels impelled to tell the facts, any suggested explanation is pure guesswork.

But whether Wolfe ever condescends to admit it, or whether he remains forever silent, his parentage can no longer be a matter of conjecture, nor can there be any doubt as to the source from which he inherited his remarkable talents.

—January 1956

NOTES

1. B. DeVoto, in *Harper's* 204 No. 1250 (July 1954), p. 8.
2. *Encyclopaedia Britannica*, 11th Ed., XVII, 766
3. *The Final Problem*.
4. *A Scandal in Bohemia*.
5. Ibid.
6. *The Empty House*.
7. Winston S. Churchill, *The Unknown War* (New York: Scribner's, 1932), pp. 331 ff.

*There are many, including your Editor, who feel that
Sherlockian pastiches fall so far short of the mark of the
original Holmes adventures that they are often worth
neither encouraging nor even mentioning. Apparently
Mr. Weiss feels much the same way. . . .*

THE CELESTIAL PASTICHE

by DAVID A. WEISS

THE DUTIES of a recording secretary are exacting at times. Mine
are no exception. For quite a while, in spite of the fact that communication between our land and yours is so difficult, the members have been insisting that I contact THE BAKER STREET JOUR-
NAL to tell its readers all about the activities of our Scion here. I
suppose you think it unusual that we have a branch society at
all. But really, Sherlock Holmes is too universal to be confined
to any one people, or any one country. Our chapter has been in
existence for over twenty years. Its name is The Avenging Angels, and that is very appropriate, particularly since our land is
so often called "The Land of the Saints."

An incident occurred at our last annual meeting that made
communication with the JOURNAL absolutely imperative. Our
procrastination in the matter had to end, because withholding
the details of this incident could only be considered a very selfish gesture on our part, and one certainly not consistent with
the true Holmesian spirit. I am not familiar with the way in
which meetings of the various Scions are held in the United
States, but here the annual meeting is by far the most important
one of the year. It is looked forward to with the greatest anticipation, and an interesting program is always planned. Lectures
and speeches are given explaining some particular phase of the
Sacred Writings, and debate is held upon one of those controversial issues so dear to the students of Sherlockiana. And the
main event of the evening, the one that is always the most interesting and enjoyable, is the reading of the winning entry in the
annual pastiche contest. Is it any wonder that every member of
The Avenging Angels moves high heaven to attend?

The night of the meeting itself held a portent that something
unusual was going to happen. White fleecy clouds were drifting

by, and the sky was a beautiful dark blue. The meeting hall was filling up early. Taking off their hats and coats, they walked down the aisles, threaded their way through the rows of wooden chairs, and joined one of the little groups that had sprung up all over the hall. Excited buzzes of conversation issued from these groups, and the noise grew in volume as more and more members filed into the hall. One group was discussing the new story by Dr. Watson that had reputedly just been discovered. Another was arguing about whether the latest interpretation given to the location of the jezail bullet was a valid one. Then suddenly a hush settled over the hall. The president, Angel No. 1, who was known as the Gabriel, had taken his seat upon the speakers' platform. It was the signal that the meeting was about to begin.

The Gabriel smiled, looked out over the audience, and coughed several times, as if to test the attention to his presence. It was an unnecessary gesture, for each member was already prepared to start the meeting. Weight and limbs had been shifted to the most comfortable position; minds had been made receptive. The president arose.

"Members and friends of The Avenging Angels. It gives me great pleasure to welcome you again to the annual meeting of our Scion Society. I know you are all waiting to hear this evening's program, and my remarks accordingly will be very brief. All I really want to do is to summarize our activities for the year. Gentlemen, it has been a very successful year; a year of which we all can be very proud. Thirty-six new members have passed the supreme qualifying test and have been admitted to our ranks. Our quarterly is flourishing, and has presented a wealth of fine and interesting writing. Our library has increased its store of books and pamphlets almost twofold, and for the first time journals published in the United States have been made available in our reading room. Our museum can also report substantial gains. We have added to our collection the five orange pips, and it can also be announced that we now possess a complete set of the famous monographs. To all those who made these gains possible, our most sincere appreciation is extended. Yes, it has been a really successful year, and I, as your Gabriel, wish to thank all you members whose cooperation has made it possible.

"Well, that just about ends my remarks for the evening. I will now turn the meeting over to the head of our program committee, Angel No. 17. He deserves a tremendous amount of credit for having planned those interesting meetings for us month after month. His program tonight is an exceptional one. Incidentally, it was he who inaugurated our annual pastiche contest, the winner of which will be announced tonight and his essay read. And I don't think I'm letting anything out of the bag in saying that it is a truly magnificent effort. Well, gentlemen, thank you. I will now turn the meeting over to Angel No. 17."

The Gabriel sat down and the audience applauded—really more in anticipation of what was to follow than at what had passed. Here and there abortive conversations sprang up, but they were quelled by the appearance of Angel No. 17 upon the platform. His comments were very brief. First, he thanked the Gabriel for his kind remarks, and then he introduced the first speaker of the evening, Angel No. 5, who was to discuss the second Mrs. Watson.

Nervously clearing his throat, Angel No. 5 plunged into his subject. As his talk unfolded, it revealed the careful preparation it had received: the extensive research into the Sacred Writings, the weighing of previous interpretations, the challenge and response to inconsistent facts. As if with one ear, the audience listened, following the avenues of thought to their logical conclusions. Finally, in one last burst of reasoning, the speaker summed up his case—and its brilliant clarity and pure deduction were worthy of the great Holmes himself.

The members showed their appreciation by a roar of applause. The clapping of hands continued long after the speaker had sat down. Yet in this clapping was concealed a variety of thoughts. Some members thought the speech a good speech simply because it echoed ideas of their own. Others were more discerning; before the speech was over, they were testing its conclusions, trying to find some weak spot into which to force the brunt of their own opinions. Nevertheless, the speech had been interesting and provocative, and more than this no one could ask.

Rapping three times on his desk with a gavel, the head of the program committee called for silence. The audience immediately responded, its attention directed to the next event on the program, a debate between Angels no. 16 and 82 upon the subject, "Resolved: Mycroft Holmes held one of the most significant posts in the British government." The debaters were excellent. Each repelled smoothly and effectively the formidable questions of their opponents, and then each hurled challenging questions of his own. All facets of the topic were exhumed, examined, explored, and explained. Mycroft Holmes was a petty thief. No, he was Moriarty himself. Mycroft Holmes was a minor government official. No, he was one of the most important men in the British government, second only to the Prime Minister. And so it went. Every possible point was covered and, in the rebuttal period, a few new ones were added. When the debate was over, some of the audience was confused, some inspired, but everyone had been thrilled.

Part of this thrill stemmed from the nervous anticipation created by the nearness of the next, and last, event on the program. It was really unnecessary to announce it. For to almost everyone there, the reading of the winning entry of the annual pastiche contest was the event of the year. Long months before, curiosities had been aroused, enthusiasms whetted, pencils sharpened, research conducted, and writing performed—and all for this one contest. It represented a goal, and a most challenging goal. The fact that almost every Avenging Angel had submitted an entry was a tribute to their devotion. The fact that they recognized that their entries could approach, but never equal, the Sacred Writings themselves was also a tribute, this time to those immortals, Holmes and Watson. For more than two months the contest entries, cut down to the proper length and typed in the correct fashion, had passed through the channels of office procedure. Collated, studied, criticized, and evaluated, they had been scrutinized by each judge, and the winning entry had at last been selected. The contest entrants had done their part, and so had the judges. Only the announcement of the winning entry remained. And until that time, which was fast approaching, every entrant, although publically disclaiming all chances of winning, was secretly hoping for the best.

The program chairman turned the meeting back to the Gabriel. The audience was breathless. The winning entry was about to be read. Whose would it be? The Gabriel arose, coughed several times, and took—ever so slowly, it seemed to the audience—a typed manuscript from his leather briefcase. He looked around, adjusted his spectacles, and began to read. The spell of the breathlessness was broken, and into that vacuum—when each member realized that the winning pastiche was not his own—rushed a multitude of fast, quick thoughts. Whose pastiche was it? Was it by one of my friends? How does my entry compare with the winning one? I'll do better next year!

Slowly but firmly, like the unrelenting grip of an anaesthetic, the words of that winning pastiche forced the attention of the audience away from all these thoughts. The pastiche demanded attention because it was enslaving the minds of the audience. As the story unfolded, the petty jealousies and insignificant curiosities aroused by the contest were supplanted by the universal joy and satisfying pleasure that a reading of the adventures of Sherlock Holmes never fails to give. It seemed a part of the Sacred Writings themselves, part of the heritage of Baker Street. It was masterful, brilliantly fresh and absorbing, like the early Holmes. Like the Holmes of the Lestrade and Gregson days, like the Holmes before that fateful day at Reichenbach Fall. The pastiche was perfect—a masterpiece.

The Gabriel sighed as he read the final words. And in that sigh was his regret, as well as the regret of every member there, that he himself could not produce such a work of art. It was the sigh that recognizes greatness and stands in awe of it.

He paused momentarily, and then began again, "Gentlemen, you have just heard the winning entry in our annual pastiche contest. It speaks for itself because it is a pastiche worthy of the name pastiche. No more need be said on that score. Besides affording us the tremendous pleasure we have experienced in hearing it, this pastiche should also provide each and every one of us with inspiration for next year's contest.

"Now a word about the author. He is Angel No. 103, one of our new members. My congratulations go to Angel No. 103 on a most extraordinary piece of work. This was his first contest entry, and he should be extremely proud. Yet I could not say that he is unfitted for this type of endeavor. On earth, he pursued a career that served him in good stead for this contest. Not only was he a physician, like the good Dr. Watson to whom we are indebted for the Sacred Writings, but he was also a well-known writer as well. Perhaps you have read some of his works.

345

Most of them are historical novels, the most famous of which are *The White Company* and *Micah Clarke*.

"Gentlemen, may I present Angel No. 103, the winner of our annual pastiche contest?"

—April 1948

*Dr. Conan Doyle was, as we know, Dr. Watson's
literary agent. But how he went about peddling the
adventures of Sherlock Holmes to the publishers of his
time is another thing again. . . .*

REJECTIO AD ABSURDUM

by HERBERT BREAN

A Talk Delivered at the Annual Meeting of The Baker Street
Irregulars, 10 January 1964

WE ARE GATHERED here tonight for a number of pleasant reasons, but the most important is of course to honour the best and
the wisest man whom we have ever known.

The key words there I think are "we have ever known." We
know Sherlock Holmes through the Sacred Writings, and without them Holmes's fame might have dwindled and even died
following his retirement.

But writings do not get into print easily. As a writer of mystery fiction and as a magazine editor for many years, I can personally testify to that. To give you some idea of the obstacles
and pitfalls which can prevent publication and hence preserva-
tion of even the finest work, I would like to take you without
further delay to the office of a famous magazine editor of many,
many years ago.

He is in his office, hard at work in his shirt sleeves. (All magazine editors work very hard, and always in their shirt sleeves.)
His secretary is over there; her job of course is to answer the
'phone and misspell words.

The 'phone rings. Br-r-ring . . . br-r-ring. He speaks:

"Hey, Gertrude, pick that up, will you?

"Who? Doyle? Who is he? . . . A literary agent?

"English, eh? Maybe I'd better talk to him. He might represent somebody good like Al Swinburne or that Anthony Trol-
lope, and God knows we need material. Put him on [picks up
'phone].

"Hello, Mr. Doyle. Nice to hear from you. . . . Fine, thanks.
And how are you, sir? . . . Fine. I, ah, gather you represent a

number of English writers. Is that correct? Only one. Oh. Who is that, Mr. Doyle? . . .

"I beg your pardon. My girl didn't say you were a doctor. . . . Okay, who is your client, ah, Doctor? . . . Have I got this straight? You're a literary agent, but you're also a doctor. Watson's a doctor who is also a writer. Is that correct? . . .

"No not at all. It's just that you English seem to be so health-conscious [chuckles]. Well, anyway, tell me about Watson's work. I'm afraid I'm not familiar with it, but I don't keep up with the European output like I should. What has he published? . . .

"Some personal reminiscences, eh? I think I know what you mean. . . . Oh, sure, we get them all the time. Usually they're the biography of some old country doctor or specialist and have a title like "My Forty Years below the Navel," or something like that. . . .

"Oh, it isn't like that. Good. . . . Mystery and romance, I see. Well, we could sure use something like that. . . . I didn't get that title, Doctor. . . .

"*A Study in Scarlet*? [Chuckles] Sort of sounds like it's about a bit of unsuccessful surgery, doesn't it, Doctor? . . .

"Oh. You didn't think that was so funny. Well, I'm sorry, Doctor. I didn't mean to—I will say this though, I don't like the title. . . .

"No, you see, a few years ago we published Nat Hawthorne's *Scarlet Letter*, and it went very big. We sold out on the news-stands that month. Of course, it was kind of sexy, and that never hurts. Is your story sexy?

"A murder story? Oh. Well, I don't know, Doctor. Personally, I don't think the public will ever give a damn about murder stories. . . .

"Well, go ahead and tell me about it. What's the plot and who's in it, and so on? . . .

"*Sherlock Holmes*? That's the name, eh. . . . Oh, no, it's as good a name as any. Names don't matter. But tell me about him, Doctor. What does this Holmes do? What's in his bag, as we say over here? . . .

"A private consultant? Oh, another doctor. . . .

"He's *not* a doctor. Good. That makes me happier. What *does* he do?

"He makes deductions? Well, Doctor, maybe I can save us

both some time. You see, since you're from overseas, I wouldn't expect you to know it, but it's getting around toward income tax time in this country and everybody is busy making deductions or thinking about the ones they're going to make. . . .

"No, but you see it's commonplace. Everyone is doing it. I don't see how you can get a plot out of it. Frankly, the subject is quite distasteful to most people. . . .

"Oh, *logical* deductions. Well, I think I see. Maybe you could give me an illustration. . . .

"This Holmes can tell a man's height by the length of his stride? The hell he can. . . .

"No, I'm not arguing, Doctor. It's just that I wonder if a reader would find that credible. I'm not sure I would. Now, just for instance, we have a guy we deal with right here at the magazine. He does illustrations for us and he's very good. We ship him a manuscript—he's over in Paris—and he does a bunch of pictures and sends them back. But I'd like to see your man Holmes deduce *his* height from the length of his stride. His name is Toulouse-Lautrec—maybe you've run into him. . . .

"You once knew a man who could do that? Really? . . . Joseph Bell, eh? . . . *Doctor* Joseph Bell. Oh, yes. You know, somehow I knew he was going to turn out to be a doctor. Small world, isn't it? . . .

"Well, frankly, Doctor, everybody's a doctor, and you make me think I'm talking to the AMA convention. Well, I still don't know what goes on in this murder story. Who does the dirty work? . . .

"Some Mormons? Oh well, Doctor, that's out, that's all. I won't try to explain it; you have to know the United States. But you'll never sell that story over here. Does your man Wharton—or Watsome, or whatever it is—have anything else? . . .

"Another in the works, eh? Well, that's good. What's this one, Doctor? . . .

"*The Sign—of the Four?* I see. I know I shouldn't ask, but who, ah, are the Four, Doctor? . . .

"Mostly Indians? Well, you see, there again you're heading right into trouble. You'll never sell a story like that over here, Doctor. . . .

"Well, maybe I *had* better explain it to you. You see, today in this country we're pretty excited about integration and segrega-

349

tion, minority groups, religious rights, discrimination—all that sort of thing. For that reason no magazine will print a story in which you lay the blame on one small, identifiable group. . . .

"Well, no, but you see what I mean. In that first story you've got the Mormons going around killing people—a minority religious group. Then in the next one it's some Indians who are responsible—a minority ethnic group. You better tell Watson about this. . . .

"No, I mean it, Doctor. Tell him if he's going to have villains in his stories they must be only native-born, white, Protestant American males. And here's another thing. Tell him to take care in naming them. Don't give them names identifiable with any special race or religion. Tell him to use simple names like Jones or Smith or Brown.

"[Shakes head] No, I wouldn't use Moriarty, Doctor. . . .

"You see, the Irish are awfully sensitive; they really are. Some months ago we ran an exposé of Tammany Hall, here in New York. You should have seen the letters I got as a result. Some of them shouldn't have been allowed to go through the mail. . . .

"On the level, Doctor. Would you believe it?—that month I learned *seven* new four-letter words. . . .

"Well, I'm sorry too, Doctor, because I'm looking for material. [Aside] Hey, Gertrude, cut in here in a minute and say James Russell Lowell is calling from Boston or something, will you? I've got to get rid of this guy. . . .

"Sorry, Doctor, I was just speaking to my secretary a moment. . . .

"Of course I understand. It's natural for an agent to want to make a sale for his client. . . .

"No, I'm afraid I don't know where you might sell it, Doctor. There was a guy in my office from the Beeton people in London, right in your stamping ground, who was looking for stuff. It seems they're getting out some kind of Christmas annual and—.

"Well, I don't know exactly how much they're paying, but I'd guess in the neighborhood of a hundred or a hundred twenty-five. . . .

"No, dollars, Doctor, not pounds. We magazines aren't made of money, you know. [Looks at watch] Well, nice talking to you, Doctor. . . .

"Thanks. You too. And stay well. If you don't, I guess you know where to get help, all right. Incidentally, do you know Bill Thackeray—William M. Thackeray—over there? We need some material, and if you run into him, tell him to get in touch with us. And, by the way, Doctor, in case you ever do come up with anything in our line, just send it in. . . . No, don't bring it to the office. Mail it—and please don't forget that old stamped, self-addressed envelope. You know, just in case. 'Bye now, Doctor [hangs up].

"Gertrude, I'm going to lunch. No more calls. But look, I'm getting desperate. Nobody's coming up with anything worth printing, and the issue after next is wide open. Tell you what. While I'm out call Nat Hawthorne up there in Concord, or wherever he is, and tell him I'd like to see a sequel to *The Scarlet Letter*. Tell him to mull it over a while, and I'll call him in a couple of days. Maybe we could call it *Daughter of Hester Prynne,* or something like that. See you, Gertrude [exits]."

—June 1964

THE BAKER STREET IRREGULARS
AND ITS SCIONS

*One of the original Baker Street Irregulars takes on the
role of Irregular historian, tracing the club's peculiar
development. . . .*

THE ORIGIN OF 221B WORSHIP

by ROBERT KEITH LEAVITT

Some Notes on the Conception, Gestation,
Parturition, and Legitimization of
The Baker Street Irregulars

"All that I saw, and part of which I was. . . ."

—Vergil's *Aeneid*

PART I
THE CHALDEAN ROOTS

SINCE THE VERY INFANCY of the society, the origins of the Baker
Street Irregulars have been the subject of a lot of ineffable
twaddle and misrepresentation, much of it embalmed in print,
and thereby doubly misleading to present-day members.

Before his lamented passing, Edgar W. Smith asked me to
gather and collate with the available records the recollections of
myself and others who were around when the ferment of origin
was taking place, and to put the result into shape for the JOUR-
NAL, with the object of correcting, if possible, some of the accumulated misunderstanding. Our present Commissionaire has
seconded the request. Hence this collation, in two parts.

In this first installment I shall try to trace the antecedents of
the BSI, since they explain many otherwise puzzling things
about the society, including particularly its Constitution and
Buy-Laws, the reading of which has become a ritual feature of
Annual Dinners, and I shall try to set down, from the recollection of those present, the hitherto unrecorded facts about the
society's practically unnoticed birth.

In the second part, to follow, I shall record the legitimization of the society, as noticed in print, supplemented with the recollection of original members.[1] Finally, I shall set down the real facts about an occasion often mistaken today by recent members for the original meeting of the society.

The BSI had a father society, a mother society, and an uncle-godfather society. All contributed in some measure to the peculiar nature of the BSI today, to its color, its customs, and its rites and observances.

The three societies in question had all been sired by Christopher Morley (and if that implies incest on the part of the two parent ones, make the most of it), Chris of the high heart, the richly-stored intellect, the prodigious imagination, the boundless curiosity, the irrepressible spirit, the elfin prankishness, the selfless generosity, the splendid, shining soul! To uncounted numbers of us he was perhaps the most interesting man we ever knew, and certainly the most lovable.

Christopher Morley, during the pre-Repeal era, was in his pre-Elizabethan, or unbearded stage. In his early forties, he was stout, lustily active, gregarious, busy, prosperous (in spite of the recent collapse of the Hoboken theater venture), and immensely popular. He rarely lunched with fewer than four people, and, often as not, with a group of a dozen or more.

Among his countless fascinating traits was the habit of forming clubs on the spur of the moment. Any agreeable gathering of friends around the table was apt to find itself, halfway through the meal, constituted into a club commemorating, and usually named for, something pleasant-to-remember about the occasion. The something might be trivial, such as the title of a book plucked off the open-air bin of a second-hand bookstore. But that didn't matter, provided it yielded a good, memorable name. Chris was hypersensitive to possible titles, even in chance-heard phrases. ("Hey! That would make a wonderful book.") So all his clubs were resoundingly named. Undoubtedly part of the BSI's viability derives from the name Chris picked out of the Canon for it.

Most of Chris's clubs (and there were scores of them) never had a second meeting, and were never heard from again, save in fond reminiscence. But three clubs, at least, had a certain measure of longevity, and ran to considerable size, one way or another.

The first and best known of these (indeed it was famous) was the Three Hours For Lunch Club, which dated from Chris's early newspaper days in downtown New York. It included, more or less, every man Chris liked enough to ask repeatedly to lunch. Of these there were scores, probably hundreds, first and last, for Chris was the most gregarious of men. The make-up of those who were habitually found lunching together changed somewhat with the changes in Chris's work, location, and interests, though a hard core of old Morley companions furnished the majority of the attendants at any one time. These included fellow toilers of early newspapering days; literary figures of the era; people from the worlds of book publishing, bookselling, and book collecting; seafaring authors and America-faring Britishers; painters and sculptors; folk of the theater; and people of no other visible distinction than that Chris considered them "kinsprits." (Yet what finer distinction could any man have had?)

Normally, there were not more than six or eight people present—a limit established by Chris's ability to reach people by phone and find them free on any given day. But on Saturday afternoons (we worked half a day on Saturdays in that age) there might be fifteen or twenty. Christ Cella's restaurant, at which we used often to meet during the early 1930s, when (and because) it was a modest-priced speakeasy, had a big back room that was a combination of kitchen and family living room, and here we ate often on Saturdays, around one big, oval table. George Ennis, the famous water-colorist, sketched a small group of the Three-Hours-For-Lunchers around this table in the winter of 1933/4. I can't say much for his picture's portrait accuracy—especially of Chris, Bill Hall, and Don Marquis—but, on the other hand, six of the nine members shown [2] were among aboriginal Irregulars, and the room was probably the chief gestation-place of the BSI.

The second club that had a part in bringing the BSI into the world—the mother society, so to speak—was the *Grillparzer Sittenpolizei Verein,* or Grillparzer Morals-Police Association. This was a sort of coeducational version of the Three Hours For Lunch Club, with special features all its own. Normally, its meetings were convened by Chris, who, whenever he had a strikingly personable feminine caller at *The Saturday Review* (a frequent occurrence, happily), would telephone a number of his friends, calling a luncheon meeting of the GSPV. The great feature of these meetings was not just that they were of mixed company, but that, by the Verein's unwritten laws,[3] if you, too, brought a handsome gal to the meeting, you were not penalized for that exemplary, Christian act. On the contrary, you were rewarded, for, at the final reckoning, you paid only one share of the total bill as split equally among all the males present, many of whom had been forced to come stag.

To ensure that there should be a modicum of girls present, Chris would usually bring along not only his office caller of the moment, but as many as possible of the gal employees of *The Saturday Review*. These were known collectively as The Mermaids, largely because early meetings of the GSPV were held in a speak of which the walls were stencilled with underwater scenes, and which was known as The Goldfish Bowl. Later meetings were often held in Cella's back room, but at least one *very* important one was held elsewhere.

The GSPV got its name from the fact that its register for the enrollment of new members was an odd volume from the *Collected Works of Franz Grillparzer* (1791–1872), Austrian dramatist, which Chris had characteristically picked up hastily on his way to the first lunch of what thereby turned out to be the GSPV. New members were initiated by 1) opening the book at random; 2) picking out, from whatever text was thus exposed, and underlining, a phrase or clause or whole passage appropriate (more or less) to the initiates or the occasion; 3) having him or her sign below it, and affix as a seal anything adhesive that happened to be handy (such as the corner of a cigarette-pack revenue stamp). 4) The whole was then attested, in stately formality (often Latinized), by Chris as Grand Master (without title) of the Verein. The original Grillparzer register volume was rescued from profane hands some years ago by Bill Hall, and is at this writing among his effects in storage, and hence inaccessible for reference.[4]

There was another feature of the GSPV, and one that survives in vestigial form in the BSI Constitution and Buy-Laws: If you had in tow for lunch a gal you were particularly anxious to impress, and couldn't raise Chris or any other of the principal members of the Verein to meet you, you were authorized—again by unwritten law—to call a Special Meeting of the GSPV, composed of just yourself and the gal, whom you then signed up in The Book, right in the same binding with H. G. Wells, not to mention the *really* immortal (in her view) Robert Montgomery.

It should be recorded that the bringing of a personable female to a meeting of the GSPV (even a Special one) did not necessarily imply the likelihood of sponsor and inductee rolling in the hay afterward—though I can understand how some wives might have come to that tempting conclusion. This should be amply clear from the fact that Elmer Davis put his name to, and Chris published, the BSI's *Constitution and Buy-Laws,* which put into words (though, as things developed, not into BSI practice) certain of the customs of the GSPV. As men of discretion, they wouldn't have done that had scandalous inferences been warranted.

The legacy of the Grillparzer Club to The Baker Street Irregulars lies only in part in the customs Elmer embalmed. More important is the fact that one of its meetings actually did turn into what might be called a parturitional occasion that delivered the infant BSI living, breathing, and (as always) yak-yacking, into this world. Of which more in its place.

The third-most-significant of Chris's clubs in the origins of the BSI was The Foundry, a club with more or less the same central core as the Three Hours For Lunch Club (from which it had sprung), but colored by the fact that it had been given special and formal organization to get together a cooperative group to angel the Hoboken theatrical venture at a time when it was getting short of breath. One of the Jersey assets it took over was a fine, century-old iron-foundry that doubled in brass as theatrical warehouse and clubhouse. By the early thirties, this base had been lost, and with it went a system of dues, etc. All that remained—and endured, certainly until the late 1930s— was a men's club of Morley associates, with emphasis especially on those in the book-publishing and theatrical fields. Unlike most of Chris's clubs, this one had a more or less formal membership list, and at this period met only on mail call, usually for dinner, but always in the evening. From it the BSI inherited these latter traits, along with certain of its early members.

So much, then, for the sources of the BSI—and, I am afraid,

at intolerable length. Perhaps, however, this will make easier the narration of the origins and early development of the BSI as aboriginal members' recollections, assisted by records, sort them out.

In the year 1930, two big things happened, as far as Holmesiana were concerned. First, Sir Arthur Conan Doyle died, the author of the Brigadier Gerard stories and of many other superb tales, as well as (it later developed) one of the greatest Literary Agents who ever lived. All over the world people rendered homage to his memory as one of the most magically thrilling of writers, and started rereading and talking about his books. Right upon this came Doubleday's publication of a collected edition of the Sacred Writings—the Memorial Edition, with an introduction by our own Chris. He had all his life been an ardent Doyle fan, as anyone who examines any of his early writings can see.

These things fanned anew a fire that had never died—the glow of interest in the Sherlock Holmes stories—and in the Holmes legend, or saga, as something transcending the mere published stories and obviously constituting, for any really intelligent person, Revealed Truth. Many people, including our own Vincent Starrett, had been writing occasional pieces along the lines of this faith for a generation.

Now, the British in particular started a splendid blaze of published speculation, fed upon the most scholarly research and sparkling with footnotes. It began with Roberts' *Dr. Watson*, in 1931, continued with Blakeney's *Sherlock Holmes, Fact or Fiction?* (1932), and in the following year Bell's *Sherlock Holmes and Dr. Watson*. Bell was an American, though his book was published in London.

On this side, or at least in Three Hours For Lunch circles, we were slower on the uptake. We didn't at once perceive the Gospel-like infallibility of the Sacred Writings. Our approach to grace came later and in a roundabout, irreverent way of our own.

Some time in late 1932 or early 1933 there arose the custom of the challenge question with a round of drinks at stake. This entailed an assumption of axiomatic truth in the Writings (subject, of course, to slips of the pen or of the Watsonian memory). Competition among speakeasies in those waning days of Prohibition had brought the price of drinks down to a seemly level, so the challenge game was a reasonable diversion for a group of six or eight, and an agreeable way of providing for their thirst over three hours—or, as often happened, more. This custom had several results:

—It set the more calculating of us to studying The Writings with care, both to dig up what were then considered real stinker questions, and to fortify ourselves against the same kind, that we rightly suspected were being combed out by our confrères. Thus, Holmesian scholarship got off to a flying start, before it was even aware of itself. I suppose that in the light of present-day learning of, say, Akron or Philadelphia level, our early questions would be laughed to scorn. But we were doing our simple-minded, troglodytic best.

—To sustain contentions that sometimes got disputed in the heat of a quiz, several of us started research of a sort, along lines that appealed to us, such as (in one case) Holmes's techniques of making detection profitable. In this, we had the British pattern to follow, and we were egged on by Chris, who was doing the same thing himself, but better.

—The fact that we quizzed literally for drinks led naturally to the drinking of toasts. It seemed only right that when someone had failed to identify Col. Moran by his best-known characterization, all those who profited by his ignorance should lift their glasses to The Second Most Dangerous Man in London.

—Some of these toasts became more or less habitual, even ritual, and so were not only the ancestors of the Conanical toasts, but important features of the actual accouchement of the BSI on the society's Natal Day, as I shall tell presently.

Out of all this, a Holmesian cult started, first in the THFLC and then in the GSPV. It didn't have any separate identity as it began, but now it can be recognized as the BSI in foetal form. There were several small meetings during the closing months of 1933, in which the talk never got far from Baker Street. And since some of these were of mixed company, it would be difficult to say whether they were Baker-Street-tinged meetings of the Grillparzer, or Grillparzer-infiltrated meetings of the larval BSI. The actual Nativity Meeting, in fact, had just that character.

There were some healthy jounces that helped bring on the labor out of which the BSI popped. Early in December, Vincent

Starrett's book *The Private Life of Sherlock Holmes* had appeared and had been reviewed by Elmer Davis in the SRL (2 December 1933). Elmer's review not only paid deserved tribute to a great Work of Scholarship, but on its own went to some length to comment on the love life of Mr. Holmes. As he said in closing, "These are all matters that deserve the serious attention of scholars, and will undoubtedly receive it." Off and on thereafter, "The Bowling Green" carried letters from people like Felix Morley commenting on points of Sherlockian lore. It was becoming evident to the world that a society of Holmesians was needed—and on 6 January 1934, the world got it, though without its—or the society's at first—realizing that a birth had taken place.

I can't say from memory, nor can any other aborigines I have consulted, just when Chris Morley began to refer to the members of the Holmesian cult as The Baker Street Irregulars. My impression is that it was not much, if any, before the actual accouchement. And the first published use of the name that I can find is in comments on the proceedings of that date, January 6th, 1934.

Piecing together my recollections with those of others, and with the fragmentary records in print, here is the story of how the BSI finally got born:

In the fall of 1933, the management of the Hotel Duane, on Madison Avenue between 36th and 37th Streets, conceived the sales-promotion idea of making their hostelry a gathering-place for the publishing and bookselling trades. They redecorated a below-stairs lounge and plugged it industriously as a luncheon and meeting place for publishers. Needless to say, they didn't neglect to urge their idea on columnists like Chris, who wrote of and to the book-publishing world.

In the closing days of 1933, Chris sat down to compile his "Bowling Green" column for the first issue of *The Saturday Review* that was scheduled to come out in 1934. He looked at the date—January 6th! Wonderful! Sherlock Holmes's birthday, as Chris had long been contending. And on a Saturday! There really ought to be a party. And so, with the Duane's publicity fresh in his mind, Chris wrote a piece—two pieces, rather—for "The Bowling Green."

The first of these was in a pattern used by every columnist

whenever he wanted a springboard for his thoughts: he wrote a letter to himself from a conveniently imagined character. Then he wrote a reply to it, and he printed the two under a single head:

SHERLOCK HOLMES AND COCKTAILS

SIR:—Last year—on what evidence I cannot guess—you announced that January 6 was the date of Sherlock Holmes's birthday, and 1853 the proper year. That seemed to be about right. I remember the beautiful Irene Adler, "*the* woman," the only one toward whom Sherlock might conceivably have felt an impulse of sentiment, was born ("in New Jersey") in 1858. (Where in New Jersey, I wonder?)

Anyhow, every year about Christmas time I get out my Conan Doyles and read Sherlock again. And your comment lately about cocktails having gone back to 25 cents reminded me that Holmes considered even that price a trifle high. In *The Adventure of the Noble Bachelor,* you remember, he examines a hotel bill in which a cocktail costs a shilling and a glass of sherry 8*d*. He deduces that the bill was from "one of the most expensive hotels."

Will not the Hotel Duane, on Madison Avenue, which you say is frequented by Sherlock Holmes's publishers, invent a Sherlock Holmes cocktail in honor of the birthday? I will offer the two-volume edition of the Complete Stories as a prize for the most appropriate formula. Of course there should really be two: the *Sherlock* and the *Mycroft*. What a subtle and influential philtre the *Mycroft* would have to be!

Another thought: what evidence can you give of Sherlock's religious feelings, if any?

CHARING CROSS
St. George, Staten Island

I like Mr. Cross's suggestion about the cocktail, and will be pleased to forward for his judgment any suggested formulae. In regard to Irene Adler ("a face that a man might die for" was Holmes's astonishing description) I have always maintained that she was born in Hoboken.

Of Holmes's religious feelings: I've always supposed the beginning of his atheistic tendency was the fact that if he hadn't been on his way to college chapel he wouldn't have been bitten by Trevor's bull terrier. (See the story of the *Gloria Scott*.) It must have been a bad bite; Holmes was laid up for ten days. But Holmes was a student of the bible (see *The Crooked Man*).

Once Chris had got this to press, he gave thought to the idea of a birthday party for Sherlock Holmes.[5] I do not know how much of a bite he put on the Duane and Doubleday on behalf of his forthcoming guests, but I do know that the hotel turned over exclusive occupancy of the newly decorated downstairs lounge to a mixed company of maybe fifteen or twenty whom Chris had invited—on Grillparzer principles as to the check. Just who was there I couldn't say at this distance in time, but I remember, beyond Chris, of course: Bill Hall, Frank Henry, Mitchell Kennerley, and some, at least, of Doubleday's sales force, among the men.

There was also present a man whom fallible memory labels Hutchinson, or Hutchins (was his first name Gene?) who had brought an early form of candid camera, complete with flashlight, and used it extensively during the party. If anyone can locate him—which I can't—and if he still has those pix, then somebody can compile an accurate roster of those who attended the Nativity of the BSI.

As the Delivery of a new-born society, it was hardly noticeable. Chris spoke of its being Sherlock Holmes's birthday, and proposed several toasts, of which there is later record. But I do not remember, nor do my collaborators, any discourse to the effect that this was a meeting—*the first* meeting—of a society devoted to the study of the Sacred Writings. I had always remembered it simply as another, and perhaps more festive, meeting of the Grillparzer. Only upon collating all records, notes, and recollections of those present, does it become unmistakably clear that Chris, at least, regarded this as *the* first meeting of the BSI. He may have had the idea only dimly on that day, but within two weeks he had it firmly fixed in mind, and was talking of the BSI in print. And the dating of the Second Annual Meeting (so termed by Chris, on the menu) is significant; it was held on *6 January* 1936, even though that day was a Monday. Perhaps some people whose records cover the '37 and other meetings may find that the January 6 date persisted.

But if this first meeting is not memorable for Holmesiana other than the drinking of birthday toasts, it will still not likely be forgotten by anyone who was there. For, after lunch we played Sardines with the pretty ladies who were our guests. This, as you may know, is a sort of Hide-and-Seek in reverse. The one person who is "It" steals away and hides. All the others look for him (or, you understand, her). Anyone finding him crawls into the same hiding place. And so for each additional finder as they accumulate. At length, as you can see, the hiders, now being sought by only one or two questers, get very sardine-compressed but (if there are enough pretty ladies) correspondingly happy. It is in terms of this game that everybody remembers that day at the Duane. And they all agree on another thing: on *no* other occasion did the BSI or the Grillparzer ever have any other meeting at the Duane. This one, in other words, was The Nativity.

Three weeks later the "Bowling Green" (of January 27, 1934) carried this small item—much more significant than it appears—

> W.S.H. [i.e., Bill Hall], secretary of the Baker Street Irregulars, has allowed us to look over the minutes of the first meeting of the club [sic]. Among other business it appears that the matter of an official toast was discussed. It was agreed that the first health must always be drunk to "*The* Woman." Suggestions for succeeding sentiments, which will have their own overtones for all genuine Sherlockians, were:—"Mrs. Hudson," "Mycroft," "The Second Mrs. Watson," "The Game Is Afoot!" and "The Second Most Dangerous Man in London."
>
> Also agreed that the club room must be exactly seventeen steps up, and the first furnishings to be a gasogene and a tantalus.

The venerable Mr. Hall, when I showed this to him the other day, denied ever having been ("at least knowingly") the secretary of the BSI, and ascribed the attribution of the toast record to the same columnist-convention that had produced the earlier-cited letter from "Charing Cross." In other words, this again was just Chris setting the record straight. Or, if you like, setting the record.

Like the incident of the dog in the night-time, there is a remarkable fact about the use of the term "Baker Street Irregulars." It has no explanation. By inference, it needs none. Yet as far as I know this is the first reference in print to the Society. Most of us aborigines agree that it didn't strike us as strange when it appeared in print—and this may argue that it had had some oral currency before the end of 1933. Or that Chris, at the January 6th meeting, did use the name, though it went in one ear and out the other, of people intent on the prospect of Sardines.

The toast to The Second Most Dangerous Man was one that was frequently drunk with a leer at meetings of the Grillparzer. I still have a copy of *The Conan Doyle Stories* inscribed by Chris:

365

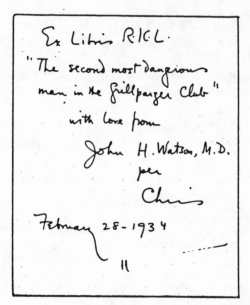

Ex Libris RICL.
" The second most dangerous
man in the Grillpanzer Club "
with love from
John H. Watson, M.D.
per
Chris
February 28 - 1934
II

By 3 February 1934 Chris was printing Holmesian correspondence (from genuine people, now) under the title THE
BAKER STREET IRREGULARS, and on February 17th he ran two
significant items.

The first was a letter from Vincent Starrett, under the title
"The Two Moriartys"—and a masterly presentation of the
puzzle of the brothers James and James that was!

Then, following it:

THE BAKER STREET IRREGULARS

> Of course it is for the study of just such savory problems that the
> BAKER STREET IRREGULARS propose to meet together. One of the most
> soundly documented Holmesians now comes forward with a suggested
> Constitution for the club. It runs as follows:—

Then appears (over the signature of Elmer Davis, and as yet
without the "Buy-Laws" part of its title) the immortal document
that constitutes the charter of this society. The fact that many of
its provisions were never intended seriously, and that most of
the rest have been chiefly honored in the breach is of no importance whatever.

The Davis Document was republished in *Profile by Gaslight*,
but since that learned work is now out of print, it may be diffi-

cult for most members to consult. Accordingly, the original is reproduced here—however illegibly—as a matter of record.

PART II

OUR OWN DEAR LITTLE GIRLIE

BECOMES A) LEGITIMATE, B) THE

SUBJECT OF UNMITIGATED BLEAT

We have seen, in the first section of these notes, the influences that gave the BSI its peculiar shape, and the events that brought it into the world as a society, though at first one that was hardly aware of itself, or clearly conscious that Chris Morley had designated it as such, on the day of its Delivery. The same installment went on to record what seem to have been the first mentions of The Baker Street Irregulars in print. These were a succession of mentions in *The Saturday Review of Literature*'s column "The Bowling Green," conducted by Chris. They led up to a Constitution, penned by charter member Elmer Davis, and the earliest, if not the only State Paper of the society. This, because it was otherwise out of print, was reproduced at the close of Part I.

Of the Davis Document, one group of provisions continues in force; another group has vanished.

Still Enduring:

§The name and concept of a separate society for what had been merely a cult until 6 January 1934.

§The purposes as stated. "The study of the Sacred Writings" is pure Davis-ese.

§In general, the designations of officers, though no one can be sure we ever had all those called for in the Constitution, and lately, all the practicing ones we have had have been rolled into one. Edgar Smith, with typical modesty, chose the title of "Buttons" when he consented to take over the burden of doing all the work and supplying all the leadership that the BSI needed. Chris's addition of "cum Commissionaire" to this title was simply a gesture to the original Musdavis Ritual.

§The designation of the meeting date still holds good, with a bow to the original Nativity Day of January 6th, but with a practical "or thereabout" added.

§The Conanical Toasts continued as specified. "Conanical" sounds like Morley-ese, and leads to the speculation that the Davis Document may have been cooked up by Chris and Elmer, with, perhaps, the help of a mermaid or two, at some Grillparzer-esque luncheon early in 1934.

Vanished—and in most cases, never observed, anyway:

§The examination-for-membership in knowledge of the Sacred Writings has completely vanished from the BSI itself. At the outset, Frank Morley's crossword puzzle did duty, in a manner shortly to be narrated, and not with much severity.

§The "Special Meetings" provision of the original charter has vanished, along with any idea of the BSI being a ladies-admitted organization. At one time or another in the years since the BSI was founded, one or two charming ladies may have seemed to cherish hopes that, in view of their looks and celebrity, the BSI might admit them, especially while refusing others of their sex, and may have even seemed to maneuver toward that end.

368

But the society has steadfastly declined to admit grit to its works, even in those charming incarnations.

§The provision in the Davis Document about "clients of the Personal Column of *The Saturday Review of Literature*" never was even meant to be taken seriously, but, perhaps on that very account, deserves some explanation. The SLR, in those days, was unprosperous to a degree equalled only by its un-noticedness among people who Really Counted in, say, the Attorney General's Department, and among Inspectors of the Post Office Department. It was also heavily un-noticed by most advertisers. So it worked up quite a business for itself in the "Personal" want ads. A good many of the ads in this column could be readily translated as, "Wanted: to meet handsome gal. Object, carnal knowledge." The paper even hinted in its editorial columns— not least in the Falstaffian Chris's "Bowling Green"—that this was a good way to invest a buck or two. Elmer was just giving Chris a lift in his high-spirited campaign by plugging the Personal Column in a document which, very obviously, neither of them thought at the time would ever achieve any permanence. Eventually the government got somebody in *its* morals-police who could read, and the SRL was constrained to mend its ways. But not until the publication's open-mindedness got memorialized forever in our Basic Document.

From then on "The Bowling Green" and its companion column, "Trade Winds" (usually also written by Chris), abounded in mentions of The Baker Street Irregulars and in learned correspondence about Holmesian affairs. E.g., Trade Winds reported "Mr. W. S. Hall, of 500 Fifth Avenue, is undertaking a Conan Doyle bibliography for the Baker Street Irregulars," while "Bowling Green" featured a letter from one Earle Walbridge commenting on some Holmesian speculations of Chris's.

There was a spate of other letters, too, many of them signed by people who appended "Baker Street Irregulars" to their names. This apparently scared Chris, lest his carefully-nurtured society should be diluted, inundated, and swept away. So he published an Examination in the Sacred Writings (as called for in the Constitution). The substance of this turned up in a communication signed by Tobias Gregson, and enclosing a Sherlock Holmes Crossword Puzzle. (Actually, this devilish work had been concocted by Frank Morley to pass the time aboard ship while returning from these shores to England a few weeks before.)

Chris published the letter and crossword in Bowling Green of 13 May 1934. They were followed in the "Green" by this challenge from Chris: " . . . I will delay printing the solution of the crossword for two weeks, to give our clients plenty of time to consider it. All those who send me correct solutions—but they must be correct in every detail—will automatically become members of the Baker Street Irregulars."

But in two weeks it became apparent that the 100% perfection requirement was a little too stiff. For only six people of the first batch of responses met its requirements. The crossword had abounded in unkeyed letters by which many already-accepted Irregulars got led astray. Accordingly, Chris relaxed his requirements and announced the following as having qualified (I combine the lists that appeared up to the issue of 19 June):

Perfect Solutions from: M. S. Packard, Brooklyn; Stuart Robertson, Philadelphia; Harvey Officer, New York City; Walter Klinefelter, Glen Rock, Pa.; Vincent Starrett, Chicago; Emily S. Coit, Pensacola, Fla.; (and on 19 June) Doris E. Barton, Hartford, Conn.; Dorothy E. Dawson, Salem, Va.; Harry W. Hazard, Jr., Montclair, N.J.; Henry H. Jackson & Family, Barre, Vt.; Joyce & George Guernsey, Jr., University City, Mo.; Staff of Mrs. Cowlin's Open Book Shop, Elgin, Ill.; Ruth M. Consdell, Hartford, Conn.; Benjamin March, Ann Arbor, Mich.

Near-perfect Solutions—failing by not more than one word: Elmer Davis, New York City; Mrs. C. C. Williams, South Hamilton, Mass.; C. Warren Force, New York City; Allan M. Price, New York City; J. Delancey Ferguson, Cleveland; Velma Long, Winamac, Ind.; Earle Walbridge, New York City; Katharine A. Fellows, Cummington, Mass.; W. S. Hall, New York City; Harrison L. Reinke, Lakeville, Conn.; George Lowther, New York City; R. K. Leavitt, New York City; Malcolm Johnson, New York City; (and on 19 June) Alexander W. Williams, Boston; L. H. and F. E. Fry, Oakmont, Pa.; Dr. Adele B. Cohn, Newark, N.J.; Basil Davenport, New York City; Cecil Spence, Brooklyn; Horace R. Stahl, Desloge, Mo.; Runyon Colie, Newark, N.J.; E. R. Bartlett and Son, Bronxville, N.Y.

While these names were accumulating, another problem was

developing and spurring Chris into action. It had really been posed by a communication published in the "Green" for 12 May:

NEWS FROM BAKER STREET

Mr. A. G. Macdonell writes that the English *Sherlock Holmes Society* has organized and sends greetings to our own *Baker Street Irregulars*. The S.H.S. is to hold its first dinner on June 6th at a restaurant in Baker Street. "June 6th being Derby Day," says Mr. Macdonell, "it was felt that *Silver Blaze* might well be discussed, together with Holmes's extraordinary conduct in running a faked horse."

The British were conceding us seniority, largely by virtue of that Nativity party on January 6th, and Chris's subsequent reports of it and of Holmesian activities conducted in the name of The Baker Street Irregulars. But if we were to maintain seniority, we had better hold a somewhat more formal meeting than that initial one, and get it in before the British sat down to dinner on June 6th.

This probably explains why the following letter was mailed on May 29th to (I suppose) all successful contestants of the male gender who had got their entries into Chris's hands by that time. Also included were certain old Morley companions who had been Baker Streeting all along, but who wouldn't have done a crossword puzzle if it had come to them from the hand of Mr. S. Holmes himself. (I am thinking, among others, of Frank Henry, Don Marquis, and Mitchell Kennerley.)

The concluding sentence of the letter must have cost Chris a few pangs, since the deadlier sex had been so prominent, not only in the mother society, but also among the successful solvers of the crossword. That may have been why he announced merely that "this first meeting" would be stag. Happily, the once-tentative decision has stuck, and all subsequent meetings of the society have been, like this one, un-cracked as to lens, whatever they may have been otherwise.

The dream of a permanent clubroom was to prove illusory, and in any event nobody ever pushed it very far. And of "the decorations or trophies" only one showed up at this dinner: Bill Hall's wife, Marjory, had made a deerstalker cap out of pieces of an old tweed jacket, and a glamorous, Holmesian headpiece it was, much admired by all the communicants. Alas, at the next dinner, in December, it was to suffer a Fate Worse Than Death, as I shall tell.

The Saturday Review

of LITERATURE

25 West 45th Street, New York City

HENRY SEIDEL CANBY, *Editor*
AMY LOVEMAN, *Managing Editor*
WILLIAM ROSE BENÉT, *Contributing Editor*
CHRISTOPHER MORLEY, *Contributing Editor*

May 29, 1934

Mr. Robert K. Leavitt
Ruthrauff & Ryan Inc.
405 Lexington Avenue
New York City

The first formal meeting of the
Baker Street Irregulars will be
at 144 East 45th Street on Tues-
day, June 5th at 6:30 P. M.
Chris Cella, the proprietor has
set aside a room for us upstairs
which we can use as permanent
headquarters. If anything occurs
to you in the way of decoration,
or trophy suitable for the clubroom, bring it along.

Dress informally of course. This
first meeting will be stag.

CM

But this "first formal meeting" was an unalloyed delight. "The upstairs room" (exactly seventeen steps up, by the way) was really two rooms, connected, in the old brownstone manner, by a wide opening for sliding doors. In the back section, a converted square piano did duty as a buffet for pre-dinner cocktails and canapés. In the forward part was the single long table, set for ten. As a matter of fact, there were only eight present[6]—since the list of eligibles had been small to begin with, and the notice had been short.

Chris presided—as Gasogene-by-acclamation. If he was elected, it was in the same sense that Noah was elected Captain of the Ark. At his suggestion—and with equal readiness—Earle Walbridge was acclaimed Tantalus, and somebody or other must have acted as Commissionaire.

Earle later wrote up the minutes of the meeting and forwarded them to Chris, but unless they turn up in the Morley files, they seem to have vanished. It is possible, however, to reconstruct from his recollections, compared with others, the high points of the meeting: The Conanical Toasts were solemnly honored. Chris presented his dissertation, "Was Sherlock Holmes an American?" This was in MS form (in fact it was already in galley proof for its later appearance in *The Saturday Review*) but Chris, like the accomplished lecturer that he was, didn't read it; he talked it. Harvey Officer spoke on "Sherlock Holmes and Music." There were challenge questions and answers in profusion (for we were getting thirsty by that time). And we played some sort of Holmesian charade game, but nobody can remember what words or phrases we acted out. The tab per person—exclusive of the challenge-round drinks—was $3.50, including tip.

Of a very different character was the next recorded meeting of the BSI, which took place on 7 December 1934. By many people this has been taken to be the first meeting of the Irregulars. Actually, as I hope I have made clear, there had been two prior meetings: the Nativity on January 6th, and the First Formal Meeting, just described.

The December meeting was a jump-the-gun Annual Dinner. I can only guess that Chris was scheduled to be out of town on the authentic Natal Day of Mr. Holmes and the society, and that the dinner was moved forward on that account. The fact that

6 January 1935 was a Sunday wouldn't explain moving the dinner up a whole month.

It was held on December 7th—a Friday night—at the same Cella rooms as the June 5th meeting. (The Second Annual Dinner—explicitly so called on its printed menu—was held in the same rooms on 6 January 1936, a Monday.) There were some eighteen or twenty people present. Those who signed my copy of the menu (and I missed a few) were: Frank Henry, W. S. Hall, Alexander Woollcott, William Gillette, Archie Macdonell, Christopher Morley, Basil Davenport, Elmer Davis, Earle Walbridge, Allan M. Price, Laurence P. Dodge, Frederic Dorr Steele, Gray C. Briggs, M.D., and H. W. Bell. Also present were Gene Tunney, Vincent Starrett, Dr. Charles Goodman, and perhaps others to whom apologies are hereby tendered in advance.

If this meeting was not the first of the BSI, it certainly does not lack identification. For it has come to be known as the Woollcott meeting, first because of the all-too-conspicuous behavior of the ineffable Alexander, second because of his self-created (and largely mendacious) account of himself on that occasion, and last because of a well-intentioned blurb by Edgar Smith, that happens to be inaccurate in nearly every particular.

This was the introductory note written by Edgar in his capacity as editor of the book *Profile by Gaslight*, which included a reprint of Woollcott's piece in *The New Yorker* for 29 December 1934. Woollcott died while *Profile* was being assembled. So Edgar Smith (who had not joined the Irregulars until 1938 and thus knew nothing of the actual circumstances, and who, in any event, was too high-minded to believe ill of anybody, let alone to speak ill of the deceased) took the Late Lamented's account at its face value in writing his introduction to the Woollcott piece.

He was probably further misled by a MS, "The Baker Street Irregulars," originally written in 1941 or 1942 by Joel Sayre, a magazine-writer of that age—though not a member of the BSI—and apparently never sold to any magazine. (The BSI later published it in mimeographed form and distributed it to members.) This bears internal evidence that the author consulted Chris and others for certain of its data (e.g., the origins of the crossword puzzle and its fifteen perfect solutions, the eight at the first dinner, the seventeen steps up, certain digs at the foibles of early members, and a version of the "Unrecorded Incident"—actually written by Chris Morley—that appears on pages 298–300 of *Profile by Gaslight*). But the Sayre MS is monstrously inaccurate in most other respects, including the attribution of a founder's rôle in the BSI to Woollcott.

Edgar seems to have accepted the Sayre–Woollcott legend,[7] for he gave Woollcott's piece an introduction in *Profile* that said: "[Woollcott] was one of the party to the original conspiracy [i.e., a charter member of the BSI] and [his] memory is revered by the membership . . . as warmly as his presence was hailed that night in 1934 . . . when Sherlock Holmes—alias Alexander Woollcott—strode into Chris Cella's . . . complete with cloak and deer-stalker."

Woollcott's own account of the evening alleged: "On a gusty night . . . there met and dined together certain raffish fellows . . . all brothers in the Baker Street Irregulars. Topped for the occasion with a plaid hunting cap, your . . . correspondent repaired to the secret assemblage. . . . The faithful were out in full force. Trampling down a negligible opposition, Christopher Morley was elected Gasogene. . . . Elmer Davis firmly read aloud what is known, I believe, as 'a paper'. . . . But the dinner turned from a mere befuddled hope into a great occasion when there entered . . . William Gillette. . . . Mr. Gillette confided to my delightful ear . . ."

These supposedly intimate confidences were, as a matter of fact, rehashes of parts of Mr. Gillette's speech for the occasion, but never mind; let us get to a correction of the record in its more significant inaccuracies:

1) Woollcott was not a "party to the original conspiracy." He was never even a member of the BSI.

2) To say that his presence was hailed "warmly" that night is true only in a sulphurous sense that I am sure Edgar, bless his heart, did not intend. Few of us who were there that evening will forget the crackling *sotto voce* Morleyan sputter when Chris discovered that Woollcott had got in. Laurence Dodge has recorded our recollection of Chris's characterization of *The New Yorker*'s "Town Crier" as "that --- -- - -----."[8] (Typography mine.) On that evening, Woollcott certainly worked hard to deserve the title. He did this by three means:

a) Though he had been invited to the dinner (by Vincent

375

Starrett) he arrived ahead of his sponsor, and omitted to mention the fact that he had one. He left us to infer—in fact, there are some who still think he wanted us to—that he had simply walked in by divine right.

b) Woollcott neglected no opportunity to impress upon his new acquaintances how different he was, in all respects, from them. Example: he sat down next to a member. The man, as one of his hosts, introduced himself by name. "What of it?" demanded Woollcott.

c) Upon the appearance of Gillette, Woollcott monopolized the attention of the aging star, so that Gillette had next to no opportunity to talk about the things the rest of us would have liked to hear, since Woollcott was incessantly bending his gentle old ear with interminable Alexandrine narratives and opinions.

3) As to the deer-stalker, in which Woollcott said in print that he had "repaired to the secret meeting place," the facts are these:

a) He came in an ordinary, Philistine hat.

b) When he saw Bill Hall wearing the fore-and-aft cap above-mentioned—the one Marjory Hall had made—he went up to Bill, lifted it off with hardly a by-your-leave, and put it on his own head.

c) The surprised Hall, thinking that this was just the whim of a minute, made no objection—and the cap stayed on Woollcott's head all the rest of the evening.

d) Not only that, but at the evening's end, Woollcott walked off with the deer-stalker (in addition to his own hat) without thanks, apology, or even good night to Hall. And Hall hasn't seen it since.

I am particularly indebted to Messrs. W. S. Hall, Frank Henry, and Earle Walbridge for reviewing and checking the MS of the foregoing.—R.K.L.

—September and December 1961

NOTES

1. These include particularly the antediluvian Messrs. W. S. Hall and Earle Walbridge. Others, too numerous to mention, have given me invaluable nuggets of information. Records consulted include the library files of *The*

Saturday Review of Literature from June 1933 through June 1934, together with fragments from the magpie files of myself and several of those I have consulted.

2. George Ennis called this "The Three Hours For Lunch Club," but actually, it shows only a small, and not at all representative, group of THFLC members. Not shown are many men of fame and brilliance, such as Bill Benét, Jo Davidson, etc., etc., and many men of charm, industry, and piety far surpassing those Innes pictured around Christ Cella's back room table. Indeed the picture greatly shrinks the size of that table, and, as in the case of most water colors, its portrait likenesses are strictly hit-or-miss. However, more or less by accident, it shows many of those who constituted the foetal BSI. Shown were, top row, left to right: Franklin Abbot, Christ Cella, Frank V. Morley*, "Torino" (a Cella waiter), Hulbert Footner, Mrs. Cella. Front row: R. K. Leavitt*, Frank C. Henry*, W. S. Hall*, Christopher Morley*, Don Marquis*, and Emile Gauvreau. (Asterisks indicate BSI members, original or early.) Among the many Holmesian aborigines of that era not shown were Mitchell Kennerley, Buckminster Fuller, Thayer Cummings, Elmer Davis, Allan Price, and others whose names escape me, and whose pardons I beg in advance. And, of course, as noted above, there were so many Three-Hour Lunchers who had no Holmesian interests that space forbids trying to name them. *I* didn't title the picture; Ennis did.

3. See Morley's essay, "On Belonging to Clubs," first published in *The New Colophon*, Part Six (June 1949), and later included in *The Ironing Board* (New York: Doubleday, 1949). Chris abhorred such formalities as hard-and-fast written rules, dues, "must" activities, and other restraints upon the spirit of any club. In the essay above-cited, he even shakes a gloomy head over the Irregulars' involvement in "a publishing business, an annual meeting, a province of pulp . . . [and] letters that have to be answered."

4. In the essay "On Belonging to Clubs," just cited, Chris is referring to this volume as the early record-book of the BSI. "Our scrapbook of minutes was stolen by some biblioklept." This was the book that Hall later recovered. Note the clear implication, in Chris's identifying two books in one, that the GSPV was more than the mother society of the BSI—that it *changed into* the BSI—as, in a sense, it did, at the Natal Meeting, to be described.

5. Frank Henry, then Sales Manager for Doubleday, who were at that time publishers of both Doyle and Chris, says the party idea was spawned in his office at 244 Madison Avenue, across the street from the Duane. "We [Chris and Frank] had with us Dan Longwell, George Siefert [both of Doubleday], and our publicity gal."

6. Earle Walbridge's photographic memory, impressed especially because of his function as the evening's Tantalus–recorder, collates the hazier recollection of the other survivors of that evening to establish this seating-order, clockwise around a rectangular table, beginning with the Gasogene at the head end: Christopher Morley, Malcolm Johnson, Allan Price, Harvey Officer, Earle Walbridge, and (across the table and up the other side) R. K. Leavitt, Frank Henry, and W. S. Hall.

7. It may be asked why Chris Morley did not set the record straight, at

least before it got into *Profile*. I can only say that while these things were going on he was up to his neck in the monumental labor of the Revised Edition of *Bartlett's Familiar Quotations*, and carrying at the same time his usual tremendous burden of current work. Later—in 1949—he did record in print his resentment that the BSI had been "taken up by that resonant sounding board, Woollcott" (see "On Belonging to Clubs").

8. BSJ (NS) 10 (1960), 117.

Writing from the vantage point of 1946, Christopher
Morley—our Founder and Gasogene-cum-Tantalus of
The Baker Street Irregulars—reminisces about the
genesis of the society. . . .

CLINICAL NOTES BY A RESIDENT PATIENT

by CHRISTOPHER MORLEY

"Not out of malevolence, you understand, but simply out of a
spirit of inquiry."   —Young Stamford

AS I LOOK OVER my case-books I can see now (what was mercifully concealed from me at the time) how strangely significant
were the spring and summer of 1930. The world is not yet prepared, and very likely never will be, for the full details of some
of those episodes. There was the Scandal on the Seacoast of Bohemia (viz. Hoboken); the Affair of Mulligan's Kitchen (opposite the old Doelger Brewery, somewhere in the East 50's); the
Decline and Fall of the Grillparzer Club (where I first met Rex
Stout); and the Story of the Autographed Bathroom (on Lexington Avenue) where I encountered Bill Hall. As the waters of
Long Island Sound grew warmer there were the Singular Circumstances of the Cruiser *Snippet*, Captain Bob Leavitt, a few
leagues off the Stamford Yacht Club. But of all these adventures, which mingled comedy and calamity in quantum suff., I
think of none which had more bearing upon our present curiosity than the Proffer of the Third Oldfashioned.

There was a basement speakeasy, then momentarily esteemed
by the Grub Street Runners of Messrs. Doubleday Doran and
Co. There, whether by chance or solicitation, I met my old
friend Mr. Francis C. Henry, at that time sales manager of that
firm. I am too proud, or too prudent, to look up dates and
memos, but my thought is that the author of the Sacred Writings had lately died (date? June 1930?) and his American
publishers planned the first complete collected edition of the
Holmes stories. I think that Mr. Henry was accompanied and
enforced by his faithful assembly men Messrs. Malcolm Johnson, Charles Halliwell Duell, Daniel Longwell, and Ogden
Nash; at any rate they were only a few olives or cherries away

379

down that shining counter. According to the ritual prescribed in the prohibition era no one talked business until the Third Drink—the one which George Herbert, my favorite poet, says is fatal; see *The Church Porch* stanza 8. With the third old-fashioned amberlucent between us (I could still drink bourbon or rye in those days) Mr. Henry and his assiduents suggested I should write a preface for the projected two-volume Holmes. I said if the fee would be generous enough for me to go to Baker Street and back I'd do it. Actually it fell short by about 200 dollars; but that was my fault, not theirs. They paid the largest price I ever heard of for a preface to any book.

By coincidence, July 16 that year, the Book of the Month Club chose the Holmes Omnibus. I think, but am not sure, it was the only time the Club has ever taken an older book as a monthly selection. I did not urge it, but was delighted. What a break for Doubleday!

On July 25, 1930, I wrote my preface.

On July 30, 1930, I got my check.

On August 2, I think it was, I sailed in RMS *Caronia*.

I've just looked it up. I was only 6 minutes wrong. According to the *Abstract of Log*, RMS *Caronia* (Twin Screw) sailed 11:54 P.M. August 1st. She had Ambrose Channel L.V. abeam at 2:06 A.M. She made Eddystone abeam at 1:18 G.M.T., August 9. Captain F. G. Brown, RNR. My wine account, as of August 9, was £2.16.6. Stateroom C 47. Table 29. Saloon steward, Wimbush.—As a matter of historic record (since I've now looked up the chits) in the year 1930, when one bought drinks for cash in the smokeroom, a Martini or a Manhattan cost 21 cents; an Old Fashioned 25 cents; a whisky sour 37 cents; and a "John Collins" (so Cunard called it) 37 cents. They called a highball a "Long Cocktail." Lemon squash was 13 cents.

I don't remember why, I stayed at the Stafford Hotel (St. James's Place) instead of the good old Wigmore Hotel as in previous years—I once, about 1926, met A.C.D. on Wigmore Street carrying a 'gripsack' of ectoplasm slides for his lecture that evening.—I see that at the Stafford in August 1930 one paid 15 bob for room and bath. Breakfast was 4 bob. Newspaper was 2d. I'm chagrined that under the rubric "Wine, cocktails, spirits, liqueurs, ale & stout, minerals" I spent nothing, so I can't check against F. H. Moulton. But I want to record that the 5-shilling lunch at the Hind's Head Hotel at Bray (where the Vicar was) was like this:—Fried fillet of haddock; Steak & Kidney Pudding; Silverside, Marrow, New Potatoes; Treacle Tart; and Cheddar Cheese.

I have always been griped because Holmes never spoke of Mrs. Hudson's treacle tart. I usually took two slices and Watson three. I don't believe there is another B.S.I. who ever had a Baker Street treacle tart; and Watson, with his experience in India, always insisted on kedgeree for breakfast. The *Orontes*, by the way, mushed up a mighty wholesome kedgeree.

The famous revival of the play *Sherlock Holmes*, by William Gillette, in the winter 1929–30; the lamented death of the Sacred Writer; the wide circulation of the new omnibus edition; and the increasing nostalgia for Victorian comedy and melodrama (certainly stimulated by the Hoboken production of *After Dark* and *The Black Crook*) were all seed on the wind. (I use this phrase à propos; it is the title of Rex Stout's first and best book.) Then came Mr. S. C. Roberts' brilliant little biography *Doctor Watson* (London: Faber & Faber, 1931). Mr. Vincent Starrett followed in 1933 with his admirable *The Private life of Sherlock Holmes*. This was reviewed (Dec. 2, 1933) in the *Saturday Review of Literature* by Mr. Elmer Davis, a stunning piece afterward revised into its present classical form "On the Emotional Geology of Baker Street" (in *221B*). The first actual suggestion that some of the devotees might join in an informal sodality, or even whisky-and-sodality, came about by devolution from the many paragraphs uttered in The Bowling Green and Trade Winds departments of the S.R.L. Mr. Elmer Davis promptly composed a pointed and humorous constitution and buy-laws, first printed in the S.R.L. of Feb. 17, 1934.

There was in those days a small back room, up the canonical count of steps, at Christ Cella's restaurant on East 45 Street. To paint 221B on the door and gather there a few appropriate memorabilia was an agreeable amusement. There were on that upper floor two retiring rooms, which we persuaded Christ Cella to label as SHERLOCK and IRENE. This puzzled some customers, but was effective for segregation. The occult and retentive 3rd Garrideb, F.V.M., amused himself about that time in the smokeroom of a Cunard liner by putting together a crossword puzzle based on Sherlockian allusions. This, printed in the Bowling Green, was used as a shibboleth for entrance into B.S.I membership. I think about a dozen correspondents answered it with 100% accuracy and were enrolled as charter members. Unexpectedly, one of these was a charming young woman from Illinois, Miss D. B., who was immediately elevated as THE Woman and given the statutory luncheon of honor (3 hours) when she visited New York a few months later. There is an appropriate fogginess of detail as to the earliest proceedings of the Irregulars; due to the fact that when Cella moved from his original quarters to a luxurious renovation next door, some brigandeering bibliophile swiped the scrapbook in which a multitude of clippings and souvenirs had been carefully preserved.

So the B.S.I. never had any strictly formal organization; and since the disappearance of the early memoranda, no one remembers who were the founding fathers. It is sad to record that Miss B. married a man who, so far as we know, has no special interest in Sherlock. The first dinner was held June 5, 1934. Mr. H. G. Wells, who had been in New York about that time, should have been there, but admitted that he could not pass the examination. One member, of a horoscopic bent, announced that zodiacal and astrological study indicated Sherlock's birthday as probably January 6, 1854. This pleased me as it coincided with the birthday, in 1894, of the 2nd Garrideb, Dr. Felix Morley. So we decided to hold the annual meeting, if possible, some time during January.

At the first of the more formal meetings, in December 1934, we were lucky enough to have William Gillette as our guest of honor; also Mr. A. G. Macdonell who had been one of the founders of the Sherlock Holmes Society in London, which started about the same time as the B.S.I. That was the occasion when the Gasogene scoured the town to find exactly the right kind of Woolworth bauble to represent the Blue Carbuncle in the guts of the Christmas Goose. The worthy Cella was considerably puzzled by our insistence that the goose be cooked with the jewel inside it. That was also the dinner to which Alec Woollcott came unbidden, made himself happily conspicuous, and afterward rather ridiculed our naïveté in his *New Yorker* piece. As none of us had had the slightest appetite for publicity, I think the original group were a trifle annoyed.

The happiest achievement of the B.S.I. was when it attracted the attention of our devoted Edgar Smith. Very different from Woollcott, he wrote in a vein of decorous modesty asking if he could be put on the waiting list and offered to undergo any sort of inquest of suitability. It was plain from the first that here was THE Man. After the Woollcott condescension most of us were content to go on without any Stated Meetings—indeed, I think several years did go by—but Mr. Edgar Smith's affectionate zeal, not less than his Sherlockian scholarship, his gusto in pamphleteering, his delight in keeping orderly records, and his access to mimeographic and parchment-engrossing and secretarial resources, all these were irresistible. I don't suppose that any society of Amateur Mendicants has ever had a more agreeable or competent fugleman. It was probably Mr. Edgar Smith who took pains to ensure the correct serving of a scroll representing the Naval Treaty, under the Murray Hill Hotel's largest dish-cover, as in the Sacred Writings; this, I think, was at an early dinner when Dr. Harrison Martland, medical examiner of the City of Newark, was our guest. The Murray Hill kitchen was always able to give us a very satisfactory replica of Mrs. Hudson's catering, including curried chicken. As these notes are written it is likely that the familiar Murray Hill may not again shelter us; Edgar Smith's suggestion of the Chelsea as a possible refuge is certainly worth notice. It is probably the only other hotel in Manhattan that still has some Baker Street flavor; I believe it actually antedates the Murray Hill by two years.

It is odd to recall, thinking back over past dinners, that one of the pleasantest talks we ever had was made by Mr. Denis Conan Doyle. He was naturally and filially moved by the profound homage implied in our proceedings. That he afterward changed his mind, and decided that in some sinister way the B.S.I. were invading the property rights of his father's estate, is likely to become a permanent liptwisting footnote in literary history.

There have been, of course, occasional hard-minded observers who thought it silly for a group of grown men to dally so intently over a literature of entertainment for which even its own author had only moderate regard. Let me repeat what I have said before, that no printed body of modern social history (including Keyserlings, Spenglers, Paretos, and other brows like Dover Cliff) either by purpose or accident contains a richer pandect of the efficient impulses of its age. It has shown itself keen forecast in many ways, and some of its allusions may yet again be painfully timely. I wouldn't be surprised at any moment to see Afghanistan, or the river Orontes, or the Coptic Patriarch, or the dynamics of an asteroid, reappear in the news.

—July 1946

383

*Mr. Nathan Bengis affords a public not generally
aware of the annual machinations of The Baker Street
Irregulars a rare glimpse of one of its meetings. . . .*

MARKED DOWN—IRREGULAR

by NATHAN BENGIS

APPROPRIATELY ENOUGH, 10 January 1964, the day of the Baker
Street Irregulars' annual dinner meeting in honour of the
110th birthday of Sherlock Holmes, started with a mystery. In
the morning mail I received a package with the typed return
address: James Moriarty, Camford University. A belated Sherlockian Christmas offering, I supposed, no doubt from someone with a pawky sense of humour. I changed my mind when I
saw the contents: a copy of the extremely rare *A Note on the
Watson Problem.* Truly a princely gift. But from whom: Ah—an
inscription from the author: "To Nathan Bengis, This rather
murky copy of an over-rated pamphlet, S. C. Roberts." How
kind of him to remember me in this way! And then I noticed
the inscribed date: 22 X 1946, and saw too that the package was
postmarked from an American post office. At last I remembered: This was the copy I had passed around at a meeting of
The Baker Street Irregulars years before and had never got
back. I recalled so well how in desperation I had asked our late
beloved Edgar W. Smith if he would please announce the loss
and request its return to its loser, Nathan Bengis of the Musgrave Ritualists. Alas, it never came back to me, and I resigned
myself to an irrevocable loss. Now at last the culprit had re-
pented of his theft and had made restitution. I felt as happy as
if I had indeed received a gift—even though an Irregular one.

As I looked through the pamphlet a slip fell out, with the following lines typed on it:

"—*Ce dessein détestable,*
S'il n'est digne de J. M., est digne du diable."

Pawky sense of humour indeed!

What was my amazement, upon relating this happy recovery to several fellow-Irregulars at the cocktail hour at Cavanaugh's Restaurant that evening, to learn that at least three others had had a similar experience that same day or the day before: Jack Hammersmith, of the Diogenes Club, Epsilon, of Trenton, New Jersey, had got back a February 1890 *Lippincott's Monthly Magazine* which he had circulated at a meeting several years before; Bob Summers, of the Penang Lawyers of Buffalo, a copy of Vincent Starrett's *The Unique Hamlet*; and a third individual, who requested complete anonymity—not even an alias—a copy of the very scarce 1913 Collier booklet with the first and only separate appearance of *The Dying Detective*. I had another surprise in store when, upon telling Miss Lisa McGaw, *the* Woman of the evening, about these strange happenings, I was informed by her that still another Irregular had just shown her a purloined Arthur Conan Doyle letter which had been returned to him that morning. She properly would not reveal this person's name, which she said had been given her in confidence.

Bob Summers had with him the very Manila envelope in which his property had been sent back. It too had the return address of James Moriarty, Camford University. There could be little doubt that all the items mentioned had been stolen and returned by the same person. All feeling of rancour we had borne the unknown culprit was wiped out with one accord. After all, as Jack Hammersmith remarked, "It is the season of forgiveness—or not too long thereafter." We drank a toast on it and went in to dinner.

All who attended that meeting will agree, I am sure, that it was one of the best we have had in years. The libations from the Tantalus flowed more freely; the roast beef was juicier; the toasts more apt (the one to Mrs. Hudson being given by Martin Swanson, the youngest, but one of the most enthusiastic Sherlockians present); the speakers wittier; the conversation spicier; the Challenges more difficult than ever to answer. Our Commissionaire, Dr. Julian Wolff, who has been carrying on splendidly in the tradition of Edgar W. Smith, had, as usual, prepared a most interesting program. Chairman Rex Stout was his customary energetic self. Frank Waters read the Constitution and Buy-Laws with gusto, with a chorus of chuckles from the assemblage at the closing jest: "There shall be no monthly meeting." Herbert Brean's imaginary telephone conversation with Edgar Allan Poe and Arthur Conan Doyle kept us rolling with laughter from beginning to end. And of all these proceedings Bill Rabe, constantly on the hop with his ubiquitous microphone, took a recording on tape.

A number of guests were introduced by Rex Stout, among them one sitting across the table from me: Luther L. Norris of Culver City, California, whom many Sherlockians here and abroad have come to know in recent months as the distributor of the attractive seventeen-inch statue of Sherlock Holmes, designed by Luques Whitmore, with a personalized brass plate on the pedestal. Mr. Norris explained he had arrived by plane that very day to attend his first meeting of The Baker Street Irregulars at the invitation of the Commissionaire, and demonstrated his eligibility for full Irregularity by giving a talk, illustrated with lantern slides, on Scotland Yard in the 1890s and 1900s. He exhibited one of the Sherlock Holmes statues and said he was, with Dr. Wolff's permission, offering it for the best score in the Owen P. Frisbie Memorial Prize Quiz to be held later in the evening.

At this point Old Irregular Charles Honce asked if the statue could be passed around for inspection. I was relieved when Peter Ruber rose and suggested that it might be better to pass out glossy prints of the sculpture, and this was accordingly done. Peter explained that orders for the statue could be taken at thirty dollars. A number of members walked right up to pay for theirs, but Rex Stout rapped his gavel and said that a more appropriate time to conduct this business would be at the intermission. Peter seemed disappointed, apparently being afraid that everyone would forget about the statue by then. Jack Ebers, of the Five Orange Pips, was heard to say that he was not going to order one, as he thought he could win first prize in the contest, but Richard W. Clarke, who had prepared the quiz, reminded him that no member of The Five Orange Pips was eligible for the prize.

Next on the agenda was the Presentation of the Neophytes, or Postulants, as the sticklers for formality insist they should be called. There were no fewer than fourteen of these, and our Chairman, with his flair for arithmetic, calculated to the second how long each one should take, just as easily as the Master calculated the speed of the train in *Silver Blaze*. The postulants stood up one by one, when presented, and briefly introduced themselves. That is, most of them were brief, but two or three were hardy enough to do more than say tritely how pleased and honoured they were to be present ("at so august a gathering," as one of them actually said, a remark at which a few were heard to snicker).

One of the more promising of these novitiates, Robert Merridew, of the firm of Kenyon and Eckhardt, spoke on "Sherlock Holmes and Advertising," showing a tie-up between the Master and such products as cigarettes, hair cream, toothpaste, coffee, and automobile tires. Another, Riccardo Ricoletti, of the Horsheim Shoe Company, spoke on shoes as a status symbol and cited cases in which Holmes had made deductions from footwear.

A considerable stir was made by Postulant Arthur Holder, who, at the age of about twenty-seven, had already—unlike his Canonical analogue—made his mark in the world as an attorney, and who dabbled in amateur theatricals. He said he would be forever indebted to his sponsor and mentor, Hill Hope, the distinguished barrister, for having given him his first real break in the legal profession and for having introduced him to the "magic of the saga," as he put it. He then spoke on "Sherlock Holmes in Disguise," and enlivened his talk with a performance that seemed magical in itself, by assuming in fast succession a number of disguises used by Holmes in the Canon, taking his equipment out of a travelling case he had brought with him. In a minute or two he had shown us the Nonconformist clergyman, Escott the plumber, the old woman, the aged mariner, the Italian priest, and the elderly deformed book collector.

"Quite a guy, isn't he?" I heard his sponsor, Hill Hope, say, beaming with admiration and looking almost the embodiment of the Master himself, in his deerstalker and Inverness cape which he invariably wore at the meetings. "My find, Mr. Norris. I tell you I couldn't be prouder of him if he were my own son."

The next item on the program was the presentation by Dr. Julian Wolff of a most unusual award to George Brady, a senior waiter at Cavanaugh's: a dinner plate, appropriately imprinted on the back, in commemoration of Mr. Brady's thirteen years of service to The Baker Street Irregulars in this restaurant. Mr. Brady was visibly touched, and said that never before in his experience had such an award been made. He added that he only hoped he would continue to serve for as many more years or longer.

There then followed the Standing on the Terrace, in memory of the Irregulars who had passed away in the preceding year. This is always a sad part of our annual dinner—unusually so this year because no fewer than six members had departed, including such prominent Sherlockians as Dr. Jay F. Christ, Clifton R. Andrew, and Owen P. Frisbie.

We were all relieved to hear our Chairman, Rex Stout, announce that there would now be an intermission of ten minutes, to give us a chance to walk about and to chat with our friends, after which the prize contest and other unfinished business would round out the meeting. For some, this break is the best part of the whole affair. They go to the bar, or are invited there, and forget to come back.

I was talking with Maurice Melas, who translates Latin and Greek with equal facility, when suddenly there was a commotion in the far corner of the room, near the bar. "Say, come over here. Get a load of this," I heard Dr. Charles Goodman shouting at the top of his voice. He was standing next to Old Irregular Bill Hall who was showing something to Dr. Goodman. A few people nearby walked over to see what all the excitement was about. No sooner had they seen whatever it was that was being shown than they let out a whoop. "Bengis, come over here quick. Look what Bill Hall has got," yelled Charles Goodman. In less time than it takes to tell about it, a crowd had gathered around Bill, all stampeding to catch a glimpse of the prize exhibit. Elbowing my way through the mob with less decorum than befits a retired teacher, I finally reached the centre and snatched the plum out of Bill's hands.

"Nathan," Bill gently reproached me, "remember what Sherlock Holmes once said: 'I would handle it gingerly if I were you.'"

"Forgive me, Bill," I said, handing it back. "Put it down to excessive zeal."

And then Bill Hall showed it to me: his unique *Beeton's Annual* for 1887, with Arthur Conan Doyle's signed inscription:

"This is the very first independent [*sic*] book of mine which ever was published. Jan. 9/14." The hubbub can better be imagined than described. It beat anything I have ever seen at a department store bargain sale.

"Gentlemen, gentlemen," I heard Rex Stout admonishing us as he rapped the gavel for the resumption of the meeting, "a little order, please. In the many years of my membership I have never yet witnessed such a display of Irregularity. The jostling of the red-headed men in Pope's Court is the nearest thing I can compare it to. I don't know what is being passed around, but surely it can't be *that* interesting."

When we had all settled down, our Chairman continued: "The next order of business, Dr. Wolff informs me, is the Owen P. Frisbie Memorial Prize Quiz, prepared by Richard W. Clarke of The Five Orange Pips. The first prize, as has been announced, is the statue of the Master designed by Luques Whitmore and presented this evening by Mr. Norris. I trust you will not disgrace yourselves with your customary low grades. After all, what is one of the prime purposes of belonging to The Baker Street Irregulars? To show we are serious students of the Canon, of course. Lord Donegall has asked me to say that he is offering a consolation prize of his complete set of six Christmas cards he has put out in as many years."

"May I correct a tiny error, Mr. Chairman," Dr. Banesh Hoffmann objected. "Six successive Christmas cards would be put out in five years, not six. It's the same mistake as Mary Morstan's six pearls all over again."

"You're absolutely right, Dr. Hoffmann," Rex Stout replied. "A real pearl of wisdom."

At this point Mr. Norris rose and blurted out excitedly: "Eminent Bodymaster, I claim urgency! I very much regret to interrupt, but I have just noticed that the Sherlock Holmes statue has disappeared."

A hush fell over the meeting, and for several seconds there was general consternation.

"Where was the statue when the intermission began?" asked Rex Stout.

"Right here on the table in front of me," said Mr. Norris, "between me and Mr. Bengis."

"Oh, I'll bet Nathan Bengis took it," said Charles Honce,

389

without the slightest malice, I'm sure. "He's always pulling jokes like that. Why, he even took my BAKER STREET JOURNAL at our New Year's Eve party."

"You know very well you gave it to me, Charles," I said reproachfully.

"Okay, okay. Please excuse my badly timed joke, Nathan. Gentlemen, Nathan didn't take it. I'm just paying him back for the terrible puns he's always springing on me."

"All this is ridiculous," said Peter Ruber, with some asperity. "Only a month ago Mr. Bengis sent me a check for one of those statues."

"Which he wrote me was duly received about two weeks ago," finished Mr. Norris. "What in blazes would he want two statues for?"

"Oh, you don't know Nathan," interpolated someone whose name I'd rather not mention, but whom I had always considered a friend. "Why does he need three whole shelves full of copies of *The Sign of the Four?* God only knows, but he's got them. I've seen them lots of times; and every time I go to his house and look, he's got more."

"These accusations against Mr. Bengis are outrageous, even if made in jest," came from a person at the far end of the table. We all looked in that direction. Martin Swanson was on his feet. "I think an apology is due Mr. Bengis," he continued with great feeling.

It was worth a gibe—it was worth many gibes—to hear this young man speak in my defense—my former student and now a devoted Sherlockian whom I myself had had the pleasure of presenting to the Irregulars only the year before. All my years of teaching English and French, of correcting reams of home-work assignments, of grading stacks of test papers, culminated in that moment of revelation of loyalty.

"Thank you, Martin," I said. "I deeply appreciate what you have said, but no apology is really needed—especially not from Charles Honce. If you knew him as I know him you would know that he has a heart of gold, and that he would not hurt a fly—much less a friend."

"Gentlemen," said Charles, "just see what I started with my ill-considered jest. Let's all forget it, I beg of you."

"Maybe a waiter cleared it off the table with the refuse," suggested another individual, whom decency forbids me to call by name—by the name he *deserves*, I mean.

At this awkward point a number of waiters who were engaged in clearing the tables stopped their work and glared at the unhappy speaker. One of them set down a number of plates he had been carrying, turned to that person, eyed him with disdain, and said in a voice of ice: "Sir, I do not know you, and it is just as well I do not. I resent your remark as much as my co-workers do. As I told Dr. Wolff when he presented me with his unusual award a short while ago, I have waited on The Baker Street Irregulars at Cavanagh's for thirteen years, and I have considered it a privilege to do so; but never before in all that time—in fact, never before in my entire career—have I heard such an insulting remark. You apparently have not been a member of this Society very long, or you would have better manners." So saying, he picked up his plates, turned on his heels, and strode out of the room. The face of the character who had caused this interruption turned a peculiar shade of purple. He stood up, mumbled a few words of apology, and—mercifully sitting near the exit—vanished in a moment.

"Gentlemen," pleaded the Chairman, again rapping for order, "I must insist that there be no more interruptions of the type just witnessed. So far we have got exactly nowhere. If the statue has indeed been stolen it behooves us, if we are worthy of being called The Baker Street Irregulars, to find the culprit. All that has been done so far is to make a lot of irrelevant—not to say irreverent—remarks. Doesn't anyone have a worthwhile suggestion?"

"Search me," said Bob Summers, whom I had spoken to during the cocktail hour, and whom I should have considered above passing so insipid a remark.

"An observation meant to be pointless," said Rex Stout, "but ironically enough it points the way to the proper *modus operandi*. None of us have pockets large enough to secrete an object seventeen inches tall. But a number of you have containers of one sort or another in which such a thing could easily be concealed. I have noticed several travelling cases, a small grip or two, even a cardboard box—the last large enough, I'm sure, to hold something bigger than human ears. I suggest, gentlemen, that all members having anything in which an object of this sort could be hidden submit willingly to having it searched."

"An excellent suggestion, Mr. Chairman," said Lord Donegall, with the alacrity so typical of him. "May I, with your permission, be the first to have my travelling case searched?"

"My dear Donegall," said Rex Stout, "I am sure the membership will agree that you are the last person in the world we would dream of submitting to anything like that."

"Thank you Rex, for the implied compliment," said Lord Donegall, "but I really can't accept for myself an exemption denied any of my fellow-Irregulars. *Holmes oblige*—and all that sort of thing, you know. Here—why be embarrassed? It's done in a moment."

Whereupon he opened his case, cleared an area on the table before him, and emptied the contents there: a profusion of books, magazines, and papers of all sorts—but no statue.

That broke the ice. One after another, Frank Waters, Bill Rabe, Arthur Levine, Thayer Cumings, and several others stood up and emptied the contents of their cases and boxes onto the table. Still no statue.

"How about the cloakroom downstairs?" suggested Howard Haycraft. "A clever thief would already have got it out of this room."

"Stop that man down there who's trying to leave!" shouted Irving Fenton.

We looked where he was pointing. I was horrified to see Arthur Holder, who had entertained us earlier in the evening with his protean disguises, rushing to the door with his travelling case. Cries went up from all over the room. "Stop him!" "Open your bag, Holder!" "Where do you think you're going?" "Sure, it's him all right. Just look at his face."

And to tell the truth he looked the picture of guilt. Perfectly self-possessed before, he seemed to go to pieces before our eyes. He stopped and faced the assemblage.

"No—you won't search m—my bag," he stammered. "You can't force me to s-submit to this humiliation. What's more, I don't want to be a member of this S-Society."

With that he made another dash toward the door. He was almost there when three Irregulars jumped up to barricade the exit. He struggled to force his way out. After a tussle he was at last held captive.

"Stop it! Stop it at once, I say!" a new voice bellowed across the room. "Leave him alone! He's innocent!"

Our eyes turned to the other end of the room. Irregular Hill Hope was on his feet. With energy we never knew him to have he shoved aside his chair and rushed down to the end of the table, across to the other side and right over to the door where the three Irregulars were still on guard. Out of respect for Hill Hope, one of the most esteemed of all the members, they had let go their captive, who stood there panting.

"Yes, gentlemen," said Hope, "this fine young man is innocent. Let me prove it to you, since you require proof." Here he took off his cape and deerstalker and laid them on a chair, then turned to Arthur Holder and put a hand on his shoulder. "Arthur, let me have your travelling case," he resumed. "Please, Arthur. Earlier this evening you said you owed me a great debt—a debt you never could repay. You were wrong, Arthur. No one owes another a debt he cannot repay. Your debt to me—if there was one—has been amply repaid to-night. Now once more I ask you"—this time with firmness—"to give me your case. Thank you, Arthur; thank you very much."

He opened the case, turned it over, and let its contents fall out on the table. All that came out were some books and the paraphernalia Holder had used earlier in the evening in doing his disguises.

"Here, Bill," he said to Bill Rabe, who was nearby with his loud-speaker. "And by the way, Bill, you *will* erase all this from your tape, won't you? 'We also have our diplomatic secrets,' you know. You haven't taped all this? Of course, I should have known you wouldn't. Thank you very much. Now please just reach into this case to make sure nothing more is in it."

Bill Rabe did so. "Nothing else inside, Mr. Hope," he said.

"Exactly," Hope resumed. "Sit down, Arthur. You do need a rest after all this." Here he paused and faced us all. "You see, gentlemen, there is no statue here. There never was. Arthur Holder never stole it. It was I who stole it. I see all of you who have known me these many years aghast with disbelief. But it is true.

"You made the capital mistake, gentlemen, against which the

393

man we honour here to-night has so often cautioned us: 'to theorize before one has data.' Merely because Mr. Holder refused to have his case searched you all jumped to the conclusion that he had the statue inside and that he had stolen it. A natural conclusion, one which Mr. Holder wanted you to reach, and you must admit he succeeded admirably. It never occurred to you, however, that there was another perfectly valid reason for his acting the way he did: to have you think he was guilty in order to prevent suspicion from falling on the one who was really guilty: myself.

"You see, I would never have stolen the statue if an opportunity had not been unexpectedly created. That opportunity came during the intermission, when Bill Hall unintentionally caused a diversion by displaying his autographed *Beeton's*. You will all recall how, within a short time, almost the entire upper part of this hall near the dais had become deserted as you rushed down near the bar to catch a look at the treasured item to which Dr. Goodman had called attention by his lusty outburst. I had just the chance I needed. If our Commissionaire and Chairman had not been so busy chatting with Lord Donegall, they would have caught me in the act. I picked up the statue, hid it in the folds of my Inverness, casually walked out, and went downstairs. There I immediately removed my Sherlockian attire in order not to appear conspicuous. I then obtained a large Manila bag and some string from an attendant in the dining room, locked myself up in the lavatory, made a package of the statue, and checked it in the cloakroom. I paid a quarter to get a second check, to guard against the possibility that the place might be searched and the package found checked with my outer wraps.

"As I turned to retrace my steps I was taken aback to see someone standing a short distance away, staring at me incredulously. It was Mr. Holder. I didn't know what to think. Had he seen me take the statue? You did, Arthur, didn't you? Yes, I thought you did, but of course I couldn't be sure. Had you followed me downstairs to see what I would do? I thought so, but I still dared to hope I was wrong.

"For the next few minutes I went through hell—not for what I had done but because I feared that Mr. Holder, who had built up of me an image of perfect integrity, had just seen his image smashed. When I saw this noble young man go so far as to assume the guilt for a theft of which he was innocent, I was sure he could have but one motive: to shield me. But tell me one thing, Arthur. Why did you have to do it? Even if you had opened your case and shown it did not contain the statue, why were you afraid suspicion would fall on me? It's the one point not clear to me. Might I still not have been safe?"

Arthur Holder looked at his mentor with a pained smile on his face. "You surmised everything else so perfectly, Mr. Hope," he said, with the slightest touch of sarcasm in his voice, "that I'm surprised you missed this one point. Someone—I think that gentleman over there," pointing to Howard Haycraft, "had just said, 'How about the cloakroom downstairs?' I was certain that in another minute, if the statue were not found, a messenger would be sent down to ask if a package had just been left there. If I were going to do something I had to do it at once. So I jumped up and tried to make off with my case."

"Of course, of course, Arthur. How could I overlook that simple explanation? So it was you, Howard, with your timely suggestion, who forced my young friend's hand. He felt he had to act, and he acted quickly—and very well too, you must all admit. If I may repeat a compliment once paid the Master, he 'would have made an actor, and a rare one.' God bless you, Arthur, for your magnanimous gesture, but how I wish you had let things take their course without involving yourself. Ironically enough, if you had not interfered, all this unpleasantness would most likely not have occurred. I doubt very much if the package would have been surrendered without my check, and if things got too uncomfortable I simply would not have claimed it. I might still, despite all my precautions, have been identified by some attendant, but those were just the chances I had to take."

"Hill," said Rex Stout, suddenly standing up, "do you seriously intend us to believe that you went to all that trouble to steal that confounded Sherlock Holmes statue? No offense, Mr. Norris, and no reflection on your statue. I have one myself, as you know, and I do like it very much, but I'll be something or other if I'd make so much fuss about it. It just doesn't make sense."

"And besides, sir," said Mr. Norris, getting up and addressing Mr. Hope, whose name at that moment was only too obviously belied by his appearance, "why didn't you just tell me you wanted one of the blasted things? They only cost thirty dollars and you certainly don't look like a person who can't afford that sum. Why, hang it all, if anyone in this society wanted one that badly and couldn't afford it, I'd make him a present of one. Believe me, sir, I would."

"I do believe you, Mr. Norris," said Mr. Hope, "and I thank you very much, but I *couldn't* ask you for it. That's just the point you don't know—none of you know." He paused for a few moments; he seemed to be in the throes of a profound conflict. "Oh well, I've gone so far I might as well go the whole way.

"I'm going to ask you all now, as Rex Stout asked us once, many years ago, when he was about to make a disclosure which shook the Sherlockian world to its foundations, to *please keep your chairs*. The sad, the shameful truth is that I am a kleptomaniac. Yes, gentlemen—in less scientific language, a thief. You are shocked, you recoil in disbelief, but it is true. It has been true for many years. My special refinement of the malady is to steal Sherlockiana—only Sherlockiana, mind you. And not always the top-drawer variety. Last year I even stooped, I'm ashamed to admit, to misappropriating a mere *Strand Magazine*, and was all but caught in the act."

"But, Mr. Hope," said Lord Donegall, rising at this point, "what possible satisfaction could you derive from your ill-gotten gains? You could never display them, for example."

"No, my dear sir, but in the privacy of my home and behind locked doors I could gloat over them to my heart's content, like Horace's miser. Remember the lines, beginning: '*Populus me sibilat . . .*'? The only difference is that, instead of being hissed by those who knew me, I was respected and esteemed for an integrity I did not possess.

"But I must not drag out these maudlin details. After more years than I care to say, I had reached a surfeit. I had decided almost a year ago to free myself from the shackles of this disgusting vice. I made a start by restoring my greatest treasure: the plaque erected outside the Criterion Restaurant in Piccadilly circus just ten years ago, to commemorate the meeting of Dr. Watson with young Stamford. Yes, gentlemen, you may well gasp in astonishment. You are now looking at the loathsome creature who stole the plaque from that hallowed spot—in broad daylight too, and practically in full view of the London bobbies. Exactly how is a story for which the world is not yet prepared. Some of you may have read a brief notice about the return of the plaque in the Winter 1963 issue of *The Sherlock Holmes Journal*; but none of you, I am sure, ever dreamt it was I who stole it. Now you know the truth.

"This last New Year's Eve I had resolved to make full restitution. I packed up the accursed treasures that had been my temptations, and returned them to their rightful owners. All except a few, that is, whose owners have either broken from the ranks or moved to addresses as yet unknown to me. One of the rarities I have yet to return is a *Beeton's Annual* for 1887 (no, not yours, Bill Hall—I see you checking on yours in your brief-case)—one abstracted from one of the most famous private collections in this country, and for which I deftly substituted one of the admirable facsimile *Beeton's* put out three years ago. A number of you I am sure have already received your Sherlockiana back in the mail. Yes, Nathan?"

"I received this morning my copy of *A Note on the Watson Problem* and need not say how pleased I was to recover it. But tell us, Mr. Hope: if you resolved, as you say, to have done with all this—kleptomania, why did you yield to the very first new temptation that came your way to-night?"

"For the same reason, I suppose, that a reformed alcoholic or drug addict will occasionally relapse. I saw the statue, desired it, and had the perfect opportunity. The syndrome went into instant operation. I struggled against it but I gave in. Even Sherlock Holmes had his tussle with cocaine, but he had Dr. Watson to warn him from time to time.

"To-night I know I have finally been cured—by the selfless action of Arthur Holder. I know I have forfeited the esteem in which I have been held by so many of you, but in confessing I feel I have taken the first honest step in my regeneration."

"It is not for us to judge you," said Dr. Wolff. "If you wish to remain I am sure there are many who will not ostracize you."

"Thank you, Julian, you are very kind, but it is I who must ostracize myself. Not until I have regained my own self-respect dare I hope to regain that of my friends and associates. Good evening, gentlemen. I am terribly sorry to have spoiled an evening that started so pleasantly. No, Arthur, please remain. I will go alone."

He picked up his cape and deerstalker, and with such dignity as he could still command he slowly walked to the door. He stood there for a little while, looking back at us and at the room with an expression of profound grief and remorse, then was gone. I felt there was none among us who did not think of Baxter's words and say to himself, "There, but for the grace of God, go I."

In a few minutes an attendant came up from downstairs with a package addressed to Mr. Norris. It was opened at once and the statue was found inside.

By this time a pall had fallen on the proceedings. No one had the heart to go on with the contest or with any other unfinished business. By common consent the meeting was adjourned, but not until a motion had been carried that the true identities of Arthur Holder and Hill Hope should never be divulged by anyone present that night. It was for that very reason that our Commissionaire, Julian Wolff, discreetly omitted any reference to this sad affair in his minutes of the meeting published in THE BAKER STREET JOURNAL.

I myself, alas, was slightly less discreet. One thoughtless action of mine enabled my friend and fellow-Sherlockian James C. Iraldi, who could not be present at the meeting in question but who was kind enough to read this account of the events in proof, to obtain a glimmering of the truth. Recently when we were downtown on Fourth Avenue we stopped outside a bookstore where, besides books, some photographs of celebrities and beauties of the day were on display in the window. I emitted an involuntary "Oh" as my eyes fixed themselves upon one of them, and following my gaze Jimmy saw the picture of a man of almost regal bearing. He looked at the high forehead, the piercing eyes, the sharply chiseled nose, the pursed lips, and the strong chin. Then he caught his breath as he read the name of the prominent attorney depicted. His eyes met mine, and I put my finger to my lips as we turned away from the window.

It must be obvious to the reader that a number of fictitious names have been used in the account of the proceedings of the 10 January 1964 meeting of The Baker Street Irregulars, as related in "Marked Down—Irregular." Aliases had to be used wherever the persons quoted refused permission for their real names to be used. In these cases the disguised names were in general chosen without any particular rhyme or reason. When it came to the man on whom suspicion unjustly falls, as well as to the real culprit, I felt that in fairness to the reader some clue to the truth—though not to their identities—should be provided in their fictitious names. Arthur Holder, as all students of the Canon know, preferred to be suspected by his father of defacing the Beryl Coronet, in order to protect his cousin Mary, whom he loved. And the name Hill Hope is of course derived from Hilda Hope—that is, Lady Hilda Trelawney Hope, who stole an important document from her husband, but returned it when she realized how disastrous the consequences of her theft would be.

The situation of a person who is suspected of theft, and who, though innocent, refuses to be searched, is of course a classic one in literature. I certainly never expected to find an example of this theme in real life. But then "life is infinitely stranger than anything which the mind of man could invent."

—December 1964

Silver Blaze was, of course the race horse in the Holmes story of the same name. But among the Irregulars, The Silver Blaze became a horse race. *The race's founder explains how. . . .*

THE SILVER BLAZE COMES OF AGE

by THOMAS L. STIX

ON THE EVENING of 18 April 1952 the United Press put out a picture of a presentation in the winner's circle at Jamaica raceway. It bore the legend:

> Turf writer Joe H. Palmer (C) presents a copy of "The Adventures of Sherlock Holmes" to Alice A. Patterson (2nd from L), half-owner of Quiet Step, winner of "The Silver Blaze" (sixth, feature, race here 4/18) in winners' circle. The Baker Street Irregulars, devotees of Sherlock Holmes, made the presentation in connection with the famous "Silver Blaze" adventure by A. Conan Doyle, author of the Holmes series. Also attending presentation are Tom Stix (L), who failed to let broken leg keep him away, and K. Jenson (R), Quiet Step's trainer. The winning jockey, Steve Di Mauro, is second from right.

That was the first Silver Blaze. Every year since then the Silver Blaze has been run at one of the New York tracks—Jamaica, Aqueduct, or Belmont. There were six Irregulars at that first race. Julian Wolff was, of course, there, or the infield board could not have flashed "Official."

Our race has progressed since then, and nowadays about sixty of us attend each year. Scion Societies have had their own Silver Blazes—Chicago, Philadelphia, San Francisco, Toronto, Baltimore, Los Angeles, Copenhagen, and Tokyo. It has been an enduring good joke and a good party.

Good horses have won the Silver Blaze, notably Find and, in Chicago, Mail Order. The best of these was Alfred Gwynne Vanderbilt's great gelding. For five years Find was listed among the ten leading money winners in the United States. Mr. Vanderbilt, in the winners' circle, interrupted Red Smith who was making the presentation for The Baker Street Irregulars with: "I don't want to hear any more—give me the book—I want to read the story."

THE SILVER BLAZE
PURSE $ 12,000
BELMONT PARK   SEPT. 15, 1972
HEXTONIA STABLES   "NURSE MADA"   B BAEZA up
G. M. BAKER trainer   1 1/16 Miles Time 1.42 2
NALEESA   2nd   PRESENTATION BY MR. THOMAS STIX   ROBA BELLA   3rd

THE 1972 SILVER BLAZE

There are any number of hunch bettors who have done well looking for clues in the names of the horses: Quiet Step (The Devil's Foot); Sweet Music (A Study in Scarlet); Find, any Sherlock Holmes story. Then the winning number 4, Silver Blaze's number.

The Colonel's colours, Black and Red, have fared well. So

have others associated with the Silver Blaze. Red Smith is a columnist of *The New York Times* and a number of other papers, and Alfred Vanderbilt has become the Chairman of the Board of the New York Racing Association. Your correspondent has graduated from using crutches to a mere cane. In 1966, worn and frazzled by his responsibilities of arranging the Silver Blaze party, he handed his responsibilities over to his son, Tom Stix, Jr.—a democratic gesture.

In 1972, the B.S.I. bowed to Women's Lib and not only allowed Mrs. Samuel DuPont to win the Silver Blaze with Nurse Nada, but also to come in second with Naleesa. The original race was run for a purse of $5000.00. In 1972 the purse was $12,000.

Come raise your glass to Sherlock Holmes; his truth goes marching on.

—June 1973

President Franklin Roosevelt was the first of two U. S.
presidents to be enrolled as a member, honoris causa,
of The Baker Street Irregulars. Here, in his own words,
are the President's musings about matters
Sherlockian. . . .

SHERLOCK HOLMES IN THE WHITE HOUSE

by FRANKLIN DELANO ROOSEVELT

. . . I AM GLAD to have a part of any movement whose purpose is to keep green the memory of Sherlock Holmes.

Now that I belong to the Baker Street Irregulars, I cannot restrain the impulse to tell you that since I have had to give up cruising on the *Potomac* I sometimes go off the record on Sundays to an undisclosed retreat. In that spot the group of little cabins which shelter the Secret Service men is known as Baker Street.

I am distressed to learn that such a serious tempest is sweeping through the ranks of the Irregulars. In my search through Dr. Watson's papers some years ago I found several pages proving that the good Doctor spent many sleepless nights trying to devise a Coat of Arms for Sherlock Holmes. These notes also proved conclusively that Holmes had no Coat of Arms. Being a foundling, his one great failure was his inability, after long search, to find his parents. Perhaps this will contribute to the calming of the tempest among the Irregulars.

On further study I am inclined to revise my former estimate that Holmes was a foundling. Actually he was born an American and was brought up by his father or a foster father in the underground world, thus learning all the tricks of the trade in the highly developed American art of crime.

At an early age he felt the urge to do something for mankind. He was too well known in top circles in this country and, therefore, chose to operate in England. His attributes were primarily American, not English. I feel that further study of this postulate will bring good results to history.

. . . I am delighted to know that my postulate with reference to Holmes's criminal background in America brought such

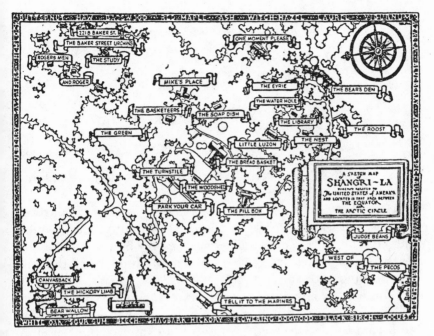

heated discussion and debate. It only goes to show that interest in the whole field of Sherlockiana is perennial.

(Only the Baker Street Irregulars knew, while he lived, that President Roosevelt was a free and accepted member of their order. The foregoing text is taken from several of the many letters Mr. Roosevelt wrote to the Buttons-cum-Commissionaire of the Irregulars during the term of his membership, from 1942 to 1945.)

—April 1955

405

With the death of Franklin D. Roosevelt, Harry S Truman not only became President of the United States but also the only honorary member of The Baker Street Irregulars. These notes about the President's Sherlockian interest come from a man who knew him personally. . . .

HARRY S TRUMAN, SHERLOCKIAN

by MILTON F. PERRY

"MR. PRESIDENT," I asked, "What did the dog do in the night-time?"

Harry S Truman grinned and looked at his glass of bourbon and branch water. "Perry," he said, "you ought to know better than test an old Holmesian like me, the only honorary member of the Baker Street Irregulars. You know damned well the dog did nothing in the night-time!"

This was my introduction to Harry Truman as a Sherlockian, a relationship I was able to develop from time to time during the years I was associated with him as Curator of the Museum at the Harry S Truman Library in Independence, Missouri, from 1958 until 1976. I was fortunate to have been able to discuss many things with him during those years, mostly in the uninterrupted privacy of his office.

He *was* a "Holmesian" and a good one too. Truman had a capacity to absorb and remember with great clarity what he had read, and he read constantly. His reading habits were established early because his eyes were never good. "I had flat eyeballs as a boy, and couldn't see well enough to play ball with the other kids, so they made me the umpire," he used to say with a laugh. "I still use the same prescription for my glasses I did then, and it forced me to read a lot, which is my favorite way of relaxing." He read everything he could find. He said that he had read all the books in the Independence Library as a child, though the collection was a small one.

He once told me of some extra-curricular reading: "I used to get those ten-cent novels of western bad men, you know, Jesse James, Cole Younger, and all, and hide them in the barn and sneak out there where I could read them. I'd get a licking from my dad whenever he caught me, but I kept it up. I first read the

Holmes stories at that period, along with *Tom Sawyer, Huck Finn,* and other books of that nature. I'm afraid, at that time, I regarded them as recreation rather than literature, and it wasn't until many years later that I came to reread them and discovered to my delight that they took an entirely different cast when read as an adult. I still like 'em and I still reread them."

That was how the conversation on Holmes began. It was in 1960 at a party at the home of my boss given for the director of a local museum who was moving on to another job. Truman and I had been making the usual party talk when I happened to mention that, though I liked to read new books, I had some favorites that I constantly went back to. His eyes brightened and he told me he did too, mentioning Mark Twain books and Sherlock Holmes.

In 1945, the Baker Street Irregulars conferred a membership upon him, *honoris causa,* and enclosed a copy of *A Baker Street Folio,* a pamphlet containing five letters about Sherlock Holmes that had been written by Franklin D. Roosevelt. (It was FDR's chauvinistic view that Holmes was an American crook who had tired of his ways and retired to England, "to do something for mankind." He also named his cabin at the Presidential retreat, "Shangri-la" [now Camp David], "Baker Street."[1]) Truman was pleased with the honor. "Far from finding you, as you suggest, 'strange and deluded creatures,'" he wrote Edgar W. Smith, "I commend your good sense in seeking escape from this troubled world into the happier and calmer world of Baker Street."

He then touched off a minor controversy when he wrote, "I had read all of the Holmes novels before I was twelve years old and I would do it again if I had time."[2]

The analytical minds of the BSI immediately jumped on that one. Truman was born in 1884 and was twelve years old in 1896. Certainly not *all* of the cases were published by then. And it was decided, after a bit of convoluted reasoning, that Truman was a good deal younger than everyone thought and was therefore the youngest president the nation had ever had: if he had indeed read them "all," he'd have been born in 1927![3]

"I guess I really upset those fellas with my acceptance," he told me. "They were too embarrassed to tell me I was wrong and had made a mistake so they went all around trying every way they knew to make me right. What I really meant was that I had read all the stories that had come out by the time I was twelve. I read the rest as they came out. By 1930 I *had* read them all, like everybody else who had followed the stories."

The BSI regularly invited Truman to the annual dinners, sent him a subscription to THE BAKER STREET JOURNAL, and asked him to write an article for the magazine. He never did, though he did see that they received replies to the invitations. He was, he told them, "looking forward to reading the JOURNAL," and, one year, claimed that if it weren't for the "heavy pressure these days in preparation for the assembly of the new Congress next week," he would "send you the message which you suggest. . . ."[4]

In early December 1948, after his stunning upset victory over Thomas E. Dewey, Truman was asked by Elmer Davis, an Irregular and a widely known radio newsman, whether he would accept the first award of the Diogenes Club, "an off-shoot" of the BSI. The award, the Lantern of Diogenes, would be given "to those who have shed the most light on this and that; and they hope the President will accept the first lantern, for having shed light on the political opinions of the American people at a time when all of us who were in the business of political analysis were groping in the dark. . . .

"I have no idea," Davis continued, "whether the lantern is something you wear in your buttonhole, or a real lantern of the kind you take down to the barn when you feed the stock before daylight."[5]

Davis' jocular invitation as expressed to Matt Connelly, Truman's secretary, was preceded by a more formal one from Dr. Charles Goodman who, using a Sherlockian metaphor, said the award was to be granted "to that American who had done the most . . . to keep the light of freedom and liberty burning, in a world where so many hostile winds are blowing hard to extinguish it."[6]

Davis sweetened the political pot by telling Connelly that Edgar Smith, who would present the award, was a General Motors Vice President for overseas relations, "a New Dealer who has long been a solitary rock of sound opinion among the breaking waves of GM ideology."[7]

The Adventure of the Blue Carbuncle, first publication of The Baker Street Irregulars, Inc., gets a page-by-page inspection by President Truman, aided and abetted by Elmer Davis and Edgar W. Smith.

The award was presented in the President's Oval Office, at 11:45 A.M., 8 December 1948. Press reports said it was for "throwing light on the state of public opinion" when "alleged experts were stumbling around in the dark."[8]

Surprisingly, the group had no lantern! Davis rather lamely admitted to reporters that the club planned to present one to the President "later on," and Goodman wrote Truman that when the lantern was made he would send it to him. No reply is found in the President's papers. Whether the group didn't expect their offer to be accepted, or accepted so soon, is unclear.[9]

In 1949, Smith and Davis made another appearance at the White House when they presented Truman with a copy of *The Adventure of the Blue Carbuncle,* the first publication of the Baker Street Irregulars, Inc. It is there today, shelved with the President's books in Harry S Truman Library at Independence, Missouri.[10]

—December 1986

NOTES

1. Edgar W. Smith to Harry S Truman, 3 Dec. 1945 and Roosevelt to Smith, 18 Dec. 1944. All documents cited are in the President's Personal File #2275, Harry S Truman Library, Independence, Mo.

2. Harry S Truman to Edgar W. Smith, 15 Dec. 1945.

3. Stephan F. Crocker, "A Declaration from Independence, Mo., or 'The Affair of the Politician,'" BSJ (os) 3 (1948), 477–78; Page Heldenbrand to HST, 24 June 1946. Heldenbrand, who was stationed aboard the USS *Franklin D. Roosevelt,* mentioned in a letter a Sherlock Holmes who was then serving in the U.S. Navy. Crocker pointed out that in 1896 only *A Study in Scarlet* (1887), *The Sign of the Four* (1890), *The Adventures* (1892), and *The Memoirs* (1894) were in print.

4. Ben Abramson to HST, 21 Dec. 1945; William D. Hassett to Abramson, 7 Feb. 1946; Edgar W. Smith to HST, 9 Sept. 1946; Charles G. Ross to Smith, 18 Sept. 1946; Smith to HST, 19 Dec. 1946.

5. Elmer Davis to Matthew Connelly, 4 Dec. 1948.

6. Goodman to HST, 3 Dec. 1948.

7. Davis to Connelly, 4 Dec. 1948.

8. Washington *Star,* 9 Dec. 1948.

9. Goodman to HST, 13 Dec. 1948.

10. BSJ (ns) 23 (1973), 61.

*While serving in the South Pacific during World War
Two, the author of this* recherché *little piece
discovered that to the U. S. government neither
Sherlock Holmes nor national security are particularly
amusing subjects. . . .*

BAKER STREET FROM GUAM

by ELLERY HUSTED

IT HAPPENED in the Pacific. After waiting around Ford Island three weeks for my orders, I was yanked out of bed by the OD's messenger the night they came.

The orders read:

Report Cincpac, Advanced Intelligence Headquarters, Guam. Passage via Air Transport. Proceed without delay. (*Cincpac* was Admiral Nimitz, Commander-in-Chief Pacific.)

An hour's paper work, fifteen minutes packing, and I made it by jeep a minute before the plane took off. There was a two-day hop ahead, and I'd forgotten to pack a book. On my way through the hangar, I saw on a chair a paper-backed volume with no visible owner. The cover said: *Six Adventures of Sherlock Holmes.* I stole it without hesitation and without shame.

Our plane was an old DC-3 lined with bucket seats and filled with mail bags and vapors of DDT. The people riding with me were mostly Army. They were bored and uncommunicative.

On the first leg to Johnson's Island, I read my borrowed volume twice. On the first reading, the tales were hauntingly familiar. On the second, there were no surprises. I wondered what I could do to make my cheerless, viewless transit of the Pacific less depressing. I pictured Sherlock Holmes and Doctor Watson seated comfortably and conversationally before their fire at 221B Baker Street, and wondered in my ex-architect's way what their rooms had looked like. Suddenly a thought burned like a sunbeam through the cloud of my ennui. I retrieved the *Six Adventures* from where I had dropped them "on the deck" and prepared for another reading with re-awakened eyes.

This reading turned out better than I had dared hope. Scattered through each of the *Six Adventures* were disconnected but explicit references to the physical arrangements of the famed

411

rooms. As I read through the pages quickly, the descriptions seemed to form an intelligible pattern. I had a pencil with me and plenty of paper (a superfluity from Personnel) so I started my fourth reading with pencil poised. All references to Baker Street I copied whole.

Like these:

"We met next day, as he had arranged, and inspected the rooms at No. 221B Baker Street. . . . They consisted of a *couple of comfortable bedrooms and a single, large, airy sitting room,* cheerfully furnished, and *illuminated by two broad windows.*"

"He would lie *upon the sofa in the sitting room.*"

"As we sat *on either side of the fire.*"

"We heard a loud knock, a deep voice below, and heavy steps *ascending the stair.*"

"A bath at Baker Street and a complete change freshened me up wonderfully. When I *came down to our rooms,* I found the breakfast laid, and Holmes pouring out the coffee."

By the time the plane reached Johnson's Island and dipped to a landing on the blazing coral, the tedious business of transcription was almost over. During the rest of the trip to Kwajelein and Guam, the work of sorting and assembling architectural references made the long hours pass easily. To my surprise, each reference, as I found it, fitted like a shaped piece into the picture puzzle of 221B. It was possible from the text to imagine the plans and elevations, the arrangement of rooms, the position of doors and windows, and even the number of risers on the stairs.

"*I know there are seventeen steps,* because I have both seen and observed."

The disposition of furniture in Holmes's and Watson's rooms was carefully described; not only the major pieces, but the minor articles as well.

"I picked up a magazine *from the table.*"

"There was a *small portmanteau* in the [sitting] room."

"Sherlock Holmes took *his bottle from the corner of the mantelpiece* and his hypodermic syringe from its neat morocco case."

"He took up *his violin from the corner.*"

When all the references had been written down, grouped, and analyzed, I decided to amuse myself by reconstructing the plans and elevations. No line was drawn without confirmation from the text. Slowly and with developing clarity the outlines of 221B began to emerge. When the work of literary restoration was complete, the written evidence had grown into a bulky package. My first concern on landing at Guam was how to rid myself of these superfluous papers. I was about to consign them to the hangar's head, when I thought of my friend Dick Clarke of The Five Orange Pips. It might amuse them to receive this bit of literary archaeology out of the blue of the Pacific. I put the papers in an envelope addressed to Clarke, and upon my arrival at Nimitz's Headquarters on Cincpac Hill, gave them to a yeoman to send by airmail, warning him to put on plenty of stamps.

Though I couldn't remember much about The Five Orange Pips, I had a vague picture of a group of cheerful and scholarly eccentrics, incurably addicted to the needle of Sherlock Holmes. Members were said to be selected solely on the basis of Holmesian erudition. At the annual dinners the members exchanged learned papers illuminating obscurities in Watson's narrative and explaining ambiguities in his text. Solemn and scholarly research was devoted to unraveling unsolved "cases" referred to by Dr. Watson. A delegation of members had once journeyed to London to call on the British Brethren, the Sherlock Holmes Society of London, and to visit the site where *The* House was ingeniously argued to have stood.

Although I was not myself (except by accident of war) a student of Sherlock Holmes, I hoped that my reconstruction of the famous lodgings might be a contribution to the archives of the Orange Pips. At any rate, the inconvenient burden of my scholarship was now disposed of, and shortly forgotten in the more serious business of war.

Some months later, new duties took me from Guam. When I returned, the war was almost over. The day I got my orders home, I was cheerfully destroying official papers, when a yeoman handed me a large and vaguely familiar envelope covered with the ink of rubber stamps. I looked at it casually and saw it was my letter to Clarke come back to roost after all these months. I assumed that it had been sent off with too few stamps, but my absorption with the task of getting home made the omission a matter of no importance. I had wangled a ride back to Pearl Harbor for the following day on Admiral Nimitz' private plane. Weight was crucial, and I knew there were better things to carry than paper. Without looking at the envelope again I chucked it into the "burn basket" with the rest of the junk.

Next morning I climbed aboard the Admiral's transport for the first half of the long journey home. The plane was a C-54 with forward-facing single seats. A blond young ensign in the seat ahead turned around when we were airborne and said "Your name's Husted?" I nodded. The ensign added with a grin: "And how's Dr. Watson doing?"

I considered the question for a minute, and realized the ensign must have been a Cincpac censor. I said "I suppose you censored that Baker Street letter." "Yeah," the ensign replied, "and *did it give us trouble*. They put the best brains in Guam on it, but nobody could make anything of it. It was obviously in code, but we couldn't break it, so we sent it back to Pearl. They spent some time on it there and sent it on to Washington, but it was no go. It came back to us, and we held it until the war was over."

I laughed at the absurdity of the incident and said, "Hell, you knew all about *me*. Why didn't you ask *me* about it?"

The ensign smiled. "Yeah, we knew all about you, but it wasn't that easy. We checked your handwriting with the letter and it didn't agree. Too jerky [apparently the eccentricities of airborne calligraphy had been overlooked] and you'll agree that all that stuff about 221b Baker Street sounded damn queer. On any basis the letter didn't make sense."

I thought of the wavy handwriting, of the drawings made shaky and unprofessional by the undulations of air travel, of my mysterious disconnected passages lifted from the text, and especially of my enigmatic letter to Clarke:

Dear Dick:
Excuse this unexpected and almost incomprehensible gibberish I am sending you. Tell your group of *Peculiar Pips* that 221b did exist, and that it has been resurrected by one who is not of you, but believes in you. I wish Holmes were with me to solve the riddle of the Empire. God bless you, and in the name of Holmes and Baker Street keep up the good fight.
            Yours,
            —Husted

I could not but agree that Cincpac's alerted censors had had some cause for their suspicions. I was ruminating pleasantly over the extent of the trouble I had probably caused, when the blond head before me revolved again to say, "And, worst of all, my friend, Baker Street was the code name for OSS Headquarters, London."

When I told the tale to Clarke back home, Clarke was not amused. He shook his head sadly. He said, "That envelope was a natural for the archives, and like an idiot you burned it with your Navy papers. You ought to have been court-martialed."

And this from Commander Clarke, the Orange Pip, who was another Navy man.

—January 1949

The Five Orange Pips of Westchester County, New York, is the oldest of the Baker Street Irregulars' "scion societies." Herewith, Mr. Clark's reminiscences of its earlier days. . . .

SOME BRIEF RECOLLECTIONS OF A PIP

by BENJAMIN S. CLARK

ROWLAND STEBBINS, our late member, was the man who introduced me to Dick Clarke. Holmes, describing brother Mycroft for Watson's benefit, said that Mycroft "occasionally *is* the British government." Dick Clarke, by contrast, *always* was the Five Orange Pips. Rowly introduced us as we were waiting for our respective wives to leave their coats upstairs before entering into the festivities of a private dance.

"Dick, I want you to meet my friend Ben Clark, who like you is an ardent Holmes enthusiast." I might interject here that Dick and I had each failed to flinch from the bottle at our respective pre-dance dinners, which may help to explain what the reader will perceive directly as Dick's arrogance and my brashness. Neither conduct is quite what is expected when strangers meet.

"Well," said Dick, without any preamble, "when it comes to Sherlock Holmes we Pips have all the answers."

"I find that statement hard to believe," said I; "you no doubt are familiar with *The Hound of the Baskervilles.*"

"Of course, who isn't?" said Dick, with scorn.

"Then perhaps you'll be good enough to tell me where the hound was bought."

"Where the hound was bought?"

"Yes, where the hound was bought."

A long pause.

"It doesn't say."

"I'm sorry, but it does say. Ross and Mangles in Fulham Road."

Dick immediately laid aside his weapons and I was invited to join the Pips. Later that year, with my fellow Pips, I enjoyed the Irregulars' dinner at the old Murray Hill Hotel. Christopher Morley, Rex Stout, Edgar Smith, and Fletcher Pratt were amongst those present, I can remember. Ironically, having entered the Pips' ranks by challenging their omniscience, I as a Pip was able to re-establish it that evening by winning the quiz, a pure fluke since I never won another.

On one of the early occasions of my playing host to the Pips at Baskerville Hall, I chose to send out the invitation by telegram. After the usual business of date, hour, black tie, etc., I concluded with a warning: "FOR GOD'S SAKE BE CAREFUL CROSSING THE MOOR." Each wire was addressed to the name of the character in the Canon that Pip had adopted, as resembling most nearly his own appearance, care of the man's real name. In at least one instance this caused a bit of embarrassment, because the wife, who took a dim view of Sherlockian doings, answering the phone insisted that there was no one named Woodley in the home. Fortunately her husband overheard the denial in time for her to retract and admit a Woodley presence. Their home was of modest size so that the admission made her appear to be a bit of a scatter-brain. Dick Clarke's wife, Kay, by contrast an enthusiast, on answering the phone immediately responded that Mr. Rucastle was there and would take the message. After delivering same, as Dick told me later, the Western Union gal said, "That other Mr. Clark, he's sort of a nut, isn't he?"

A footnote. We had close friends as neighbors who were most cooperative in providing sound effects. They had a coon hound of local breed who could deliver a wonderfully lugubrious bay when stimulated by a gentle but firm poke. It was arranged that when we rang their number they'd not bother to answer the phone, but simply poke the dog. My guests were horribly impressed.

The Adventure of the Cardboard Box has a low ranking amongst the adventures, but it provided me with material for a joke that turned out better by far than what I could have hoped for. A close friend of mine, at the time music critic for *The Boston Herald,* was well read in the Canon, and though not an Irregular did at least on one occasion attend as a guest a gathering of The Speckled Band of Boston—where, incidentally, no slouch in that line himself, he was most impressed with the quantity of fire-water taken aboard in the course of an evening.

Taking great pains, I procured from a shop which dealt in

the fixings for parties and jokes two plastic ears which I placed in a box of coarse salt. The box was then wrapped in brown paper which, I've forgotten how, I impregnated with a strong odor of coffee and then tied up with tarred twine, carefully using only nautical knots. The package was mailed to Miss S. Cushing, c/o A. W. Williams [my friend's name], The Somerset Club, 42 Beacon Street, Boston. I was singularly favored by fortune. The package arrived on a Friday and was delivered to Alex as he was about to take his guest, an older lady, in to lunch before attending the Boston Symphony. He told me he was struck with terror that in some way through a medical student I'd procured real human ears. (As a good student of the Canon he knew what the package might contain.) He didn't dare open the package then, but asked that it be kept for him in the cloak room. By lunch it was placed near a radiator and when he returned alone to the club he felt his worst fears were confirmed when he saw a liquid stream coming apparently from the package. (It was, of course, the radiator acting on the plastic.) Embalming fluid, he was sure. He did finally open the box. Relief at last.

Some of you may have seen, many years back, at the Plaza Gallery, now no more, the Sherlock Holmes exhibit brought from London. A realistic duplication of Holmes's and Watson's "digs." On the wall was a copy of the manuscript of the Baskerville family legend. At his request, I loaned this to Adrian Conan Doyle. It had been given to me by my friend and fellow Pip, Owen Frisbie, who wrote a beautiful copperplate hand, to produce a real work of art. At the end of the exhibition this manuscript was not returned. Several years later, a partner of mine visiting our London office was taken one evening to the Sherlock Holmes Pub. He knew of my Holmesian interest and on his return to New York said he was impressed with my generosity in lending my Baskerville manuscript to the Sherlock Holmes Pub. I saw it there some years later, but the man in charge of the Pub that day at lunchtime pulled a complete blank when I identified myself as the lender and said they could keep the loan. His response was as much as to say, "who dat Sherlock Holmes?"

—September 1987

For most devotees of the Master, entrance into
organized Sherlockiana is a consummation devoutly to
be wished. For some, however, things just don't happen
the way they're supposed to. . . .

TRAVELS WITH A PUMPKIN

by TERRY BELANGER

WHEN I JOINED The Sons of the Cooper Beeches several years ago as an undergraduate of Haverford College, I became the youngest member of the BSI's Scion Society in Philadelphia. I felt like an unsanctified Littlest Angel at my first meeting, where everyone seemed to be twice my age and a doctor, lawyer, or at least a college professor. After a trip to the bar, I ensconced myself in a dark corner and there I remained, hoping no one would notice me.

Eventually a man came over, introduced himself as a coroner of the City of Philadelphia, and gave me a cigar, which I combined with my highball-glass Martini. Toast after Canonical toast soon finished me off, and it took all of my self-control to keep from disgracing myself over a plate of Chicken Jonas Oldacre at dinner.

Glittering conversation crossed and recrossed my end of the table, as I did my best to ask for the butter, and would someone pass the celery. I determined then that I should either make a better showing at the next meeting, or give up going altogether.

The next Philadelphia meeting was scheduled for the last Friday in October. On the morning of the 24th I went down to Haverford's Penn Fruit market and selected a large watermelon-shaped pumpkin. I used construction paper, cardboard, and a Magic Marker to make a gray cap, then carved a hawk-like face on my pumpkin, inserted a candle in its belly and a calabash pipe in its mouth, and the result was a Canonical jack o'lantern. I would bring this with me to the meeting in honor of Hallowe'en.

But I was not about to exhibit myself with a Sherlock Holmes jack o'lantern on the train into the city. Fortunately, my creation fitted snugly into a Haverford College laundry bag, and I

419

in my tux and Holmes in his sack adjourned for Philadelphia and fame on the Paoli Local.

The SOCB meets at the Orpheus Club on South Van Pelt Street. Their rather formidable building serves as the headquarters of a group of singing businessmen, with a lounge downstairs and a dining-room for dinner.

Outside the Orpheus Club I lit my pipe on the doorstep, resolutely shouldered my laundry bag, and went into the vestibule.

A dozen men eyed me coldly from the bar in the next room. I had never seen any of them before, and I remembered thinking that I'd never be able to recognize all of our 90-odd members. Realizing that the twelve men were undoubtedly wondering whose little boy I was, I took off my coat, reorganized my composure and the front of my dress shirt, and prepared my jack o'lantern for its entrance into the Society.

I wormed Sherlock's head out of his laundry bag and dressed him artistically in the deerstalker and calabash. My supply of matches had run out on the doorstep, but there would be piles of Orpheus Club matches on a stand in the lounge. I strolled into the main room as nonchalantly as only one who is carrying a large pumpkin can, nodded pleasantly to the jury at the bar, and went over to the matchbook stand to help myself.

Setting Sherlock on the floor, I got the candle going, straightened up and turned around, and there were my dozen friends from the bar, lined up in front of me and staring at my pumpkin in picturesque attitudes of total disbelief.

"Can we help you?" said one of the men.

"I'm here for the SOCB meeting," said I.

"You're here for the *what*?" asked the man.

"For The Sons of the Copper Beeches meeting," I said.

"The Sons of the *What*?"

I began to shake. "Now look," I said, "the Philadelphia Sherlock Holmes Society has been meeting here for years."

"When does it meet here?"

"On the last Friday in October. Isn't this the twenty-fourth?"

"And what, young man, gave you the idea that the twenty-fourth of October is the last Friday in October?"

Yes indeed, I had made an impression at the Orpheus Club this time. I asked if I could use an Orpheus Club telephone and called our Headmastiff. When he could stop laughing, he hoped

420

I could make it to the meeting on the 31st of October. I told him I'd try again on the following Friday, and I returned to the lounge, apologized to the gentlemen, put Sherlock back in his bag and my tail between my legs, and disappeared into the night.

But my evening was not yet over.

I dashed back to the railroad station to get to Haverford in time for supper. Across from me on the Paoli Local sat two high-school girls, who looked at me and began to snicker. I lit my pipe and looked severe.

After some whispered debate between them, one of the girls leaned forward and, looking at my dinner jacket, said, "Excuse me, but where are you going?"

"I'm going out to dinner," said I, simplifying the matter somewhat.

"But what are you dressed as? I mean, are you going to be a waiter, or something?"

"No," said I, "I'm just—just going out to dinner."

"Oh. Do you go to Villanova?"

"No, Haverford."

"Haverford Prep School?"

"No, Haverford College."

"Gee, what a liar!" said one to the other.

Then came the question I had been expecting: "What d'you have in the bag?"

"Well," said I, "if you really want to know, it's a fifteen-pound pumpkin."

"And what d'you have in the pumpkin?"

"Seeds."

A ripple of laughter spread from the other passengers in the coach, who had tuned in to our conversation. This was getting better than a minstrel show; the girls dey laffed 'n' dey laffed, and one said to the other, "Gee, he's *great!* Let's ask him some more questions." And to me, "We don't believe you've really got a pumpkin in the bag. Take it out and show it to us."

"I can't do that," said I. "It's hard to get it out of the bag—as a matter of fact I wish it was impossible to get it out of the bag. Besides, I'm getting off soon. But if you want to, you can come over here and feel the pumpkin through the bag and find out for yourselves."

And the two girls came over and felt my fifteen-pound pump-

421

kin, and they were convinced. Then I got off the train to tell the tale over a late supper at Haverford.

I retold the story at the SOCB meeting on the following Friday. For a long time afterwards I was generally known to the Society as that young man with the pumpkin. The members still remind me of the time I tried to make a name for myself when our fall meeting falls on or near Hallowe'en.

I believe that I'm still the youngest member of the SOCB, but I've been thinking of proposing a young friend of mine for membership in the Society.

—March 1967

SELECT BIBLIOGRAPHY

The Annotated Sherlock Holmes, ed. William S. Baring-Gould. New York: Potter, 1967.

The Misadventures of Sherlock Holmes, ed. Ellery Queen. Boston: Little, Brown, 1944.

The Private Life of Sherlock Holmes, by Vincent Starrett. New York: Macmillan, 1933.

Profile by Gaslight: An Irregular Reader about the Private Life of Sherlock Holmes, ed. Edgar W. Smith. New York: Simon and Schuster, 1944.

Sherlock Holmes: Fact or Fiction?, by T. S. Blakeney. London: Murray, 1932.

Sherlock Holmes and Dr. Watson: The Chronology of Their Adventures, by H. W. Bell. London: Constable, 1932.

A Sherlock Holmes Commentary, by D. Martin Dakin. New York: Drake, 1972.

221B: Studies in Sherlock Holmes, ed. Vincent Starrett. New York: Macmillan, 1940.